That Vital Spark

 MUNRO ANTHOLOGY

???

That Vital Spark

A NEIL MUNRO ANTHOLOGY

Edited by
BRIAN D. OSBORNE
and
RONALD ARMSTRONG

Birlinn

First published in 2002 by
Birlinn Limited
West Newington House
10 Newington Road
Edinburgh EH9 1QS

www.birlinn.co.uk

ISBN 1 84158 204 2

The publisher acknowledges subsidy from

THE SCOTTISH ARTS COUNCIL

towards the publication of this book

Typeset by Textype, Cambridge
Printed and bound by Creative Print and Design, Ebbw Vale

Contents

✝

1
Foreword

†

The fact that seventy per cent of the material in this anthology is not currently in print, and that more than half of that seventy per cent has never been available in book form may suggest that our view of Neil Munro's writing has been, perforce, a restricted and narrow one.

However true this may be, the situation in 2002 is considerably healthier than in the late 1980s when Munro's sole representation in the bookshops was an incomplete edition of the *Para Handy* stories. Even the great historical novels, on which Munro's reputation as the successor to Robert Louis Stevenson had been based, had vanished from the catalogue. A revival set in with the publication by Birlinn Ltd of the present editors' complete edition of *Para Handy* in 1992 and of the Erchie MacPherson and Jimmy Swan series of short stories in 1993. These editions went back to the original source, the *Glasgow Evening News*, to find stories that had, for various reasons, not been used in the editions produced in Munro's lifetime and added a critical apparatus of introductory essays and explanatory notes on language and on local and topical references.

The Munro revival moved on with the reprinting of *The New Road, John Splendid, Doom Castle* and *Gilian the Dreamer* between 1994 and 1999 and the republication of *The Lost Pibroch* in 1996 and *Jaunty Jock* in 1999. The formation of a Neil Munro Society in 1996 and its organisation of a programme of lectures and events and the publication of a twice-yearly magazine underlines the continuing interest in Munro and his works in both academic and lay circles. *The New Road* was selected as one of thirty-six Scottish novels to be placed in multiple copies in schools as part of a lottery-funded project organised by the Scottish Library Association.

Despite the renewed availability of much of his more serious work, and perhaps inevitably, Munro is still most popularly associated with Para Handy, that wily, Odysseus-like, master mariner who still pilots the *Vital Spark* round the Clyde and West Highland waters nearly a century after he first sailed into the hearts and minds of the readers of the *Glasgow Evening News*. Para Handy rapidly became, and remarkably has remained, an iconic figure, transcending radio, television and film adaptation. And there seems no reason why he should ever lose that place. Despite Munro's own concern to distance himself from his lighter comic creations by the use of the pen-name Hugh Foulis, there is no reason why the reader should think less of the adventures of Para Handy than of those of Æneas in *The New Road*. They are obviously different in tone and in kind, but both are recounted by a writer of imagination, integrity and much more than common skill. Munro, the critically acclaimed novelist, did not forget his talent when he turned his attention to telling a 'baur' about Para Handy and his crew-mates.

In selecting material for this anthology we have chosen some familiar landmarks and a great deal that will be quite unknown to all but a very few Munro researchers. The selection bridges the Neil Munro/Hugh Foulis gap (if gap there be) and is encouraged in this eclecticism by the comment of R. B. Cunninghame Graham on Munro:

> The exigencies of life bound him to journalism, but in all he wrote there was a literary twang. And why for not, as some of his own characters might have said, for much of journalism is as good literature as the greater part of epoch-making novels . . .

The obvious, and inevitable, exclusions from the anthology are the novels, not only the historical novels mentioned above (to which can be added *Shoes of Fortune* and *Children of Tempest*) and Munro's two ventures into contemporary fiction, *The Daft Days* and *Fancy Farm*. It would be hard to do justice to these novels in an extract and we hope that readers who develop a taste for Munro may explore these riches for themselves at rewarding length. Our selections are all self-contained pieces which have been grouped to reflect the main areas of Munro's work and the phases of his literary career. Each group has an introduction setting this aspect of Munro's life and work in context and providing information about the items printed.

What we have provided, however, is the text of Munro's last, unfinished novel *The Search* – a work which has never before been publicly available. Though not strictly a sequel to *The New Road* it does reintroduce us to the cunning, experienced, Highland secret-agent Ninian MacGregor Campbell, who so enlivens that novel.

Munro's reputation underwent a severe decline in the years after his death in 1930 at the age of sixty-seven. This type of posthumous depreci-ation is commonplace but Munro perhaps took longer to recover than is the norm. In part this may have because he had further to fall than others – his reputation in the first quarter of the twentieth century was a very considerable one indeed. The publication of *The Lost Pibroch* collection marked him out as a singular talent and *John Splendid* (1898) confirmed this position. His reputation was crowned by the publication in 1914 of *The New Road* – a work of which John Buchan wrote in the most glowing terms, describing Munro as: '. . . the foremost of living Scottish writers, both in regard to the scope and variety of his work and its rare quality'.

Along the way Munro had been given an honorary degree of Doctor of Laws by Glasgow University (in a period when such honours were more parsimoniously distributed than is the case today) and made a Freeman of his native Burgh of Inveraray.

When Munro died tributes were paid by great men and lesser mortals alike. Poems were written in Gaelic and English to mark the passing of one who was seen as a figure in a great tradition of Scottish letters. Robert Bontine Cunninghame Graham in an appreciation of him for his old paper wrote:

> In some ways he occupied a unique position. Born as he was, bilingual, he had a foot both in the Celtic and the Saxon camp. Had he elected to be a Gaelic writer he might have been a worthy successor to Alister McDonald of Ardnamurchan, the last of the Scottish bards.
>
> His poetic mind, I fancy, had he chosen to write in Gaelic, would have inspired him to write verse. As it is, we owe him the 'Lost Pibroch,' perhaps the tale most inspired with Celtic spirit written in modern times.

The *Evening News* made Munro's death its lead news item on Monday 22 December 1930 with the headlines 'Passing of a great novelist' and 'Genius in Journalism'.

The leading Glasgow morning paper the *Glasgow Herald* headlined its obituary 'The Spirit of the Gael' and wrote: 'The death of Neil Munro has taken away one of the few really distinguished Scottish men of letters', and went on to speak of his work as a critic on the *News*:

> No man exercised a more subtle literary influence on the West of Scotland than Neil Munro. His discriminating praise was sufficient to set aglow the heart of the young writer, for he instinctively sympathised with the aspiring. Indeed he loved all dreamers.

In a memorial service in Glasgow Cathedral, the Minister of the Cathedral, Dr Lauchlan MacLean Watt, himself a writer and critic of note, described Munro as 'the greatest Scottish novelist since Sir Walter Scott, and in the matter of Celtic story and character he excelled Sir Walter because of his more deeply intimate knowledge of that elusive mystery.'

Nor was Munro's reputation confined to Scotland. His works had been eagerly received and glowingly reviewed in the London literary press, and indeed also in the United States and Canada. On his death *The Times* devoted fourteen column inches to an obituary which described him as 'one of the most distinguished Scottish novelists and journalists of recent times'. It went on to remark:

> Few writers have caught more truly the spirit of the Highlands, its romanticism, its mysticism, the spell and wonder of the mountains, the glens, and the lochs, enveloped in the deep mists that scatter so quickly before the sun.

After speaking highly of the comic short fiction where 'he let himself go with an abandon which was impossible in his more serious work' the obituarist concluded that Munro's 'skill and success as a writer were largely due to his command over simple and direct English'.

After Munro's death the Gaelic-language society An Comunn Gaidhealach raised funds for a monument to Munro which, after some debate as to its form and location, was unveiled in Glen Aray in 1935. Here, again, generous tribute was paid to Munro's gifts with Cunninghame Graham describing Munro as 'the apostolic successor of Sir Walter Scott'.

Not all critical reaction was, or has been, positive. C. M. Grieve ('Hugh MacDiarmid') thought Munro an inferior stylist to 'Fiona MacLeod' (William Sharp) and that he lacked MacLeod's powers of word-painting and spiritual insight. He also wrote that Munro was 'the lost leader of Scottish Nationalism' who had chosen to be 'without following and without influence' and had 'preferred the little wars of Lorn to the conflict of real life in which he ought to have engaged'. MacDiarmid dedicated his 1920 Scottish verse anthology *Northern Numbers* to Munro, only to find Munro rejected MacDiarmid's notion of a group approach to literature. Much of what MacDiarmid wrote about Munro can be seen as the reaction of a rejected suitor who pretends that the object of his desire was unworthy all the time.

If there is any substance in MacDiarmid's charge then it is that Munro wrote about safely distant crises in Highland life – the wars of Montrose, the Jacobite movement – rather than more recent crises, such as the Clearances or the land-raids of the 1890s and 1900s. However, this is at least debatable. The process of change in the Highlands is the great theme of Munro's work and it is surely possible to argue that, for example, in *The New Road*, with its attack on the negative side of traditional Highland life and the mixture of hope for change and regret for the loss of that which was of value he is addressing a universal situation, that Munro was writing a text of more general application and that metaphor, is, after all, a recognised and legitimate literary device. This view about the gains and losses of change is expressed movingly and effectively in Æneas's words to Janet about General Wade's military roads which were driving through the Highlands and spelling the end of Highland isolation, lawlessness and the dark forces he had seen demonstrated by Simon Fraser of Lovat and Coll Barrisdale. Janet Campbell has just expressed her hatred of the new road, but Æneas tells her:

> There is something in me, too, that little likes it. It means the end of many things, I doubt, not all to be despised, – the last stand of Scotland, and she destroyed. And yet – and yet, this New Road will some day be the Old Road, too, with ghosts on it and memories.

Neil Munro was born in Inveraray, Argyll, in 1863 into a difficult and poor environment. He was the son of Anne Munro, an unmarried maidservant. His father has never been convincingly identified but persistent legend identifies him as a member of the Ducal House of Argyll. Anne Munro's father had been a shepherd in Glen Aray and her mother an agricultural worker. Munro's correct birth-date of 1863 appears on the Glen Aray monument and is of course vouched for by the official record of his birth. However the date is still given in most standard sources as 1864 and indeed this date was provided by him to such reference works as *Who's Who*. Quite what purpose this apparent deceit was intended to serve is unclear.

Munro's mother married Malcolm Thomson, the Governor of Inveraray Jail, in 1875. The following year Munro left Inveraray School and became a junior clerk in the law office of William Douglas in Inveraray. In his own words he was: 'insinuated, without any regard for my own desires, into a country lawyer's office, wherefrom I withdrew myself as soon as I arrived at years of discretion and revolt'.

Douglas was not simply a country solicitor, he was Clerk to the Commissioners of Supply of Argyll and Clerk to the Lieutenancy of Argyll. He later became Sheriff Clerk of Argyll and Clerk to the Justices of the Peace. Munro's position with this firm, close to the centres of power and influence in Argyll, was hardly the most likely career move for one of his background and origins and the clear suggestion that the position was arranged for young Neil does suggest a certain degree of influence being used on his behalf and may be felt to add credence to the rumours regarding his paternity.

In June 1881 Munro, who had already shown signs of literary ability, left Inveraray for Glasgow and two years' clerical work in the city, during which time he practised his shorthand and submitted articles and poems to the *Oban Times*. In 1884 he obtained a post on the *Greenock Advertiser* – this paper, however, closed shortly thereafter and Munro returned to Glasgow, joining the *Glasgow News* and lodging in the house of Hugh Adam, a mechanic. In July 1885 he married Jessie Ewing Adam, the eldest daughter of the house, and later that year they moved to Falkirk where Munro took up a post on the *Falkirk Herald*. In April 1887 he returned to Glasgow to work on a morning paper, the *Glasgow News,* which in 1888 was absorbed by the *Glasgow Evening News* on which he became the Chief Reporter. He gave up his staff post in 1897 to work as a freelance and to concentrate on writing fiction. The First World War saw him drawn back to the *News* as a war correspondent and then as editor. His elder son, Hugh, was killed in action in 1915, a blow from which Munro perhaps never quite recovered.

The path of his career in journalism and literature will be sketched out in the introduction to the various sections of this anthology and need not be rehearsed here. What should be emphasised is the very wide range of writing Munro undertook quite apart from his routine work as a journalist: light verse, humorous articles, thrillers, travel writing, sermon reporting – and all this before the publication of his first serious short story in *Blackwood's Magazine*.

Nor were Munro's interests confined to books and literature – a keen member of the Glasgow Art Club and an art critic of strong opinions (as may be seen from his polemical poem *The New Woman in Art)* he was a friend of many artists including George Houston, his collaborator on *Ayrshire Idylls,* the sculptor Pittendrigh MacGillivray, Macaulay Stevenson, and Edward A. Hornel. Indeed he was made an honorary member of the Scottish Arts Club in Edinburgh in 1907.

Munro had a gift for friendship and knew most of the leading literary figures of the day. Joseph Conrad was a long-standing friend, as were Cunninghame Graham, J. M. Barrie and John Buchan. Three successive entries from his diary for April 1909 suggest the significant place he had in wider literary circles:

17th April: London – visit Barrie
18th April: Lunch with Galsworthy
19th April: Lunch with Arnold Bennett

When his Glasgow honorary degree was announced the *British Weekly* wrote:

Few men are more admired by those who care for literature than Neil Munro. Of course, he has his genius to begin with, but he has put that genius to a high use, and has kept the flag of literature flying when many around him succumbed to temptation. Some of his books will live, and there is not one of them that does not richly reward the reader. Neil Munro is also one of the best and widest-minded of our literary critics – too shrewd and too humorous to be led into extravagance, but always generous to merit in whatever quarter it is to be found.

By 1927 when Munro finally won free, for the second time, of the burdens of daily work in a newspaper office, he was no longer a young man and his health had deteriorated. It was perhaps too late to expect a renaissance of the pioneering novelist of the Celtic revival who had startled the literary world with the *Lost Pibroch* stories or the historical novelist who had delighted so many with books like *John Splendid* and *The New Road.* In one area, however, there was no diminution of his powers – his short fiction and journalism, to the end, was the work of a master. The last Para Handy story 'Wireless on the Vital Spark', published in the *News* in 1924, is as fresh and lively as any of the Para Handy tales written almost twenty years earlier and in its subject matter reflected Munro's lively interest in the new and exciting world of radio. Similarly his other contributions to 'The Looker-On', such as the 1926 fantasy about Glasgow fox-hunting, 'The Sport Royal', maintained the quality and imagination which had made his columns the delight of readers for three decades.

In the last months of Munro's life, J. M. Barrie, newly appointed as Chancellor of Edinburgh University, exercised his prerogative of choosing the honorary graduands to be honoured at his installation and had Munro given an Honorary Doctorate from Edinburgh to add to his Glasgow Doctorate.

Munro died at his home, 'Cromalt', (renamed when he bought it in 1918 after a stream in his native Inveraray) in Helensburgh on 22 December 1930 of cerebral thrombosis, although the death certificate indicated that he had been suffering from arteriosclerosis for ten years. He was buried in the old graveyard of Inveraray at Kilmalieu on 24 December.

We hope that this anthology will, in addition to giving pleasure to its readers, also help in the process of the re-evaluation of Munro, who has surely been one of the most under-rated of Scottish writers, marginalised when he has not been ignored. One distinguished exception to this treatment of Munro is the American scholar Francis Russell Hart who, in his *The Scottish Novel from Smollett to Spark* (1978), integrates the two areas of Munro's writing. After giving a sensitive and subtle account of the charm and appeal of the Para Handy stories he writes:

The 'tales' are attributed to Munro's alter ego 'Hugh Foulis' as a holiday from serious fiction. George Blake sees through this disguise: Munro's finest characters, he notes, are always complex humorous figures of this sort. Para Handy is not out of place in the romantic, ironic world of Gilian the Dreamer, Ninian Campbell, and John Splendid.

It is a pleasure to acknowledge the help received in the preparation of this anthology from many sources, but particular thanks must go to Lesley Bratton (Munro's granddaughter), Bob Preston and Ronnie Renton. The extracts used from Munro's correspondence are from the Blackwood & Sons and Neil Munro papers in the National Library of Scotland and are given here as printed in Hermann Völkel's *Das Literarische Werk Neil Munros* (Frankfurt, 1996).

Brian D. Osborne
Ronald Armstrong
January 2002

2
The Apprentice Writer

INTRODUCTION

†

Munro started work as a journalist in 1884 on the Greenock Advertiser, *thereafter working on a Glasgow morning paper, the* Glasgow News, *before going, in 1885, to the* Falkirk Herald. *He returned to the* Glasgow News *in 1887 and in 1888 transferred to the* Glasgow Evening News *and was appointed Chief Reporter at a salary of £100 per annum. It was with the* Glasgow Evening News *(under either that title or the* Glasgow News *(1905–15) or the* Evening News *(1915–) that he was associated for most of the rest of his life.*

Apart from his journalism for the News *Munro undertook a considerable amount of extra-curricular work, ranging from writing local content for the Christmas 1888 Glasgow Grand Theatre pantomime 'Babes in the Wood' to reporting sermons for the* Scottish Pulpit. *He also supplied material for the* Dundee Evening Telegraph *from 1890.*

He was ambitious and took every opportunity to place his writing outside Scotland; indeed in 1890 he applied for a post on the London-based daily The Star. *One less obvious source for his work opened up in 1891 when a* News *colleague, John Harvey, left to become editor of the* Newcastle Weekly Courant. *In June of that year he wrote a crime story 'How the Jeweller of Alnbury was Duped' which appeared in the* Courant *and earned him £1. We include it here to mark his breakthrough into fiction.*

Munro developed his expertise in crime/thriller fiction with 'Dr Everton Sharp's Experiment', written for the Christmas 1891 number of the Newcastle Courant. *This story, which sits somewhere between science fiction and the thriller genre, makes few demands on the reader apart from a certain suspension of disbelief. The experiment in question is a human brain transplant and Munro gets round the not inconsiderable difficulty of explaining how this operation was done by his equivalent of the comic book 'With one bound he was free': 'The exact details of what followed would, on account of its technicality, be a mere puzzle to the non-professional reader, and in most cases even to the professional surgeon, many of the methods being absolutely novel.'*

While neither of these stories, which might be characterised as commercial rather than literary, display any outstanding talent, 'Dr Everton Sharp's Experiment' does have overtones of 'The Strange Case of Dr Jekyll and Mr Hyde', with its very Scottish emphasis on duality – a tradition extending back at least to Hogg. It is also rather reminiscent of some of the scientific stories of Conan Doyle. In any event they are of considerable interest in plotting the development of Munro from journalist into short-story writer and novelist. These genre pieces pre-date his first submission of a story on The Lost Pibroch *model to* Blackwoods *in August 1892. The first publication of one of the West Highland stories was of 'Red Hand' which was published in W. E. Henley's* National Observer *in May 1892.*

A novella-length crime story, 'The Afton Moor Mystery', was serialised in a short-lived story paper Quips *in 1893–94. Unfortunately we are unable to present this story as the issue of* Quips *containing the first instalment of the tale is missing from the British Library.*

Munro was able to contribute a wide range of material to a variety of publications and as time went on his record of publication became very substantial – The Globe, The Speaker, Cassell's Saturday Journal, The National Observer *and* Black and White *all published material in 1892. From this collection of fiction, humorous articles and travel pieces we have selected his first successful submission to the recently launched illustrated magazine* Black and White *– a short article on his native county of Argyll, 'Hell's Glen', which appeared in September 1892.*

By the mid 1890s Munro was a well-established writer with most of what would be The Lost Pibroch *stories having appeared in* Blackwood's Magazine *or* The National Observer. *By October 1896 with* The Lost Pibroch *collection published Munro was considered of sufficient literary status to be asked to review J. M. Barrie's* Sentimental Tommy *for* The Bookman *and the idea of retiring to Inveraray, giving up journalism, and living by his literary earnings was beginning to appeal to him.*

In the winter of 1897–98 he carried out part of this idea by resigning his staff appointment with the News, *while continuing as a columnist, and moving out of Glasgow to a house in the village of Waterfoot, near Newton Mearns, a few miles south of Glasgow.*

✝

HOW THE JEWELLER OF ALNBURY WAS DUPED

from the Newcastle Courant, *20 June 1891*

CHAPTER 1

Business was decidedly dull at Alnbury. The next fair was not due for at least six weeks, and the circus which had a fortnight ago gone south to Morpeth had evidently drained the pockets of the burghers, and left them not a single stiver wherewithal to patronise the old-established shop of Joseph B. Wright. Alnbury evidently had no pressing necessity for new watches, or for the repair of old ones for that matter; Alnbury was struggling along without any new investments in eighteen carat gold studs or silver lovers'-knot brooches; Alnbury, in short, had made up its mind to eschew for the time being the vanities that minister to the pride of the eye, and confine the expenditure of its available finances to the absolute necessities of life.

Therefore, it was that Joseph B. Wright – 'Cockney Joe' as the townspeople called him behind his back, in recognition of his London extraction and his occasional lapses into the Cockney tongue – growled grievously at everything and everybody from behind his shop-counter at 67, High Street.

He had been growling with unusual fierceness at his son Jack, whose little peccadillos at the bar of the Red Lion had just come to his father's ears, and was administering to that volatile and hair-brained youth a regular Exeter Hall lecture, when the rattle of carriage wheels in the street directed his attention from his paternal task. The frown that had sat upon his visage a moment before cleared away, and gave place to a bland smile, as the jeweller watched with interest the descent of a well-dressed, aristocratic, middle-aged lady from a neat little barouche, which had just pulled up in front of the shop. Having satisfied himself that the lady's intention was to enter his premises, and not those of John Bolus, the chemist, adjoining, he leaned over the narrow counter, and at the risk of causing an undignified flushed face and ruffled white vest, saved the lady the trouble of opening his glass door by performing the operation himself from the inside.

It was one of those terribly hot days towards the end of July, when a three months' trip to Khamschatka under the personal conductorship of Mr Cook or Mr Gaze would be a paying speculation for either of these gentlemen, if only he had the enterprise to carry it out. Joseph B. Wright, big, broad, and bland, had off his shop coat, and with the easy manners of a true provincial, received the lady in all the starchy grandeur of a six shilling Oxford shirt.

'Mr Wright, I presume?' queried the lady, in a careless, languid tone, as she drew up her veil, and laid a neat silver-clasped portmonniae on the glass-covered case which extended along the counter.

'H'at your service, ma'am,' replied Mr W., showing his elegant two-guinea set of artificial incisors. 'What can I do for you to-day?'

'Well, you see, Mr Wright, we have just come on a somewhat lengthy visit to The Oaks, and Sir William –'

'Jack, give the lady a chair,' said Mr Wright to his son.

'And Sir William, in kindly giving us hints about the shops in Alnbury, mentioned your name as –'

'Yes, ma'am, Sir William has always been a good customer with hus. He even comes 'ere for some of his jewellery hin preference to getting it in the city. In fact,' rattled on the honest shopkeeper, with that petty vanity which likes to puff up its possessor before a stranger – 'in fact, I have in my safe at the present moment a diamond suite I recently procured from London for his lady, an' the settin' of which I am at present making a trifling alteration upon.'

'Mentioned your name as a suitable person to undertake any work for us during our stay at The Oaks,' resumed madame in a tone of hauteur, as if she was determined not to hear the good man's interruption.

'Very proud, ma'am – good stock – good workmen – connection with the best 'ouses in London – all the county families my customers,' Mr Wright muttered disjointedly, with an apologetic cough, for he observed that his customer was a practical person who meant business and not babble.

'We are desirous, Mr Wright,' proceeded the lady, as she condescended to subside into the chair Jack had placed beside her, 'of presenting to the church bazaar at Dillington next week a few trifling presents, and in addition to some crewel work and other little needlework trifles which my daughter has made, my husband – Colonel Wilson – suggests that a couple of cheap watches might be novel, and at the same time, useful articles for Lady William's stall.'

'Certainly ma'am. I shall be delighted to show you watches at all prices. This one at a low figure – only three guineas, English make, double case, compensation –'

'Oh! These are too dear – decidedly too dear for a mere bazaar, Mr – Mr –'

'Wright, if you please, ma'am,' meekly suggested the watchmaker, with the same suave smile on his face, but with a sudden fall of twenty degrees in his estimation of his customer.

'I'm very sorry we 'aven't anything cheaper, ma'am, except – Jack, bring the Waterburys here.'

Jack, having ceased his mild recreation of tossing with a lucky halfpenny for drinks with an imaginary chum, stuck a microscope over his dexter optic to convey the impression that he had been investigating the intestines of a very intricate chronometer, and came out of the back workshop with a box of Waterburys in his hand.

Mrs Wilson glanced at the watches, found what they cost, beat the price down a shilling, and ordered two, paying for them out of her apparently well-filled purse, as Mr Wright put them into a box and tied them up.

'Anything else today, ma'am?'

'No, not today. You can send these watches with Lady William's diamonds to The Oaks.'

'Certainly, ma'am,' said Mr Wright.

'Good day,' frigidly remarked the lady, as she shook her skirts about her and rose to go.

'Good day, ma'am,' said Mr Wright, hastening round the counter, and opening the door to let his customer out.

Mrs Wilson, in a tone that was heard by Mr Wright said, 'The Oaks' to the driver as she was about to step lazily into the barouche, and then, apparently struck with a sudden thought, she stepped back into the watchmaker's shop again.

'By the way, Mr White –'

'Wright, ma'am,' corrected the watchmaker.

'Mr Wright then. Sir William spoke to me about the beautiful design of that diamond suite of his wife's, and as I have never seen them, may I have a look at them?' and she lifted up her veil, laid down her portmonniae, and drew off her gloves, as if there was no 'probable, possible shadow of doubt' about her seeing them.

And neither there was. Why, indeed, should there be?

Mr Wright hastened to open his safe ('proof against the flames of Hetna and the skill of all the burglars in the kingdom' as he was about to brag), and in half a minute Lady William's diamonds lay before Mrs Wilson in all their brilliancy and beauty.

She was charmed! She was delighted and astonished! Such beautiful gems! Such sparkle, such elegance of design she had never seen for years! They even surpassed the much vaunted set of her friend, the Duchess of Draytons!

Mr Wright was pleased, and he rubbed his hands unctuously together. They were a pretty lot of stones, he knew, though – between him and Sir William and the London house – not of the first-class, and he was proud that the bosom friend of the Duchess of What-did-she-call-her and Sir William acknowledged it.

'I must really have such a suite,' said Mrs Wilson, with a decisive snap of the mouth, holding the gems up to let the sun strike the prismatic fire from them.

'They are very valuable stones, ma'am – very valuable, though few in number, and the second set would cost more than the first. A second set would cost, now-a-well-a-about £350, ma'am.' ('She's not a likely one to go in for that,' thought the watchmaker, 'and if she does, £50 is neither here nor there.')

But Mrs Wilson was a likely person to go in for the gems. In fact, before she had left Mr Wright's shop she had given him positive instructions to telegraph immediately to London for a similar suite to be worn on a particular occasion next night, as she explained to Mr Wright, as that gentleman bowed her out with all the grace his somewhat porcine figure was capable of.

'And, oh! by the way,' exclaimed the lady, as she seated herself in her carriage, 'you will observe I have taken the Waterburys with me. It will save you sending them to The Oaks.'

'Thank you, ma'am,' said Mr Joseph B. Wright.

CHAPTER 2

Next day, after dinner, there was little or nothing doing in the way of business, and Mr Wright, leaving his premises in charge of his son, crossed the street to have a talk with his friend Wilkinson, the grocer, who stood with his hands deep in his trousers' pockets in front of his shop, studying with a pleased eye the effect of a recent artistic arrangement of beef cans and mustard tins in his single-show window.

The weather was still warm – so warm indeed that the long High Street was all deserted save for the two worthy shopkeepers, the only police sergeant in the place, who meandered with half-open tunic under the shop-awnings, and a dog, which, with protruding tongue, waiting eagerly in the vicinity of the empty trough at the pump at the head of the street, for the arrival of some kind soul to supply him with a cooling drink of water. The policeman disappeared in a few minutes up the wide entry leading to the smithy; and the dog became impatient and made tracks for some other prospective water supply. The cheeky little sparrows chirped wildly in the eaves of the Red Lion Inn, and the rooks were having a noisy palaver in the beech trees which topped the eminence at the head of the street; but neither sparrows nor rooks were visible from the pavement, and the watchmaker and his friends, leaning lazily against an empty sugar cask, were the only vestiges of life in a thoroughfare as deserted as any in slumbering Pompeii or Herculaneum.

The two worthies stood there long enough to finish their conversation about the coming bazaar at Dillington, and had drifted into a desultory discussion regarding a prospective bowling tournament, when a tall, well-built, 'well put-on' gentleman – who might be either a commercial traveller, or one of the occasional tourists who were beginning to appreciate the sylvan beauties of Alnbury – stepped out of the Red Lion with a toothpick between his teeth, and sauntered up the street past the two natives.

At certain periods of the summer, the advent of a stranger was not unusual enough to create any great amount of curiosity in Alnbury, but this was the dullest month of the Alnbury 'season', so far as the incursion of strangers was concerned; and for that reason, and partly because all the good people of the Sleepy Hollow were naturally fond of poking their noses into matters they had no earthly business with, our two friends, when he of the toothpick had gone out of earshot, began to conjecture who he was.

He wasn't a commercial, Mr Wilkinson thought, for there were no big leather bags in front of the inn, and he did not enter any of the shops on his way up the street.

'He's perhaps one of the visitors at the Hoaks,' hazarded Mr Wright. 'There's a great many toffs there just now, and they may have sent him out to the h'inn for want of sleeping accommodation.'

'More likely he's one of the telegraph people down about the extension of the wires to Danton,' said Mr Wilkinson: and he added immediately afterwards, 'I told you so; he's away into the Post Office,' as the stranger turned into the last shop in the street, which did duty as Her Majesty's Post Office in Alnbury, and was kept by Jem Smith, stationer and newsagent.

Could the two worthy gossips have followed him into the Post Office, however, they would have found that he was not connected with the Telegraph Department. He merely asked the gaunt, keen-eyed custodian of the office if there were any letters 'to be left till called for' by a Mr Morton, and finding that there were none, he leaned over the well-scrubbed, white pine counter, half hidden by its collection of gaudy-coloured 'love and murder' weekly papers, and entered into a desultory conversation with the post-master, who was only too glad to join in a 'two-handed crack' with a stranger, on such a dull gossipless day.

An insinuating rogue was Mr Smith – 'deep, devilish deep', like Major Bagstock – and before the conversation was many minutes old he had wormed out of the stranger – who appeared to be a simple, good-natured, easy-going individual – a few disjointed fragments of information which could not but lead him to the astounding conclusion that Mr Morton was nothing more nor less than a detective after some swindler or swindlers who were hovering about somewhere in the vicinity of unsuspicious Alnbury.

Need it be wondered at, if that afternoon, within half an hour of Mr Morton's retirement to his inn, the entire population of Alnbury were made aware of his calling and his business in the village, by the energetic Mr Smith, who did not fail to convey the idea that he had adroitly 'pumped' the facts out of the ductile stranger.

'And a jolly soft detective he must have been to let such a bass as old Smith know his business in Alnbury,' said Mr J.B. Wright, when Wilkinson had stepped across the road and told him the tidings.

CHAPTER 3

That same evening – five minutes after the village letter-carrier had gone his rounds for the second and last time for the day – the smart barouche of the gallant Captain Wilson (for it was not one of The Oaks vehicles, as Mr Wright observed when he first saw it) dashed up to the watchmaker's shop, and Mrs Wilson, entering, eagerly inquired if the diamonds had yet arrived.

'They've just been handed in this moment by the letter-carrier ma'am. I risked getting them by the registered parcels post, so here they are safe and sound.' And the burly watchmaker opened a little morocco case and showed the gems nestling snugly among the satin of the interior.

'How nice!' said madam, with a sigh of relief. 'I was so afraid they might not come after all. If you wrap them up I shall take them with me. And here are bank notes from which you will please deduct the price of them. I think you said £300 – or was it £350, Mr Wright?'

'Three-fifty, ma'am. You see they were a second –'

'Oh, just so. £350, then. I daresay it was £350. That will be £5 I get back,' putting a bundle of bank-notes on the counter.

Mr Wright moistened his right forefinger, and carefully counted over the flimsies. They were crisp, clean notes, and Mr Joseph mentally wished they had been gold. As he carefully went over them a second time, he cautiously concocted a plan to test them before the lady left, without in any way incurring her displeasure.

'Jack,' he cried to his son, who was carrying out the shutters from the back shop, preparatory to shutting up for the evening, 'go over to Mr Edred, the banker's house – the bank will be shut for the day – and ask him to oblige me with change for this £10 note.'

'I haven't got sufficient change, ma'am,' he smilingly explained to his customer. 'The lad won't be a moment, and during his absence I shall wrap the case up carefully.'

The fact of the matter was that Mr Wright knew very well that if the note was changed by the banker there was no danger of its being anything but genuine.

While Jack was away for the change, Mr Wright and his customer talked of the good weather, the coming bazaar, and the visit of the detective to Alnbury – the last subject being broached by the watchmaker. They mutually agreed that Alnbury was the last place on earth where one would dream of hunting for swindlers, and Mrs Wilson hoped that Mr Morton might be successful in catching them wherever they were.

In a few minutes Jack came back with ten good solid gold pieces, and Mr Wright gave the lady her change, and a receipt for the £350, signing his name in the big bold calligraphy that looked so impressive everywhere it appeared.

Mrs Wilson took her jewels, and put them in her dainty handbag. Mr Wright hastened to show her into her carriage, and with his bald head reflecting the effulgence of the setting sun, beamed blandly after her as the vehicle swept down the street. Then he returned to his shop, whistling joyfully in the exuberance of his pleasure at the thought of the good day's work he had done. Mentally, he promised Mrs Wright a new dress, and himself, as early as possible, an extra glass of his favourite tipple before bed-time, over his profitable diamond transaction.

The barouche could not have been five minutes out of sight, and the watchmaker was putting the more valuable articles from his cases into his safe, when Mr Morton, breathless and excited, rushed into the shop, and astonished its proprietor by abruptly asking if the lady who had just driven off in the barouche had purchased anything.

'She has,' said Mr Wright, 'and she has paid for it, too.'

'She has, has she!' said Mr Morton. 'Then, may I, as an officer of the law, ask what she has purchased, and what she has paid for it?'

'She bought a diamond suite, and paid £350 in notes for them.' Replied the watchmaker, becoming afraid something serious was wrong.

Mr Morton tilted his glossy silk hat well back on his head, leant on his two hands over the counter, stared blankly in the watchmaker's face, and whistled a long whistle of astonishment.

'Well,' he said, in forcible, if not elegant language, when he found voice, 'that's the biggest haul the old lady's had for years.'

With a look of terror on his face, and a sinking at the heart, Mr Wright exclaimed, 'For God's sake, tell me what's wrong, there ain't hanything amiss with the lady, is there?'

'Well,' said the detective, shrugging his shoulders, 'you might as well have thrown the jewels into the sea as give them to the lady you gave them to, for old Mrs Montey is the greatest swindler on this earth, and if she hasn't cheated you –'

'But she paid me for the stones, man,' eagerly burst in the watchmaker, drawing forth and exhibiting to Mr Morton the crisp notes with which he had been paid for the gems. 'And they're straight notes, too, for the banker over the way saw one of them and changed it.'

'Changed the devil,' brusquely said the detective, turning over the notes with a contemptuous flicking of the fingers. 'Only one of these notes – this fiver – is genuine, but every other blessed one of them is rubbish, nothing but rubbish. You have been sold by Montey, who is at her old game of passing flash money again.'

The honest watchmaker almost sank in a swoon on the floor, and he gasped out, 'What's to be done?'

'Done,' echoed Mr Morton, 'why, the best we can, certainly. Put all these bogus notes in a stout envelope, seal it up in the presence of two witnesses. I'll take the notes with me and give you a receipt. You must also give me a short written description of the diamonds, and while you are getting the things ready I'll order a trap at the Red Lion, and if I don't catch up on Mrs Montey before she reaches the city, then I'm a Dutchman.'

With trembling fingers poor Mr Wright did as directed, and Mr Morton, when he returned to the shop, signed the receipt for the alleged bogus notes, which he very carefully placed in his pocket-book along with the hastily written description of the jewels, and having signified his intention of telegraphing the result of his chase from the city ere tomorrow forenoon, mounted the dogcart which awaited him, and swept rapidly towards the city.

Mr Wright was a guileless soul. Mr Wright was trustful as a lamb. Mr Wright waited a week for intelligence of the *soi-disant* Montey, *alias* Mrs Wilson.

When Mr Wright called a meeting of his creditors at the end of the month, they were unanimous in thinking that any man who could be cheated by such a device as that of the ingenious 'Mr Morton' and his female partner in crime, was a fool of the first water, on whom sympathy would be wasted.

'Joe might have known better than to fork out over £300 in good Bank of England notes to any stranger, detective or no detective,' said Wilkinson, the grocer.

'Pooh! any man might have seen that the man Morton was no more a detective than I am!' said the forgetful Mr Smith.

✝

DR SHARP'S EXPERIMENT: A STORY OF
DOUBLE IDENTITY

from the Newcastle Courant, *26 December 1891*

CHAPTER 1

To one in the full vigour of life, with the lusty blood rushing wholesomely through the arteries, there is always a grim repulsiveness about an hospital ward. The very look of the long clean rows of beds, each with its suffering load, brings a chill to the heart; the severe spotlessness of the white bedclothes seem coldly uncomfortable to the eye that is accustomed to unsubdued colours, the atmosphere laden with the suggestive malodour of carbolic is absolutely sickening. In the dim watches of the night when the lights are dulled, when the soft shuffle of the nurses' slippers is only broken by the sudden irresistible moan of an agonised patient, such a place is calculated to bring gloom and misgivings to the stoutest breast.

But a doctor, and especially a doctor with the experience and scientific enthusiasm of Paul Everton Sharp, M.D., if he is not what the unprofessional mind would consider callous, is at least emotionally unaffected by such surroundings. There was doubtless a time when his heart felt sick as he walked the wards and, with the youthful philosophy of the university, vaguely wondered at the mysteries of pain and death, but the doctor more than any other man finds, in the associations of his profession, an early proof of the proverb that 'familiarity breeds contempt' – even of disease, which can sometimes be science, and Death, which is really only a simple cessation of the nervous and circulating systems.

Dr Sharp of St Silas Hospital was, at the period of the Jones-D'Albert Experiment, without doubt one of the most celebrated surgeons in Europe. He was as yet a young man, despite the grey hairs in his beard and the dark furrows on his face. His professional brethren spoke of him confidently as one who, with years might easily acquire the fame of a Jenner, a Pasteur, or a Koch. Even those who do not pretend to technical knowledge will remember the sensation created by his paper on 'Sarcoma' read before one of the sections of the Medical Congress in 188- and the revolution which was caused by his successful experiments in antiseptic operations for tumour of the brain.

The Berlin Medical Guide in reference to his admirable treatise on 'Trepanning for Meningitis', wrote of him as 'Sharp, the English surgeon, who knows more of craniology than any other man living', and it was with no less enthusiasm that that remarkable work was hailed by our own somewhat apathetic *Lancet*, and sceptical *Medical Press*. To his intimate professional acquaintances he was more than a great surgeon – he was in some sort a veritable wizard, whose physiological practice held in contempt the traditions of the past, and whose secret operations gave results which, if openly spoken of, would bring incredulity and contempt upon the narrator who admitted his belief in them.

It was the small hours of the morning when the surgeon, wearing a pair of list slippers to make no noise upon the floor, passed with a half-jaunty air betraying anything but emotional sympathy, between the long rows of beds in the casualty ward of St Silas, and entered a long corridor ending *cul de sac* wise in a wall, in which was set a thick oak door. The door opened on a small apartment usually set aside for patients *in extremis*. It was an airy, though small apartment, of about 12 by 14 feet, and it accommodated two beds. One of these was occupied by an old man, with a strikingly intellectual face; the other by a man of middle age with a particularly low cast of countenance, in which crime and dissipation and the rough impress of the passions had made their indelible mark.

It needed no professional eye to see that both men were on the brink of the grave.

Reading at a study lamp, with green shade, sat Dr Wilson, one of the most trusted and talented of Dr Sharp's assistants. He was a narrow-chested, pale-faced young man, of less than 30 years, full of the enthusiasm of his chief, and he, too, had attained a certain degree of celebrity as a craniologist.

He rose as Dr Sharp entered, looked at his watch, and said, 'So soon? Didn't expect you for half-an-hour, yet.'

'Well, I thought it best to get the business over. I was here before supper, and saw from D'Albert's temperature that he could not be depended upon many hours longer. You have still both of them under the influence of the passes, I suppose?'

'Yes, Jones was restless, and I had a little trouble with him for a time. What a powerful brute he must have been in his normal condition.'

'He was a prize-fighter, I understand, and he has been in the hulks more than once. That massive lower jaw of his looks deadly, and I never knew a man with eyebrows of that peculiar drop who was not a scoundrel. Had you any difficulty in hypnotising him, Wilson?'

'Not the slightest. He went over much more easily than old D'Albert, whose will power is fairly normal, though there's only the faint flicker of life in him.'

A chime on a distant church tower struck the hour of three with solemn cadence, and the sound found its way even into the unconsciousness of the older sleeper. He sighed with the short breath of weak lungs, and stirred uneasily. He was within a span of man's allotted years, and was a victim of pneumonia. A few brief moments and he should be dead.

Dr Sharp was moving noiselessly but rapidly about the room, which had been specially prepared for one of the most daring operations that was ever conceived by the wit of man. An experiment was to be performed which would take the scientific world by storm, and it had been prepared for with the utmost care during the three weeks D'Albert and Jones had been in the hospital.

An extra broad operating table lay in the middle of the floor, underneath a powerful light, meanwhile turned low. Instruments, bandages, sutures, antiseptic solutions, every article that could possibly be needed in the circumstances was within reach, and the room itself, by an ingenious mechanical device, could in five minutes be rendered perfectly aseptic or free from germs, and kept in this condition by constant airing with a sterilised atmosphere.

Jones, the younger patient, was suffering from hydrocephalus, popularly known as water in the head, probably the effect of an hereditary taint. A careful diagnosis by Dr Sharp, and a fortnight's study and treatment of the case, had convinced the latter that Jones could be cured by a surgical operation. Both Jones and D'Albert had become patients of St Silas on the one day, the doctor had examined them both as they lay in adjoining beds, and there had there and then come to him the sudden thought that here at last was the opportunity he had long wished for. It made his pulse beat swift as the idea flashed on him. The old man, with a powerful brain, that had coped successfully with the greatest problems of time and philosophy, it was evident could not by any possibility elude the grim leveller, but the younger man, whose physique was marvellous, might, by the exercise of careful surgical skill be yet brought round to health and strength.

For many months it had been the surgeon's desire to make an experiment, which to men of less genius would be considered madness of the most awful character. The time had come, he thought, when surgical science had reached such a state of perfection that Goethe's conception of Faust's demoniac transformation, or of Byron's 'Deformed Transformed' – a weak old man's brain surmounting the frame, and fed by the life blood of a young and vigorous giant, might be realised in the most practical manner. Here was the very chance he sought. Here were the very subjects on which such an operation could best be carried out, not only at no loss to humanity in the case of failure, but with the prospect of ridding the world of one villain, and saving for it a brilliant and noble intellect. D'Albert's brain was as vigorous as ever it was, as a lecture he had delivered a month ago to the Philosophical Society admirably demonstrated;

were the experiment a success, that wonderful intellect, grafted on to a healthy young body, would enrich the world of thought for many years to come, and all that would be lost would be the body of D'Albert, doomed at any rate, and the weak brain of the prize-fighter.

It was an experiment that must be carried out secretly, and yet it was one that necessitated at the very least a colleague. With a certain amount of natural reluctance Dr Sharp confided his scheme to his assistant, who gratified him beyond measure by entering into the project with the utmost enthusiasm.

For days the subjects were the object of ceaseless attention. Their diet was regulated with the utmost care. Never in the history of surgery had patients been so carefully prepared for a capital operation.

With cats for subjects, fully a dozen preliminary tests were made of the new and startling operation, and though the three first of these were unsuccessful, owing to apparently trivial, but really all-important, mistakes on the part of the operators, the following tests were carried through with a success which astonished the surgeons themselves.

At early morning, then, in the small ward of St Silas, the two surgeons were now prepared to exercise on human beings instead of dumb animals the most extraordinary surgical operation ever attempted in the annals of surgical science.

Wilson, with a few rapid passes intensified the hypnotic condition of both subjects. Hypnotism, as applied to surgery and as a means of suggestion, was an art he had learned in the course of a twelvemonth's experience at the Salpêtrière in Paris.

Then the patients were lifted on to the operating table.

The exact details of what followed would, on account of its technicality, be a mere puzzle to the non-professional reader, and in most cases even to the professional surgeon, many of the methods being absolutely novel. It is sufficient to say that the first part of the process consisted simply in the dissection of the contents of the cranium of the unconscious subjects. This done the brain of Jones was removed from the now collapsed parasitical water-sac of the prize-fighter, and that of D'Albert was substituted.

Careful measurements made in advance had satisfied the operators that D'Albert's brain could be accommodated in its new home. With rapid but skilled fingers, arteries, nerves and veins were brought into apposition and connected. Each strand of the nervous and circulating system was made fast to its proper combination. Differences in the position of the various apertures and nerve currents in D'Albert's brain as compared with the smaller brain of Jones had been allowed for in dissection, and little difficulty was experienced in making all the connections. By this time the body of D'Albert was dead and *rigor mortis* had already set in.

Jones, on the other hand, having his respiratory organs kept in operation by ceaseless artificial means on the part of Dr Wilson, had a circulation so sluggish that scarcely a drop of blood was lost.

'So far we are all right,' whispered Sharp. 'There is not a single sign of haemorrhage in the cavity, and it was the only thing I feared.'

'The healthy circulation must be more fully restored, sir,' suggested Wilson, and as this only demanded a very simple mode of assistance to nature it was soon accomplished.

All this time Jones – or, to speak with literal correctness, Jones-D'Albert – lay inert. The whole operation was carried through in a marvellously short space of time, and when the head had been closed and carefully covered with antiseptic wrapping, the sad grey dawn was creeping in at the window.

Jones-D'Albert was carefully restored to his bed, all traces of his part in the great operation were removed, and when the active day of the institution began, the porters had to take to the mortuary the body of the old man who 'had succumbed during a critical operation on the part of Dr Sharp.'

An hour later the two surgeons – Sharp elate and talkative, Wilson unusually quiet and sad – sat at their breakfast table.

'If it pulls through,' said Sharp, chipping the top of an egg, 'we shall astonish the world.'

'Yes,' answered the younger man, somewhat dubiously. 'But I'm afraid our failure to remove the whole of the medulla oblongata may have a serious effect on the result.'

It took three weeks before the mental result of the great operation could be ascertained. Watched day and night with more assiduity than if he had been an emperor upon whose fate lay the peace of Europe, Jones-D'Albert slowly drew back from the gates of death. The wound healed, the physical union of the new brain with the old cavity was, so far as could yet be known, complete. But the brain of D'Albert was still under the hypnotic influence of the surgeon, and its mental energy could only be roused, if it could be roused at all, by the 'suggestion' of Dr Wilson.

Nourishment in carefully measured doses, and at mathematically regular periods was administered to the patient, and it became evident at last that his system was fully recovered from the shock of scalpel and saw. As his physical strength increased, he became impatient in his unconsciousness, and the critical day arrived when it was considered safe to make the final and crucial test of the experiment, to see if he were a mere automaton, or a man with the intellect of a human being.

In the little room which – unknown to all the other members of the hospital staff – contained the mental half of one man and the physical half of the other – in other words, a body and soul which had not originally belonged to each other, Sharp and Wilson, three weeks and two days after the thrilling experiment at early dawn, put that experiment to its final test.

Strong stimulants were applied to the patient, and with a few hypnotic passes, 'suggestion' was imparted by the younger surgeon.

A strange expectant look came over the face of the subject, his lips parted, a guttural sound came from his larynx. Eagerly Sharp bent down to hear what should follow. There was a faint muttering, altogether unintelligible at first, then a clear whisper, and a gleam of triumph shot over the countenance of the scientist as the subject, in words which Jones's meagre vocabulary never knew, incoherently framed some inconsequent sentences. In themselves the words meant nothing, but in the ears of Sharp they came as joy bells, for they told him that the complex being lying before him was in a half-dream, working out some unsolved mathematical problem which had engrossed the mind of the dead *savant* ere he became ill.

A few moments later and the patient sat up in bed, passed a nervous hand over his eyes, and glanced inquiringly around him. It was curious to note how the evil countenance of Jones was to a great extent transfigured, as it were, by the refinement of its new soul. The eyes were softer, the mouth less cruel – it was as if a strain of sweet music, suggestive of love and home and the innocence of youth had fallen on the ear of a prodigal son and for a moment blotted out a life-recollection of evil days and devious ways.

'I am better, doctor,' he stammered forth rather weakly, looking at Dr Sharp, who handed him a cordial. 'I feel wonderfully refreshed in my sleep, and I breathe quite easily.'

'Yes, you are very much better,' replied Sharp, 'quite a different man in fact. We have had an operation which has been successful I am glad to say, and you have got over it admirably.'

'Ah! I knew there was something. I felt during my sleep that something was happening or had happened. I dreamt of Paradise and the Celestial Choristers, and then I felt purgatorial pains in my head.'

'The hypnotic suggestion, that was all,' interrupted the practical Wilson.

'Dear me, I feel better than I have done for twenty years, and I have actually gained flesh. How long have I been unconscious?'

'Oh, a pretty long time,' replied Dr Sharp. 'But lie down just now and do not exert yourself. It will be necessary to exercise great caution for some time.'

Jones-D'Albert lay down and slept that night the sleep of health.

In a few days he was able to rise and take brief airings on the south balconies.

Sharp and Wilson had every day more reason to be satisfied with the success of the experiment. The man was a perfect miracle of physical and mental perfection. Nature herself rarely turns out such a combination of virtues as were in this product of nineteenth-century science. He was vivacious, happy, and talked with scholarly charm to his creators, and he was never done extolling that skill which had restored him to such health and strength.

There was one thing which for a time troubled the doctors. Jones-D'Albert had at all hazards to be kept from seeing his face in a mirror. His wonder had been early aroused by the fact that the callosities of hard work were in the palms of his hands, and that his finger nails were not of the taper shape which they had before he became ill. His limbs, too, seemed in a way 'a bad fit'. He was awkward in many things, and they were in some inexplicable way unfamiliar to him.

He had no relatives, and friends who called to inquire for him were never afforded an interview.

'We must explain the affair to him sooner or later,' said Sharp, one day. 'He must leave here in a few days, and it will be better for us to break the matter to him judiciously, than if it should be brought home to him suddenly and hastily.'

The revelation was diplomatic and gentle. A casual conversation on surgery between D'Albert and Dr Sharp led on to the particular subject of grafting, with which D'Albert had something of a layman's acquaintance. His views on a hypothetical case were ascertained – a case of brain grafting instead of mere bone and cuticle. He smiled with a blandness which sat tolerably well on the countenance of Jones, whose facial muscles were unused to such contractions, and he interrupted the doctor to say: 'I suspect what this is going to lead to. On my right arm this morning, for the first time I noticed a tattooed ship with full sails set. The marks are years old and yet I was not tattooed on the body which I brought to St Silas with me.'

Three days later, when Sharp was ready to produce to a select meeting of medical men the greatest wonder of the age, it was found that the interesting subject of one of the most marvellous experiments in the domain of psychological science had disappeared mysteriously from the hospital of St Silas. No one had seen his departure, and his whereabouts could not be discovered, even by the best-trained sleuth hounds of Scotland Yard. Jones-D'Albert was to all intents and purposes blotted out of existence.

CHAPTER 2

Dr Paul Everton Sharp, M.D., died six months after the eventful affair reported in the previous chapter. The most promising, and in some departments already the most eminent craniologist in Europe, met the ultimate fate which science can never avert. Death, who chuckles – if so solemn a mystery can chuckle – over the vain groping and the impotent self-assurance of the scientist, cut off the doctor with exactly the same sort of weapons with which he daily dispatches men of far less eminence and far less practical medical skill. A rapid rush for a train – a chill unheeded – acute congestion – and that was all.

Dr Wilson, by natural promotion, fell into the office of senior surgeon and filled it successfully, if not with the same eminence as his predecessor.

It was three years after the mysterious disappearance of D'Albert – the full details connected with which the two surgeons never made public – that Dr Wilson, reading his evening paper one afternoon, had his attention attracted by the following report, heavily 'leaded' to use the phraseology of the printer, and headed by 'scare' lines in the boldest and blackest type contained in the cases of the *News*.

MYTERIOUS MURDER IN DOLCHESTER
A Crime of Christmas Day
(From Our Own Correspondent)

At an early hour this morning, a tragedy of the most terrible character was enacted in the town of Dolchester. The private residence of Mr Frank R Sutton, bank agent, was broken into, evidently at some time after midnight, and an attempt was made to force open a safe containing a large and valuable collection of uncut diamonds which had been put under the charge of the banker by Sir George Home of Hatterley House, South Doulton, to be kept during the absence of the latter gentleman, who is wintering at the Riviera. Foiled in his attempts to burst open the safe, after arduous efforts, in which every appliance known to the burglar's craft was brought into play, the burglar evidently determined to vent his disappointment and rage on the unfortunate banker, who was asleep in a remote part of the house. The door of the banker's bedroom was burst open, and a couple of merciless slashes with a sheath knife ended the career of one of the most highly regarded gentlemen in the West. There was evidently no warning for the victim; his position and the appearance of his features showed that he had been done to death in his sleep.

The murderer would appear to have been alarmed in the execution of his awful deed, for the sheath knife, an ugly weapon with a blade fully four inches long, was left lying on the bed, although it afforded an unerring clue to the identity of the murderer in the name of 'Jeff Jones' cut rudely on its bone handle. When the murder was discovered by the housemaid at the Bank, and the police were communicated with, they were speedily on the track of Jeff Jones, who is a convict out on ticket-of-leave. According to the terms of his parole Jones had at regular stated periods reported himself to the police of Dolchester, and did so as late as Monday last. He then reported that he was still carrying out his old occupation of hawking, showed his hawker's licence, and gave an account of his last trip, which extended, he said, as far north as Carlisle. On Tuesday, Jones was seen at a local tavern called 'The Green Man', and that night, as well as on Monday night, he lodged at a common lodging-house kept by an Irishman named Donnelly. He left Donnelly's yesterday morning, carrying a small bag, and his movements since then are not known with exactitude.

LATER

Inquiries made today by the police have completely satisfied them that the account given by Jones of his hawking expedition was absolutely false. It has transpired that on several occasions during the past two months at the time he was supposed to be up in the vicinity of the Border, he was seen at various points within thirty miles of Dolchester, his actions on these occasions being of such a character as to create suspicion. Jones's behaviour within the last three years has been of a very curious character. He has only been seen at Dolchester when reporting himself to the police, and it is now evident that in the towns and villages where he was supposed to be carrying on his calling he was altogether unknown. As yet the police have, however, failed to find out where he spent his time during these long periodical absences from Dolchester. The circumstances connected with the tragedy have acquired a fresh mystery. The diamonds were only deposited at Mr Sutton's on Tuesday night. No one can understand how Jones could have known of their being there. Under ordinary circumstances they should have been placed in the bank strong-room, but they arrived at an hour when the bank was closed for the day, and were meant to be only temporarily accommodated in the safe in Mr Sutton's house, which forms one of the wings of the bank building. The depositing of the jewels was carried out by Sir George Home himself, and the fact that they were there could be known only to himself, the steward, and the bankers.

Dr Wilson, who had begun the perusal of the above report with indifference, had his interest quickly aroused when he came upon the name of Jeff Jones.

'Why,' he exclaimed aloud to himself, 'that was the name of the ex-prize fighter who was one of the subjects of our brain transfer experiment. The idea may be absurd, but there is just the faintest chance that the perpetrator of this outrage at Dolchester may be the very gentleman whose disappearance three years ago effectively destroyed the final scene in our performance. But if this wild fancy of mine should prove correct, how are we to account for the loss of those very fine moral characteristics which by right belonged to the brain of D'Albert?'

To think, with Dr Wilson, was to act. It was in a sense an off-day with him, though Christmas holidays were not popular at St Silas. So an hour later he was at the railway station purchasing a return ticket for Dolchester.

Police-Superintendent George, a Scotch inspector, and a detective from Leeds were discussing the murder when Dr Wilson appeared at Dolchester Police Station. His card was enough to secure for him the utmost deference.

'I may be wrong,' he said, 'but I fancy I may be able to throw some light upon the tragedy.'

'Delighted to hear it, sir,' said the superintendent. 'Fact of the matter is, we are completely off the scent. We don't pretend to be so sharp as those Scotland Yard fellows, but up till half an hour ago we did think that to lay hands on our man was as easy as –'

'Knocking the head off a glass of beer,' broke in the detective, who seemed to have a humorous faculty in simile.

'We have traced Jones,' continued the superintendent, 'to the 7.15 a.m. train, which he left at South Doulton, fifteen miles from here. But we have completely lost track of him there.'

'What sort of a place is South Doulton?' asked the doctor.

'Oh, a little village of a thousand inhabitants or so, where a man of his stamp could readily be laid hands on.'

'Have you a photograph of Jones?' then asked the doctor, anxious that the conclusions he was forming in his own mind should not be based upon false premises.

'We have,' said the superintendent, who very soon produced the Rogues Album, that strange pictorial record of criminal physiognomy, which can be found in every well regulated police station. Thieves, garrotters, burglars, murderers – their portraits faithfully caught by the camera of the criminal officer, were rapidly run over until the lineaments of Jeff Jones were exposed to view.

There was no mistake about it; the portrait presented to the gaze of the house surgeon of St Silas was undoubtedly that of the man who three years ago lay upon the operating table, the unconscious subject of the Everton-Sharp experiment. The firm jaw, the broad nose, the drooping eyebrows, were without question familiar to the doctor, and if any further confirmation of his suspicion were needed, he found it in the descriptive footnote attached to the portrait.

According to this description the most prominent mark on the body of the ticket-of-leave man was a full-rigged ship tattooed indelibly on his left arm.

'Just as I thought,' said the doctor. 'Now, do you know of any *alias* he was in the habit of using?'

'No, you see he never stayed here long at a time, and being a ticket-of-leave man, there was little use of his assuming an *alias*.'

'Did he never assume the name of D'Albert?'

'Not that I know,' replied the superintendent.

'D'Albert!' said the Scotch inspector musingly. 'That is the name of Sir George Home's steward, if I'm not mistaken.'

'Ah!' cried the doctor, 'and Sir George is the man to whom the jewels belonged?'

'That's so.'

'Have any of you ever seen this steward?'

The officers admitted that none of them had seen the gentleman in question. He lived on Sir George's estate, a mile or two out of South Doulton, was a very retired man, and was greatly esteemed by Sir George, whose service he had entered a few years ago, and who found in him an invaluable assistant in those archaeological and philological researches which were the hobbies of the baronet of Hatterley.

'Where did he come from?' followed up the doctor.

On this point the officers were unable to enlighten him. All that they could say was that the steward had never previously held a similar appointment, and that as his antecedents were remarkably obscure, other county families had been surprised at the readiness of Sir George to entrust him with a post of so much responsibility.

'So! Then I think I have got at the bottom of two mysteries. If I am not greatly mistaken, you will find that D'Albert the steward is one and the same man as Jeff Jones the murderer.

'I had always,' he continued, more to himself than to his hearers, 'a suspicion that the half-inch of the original medulla oblongata which Dr Sharp left in the cavity of Jones would result in curious eccentricities of mental character.'

Extract from Evening News *of 3 January, 188–:*

Unfortunately, or fortunately, as it may occur to the minds of some people, Jeff Jones alias Samuel W. D'Albert, has by his own hand expiated the horrible crime of which he was guilty on Christmas Day. When Superintendent George, acting upon the information of the celebrated surgeon already mentioned, yesterday reached the residence of Sir George Home's steward, and told him that he was under arrest for murder, the latter, with a promptness which showed that he was prepared for discovery at any moment, took a revolver from his pocket and shot himself dead. It appears that the success with which D'Albert the steward concealed his identity from the people of South Doulton, who knew Jeff Jones fairly well, was that he invariably wore in the former character blue-tinted spectacles and a grey wig, which most effectively altered his appearance. It is without his disguising wig and glasses that Jeff Jones, or Samuel W. D'Albert, lies today at the mortuary at Dolchester with a suicide's bullet in his brain.

'Not exactly in *his* brain either,' was the mental comment of Dr Wilson, as he turned over the pages of the *News* in his comfortable sitting room in St Silas' Hospital.

HELL'S GLEN

The wild and awful grandeur of Loch Coruisk, the loneliness and mystery of the great Moor of Rannoch, and the sadness and desolation of Glencoe have so much claimed the attention of the tourist in Scotland that Hell's Glen is practically unknown. It lies out of the route of those who are seeking the higher altitudes of the 'true and tender north', *via* the North British and Highland Railways, and, it is equally inaccessible to those who go west to the dim Hebrides by way of the turbulent 'Moil' of Kintyre, or the placid and somewhat monotonous Crinan Canal. Yet Glasgow is practically at its gates, and in little over three hours after the malodorous Broomielaw is left astern, one can reach our charmèd gorge of ominous name, with its huge stern dignity, its eternal repose and that fine spiritual influence that comes from 'the sleep that is among the lonely hills'.

Less than half-an-hour's sail from Greenock the villadom of Glasgow's merchants is for the most part left behind as the steamer enters Loch Long. The far reaching sea-arm pierces the mountains like a Norwegian fjord. But the slopes of the hillsides are softer, the far-off peaks that close the vista swim in a haze that gives a magic and a poetry the Norwegian summits never know. The Hartz Hills, the tree-clad Schwarzwald, the Feldberg, and the Belchen may be higher, and more fully fill the eye that seeks form alone, but they lack the opulent colour, the positive delirium of that Montichellian palette with which nature has painted those softly curved Argyllshire hills. The loch, if the day be calm, captures the reflection of the most infinite detail upon the coast – farms, cots, fields, sheep-drains, and purple heather. A tiny ripple, or the dip of a seagull, may quiver the picture into pieces for a moment, but that is all.

Hell's Glen lies two miles west of the hamlet at the head of Lochgoil, which breaks off from Loch Long before the rugged peaks of 'Argyll's Bowling Green' have been reached. A coach of the old order drawn by a quartette of horses handled by an old Highlander, runs through the glen to St Catherines on the shores of Loch Fyne, but the nine miles which divide the two sea-arms can easily be negotiated by a stout heart and a strong pair of boots. In truth, the walk is preferable to the drive, for honest old Hugh Cameron, who has toiled over the rough road for nearly a decade, has learned by long experience to keep his horses preternaturally cool, greatly to his own ultimate gain, but rather to the harrassment of impatient passengers. Two miles of flat white road, bordered by arable and pasture land, bring us to the steep ascent which must be scaled before Hell's Glen is entered. A keen eye, even in the adventurer to whom the region is unknown, discovers a footpath through the wood which makes the climb easier. It is half lost in the errant water of a peat-tanned burn which in broken courseless flatness flows vagrantly anywhere. The burn being forded, the path zig-zags uphill under a profusion of young trees. The birch, sweet scented and silver barked, swings its feathered bough across to caress the rowan's scarlet bunches; the hazel, nut-laden and downy green, the moss-grown oak, 'tenacious of its leaves of russet brown', the slender ash and fast-fading lime mingle their plumage in an arch of undescribably beautiful green through which the sun's hot shafts filter cool and pleasant.

The short cut counts nearly half a mile off our estimated nine miles, and lands us at the mouth of the glen. Like a white ribbon, the sinuous road winds before. The arable land is behind, only rock, torrent and huge towering mountain lies beyond. Past the rock, from whose lion face spouts a cool stream of spring water, is Desolation. The solitude is oppressive, the silence profound; only in nightmares do we behold such vast o'er-towering rocks. They hem us in – close, weak, puny, helpless! Ages of elemental storm and strife, the jar of earthquakes, the dash of thunderstorms, the leverage of frost and rain have sundered the Titans from their solid mother mountains and scattered them over the hill face on either side. Some of them, hundreds of tons in weight, have slipped and torn great gashes down the hills for a thousand yards, leaving cavernous gaps over which the harebell or the purple heath dizzily nods, and the stray sheep sometimes crumbles, to be dashed to death on the quartz floor below. Other blocks, poised as on a finger tip, seem to invite the faintest breath of wind to hurl their colossal proportions into the valley. Between the rocks, high up, the short grass tempts the adventurous black-faced sheep, whose position seems absolutely inaccessible, but is, nevertheless, frequently surmounted by the shepherd and his collie. Noisy streams hurry down with many an unexpected leap over some moss-grown giant stone, but not a single tree meets the eye to relieve the monotony of rude, primeval rock-rib and scantily sown quartz soil. The autumn echo of the cuckoo sounds curiously enough in a glen without a coppice; much more to be expected is the incessant shrilling of the lapwing which, with quaint flicker of wing, darts hither and yond below the brown bald forehead of Clach-na-coû. Even the red deer finds in this desolate region no encouragement to linger when they seek its shade in the hot days, the grouse may find a precarious living among the bleached heather roots, but the ptarmigan and the white hare in their season are more at home on the cloud kissed summits. A thousand sweet odours fill the air, but the bog-myrtle tops them all. There is here a dreariness almost oppressive, even in the height of summer when the sun brings out the richest colour harmonies in nature; in autumn, when the whole world seems sobered down to a sombre grey brown, it is heartbreaking in its desolation and suggestivesness of the weakness and the mutability of life; but in winter –! Hugh Cameron can tell of the grim terror of that season in Hell's Glen, of the dim, cloud-wrapped brief days, when the rains batter down ceaseless and relentless, and the road sogs below the horses' feet, and the mist lies close in on the leader's ears, when the sheep drains swell to brawling mountain torrents, and wash the great o'er-hanging rocks across the highways. Or he can make one shiver in hot July with the chill, chill tale of snowstorm and black frost – road like iron and only to be vaguely guessed at in the wreaths, burns chrystalled, resonant like bells muffled, peaks unfamiliar below their dazzling whiteness, sheep 'smoored' in the drift that swirls furiously through the Pass!

3

The Lost Pibroch and Other
Sheiling Stories (1896)

INTRODUCTION

†

The publication of The Lost Pibroch *collection in 1896 by William Blackwood & Son marked the arrival of a new and considerable talent on the literary scene. Munro, then aged 33, was an established figure in the world of journalism and had published a wide range of commercial short fiction in a variety of publications.*

The Edinburgh based Blackwood's Magazine, *on the other hand, was one of the longest-established and most distinguished literary journals of the period.* Maga *(as it was popularly known) had a great tradition and a distinguished list of contributors and its approval was an eagerly sought prize. Munro had first applied to* Maga *in 1887 with a poem, which was rejected. In 1892 he submitted 'Anapla's Boy' – 'a West Highland sketch.' This was also rejected, but with, as William Blackwood observed to Munro, a degree of hesitation and regret. 'Anapla's Boy' was never published although Munro retained the manuscript despite a suggestion in his diary that he had destroyed it. Blackwood's rejection was sufficiently encouraging for Munro to swiftly respond by submitting 'The Secret of the Heather Ale', and in 1893 'Shudderman Soldier'. This latter story was accepted and appeared in the October 1893 edition. A number of other of the stories which were to form the collection appeared over the next couple of years and in 1896* The Lost Pibroch and Other Sheiling Stories *was published in an edition of 1,500 copies – a reasonable print-run for a work by a relatively unknown author.*

In February 1897 Blackwoods were able to report to Munro that although stock still remained the production costs had been covered, and they sent him his first royalty payment for the book – £4 13s. 4d. More interestingly, they reported approaches from the US publishers, Harpers, who wished to purchase an edition of 1,600 copies for the American market – a significant breakthrough for a new writer and a good omen for the success in the US of his first novel, John Splendid, *on which Munro was then at work.*

The Lost Pibroch *was a considerable critical success. Andrew Lang, perhaps the leading critic of the day wrote:*

In The Lost Pibroch *we meet genius as obvious and undeniable as that of Mr Kipling . . . Mr Munro's powers are directed to old Highland life, and he does what genius alone can do – he makes it alive again, and makes our imagination share its life – his knowledge being copious, original, at first hand.*

He did also say, in the context of a review of John Splendid, *that* The Lost Pibroch *was 'esoteric and appealed to the few'. In fact* The Lost Pibroch *proved to be not only a critical success but also a popular one. After a few years of steady sales of the full price and cheap editions, a 6d. edition was produced which sold over 21,000 copies in its first year on the market – a remarkable figure for a collection of short stories, 'esoteric' or otherwise.*

Lang's epithet may perhaps be true of our first choice from the collection – the title story The Lost Pibroch. *At first glance the sprinkling of Gaelic words through the text looks off-putting to an English-speaking audience but in fact most can be easily enough deduced from their context. Perhaps more problematical is the use of a heavily Gaelic influenced syntax. Munro, brought up in a Gaelic-speaking environment, rejected the mock Gaelic of Scott and Hogg and their later imitators, what he described as 'bagpipes and bad English'. As he wrote to William Blackwood in 1893: 'I am a Highlander by birth and upbringing; I know the language and I believe I know the heart of the Highland people. If I have but the technical ability, I have, I think, the imagination and the ability to make good stuff of a style no modern writer is attempting.'*

Certainly, Munro's Gaelic-influenced prose was original. The absence of a prose fiction tradition in Gaelic until the twentieth century meant that, even for Gaelic speakers, there had been no fiction which truly reflected Gaelic life, language and feeling. Munro would develop this in his later novels, perhaps most strikingly in Children of Tempest *his 1903 novel set in the Western Isles.*

Ronnie Renton in his edition of The Lost Pibroch *stories (House of Lochar, 1996) has suggested of this story that 'It is possible to see it as an allegory of the history of the Highlands depicting the dereliction of the Highland way of life after Culloden, the Clearances and the years of emigration.' Certainly the process of change in the Highlands would be a major theme of much of Munro's historical fiction.*

Less esoteric perhaps is our second selection – a short but grim story which recycles the old Scottish legend of the secret of the Heather Ale. A secret which, in some versions, such as that recounted in verse by Robert

Louis Stevenson, sets the story in the period around the supplanting of the supposedly dwarfish, undergound-dwelling Picts by the Scots:

> *From the bonny bells of heather*
> *They brewed a drink long-syne,*
> *Was sweeter far than honey,*
> *Was stronger far than wine.*
> *They brewed it and they drank it,*
> *And lay in blessed swound*
> *For days and day together*
> *In their dwellings undergound.*

Munro's version is set around Inveraray and at the time of the 1st Marquis of Argyll, Archibald Campbell, 'Gillesbeg Gruamach' (1607–61) – a period and a character who were to feature in John Splendid. *The 'Pictish' possessors of the secret of heather ale are represented by the Mackellars, while those who seek the secret are MacArthurs – allies of Clan Campbell and part of the House of Diarmid – the mythical progenitor of the Campbells. In Munro's version, as in Stevenson's, the possessor of the secret dies rather than share it with the hated enemy.*

THE LOST PIBROCH

To the make of a piper go seven years of his own learning and seven generations before. If it is in, it will out, as the Gaelic old-word says; if not, let him take to the net or sword. At the end of his seven years one born to it will stand at the start of knowledge, and leaning a fond ear to the drone, he may have parley with old folks of old affairs. Playing the tune of the 'Fairy Harp', he can hear his forefolks, plaided in skins, towsy-headed and terrible, grunting at the oars and snoring in the caves; he has his whittle and club in the 'Desperate Battle' (my own tune, my darling!), where the white-haired sea-rovers are on the shore, and a stain's on the edge of the tide; or, trying his art on Laments, he can stand by the cairn of kings, ken the colour of Fingal's hair, and see the moon-glint on the hook of the Druids!

Today there are but three pipers in the wide world, from the Sound of Sleat to the Wall of France. Who they are, and what their tartan, it is not for one to tell who has no heed for a thousand dirks in his doublet, but they may be known by the lucky ones who hear them. Namely players tickle the chanter and take out but the sound; the three give a tune the charm that I mention – a long thought and a bard's thought, and they bring the notes from the deeps of time, and the tale from the heart of the man who made it.

But not of the three best in Albainn to-day is my story, for they have not the Lost Pibroch. It is of the three best, who were not bad, in a place I ken – Half Town that stands in the wood.

You may rove for a thousand years on league-long brogues, or hurry on fairy wings from isle to isle and deep to deep, and find no equal to that same Half Town. It is not the splendour of it, nor the riches of its folk; it is not any great routh of field or sheep-fank, but the scented winds of it, and the comfort of the pine-trees round and about it on every hand. My mother used to be saying (when I had the notion of fairy tales), that once on a time, when the woods were young and thin, there was a road through them, and the pick of children of a countryside wandered among them into this place to play at sheilings. Up grew the trees, fast and tall, and shut the little folks in so that the way out they could not get if they had the mind for it. But never an out they wished for. They grew with the firs and alders, a quiet clan in the heart of the big wood, clear of the world out-by.

But now and then wanderers would come to Half Town, through the gloomy coves, under the tall trees. There were packmen with tales of the out-world. There were broken men flying from rope or hatchet. And once on a day of days came two pipers – Gilian, of Clan Lachlan of Strathlachlan, and Rory Ban, of the Macnaghtons of Dundarave. They had seen Half Town from the sea – smoking to the clear air on the hillside; and through the weary woods they came, and the dead quiet of them, and they stood on the edge of the fir-belt.

Before them was what might be a township in a dream, and to be seen at the one look, for it stood on the rising hill that goes back on Lochow.

The dogs barked, and out from the houses and in from the fields came the quiet clan to see who could be here. Biggest of all the men, one they named Coll, cried on the strangers to come forward; so out they went from the wood-edge, neither coy nor crouse, but the equal of friend or foe, and they passed the word of day.

'Hunting,' they said, 'in Easachosain, we found the roe come this way.'

'If this way she came, she's at Duglas Water by now, so you may bide and eat. Few, indeed, come calling on us in Half Town; but whoever they are, here's the open door, and the horn spoon, and the stool by the fire.'

He took them in and he fed them, nor asked their names nor calling, but when they had eaten well he said to Rory, 'You have skill of the pipes; I know by the drum of your fingers on the horn spoon.'

'I have tried them,' said Rory, with a laugh, 'a bit – a bit. My friend here is a player.'

'You have the art?' asked Coll.

'Well, not what you might call the whole art,' said Gilian, 'but I can play – oh yes! I can play two or three ports.'

'You can that!' said Rory.

'No better than yourself, Rory.'

'Well, maybe not, but – anyway, not all tunes; I allow you do "Mackay's Banner" in a pretty style.'

'Pipers,' said Coll, with a quick eye to a coming quarrel, 'I will take you to one of your own trade in this place – Paruig Dall, who is namely for music.'

'It's a name that's new to me,' said Rory, short and sharp, but up they rose and followed Big Coll.

He took them to a bothy behind the Half Town, a place with turf walls and never a window, where a blind man sat winding pirns for the weaver-folks.

'This,' said Coll, showing the strangers in at the door 'is a piper of parts, or I'm no judge, and he has as rare a stand of great pipes as ever my eyes sat on.'

'I have that same,' said the blind man, with his face to the door. 'Your friends, Coll?'

'Two pipers of the neighbourhood,' Rory made answer. 'It was for no piping we came here, but by the accident of the chase. Still and on, if pipes are here, piping there might be.'

'So be it,' cried Coll; 'but I must go back to my cattle till night comes. Get you to the playing with Paruig Dall and I'll find you here when I come back.' And with that he turned about and went off.

Paruig put down the ale and cake before the two men, and 'Welcome you are,' said he.

They ate the stranger's bite, and lipped the stranger's cup, and then, 'Whistle "The Macraes' March", my fair fellow,' said the blind man.

'How ken you I'm fair?' asked Rory.

'Your tongue tells that. A fair man has aye a soft bit in his speech, like the lapping of milk in a cogie; and a black one, like your friend there, has the sharp ring of a thin burn in frost running into an iron pot. "The Macraes' March", *laochain*.'

Rory put a pucker on his mouth and played a little of the fine tune.

'So!' said the blind man, with his head to a side, 'you had your lesson. And you, my Strathlachlan boy without beard, do you ken "Muinntir a'Ghlinne so"?'

'How ken ye I'm Strathlachlan and beardless?' asked Gilian.

'Strathlachlan by the smell of herring-scale from your side of the house (for they told me yesterday the gannets were flying down Strathlachlan way, and that means fishing), and you have no beard I know, but in what way I know I do not know.'

Gilian had the *siubhal* of the pibroch but begun when the blind man stopped him.

'You have it,' he said, 'you have it in a way, the Macarthur's way and that's not my way. But, no matter, let us to our piping.'

The three men sat them down on three stools on the clay floor, and the blind man's pipes passed round between them.

'First,' said Paruig (being the man of the house, and to get the vein of his own pipes) – 'first I'll put on them "The Vaunting".' He stood to his shanks, a lean old man and straight, and the big drone came nigh on the black rafters. He filled the bag at a breath and swung a lover's arm round about it. To those who know not the pipes, the feel of the bag in the oxter is a gaiety lost. The sweet round curve is like a girl's waist; it is friendly and warm in the crook of the elbow and against a man's side, and to press it is to bring laughing or tears.

The bothy roared with the tuning, and then the air came melting and sweet from the chanter. Eight steps up, four to the turn, and eight down went Paruig, and the *piobaireachd* rolled to his fingers like a man's rhyming. The two men sat on the stools, with their elbows on their knees, and listened.

He played but the *urlar*, and the *crunluadh* to save time, and he played them well.

'Good indeed! Splendid, my old fellow!' cried the two; and said Gillian, 'You have a way of it in the *crunluadh* not my way, but as good as ever I heard.'

'It is the way of Padruig Og,' said Rory. 'Well I know it! There are tunes and tunes, and "The Vaunting" is not bad in its way, but give me "The Macraes' March".'

He jumped to his feet and took the pipes from the old man's hands, and over his shoulder with the drones.

'Stand back, lad!' he cried to Gilian, and Gilian went nearer the door.

The march came fast to the chanter – the old tune, the fine tune that Kintail has heard before, when the wild men in their red tartan came over hill and moor; the tune with the river in it, the fast river and the courageous that kens not stop nor tarry, that runs round rock and over gall with a good humour, yet no mood for anything but the way before it. The tune of the heroes, the tune of the pinelands and the broad straths, the tune that the eagles of Loch Duich crack their beaks together when they hear, and the crows of country-side would as soon listen to as the squeal of their babies.

'Well! mighty well!' said Paruig Dall. 'You have the tartan of the clan in it.'

'Not bad, I'll allow,' said Gilian. 'Let me try.'

He put his fingers on the holes, and his heart took a leap back over two generations, and yonder was Glencoe! The grey day crawled on the white hills and the black roofs smoked below. Snow choked the pass, *eas* and corri filled with drift and flatted to the brae-face; the wind tossed quirky and cruel in the little bushes and among the smooring lintels and joists; the blood of old and young lappered on the hearthstone, and the bairn, with a knifed throat, had an icy lip on a frozen teat. Out of the place went the tramped path of the Campbell butchers – far on their way to Glenlyon and the towns of paper and ink and liars – 'Muinntir a' ghlinne so, muinntir a' ghlinne so! – People, people, people of this glen, this glen, this glen!'

'Dogs! dogs! O God of grace – dogs and cowards!' cried Rory. 'I could be dirking a Diarmaid or two if by luck they were near me.'

'It is piping that is to be here,' said Paruig, 'and it is not piping for an hour nor piping for an evening, but the piping of Dunvegan that stops for sleep nor supper.'

So the three stayed in the bothy and played tune about while time went by the door. The birds flew home to the branches, the long-necked beasts flapped off to the shore to spear their flat fish; the rutting deers bellowed with loud throats in the deeps of the wood that stands round Half Town, and the scents of the moist night came gusty round the door. Over the back of Auchnabreac the sun trailed his plaid of red and yellow, and the loch stretched salt and dark from Cairn Dubh to Creaggans.

In from the hill the men and the women came, weary-legged, and the bairns nodded at their heels. Sleepiness was on the land, but the pipers, piping in the bothy, kept the world awake.

'We will go to bed in good time,' said the folks, eating their suppers at their doors; 'in good time when their tune is ended.' But tune came on tune, and every tune better than its neighbour, and they waited.

A cruisie-light was set alowe in the blind man's bothy, and the three men played old tunes and new tunes – salute and lament and brisk dances and marches that coax tired brogues on the long roads.

'Here's "Tulloch Ard" for you, and tell me who made it,' said Rory.

'Who kens that? Here's "Raasay's Lament", the best port Padruig Mor ever put together.'

'Tunes and tunes. I'm for "A Kiss o'the King's Hand".'

Thug mi pòg 'us pòg 'us pòg,
Thug mi pòg do làmh an righ,
Cha do chuir gaoth an craicionn caorach,
Fear a fhuair an fhaoilt ach mi!

Then a quietness came on Half Town, for the piping stopped, and the people at their doors heard but their blood thumping and the night-hags in the dark of the firwood

'A little longer and maybe there will be more,' they said to each other, and they waited; but no more music came from the drones, so they went in to bed.

There was quiet over Half Town, for the three pipers talked about the Lost Tune.

'A man my father knew,' said Gilian, 'heard a bit of it once in Moideart. A terrible fine tune he said it was, but sore on the mind.'

'It would be the tripling,' said the Macnaghton, stroking a reed with a fond hand.

'Maybe. Tripling is ill enough, but what is tripling? There is more in piping than brisk fingers. Am I not right, Paruig?'

'Right, oh! right. The Lost *Piobaireachd* asks for skilly tripling, but Macruimen himself could not get at the core of it for all his art.'

'You have heard it then!' cried Gilian.

The blind man stood up and filled out his breast.

'Heard it!' he said; 'I heard it, and I play it – on the *feadan*, but not on the full set. To play the tune I mention on the full set is what I have not done since I came to Half Town.'

'I have ten round pieces in my sporran, and a bonnet-brooch it would take much to part me from; but they're there for the man who'll play me the Lost *Piobaireachd*,' said Gilian, with the words tripping each other to the tip of his tongue.

'And here's a Macnaghton's fortune on the top of the round pieces,' cried Rory, emptying his purse on the table.

The old man's face got hot and angry. 'I am not,' he said, 'a tinker's minstrel, to give my tuning for bawbees and a quaich of ale. The king himself could not buy the tune I ken if he had but a whim for it. But when pipers ask it they can have it, and it's yours without a fee. Still if you think to learn the tune by my piping once, poor's the delusion. It is not a port to be picked up like a cockle on the sand, for it takes the schooling of years and blindness forbye.'

'Blindness?'

'Blindness indeed. The thought of it is only for the dark eye.'

'If we could hear it on the full set!'

'Come out, then, on the grass, and you'll hear it, if Half Town should sleep no sleep this night.'

They went out of the bothy to the wet short grass. Ragged mists shook o'er Cowal, and on Ben Ime sat a horned moon like a galley of Lorn.

'I heard this tune from the Moideart man – the last in Albainn who knew it then, and he's in the clods,' said the blind fellow.

He had the mouthpiece at his lip, and his hand was coaxing the bag, when a bairn's cry came from a house in the Half Town – a suckling's whimper, that, heard in the night, sets a man's mind busy on the sorrows that folks are born to. The drones clattered together on the piper's elbow and he stayed.

'I have a notion,' he said to the two men. 'I did not tell you that the Lost *Piobaireachd* is the *piobaireachd* of good-byes. It is the tune of broken clans, that sets the men on the foray and makes cold hearthstones. It was played in Glenshira when Gilleasbuig Gruamach could stretch stout swordsmen from Boshang to Ben Bhuidhe, and where are the folks of Glenshira this day? I saw a cheery night in Carnus that's over Lochow, and song and story busy about the fire, and the Moideart man played it for a wager. In the morning the weans were without fathers, and Carnus men were scattered about the wide world.'

'It must be the magic tune, sure enough,' said Gilian.

'Magic indeed, *laochain!* It is the tune that puts men on the open road, that makes restless lads and seeking women. Here's a Half Town of dreamers and men fattening for want of men's work. They forget the world is wide and round about their fir-trees, and I can make them crave for something they cannot name.'

'Good or bad, out with it,' said Rory, 'if you know it at all.'

'Maybe no', maybe no'. I am old and done. Perhaps I have lost the right skill of the tune, for it's long since I put it on the great pipe. There's in me the strong notion to try it whatever may come of it, and here's for it.'

He put his pipe up again, filled the bag at a breath, brought the booming to the drones, and then the chanter-reed cried sharp and high.

'He's on it,' said Rory in Gillian's ear.

The groundwork of the tune was a drumming on the deep notes where the sorrows lie – 'Come, come, come, my children, rain on the brae and the wind blowing.'

'It is a salute,' said Rory.

'It's the strange tune anyway,' said Gilian; 'listen to the time of yon!'

The tune searched through Half Town and into the gloomy pinewood; it put an end to the whoop of the night-hag and rang to Ben Bhreac. Boatmen deep and far on the loch could hear it, and Half Town folks sat up to listen.

Its story was the story that's ill to tell – something of the heart's longing and the curious chances of life. It bound up all the tales of all the clans, and made one tale of the Gaels' past. Dirk nor sword against the tartan, but the tartan against all else, and the Gaels' target fending the hill-land and the juicy straths from the pock-pitted little black men. The winters and the summers passing fast and furious, day and night roaring in the ears, and then again the clans at variance, and warders on every pass and on every parish.

Then the tune changed.

'Folks,' said the reeds, coaxing. 'Wide's the world and merry the road. Here's but the old story and the women we kissed before. Come, come to the flat-lands rich and full, where the wonderful new things happen and the women's lips are still to try!'

'To-morrow,' said Gilian in his friend's ear – 'tomorrow I will go jaunting to the North. It has been in my mind since Beltane.'

'One might be doing worse,' said Rory, 'and I have the notion to try a trip with my cousin to the foreign wars.'

The blind piper put up his shoulder higher and rolled the air into the *crunluadh breabach* that comes prancing with variations. Pride stiffened him from heel to hip, and hip to head, and set his sinews like steel.

He was telling of the gold to get for the searching and the bucks that may be had for the hunting. 'What,' said the reeds, 'are your poor crops, slashed by the constant rain and rotting, all for a scart in the bottom of a pot? What are your stots and heifers – black, dun, and yellow – to milch-cows and horses? Here's but the same for ever – toil and sleep, sleep and toil even on, no feud nor foray nor castles to harry – only the starved field and the sleeping moss. Let us to a brisker place! Over yonder are the long straths and the deep rivers and townships strewn thick as your corn-rigs; over yonder's the place of the packmen's tales and the packmen's wares: steep we the withies and go!'

The two men stood with heads full of bravery and dreaming – men in a carouse. 'This,' said they, 'is the notion we had, but had no words for. It's a poor trade piping and eating and making amusement when one might be wandering up and down the world. We must be packing the haversacks.'

Then the *crunluadh mach* came fast and furious on the chanter, and Half Town shook with it. It buzzed in the ear like the flowers in the Honey Croft and made commotion among the birds rocking on their eggs in the wood.

'*So! so!*' barked the *iolair* on Craig-an-eas. 'I have heard before it was an ill thing to be satisfied; in the morning I'll try the kids on Maam-side, for the hares here are wersh and tough.' 'Hearken, dear,' said the *londubh*. 'I know now why my beak is gold; it is because I once ate richer berries than the whortle, and in season I'll look for them on the braes of Glenfinne.' 'Honk-unk,' said the fox, the cunning red fellow, 'am not I the fool to be staying on this little brae when I know so many roads elsewhere?'

And the people sitting up in their beds in Half Town moaned for something new. 'Paruig Dall is putting the strange tune on her there,' said they. 'What the meaning of it is we must ask in the morning, but, *ochanoch!* it leaves one hungry at the heart.' And then gusty winds came snell from the north, and where the dark crept first, the day made his first showing, so that Ben Ime rose black against a grey sky.

'That's the Lost *Piobaireachd*,' said Paruig Dall when the bag sunk on his arm.

And the two men looked at him in a daze.

Sometimes in the spring of the year the winds from Lorn have it their own way with the Highlands. They will come tearing furious over the hundred hills, spurred the faster by the prongs of Cruachan and Dunchuach, and the large woods of home toss before them like corn before the hook. Up come the poor roots and over on their broken arms go the tall trees, and in the morning the deer will trot through new lanes cut in the forest.

A wind of that sort came on the full of the day when the two pipers were leaving Half Town.

'Stay till the storm is over,' said the kind folks; and 'Your bed and board are here for the pipers forty days,' said Paruig Dall. But 'No' said the two; 'we have business that your *piobaireachd* put us in mind of.'

'I'm hoping that I did not play yon with too much skill,' said the old man.

'Skill or no skill,' said Gilian, 'the like of yon I never heard. You played a port that makes poor enough all ports ever one listened to, and piping's no more for us wanderers.'

'Blessings with thee!' said the folks all, and the two men went down into the black wood among the cracking trees.

Six lads looked after them, and one said, 'It is an ill day for a body to take the world for his pillow, but what say you to following the pipers?'

'It might,' said one, 'be the beginning of fortune. I am weary enough of this poor place, with nothing about it but wood and water and tufty grass. If we went now there might be gold and girls at the other end.'

They took crooks and bonnets and went after the two pipers. And when they were gone half a day, six women said to their men, 'Where can the lads be?'

'We do not know that,' said the men, with hot faces, 'but we might be looking.' They kissed their children and went, with *cromags* in their hands, and the road they took was the road the King of Errin rides, and that is the road to the end of days.

A weary season fell on Half Town, and the very bairns dwined at the breast for a change of fortune. The women lost their strength, and said, 'To-day my back is weak, tomorrow I will put things to right,' and they looked slack-mouthed and heedless-eyed at the sun wheeling round the trees. Every week a man or two would go to seek something – a lost heifer or a wounded roe that was never brought back – and a new trade came to the place, the selling of herds. Far away in the low country, where the winds are warm and the poorest have money, black cattle were wanted, so the men of Half Town made up long droves and took them round Glen Beag and the Rest.

Wherever they went they stayed, or the clans on the roadside put them to steel, for Half Town saw them no more. And a day came when all that was left in that fine place were but women and children and a blind piper.

'Am I the only man here?' asked Paruig Dall when it came to the bit, and they told him he was.

'Then here's another for fortune!' said he, and he went down through the woods with his pipes in his oxter.

THE SECRET OF THE HEATHER ALE

Down Glenaora threescore and ten of Diarmaid's stout fellows took the road on a fine day. They were men from Carnus, with more of Clan Artair than Campbell in them; but they wore Gilleasbuig Gruamach's tartan, and if they were not on Gilleasbuig Gruamach's errand, it makes little difference on our story. It was about the time Antrim and his dirty Irishers came scouring through our glens with flambeaux, dirk and sword and other arms invasive, and the country was back at its old trade of fighting, with not a sheiling from end to end, except on the slopes of Shira Glen, where a clan kept free of battle and drank the finest of heather-ale that the world envied the secret of.

'Lift we and go, for the Cattle's before!' said Alasdair Piobaire on the chanter of a Dunvegan great-pipe – a neat tune that roared gallant and far from Carnus to Baracaldine; so there they were, the pick of swank fellows on the road!

At the head of them was Niall Mor a' Chamais – the same gentleman namely in story for many an art and the slaughter of the strongest man in the world, as you'll find in the writings of my Lord Archie. 'God! look at us!' said he, when his lads came over the hill in the grey mouth of day. 'Are not we the splendid men? Fleas will there be this day in the hose of the Glenshira folk.' And he sent his targe in the air in a bravado, catching it by the prong in its navel, smart and clean, when it whirled back.

Hawks yelped as they passed; far up on Tullich there was barking of eagles; the brogues met the road as light as the stag-slot; laughing, singing, roaring; sword-heads and pikes dunting on wooden targets – and only once they looked back at their women high on the brae-face.

The nuts were thick on the roadside, hanging heavy from swinging branches, and some of the men pulled them off as they passed, stayed for more, straggled, and sang bits of rough songs they ken over many of on Lochowside to this day. So Niall Mor glunched at his corps from under his bonnet and showed his teeth.

'Gather in, gather in,' said he; 'Ye march like a drove of low-country cattle. Alasdair, put "Baile Inneraora" on her!'

Alasdair changed his tune, and the good march of Clan Diarmaid went swinging down the glen.

The time passed; the sun stood high and hot; clucking from the fir-plantings came woodcock and cailzie; the two rivers were crossed, and the Diarmaids slockened their thirst at the water of Altan Aluinn, whose birth is somewhere in the bogs beside tall Bhuidhe Ben.

Where the clans met was at the Foal's Gap, past Maam. A score of the

MacKellars ran out in a line from the bushes, and stotted back from the solid weight of Diarmaid moving in a lump and close-shouldered in the style Niall Mor got from the Italian soldier. Some fell, hacked on the head by the heavy slash of the dry sword; some gripped too late at the pikes that kittled them cruelly; and one – Iver-of-the-Oars – tripped on a root of heather, and fell with his breast on the point of a Diarmaid's dirk.

To the hills went a fast summons, and soon at the mouth of the gap came twoscore of the MacKellars. They took a new plan, and close together faced the green tartan, keeping it back at the point of steel, though the pick of Glenaora wore it, and the brogues slipped on the brae-face. It was fast cut and drive, quick flash of the dirk, with the palm up and the hand low to find the groin, and a long reach with the short black knife. The choked breath hissed at teeth and nose, the salt smell of new blood brought a shiver to birch-leaf and gall. But ever the green tartan had the best of it.

'*Bas, bas, Dhiarmaid!*' cried Calum Dubh, coming up on the back of his breaking two-score with fresh lads from Elerigmor, bed-naked to the hide, and a new fury fell on the two clans tearing at it in the narrow hollow in between the rocky hills. So close they were, there was small room for the whirl of the basket-hilt, and 'Mind Tom-a-Phubaill and the shortened steel!' cried Niall Mor, smashing a pretty man's face with a blow from the iron guard of his Ferrara sword. The halberts, snapped at the haft to make whittles, hammered on the target-hides like stones on a coffin, or rang on the bosses; the tartan ripped when the stuck one rolled on his side before the steel could be twisted out; below the foot the grass felt warm and greasy, and the reason was not ill to seek.

Once it looked like the last of Calum Dubh. He was facing Niall Mor, sword and targe, and Niall Mor changed the sword to the other hand, pulled the *sgian-dubh* from his garter, and with snapping teeth pushed like a lightning fork below MacKellar's target. An Elerigmor man ran in between; the little black knife sunk into his belly with a moist plunge, and the blood spouted on the deer-horn haft.

'*Mallachd ort*! I meant yon for a better man,' cried Niall Mor; 'but it's well as it is, for the secret's to the fore,' and he stood up dour and tall against a new front of MacKellar's men.

Then the sky changed, and a thin smirr of warm rains fell on the glen like smoke; some black-cattle bellowed at the ford in a wonder at where their herds could be, and the herds – stuck, slashed, and cudgelled – lay stiffening on the torn grass between the gap and MacKellar's house. From end to end of the glen there was no man left but was at the fighting. The hook was tossed among the corn; the man hot-foot behind the roe, turned when he had his knife at its throat, to go to war; a lover left his lass among the heather; and all, with tightened belts, were at the old game with Clan Diarmaid, while their women, far up on the sappy levels between the hill-tops and beside the moor-lochs, span at the wheel or carded wool, singing songs with light hearts and thinking no danger.

Back went MacKellar's men before Niall Mor and his sturdy lads from Carnus, the breeder of soldiers – back through the gap and down on the brae to the walls of Calum Dubh.

"*Illean, 'illean!*' cried Calum; 'lads, lads! they have us, sure enough. Oh! pigs and thieves! squint mouths and sons of liars!'

The cry gathered up the strength of all that was left of his clan, Art and Uileam, the Maamlads, the brothers from Drumlea and two from over Stron hill, and they stood up together against the Carnus men – a gallant madness! They died fast and hard, and soon but Calum and his two sons were left fencing, till a rush of Diarmaids sent them through the door of the house and tossed among the peats.

'Give in and your lives are your own,' said Niall Mor, wiping his sword on his shirt-sleeve, and with all that were left of his Diarmaids behind his back.

To their feet stood the three MacKellars. Calum looked at the folk in front of him, and had mind of other ends to battles. 'To die in a house like a rat were no great credit,' said he, and he threw his sword on the floor, where the blades of Art and Uileam soon joined it.

With tied arms the father and his sons were taken outside, where the air was full of the scents of birch and gall new-washed. The glen, clearing fast of mist, lay green and sweet for mile and mile, and far at its mouth the fat Blaranbuie woods chuckled in the sun.

'I have you now,' said Niall Mor. 'Ye ken what we seek. It's the old ploy – the secret of the ale.'

Calum laughed in his face, and the two sons said things that cut like knives.

'Man! I'm feared ye'll rue this,' said Niall Mior, calm enough. 'Ye may laugh, but – what would ye call a gentleman's death?'

'With the sword or the dagger in the hand, and a Diarmaid or two before me,' cried Calum.

'Well, there might be worse ways of travelling yont – indeed there could ill be better; but if the secret of the ale is not to be ours for the asking, ye'll die a less well-bred death.'

'Name it, man, name it,' said Calum. 'Might it be tow at the throat and a fir-branch.'

'Troth,' said Niall Mor, 'and that were too gentle a travelling. The Scaurnoch's on our way, and the crows at the foot of it might relish a Glen Shira carcass.'

Uileam whitened at the notion of so ugly an end, but Calum only said, 'Die we must any way,' and Art whistled a bit of a pipe-tune, grinding his heel on the moss.

Niall Mor made to strike the father on the face, but stayed his hand and ordered the three in-by, with a few of his corps to guard them. Up and down Glen Shira went the Diarmaids, seeking the brewing-cave, giving hut and home to the flame, and making black hearths and low lintels for the women away in the sheilings. They buried their dead at Kilblaan, and, with no secret the better, set out for Scaurnoch with Calum and his sons.

The MacKellars were before, like a *spreidh* of stolen cattle, and the lot of the driven herd was theirs. They were laughed at and spat on, and dirk-hilts and *cromags* hammered on their shoulders, and through Blaranbuie wood they went to the bosky elbow of Dun Corrbhile and round to the Dun beyond.

Calum, for all his weariness, stepped like a man with a lifetime's plans before his mind; Art looked about him in the fashion of one with an eye to woodcraft; Uileam slouched with a heavy foot, white at the jaw and wild of eye.

The wood opened, the hunting-road bent about the hill-face to give a level that the eye might catch the country spread below. Loch Finne stretched far, from Ardno to French Foreland, a glassy field, specked with one sail off Creaggans. When the company came to a stand, Calum Dubh tossed his head to send the hair from his eyes, and looked at what lay below. The Scaurnoch broke at his feet, the grey rock-face falling to a depth so deep that weary mists still hung upon the sides, jagged here and there by the top of a fir-tree. The sun, behind the Dun, gave the last of her glory to the Cowal Hills; Hell's Glen filled with wheeling mists; Ben Ime, Ben Vane, and Ben Arthur crept together and held princely converse on the other side of the sea.

All in a daze of weariness and thinking the Diarmaids stood, and looked and listened, and the curlews were crying bitter on the shore.

'Oh, haste ye, lads, or it's not Carnus for us to-night,' cried Niall Mor. 'We have business before us, and long's the march to follow. The secret, black fellow!'

Calum Dubh laughed, and spat in a bravado over the edge of the rock.

'Come, fool, if we have not the word from you before the sun's off Sithean Sluaidhe, your sleep this night is yonder,' and he pointed at the pit below.

Calum laughed the more. 'If it was hell itself,' said he, 'I would not save my soul from it.'

'Look, man, look! the Sithean Sluaidhe's getting black, and any one of ye can save the three yet. I swear it on the cross of my knife.'

Behind the brothers, one, John-Without-Asking, stood, with a gash on his face, eager to give them to the crows below.

A shiver came to Uileam's lips; he looked at his father with a questioning face, and then stepped back a bit from the edge, making to speak to the tall man of Chamis.

Calum saw the meaning, and spoke fast and thick.

'Stop, stop,' said he; 'it's a trifle of a secret, after all, and to save life ye can have it.'

Art took but a little look at his father's face, then turned round on Shira Glen and looked on the hills where the hunting had many a time been sweet. 'Maam no more,' said he to himself; 'but here's death in the hero's style!'

'I thought you would tell it,' laughed Niall Mor. 'There was never one of your clan but had a tight grip of his little life.'

'Ay!' said Calum Dubh; 'but it's *my* secret. I had it from one who made me swear on the holy steel to keep it; but take me to Carnus, and I'll make you the heather-ale.'

'So be't, and –'

'But there's this in it, I can look no clansmen nor kin in the face after telling it, so Art and Uileam must be out of the way first.'

'Death, MacKellar?'

'That same.'

Uileam shook like a leaf, and Art laughed, with his face still to Shira, for he had guessed his father's mind.

'Faith!' said Niall Mor, 'and that's an easy thing enough,' and he nodded to John-Without-Asking.

The man made stay nor tarry. He put a hand on each son's back and pushed them over the edge to their death below. One cry came up to the listening Diarmaids, one cry and no more – the last gasp of a craven.

'Now we'll take you to Carnus, and you'll make us the ale, the fine ale, the cream of rich heather-ale,' said Niall Mor putting a knife to the thongs that tied MacKellar's arms to his side.

With a laugh and a fast leap Calum Dubh stood back on the edge of the rock again.

'Crook-mouths, fools, pigs' sons! did ye think it?' he cried. 'Come with me and my sons and ye'll get ale, ay, and death's black wine, at the foot of Scaurnoch.' He caught fast and firm at John-Without-Asking, and threw himself over the rock-face. They fell as the scart dives, straight to the dim sea of mist and pine-tip, and the Diarmaids threw themselves on their breasts to look over. There was nothing to see of life but the crows swinging on black feathers; there was nothing to hear but the crows scolding.

Niall Mor put the bonnet on his head and said his first and last friendly thing of a foe.

'Yon,' said he, 'had the heart of a man!'

4

Some Contemporaries (1898)

INTRODUCTION

Munro's seven pastiches of distinguished contemporary writers which appeared in his 'Views and Reviews' column on Thursday 24 November 1898 are not just admirable and amusing exercises in the styles of Kipling, Meredith, Barrie, Newbolt, Conrad, Cunninghame Graham and Neil Munro but each also offers a satirical comment on a recent event or on a literary fashion.

Clutha No. 90
A month before this piece appeared Munro had reviewed Rudyard Kipling's collection of short stories, The Day's Work, *and, while acknowledging Kipling's greatness, had commented that his listing of engine parts and technical details in some of the stories in the collection was not art but 'simply Technical Dictionary and notebook'. The Cluthas were passenger ferries running up and down the Clyde and operated by the Clyde Trust – the C.T. of the story. Kipling's great poem 'M'Andrew's Hymn' – which certainly transcends the Technical Dictionary – provides Munro's Clutha engineer with his name.*

The Principal
This sketch, after George Meredith, which captures the great Victorian novelist's dense and convoluted style was, as all Munro's 1898 readers would have instantly known, a commentary on the events surrounding the installation of Robert H. Story as Principal of Glasgow University. Story, a former Moderator of the General Assembly of the Church of Scotland ('a leg for knee-breeches') had been Professor of Church History at Glasgow and was a less than universally popular appointment. His installation at Gilmorehill ('revels on the Mount') was marked by a not untypical outburst of student rowdyism ('The students raised the son of our common ancestor' = raised Cain [the son of Adam]). The Queen Margaret's of which Miss Jerkoway is the fair sibyl was the associated Women's College of Glasgow University. Munro's depiction of Principal

Story is hardly flattering – he suggests a certain worldliness and arrogance ('the Gallinule [cock] of the walk.)' Readers with a taste for conspiracy theory may care to reflect on the fact that Story was Principal of Glasgow University from 1898 until his death in 1907 and that Neil Munro was given an Honorary Doctorate by the University in 1908 as one of the first acts of Story's successor. On the other hand Munro did lunch and dine with Principal Story on at least two occasions – so perhaps he was forgiven. Incidentally, Munro recorded in his diary for August 1890 that he had read Meredith's The Ordeal of Richard Feveral – which he described as a very good book but one which gave him the 'melancholy hump'.

Fee Market Day
Munro thought better of J. M. Barrie's writings than of some other practitioners of the Kailyard school but this did not prevent his poking a little gentle fun at the genre in this everyday story of country folk. In 1930, at the end of Munro's life, Barrie, on the occasion of his installation as Chancellor of Edinburgh University, exercised his prerogative as the new Chancellor to award Munro an honorary Doctorate of Laws.

St Mungo's Marineer
Henry Newbolt is now probably best remembered for his Drake's Drum (1896) and this poem in the Newbolt style makes ingenious reference to another Drake – HMS Drake which had served as a training ship for the Clyde Naval Brigade and which had lain at anchor in the heart of Glasgow. The naval volunteers' services had been dispensed with some years earlier and a public meeting had been called in the city, shortly before this column appeared, to press for their re-embodiment. The Ailsa referred to was the 3rd Marquis of Ailsa who had commanded the Clyde Naval Brigade and would become Honorary Commodore of the re-formed Clyde Division of the Royal Navy Volunteer Reserve.

The Canal Boatman
Joseph Conrad was perhaps Munro's greatest literary enthusiasm and he repeatedly praised the Polish novelist's work in his columns. On 1 September 1898 he wrote 'we shall waken up to find that Joseph Conrad has been the most wonderful writer of the sea English literature has produced.' The two men met for the first time when Conrad came to Glasgow in late September 1898 in a vain attempt to find a Scottish ship to command. At this point in his career Conrad was disillusioned with literature and thought that he would be better returning to his profession as a sailor. The friendly relationship then established lasted for the rest of

Conrad's life. Respect and friendship did not stop Munro writing this amusing pastiche of Conrad's epic 'man against the elements' style – translated to the somewhat less threatening environment of the Forth and Clyde Canal at Kirkintilloch.

East of the Tron
Another writer who Munro liked and admired, and who more than reciprocated these feelings was the colourful, aristocratic, socialist, nationalist, travel writer Robert Bontine Cunninghame Graham. His works tended to be set in South America or North Africa and although he wrote some Scottish sketches, many based on his ancestral Menteith, none of them seem to be set 'East of the Tron'. The Tron steeple in Glasgow's Trongate is at the heart of the old Merchant City and marks the start of the city's east end – the home of the Glasgow keelie, or, as Munro has Cunninghame Graham express it 'the Keeley boy'. The Concise Scottish National Dictionary defines a keelie as 'a rough male city-dweller, a tough, now especially from the Glasgow area, originally with an implication of criminal tendencies'.

The Celtic Pilgrim
The final sketch in this collection is Munro imitating Munro and was intended to awaken memories of The Lost Pibroch collection – translated to the southern suburbs of Glasgow. Strathbungo and Mount Florida are, sad to tell, not romantic and remote locations in Argyll, but douce commuter-belt settlements that Munro passed on his way into the city from his home at Waterfoot. The most probable noise to hear at Mount Florida would be the roar of the crowds at Hampden Park, rather than the bark of an eagle. The 'Celtic Bazaar' to which Black John is making his way was a fund-raising event organised by the Duke of Argyll to raise funds for the Argyllshire Nursing Association and would take place in Glasgow two days after this column appeared.

   Munro may well have been inspired to parody himself by reading a somewhat less skilful parody of his style which appeared in the London literary magazine The Academy on 5 November 1898. The Academy noted: 'To be parodied is to have achieved a certain popularity, or at least recognition. Hence we congratulate Mr Neil Munro, the author of The Lost Pibroch and John Splendid on having already been made the victim of a literary sharpshooter. A correspondent, Mr John Macleay, sends us the following experiment in Mr Munro's genre:

EVENING IN THE HIGHLANDS
With Apologies to Mr Neil Munro

'I'm off,' said the sun on the sea out-bye, and the first shadow crept shyly into Glen Mor. The half-closed daisies there whispered to the wind, and the wind took the news of the day's ending to Glen Beag, to the lisping birches on Sgur Oman-side and on to the rugged land of the raiding Callums. The twilight rose in the glens and up the mountain sides, and the sun had its last smile for old, old Ben Mor. 'Gone is the light for the fishing,' croaked a heron flying slowly inland. 'And for howling, too,' squawked the crows in the wood at Craggan Dhu. And there was the glint of the sun off Ben Mor and the same greyness everywhere, and never a sound but the sigh of an evening wind in Corryarich, like a great man ganting.

John Macleay went on to write a now-forgotten short novel, Smith, Clan Chief, *in which Munro's style is parodied.*

William Blackwood wrote to Munro in January 1899 praising his set of skilfully crafted miniatures:

You must not allow your talent for clever parody and satire to lie fallow. Your burlesque stories in the News *were delightful, & I should be greatly pleased if you were to hit out something on somewhat similar lines suitable for* Maga *in prose & verse which you could turn to whenever you felt in the humour & subjects presented themselves.*

Perhaps Blackwood was being a little unrealistic in his expectations – there were, after all, only a limited number of authors as recognisable and as parodiable as those whom Munro had so deftly dealt with in this column.

Munro did not provide an overall title for this group of miniatures but 'Some Contemporaries' seems apt enough.

SOME CONTEMPORARIES

In the absence of any manuscript this week from our regular contributor, we are compelled at the last moment to fill up the column with the following brief articles secured for us by telegram, through the well-known Literary Agent Mr A. P. W---t. We simply sent him the names of the authors from whom we wanted to hear, leaving them to select their own subjects. The following are the dire results.

'Clutha No. 90'
by R--y--d K-pl--g
Number Ninety, 'Old Snort' as they call her on the Quays, had something wrong with her intestines. The simplest thing in the world; it might have happened any day in the week to a Cunarder let alone a senile, doddering, scabby-boilered rattle-trap with kinks in her plummet-block, her tail-rods all slivered up like the *chutpoo* head-drone of a Madras *ghat mullah,* and her crank-throws retching like the day after a sergeants' mess smoking concert. She had got on Finnieston on the old trail, the home trail, and all well when M'Andrew blanched at a terrific sound from the engine room.

'Damned ijjits!' said he, as Old Snort canted round defiant of her helm, and the passengers were lost to sight in the escaping steam.

There was Old Tommy to pay on the river! Through the fog loomed up the bows of the *Circassian*, huge, towering, arrogant as Fate, and as the captain from the bridge jerked the reins and threw her back on her haunches, he said things in an impatient tone of voice, hard things, unpleasant things, with imputations upon the respectability of M'Andrew's mother and passing allusion to the C.T. as a suitable candidate for honours on a dark plutonic shore. On the top of the liner came down a green-hulled, pink-bottomed Norwegian, and her propelling force in the shape of the *Firelight* tug; then the hilarity of the proceedings were enhanced by the arrival of a MacGuffie tramp with a cargo of guano from Iquique. It was lovely. For twenty minutes the river was in a roar. Tug-boats twittered with their thin gas-pipe whistles; in a dulcet chorus the ululation of the jammed passenger-boats rose high and far; the great liners, angry at this impudent cheek from a penny pick-me-up, pulled out all the stops in their sirens and rent heaven with cacophonous yawp.

M'Andrew went below.

It was the simplest thing in the world, as I have said. The second greaser, a lobscouse, swivel-eyed son of a gun, had been swilling out the cap of the main eccentric with a pale-looking lubricant contained in a flat bottle. The first greaser, standing by, had let a spark from his pipe fall in the cap, a blue flame at once arose, spread to the sheaves, lingered a second among the cheap metallic packing of the thrust-blocks (the C.T., being economic owners, never used zuglosite packing), and exploded the condenser. The spectacle was appalling. The projecting flange on the left of the oscillator below the hanging-links was curled up like the dog-ears of a child's book. Then the throttle-valve of the governor fell among the injector-pipes, taking the shock off the central journal and breaking the nut that binds the guide-rods and the crank-shafts. The valve of the manhole was fully .09 off the vertical.

'It's fore-ordained that Man the Arrtifex is to ha'e his life vexed oot o' him eternally by brutes wi' breeks on. Wha did this?' asked M'Andrew.

The greaser handed him the bottle and M'Andrew smelled it. 'Just as I thocht,' said he; 'ye dinna ken the difference between ile and Auld Moses. Drunk again, Lord help ye, drunk again! Wha' took this gill bottle oot o' my pooch?'

And the river still was roaring.

'The Principal'
by G---ge M---d-th

I remember when he came, though that were scarce the adequate verb. Rather he occurred. To have come would in his case have been to surrender the poetry of motion to a lop-sided, undignified amble, and then Olympus (whereto they talk of a railway now, the Vandals, as to another Mont Blanc) would have cacchinated consumedly. The prankish monster that he was, always the seigneur grand, with ancestral satyrs – Romany too, they said – rampant in his corpuscles, a very devil of a fellow! Well, he occurred. People wondered. Dame Rumour, a mendacious jade, had mentioned others, but he knew the High Wires. He was ground and lofty tumbler (no clown he) in the gaff of Signor La Monde. There was a flutter in Academia, and his occurrence was celebrated by revels on the Mount. When he entered among them for the first time he bore himself so domineeringly, so much the Gallinule of the walk, that youth rebelled. Its voracious aesthetic gluttony craved insatiably for something human, and what was given to it was the miserably inadequate and monotonous letter 'I'. The students raised the son of our common ancestor. It is a well-known Story now.

He had a way of wearing clothes. Most of us simply cover our nudity fortuitously, a coat here, a shirt there, our legs immersed in bifurcations. The Principal adorned his clothing, and to see him at an evening party, braid haunting him like a passion, shoes fantastically buckled, his noble chevelure crisp, silvern in corybantic ends, was one of the acknowledged sights of the city. He had a cavalier court suit in his wardrobe as well as that elusive touch of the Romany. And his leg! It was like the feet of Suckling's poem, stealing out and in – to your compelled attention, a leg that smiled, that was obsequious to you, twinkled to a tender medium between imperiousness and seductiveness, audacity and indiscretion. A sheen of amiability could not have been more fatal than that leg. Miss Jerkoway – fair sybil of Queen Margaret's – noticed it first, a portent and a valiance.

'He has a leg for knee-breeches,' she said in a rapture to a Dame Blunt.

Dame Blunt (a wholesome fleshly personage of no allusions) sniffed. Her sniff was at once a challenge and a Creed.

'I am more struck by his cheek,' said she. Thus the Comedy of Farce.

'Fee Market Day'
by J.M. B-r-ie

The station was crowded with Jocks and Jennies. Mysie came up to see if the East Kilbride 5.5 was away; its tail light was just passing the signal box.

'It disna maitter a fall-tall,' said she, 'I'll just bide till the next yin,' and she sat on a porter's barrow waiting for the 6.15. At the Dreeps farm time is more plentiful than anything else. In a little Tam o' the Heugh came up to her, and being a humourist, he bit her merrily on the ear, then played a bar on his melodeon. Let us thank God there is still music in the Scots heart.

'Fee'd,' said he.

'Ye're speirin'.'

'Ow aye.'

'Ye'll no' clype?'

'Cut ma throat if I dae.'

'Sae dagont.'

He looked uneasy, and wished he had not come. He had a small bible and two catechisms in his coat pocket, and he could not but think of his mother.

'I canna say dagont,' he answered at last.

'Ye must dae it,' said she helplessly, 'for its in a' the buiks. Hoots, jaups, get awa' wi ye!'

'Well – Dagont!' said he bravely.

She whispered in his ear and he steadied himself against the trams of the barrow.

'I'm gaun to Macwhiggits o' the Slaps, and dae ye ken whit pey they're giein' me? Twal pun the hauf year.'

'It's a dawm lee,' said he.

'St Mungo's Marineer'
by H---y N-wb--t

O! heave the ensign to the truck
Set high the spare burgee;
Shake out the capstan to the stars,
And fling the taffrail free,
And let our clinkered cats-heads gleam
Athwart the tackling gear,
For he's bound to come
(What ho! the drum)
St Mungo's Marineer.

For our disgrace they took from us
Our citizen of war,
Because the Drake (God bless the ship!)
Cost quite a lot of tar,
The men that Ailsa led of yore
To Norway's waters clear,
Must gird their cutlasses agen
(Abaft, alow, aloft, ahead)
St Mungo's Marineer.

'The Canal Boatman'
by J----h C-nr-d

A curious craft, surely, combining in her lines and utilities little of the speed of the felucca, galley, galleot, pram or dhow, yet in her vast, heavy illusion of beam recalling some of the *chasses-marees,* or corvets I have seen lurking off the little lost cays and lagoons between the Ladrones and the Salomon Islands. It had begun to blow immediately after leaving Lock 16. We hove to at Camelon, pumped, spliced the main brace, pumped and spliced the main brace again. It was terrible, and yet, somehow, I was proud of the ship and felt something – you know the feeling – one of exaltation, of zest, of triumph. We set out again, and near Kirkintilloch the hurricane struck us, a cruel, unrelenting sou'-wester, setting the waves mountain high, blinding our poor brutes of horses as they laboured incessantly on the towing-path. That night had a quality of dark I have seen at no other time or place. Faint phospherent gleams in the far distance but accentuated it, and through the night came the most wonderful and elusive odours. Something indescribable, a devil's impulse, a supernatural allurement in the night seemed to call on us to quit the ship so fearfully weltering in the storm and risk all in the long boat. We felt we could make land somehow, for we were young, and all the poignances, the essence, the infatuation of youth were ours. I think of it often under the most ludicrous circumstances – of the *Mary Jane* churning in a velvet-black night, the galley fire showing up MacTaggart's legs as he stood at the wheel, the horses breathing hard, bent over the cable tow, the impenetrable and vast and terrible darkness. Not a sound came from the land. We were the serfs of the sea, to be knocked about, and get up, again, and fall again, and again stand up square to that old bully of the night.

For some inscrutable reason the skipper was anxious to get ahead and make an early landfall at Kirkintilloch. He was a man with a red nose and it was his first voyage on that route.

'We'll do it, we'll do it, it's only ten minutes past ten,' he cried, as we tied up at the pawls at Kirkintilloch. There was a strange exultation in his utterance. He hurried up to a house of refreshment and I shall never forget his look of surprise and pain to find it shut.

'Blind me!' said he, 'have they the ten o'clock closing here too?' And he put his face in his hands and wept like a child.

Ah! old times, old times, will they ever come back again with the zest, the hope, the joy, the illusion?

'East of the Tron'
by C----ng--m Gr-h-m

I have believe me by the grace of Allah and the inheritance of unscrupulous old landowning ancestors of mine seen the world after a fashion. My Sus journey is a matter of common knowledge. I can show the flea-bites of Tartary, the scars of Guachd sword wounds and the receipts of Oban hotelkeepers. Yet I confess my first impressions of the country east of the Tron were striking and novel. I say nothing of the architecture of the territory what could one say of grey Noah's Arks pierced by holes called closes where miserly lights o' night from rat-tail burners throw a discreet crepuscule upon courting lovers? But the people themselves? Turbaned Lascars, fezzed Greeks, Ebo slaves from the West Indies, from Barbadoes, 'true ''Badian, born neither crab nor Creole,' slit-eyed Chinese, Mandingoes, Jollofis and Krooboys from the West Coast of Africa, Kaffirs from the Cape, tattooed Kanakas – every shade of colour, black, brown and yellow, have I seen, and the Keeley boy of east the Tron gave me pause. And yet the Keeley boy (if one may venture to say as much to a hide-bound, respectable, self-righteous people who think a small deposit in the Post Office Savings Bank a sure free pass to Heaven), is not without certain virtues and graces one would have liked to see among the gentry who haunt the Stock Exchange worshipping their god each after his kind. I found no divorce scandals among them, and no superstitious regard for the 'Sawbath'. Instead of adorning themselves with cylinder hats and frock coats, sealskin jackets and millinery confections, to sit in a temple and envy each others' clothes, they stayed at home and read improving literature. An almost Castilian politeness characterised their deportment towards strangers, over and over again they have offered me their quaint drinking vessels and invited me to help myself without any formality about a cup or class. They beat their wives, it is true, but what proof have we that their wives do not prize rather than resent those conjugal attentions? I know that on one occasion I tried to rescue one lady from her husband who was enthusiastically kicking her and instead of gratitude I got from her the height of abuse for my interference. Bismillah! and 'tis a right odd world and the Spanish proverb of my old friend Don Guzmun el Colero de Guesda has truth in it – 'Buen abogado mal vecino.'

'The Celtic Pilgrim'
by N--l M-n-o

There was a soft smirr of rain as he went through Strathbungo with the heather sticking out of his brogues and a large claymore dangling at his side. It was he was the stout fellow; Black John they called him in the bye-name of the clan he came off, and from Kintyre to Cape Wrath there was not a prettier man with the Pibroch. He had the Instrument under his oxter, and now and then as he went down the Strath he would stop and play 'Bundle and Go' and 'Cock o' the North', and the fine tune 'Xythrobuidhknaskbz quibhodh', which the Macgregors, for reasons, do not like at all. The smirr was a shower when he got to the foot of the Strath, and by now it was the mouth of night and 'Ochan ciamar aha oo,' said he, minding of the days that were among the heather and the gall. And the eagles barked on Mount Florida, It was a wet, wet night. By and by he met a man of another clan, with a long blue 'hgwapho' coat, and he said to him, 'Sir, is it that you have the language?' The rain by this time was sweeshing in his brogues. Mists rose and swirled all about, a doleful wind soughed in the trees in the front plots.

'O lochain,' said he, and they swapped slogan.

'And whither art thou going?' asked the stranger, a black-avised fellow.

'Where, but the Celtic Bazaar,' answered Black John, pouring the rain out of the top of his Glengarry bonnet.

'O lochain, I know what you are going to do there,' said the stranger, and the rain was drooking him and the eagles were at the barking still on Cross Hill. 'You will be coming to keep a stall and not to buy at all.'

'How do you know that?' asked Black John, sick-sorry they had swapped slogans.

'Because I see your sporran is very empty' said the stranger.

The gloom fell on Black John. 'The Red Curse on you!' said he, and he went on his way. And the rain –

5

'Hugh Foulis'

INTRODUCTION

✝

By the autumn of 1897 Neil Munro had semi-retired from his position on the staff of the Glasgow Evening News – *where he was art and literary critic, leader writer and columnist – to concentrate on his developing career as a novelist.* The Lost Pibroch *had been published to a warm critical reception;* John Splendid *had been accepted for* Blackwood's Magazine *and* Gilian the Dreamer *was contracted for* Good Words – *a highly popular London-based magazine. Both could be sure of publication in book form after their periodical serialisation.*

Munro's semi-retirement meant that he would continue to write two regular weekly columns for the News. *The longest established of these was 'Views and Reviews' – a literary causerie which blended straight book reviewing (although there was a separate review column) with Munro's reflections on literary matters. This was a highly influential column and some of Munro's articles from 'Views and Reviews' are printed elsewhere in this anthology. The second column, 'The Looker-On', which blended fiction with opinion pieces and reportage, had just been started when Munro gave up his staff post.*

'The Looker-On' became a major feature of the News *and many a Glaswegian must have picked up Monday's* News *with a real sense of anticipation to see what was in the column this week. In the new century much of the success of the column came from its hosting three series of comic sketches, each quite distinct in character but each marked with Munro's wit and lightness of touch. Erchie MacPherson, Para Handy and Jimmy Swan would for a quarter of a century grace the columns of the* News *and delight its readers.*

These sketches were much too good to be confined to the ephemeral columns of a newspaper, and in October 1903 Blackwoods wrote to Munro expressing interest in publishing a volume of sketches about Erchie, the waiter and kirk beadle. Munro was keen on the idea but felt that he would not want to publish them under his own name. He also believed that the market for such light sketches was glutted at the time. J. J. Bell's Wee

MacGreegor *stories, which had run in the rival* Glasgow Evening Times, *had just been published, to great success, in book form.*

However in the spring of 1904 Erchie, My Droll Friend *appeared under the pen name of 'Hugh Foulis'. His ten-year-old son, Hugh, presumably contributed the first part of this thin disguise. Foulis is most obviously a compliment to his ancestry – the chief of Clan Munro is Munro of Foulis with his seat at Foulis Castle in Easter Ross. On another level the name Foulis was apt for a series of Glasgow stories and could be taken as a reference to the distinguished eighteenth-century Glasgow publishing house established by the brothers Andrew and Robert Foulis.*

The 'Hugh Foulis' identity was used again in 1906, when the first collection of Para Handy stories was published, and for Jimmy Swan's venture into book form in 1917.

While the identity of 'Hugh Foulis' or indeed that of 'The Looker-On' could not have been a secret to anyone in Scottish press, publishing or literary circles the formal identification of these stories with Neil Munro had to wait until after his death and the publication of an omnibus volume of all three sets of tales in November 1931.

Munro returned to a staff position on the News *during the First World War and acted as its editor until 1924. After that time he continued as literary editor and a director of the publishing company that owned the* News *for another three years. Munro would complain regularly about being tied to the newspaper – once famously comparing journalism to the 'jawbox' (the Glaswegian kitchen sink). The implication was that he was thirled to his newspaper desk just as a tenement housewife was tied to her sink. Perhaps Munro's protests need to be taken with a grain of salt – after all he had no sooner extricated himself from his editorial, directorial and columnist's responsibilities at the* News *than he commenced writing another series of reminiscences and reflections in the* Daily Record *under the pseudonym of 'Mr Incognito'.*

Nor, perhaps, need too much anguish be devoted to the difference between Neil Munro and 'Hugh Foulis' because each was, in his own way, a brilliantly talented craftsman. Although for a considerable period of time in the latter half of the twentieth century the only works of Munro/Foulis that were readily available were these products of daily journalism – the adventures of Erchie, Jimmy Swan and, above all, Para Handy – we now have available again a much wider range of Munro's work and can better judge the totality of his artistic creation.

One additional factor which has assisted this process of re-evaluation of Munro has been the publication of a rich treasure trove of short stories which were not included in the five volumes of 'Hugh Foulis' tales published in Munro's lifetime or in the 1931 omnibus volume. Although Erchie *appeared in book form in 1904 Munro, as we shall see, went on writing about him right up to the time of the 1926 General Strike, and the present editors' edition* (Birlinn, 2002), contains 112 stories which did not appear in book form in Munro's lifetime. The parallel edition of *Jimmy Swan the Joy Traveller* adds seven uncollected stories to the thirty published in the 1917 edition. *The Birlinn edition of* Para Handy *(1992) adds 18 stories, dating from 1905 to 1924, to add to the canon. The 1931 omnibus edition published a total of 140 stories. The recent Birlinn editions add 177 to this total and the additions serve as a forceful reminder to us that these characters appealed to Munro as a vehicle for his creativity over almost a quarter of a century. If this was the 'jaw-box' it was one that Munro showed immense aptitude for working, at, and therefore it would be difficult to imagine these witty and lively pieces being done as 'just another job'. It is remarkable, given the often transitory nature of humorous writing, that these stories have survived in popular affection and esteem for close on a hundred years. Para Handy in particular has become an iconic figure, flourishing in various editions over the century, never being out of print, and surviving translation into radio, television and film.*

We have selected a few typical stories from each of the series, Erchie, Para Handy and Jimmy Swan. Each group of stories is prefaced with a brief note about the character and Munro's approach to this distinctive genre of short fiction.

'Erchie, My Droll Friend' (1904)

INTRODUCTION

In the first years of the twentieth century Munro created a remarkable comic character, Erchie MacPherson, a Glasgow waiter and beadle of St Kentigern's Kirk. He used Erchie for the next quarter century to comment on royal visits, flying machines, the transfer market for footballers, the marital habits of film stars, art nouveau and the Glasgow tramway system.

Despite this longevity Erchie only ever appeared in one collection of stories published in 1904. The print-run ordered was a remarkable 107,000 copies. Had they all sold Munro's royalties would have been about £1,000 – a figure which needs to be multiplied by about 50 times to get a modern equivalent. Sadly the sales were not quite as large as had been hoped, despite Blackwood's energetic marketing. In the first year some 54,000 copies were sold but sales dropped off sharply and the remaining stock had to be sold off as a sixpenny edition – with a dramatic reduction in Munro's royalties.

Nonetheless Erchie was close to Munro's heart. As a Glasgow tenement dweller Erchie (whose motto was 'a flet fit but a warm hert') and his friend, the coal-merchant Duffy, provided Munro with apt voices to comment on all the follies and fashions of the age.

These stories were written in the era of the 'Kailyard School' – and the chronicler of the Glasgow novel, Moira Burgess, has coined the term 'Urban Kailyard', which might, at first glance, be thought an apt description of these stories. However a closer reading suggests that their sharpness of vision, unsentimental realism and, at times, surreal humour, place them well outside the cosy, couthy, depiction of life in either an idealised rural or urban community.

Munro's reluctance to sanction any further collections of Erchie stories might have been due to the very strongly Glaswegian speech patterns of the principal characters and the limitations this put on their acceptance. When suggesting a book devoted to his second great comic creation, Para Handy, he wrote: 'The dialect, for one thing, is reduced to a minimum and the articles are quite within the comprehension of the English reader without any glossary.' Modern readers, trained in Glasgow dialect by books from No Mean City to Jim Kelman, need have few fears.

We offer for your delight 'Erchie in an Art Tea Room' – with Erchie and Duffy encountering the splendours of Miss Cranston's Willow Tea Rooms and the works of Charles Rennie Mackintosh and two later stories from the Birlinn complete edition. 'Erchie on Prohibition', from April 1915, reflects the wartime Government's attempts to reduce alcohol consumption, while 'The Grand Old Man Comes Down', from March 1923, is a surrealistic commentary on the rearrangement of the statues in Glasgow's George Square to make way for a war memorial.

ERCHIE IN AN ART TEA-ROOM

'I saw you and Duffy looking wonderfully smart in Sauchiehall Street on Saturday,' I said to Erchie one morning.

'Man, were we no'?' replied the old man, with an amused countence. 'I must tell ye the pant we had. Ye'll no' guess where I had Duffy. Him and me was in thon new tea-room wi' the comic windows.[1] Yin o' his horses dee'd on him, and he was doon the toon liftin' the insurance for't. I met him comin' hame wi' his Sunday claes on, and the three pound ten he got for the horse. He was that prood he was walkin' sae far back on his heels that a waff o' win' wad hae couped him, and whustlin' 'Dark Lochnagar'.

'Come on in somewhere and hae something,' says he, quite joco.

"Not me," says I – "I'm name o' the kind; a beadle's a public man, and he disna ken wha may be lookin' at him, but I'll tell ye whit I'll dae wi' ye – I'll tak' ye into a tea-room." "A' richt," says Duffy; "I'm game for a pie or onything."

'And I took him like a lamb to the new place.

'When we came fornent it, he glowered, and "Michty!" says he, "wha did this?"

"'Miss Cranston[2]," says I.

"'Was she tryin'?" says Duffy.

"'She took baith hands to't," I tellt him. "And a gey smert wumman, too, if ye ask me."

'He stood five meenutes afore I could get him in, wi' his een glued on the fancy doors.

"'Do ye hae to break yer wey in?" says he.

"'No, nor in, I tells him; look slippy in case some o' yer customers sees ye!"

"'Och! I havena claes for a place o' the kind," says he, and his face red.

"'Man!' I says, "ye've henned – that's whit's wrang wi' ye: come in jist for the pant; naebody 'll touch ye, and ye'll can come oot if it's sore."

'In we goes, Duffy wi' his kep aff. He gave the wan look roond him, and put his hand in his pooch to feel his money. "Mind I have only the three flaffers and a half[3], Erchie," says he.

'"It'll cost ye nae mair than the Mull o' Kintyre Vaults,' I tellt him, and we began sclimmin' the stairs. Between every rail there was a piece o' gless like the bottom o' a soda-water bottle, hangin' on a wire; Duffy touched every yin o' them for luck.

'"Whit dae ye think o' that, noo?" I asked him.

'"It's gey fancy", says Duffy; "will we be lang?"

'"Ye puir ignorant cratur!" I says, losin' my patience a'thegither, "ye havena a mind in the dietin' line above a sate on the trams o' a lorry[4] wi' a can o' soup in your hand."

'I may tell ye I was a wee bit put aboot mysel', though I'm a waiter by tred, and seen mony a dydo in my time. There was naething in the hale place was the way I was accustomed to; the very snecks o' the doors were kind o' contrairy.

'"This way for the threepenny cups and the guid bargains,' says I to Duffy, and I lands him into whit they ca' the Room de Looks[5]. Maybe ye havena seen the Room de Looks; it's the colour o' a goon Jinnet use to hae afore we mairried: there's whit Jinnet ca's insertion on the tablecloths, and wee beeds stitched a' ower the wa's the same as if somebody had done it themsel's. The chairs is no' like ony other chairs ever I clapped eyes on, but ye could easy guess they were chairs; and a' roond the place there's a lump o' lookin'-gless wi' purple leeks[6] pented on it every noo and then. The gasalier in the middle was the thing that stunned me. It's hung a' roon wi' hunners o' big gless bools'[7] the size o' yer nief – but ye don't get pappin' onything at them.

'Duffy could only speak in whispers. "My Jove!" says he, "ye'll no' get smokin' here, I'll bate."

'"Smokin"!' says I; "ye micht as weel talk o' gowfin'."

'"I never in a' my life saw the like o't afore. This cows a'!" says he, quite nervous and frichtened lookin'.

'"Och!' says I, "it's no your fau't; you didna dae't onywye. Sit doon."

'There was a wheen lassies wi' white frocks and tippets on for waitresses, and every yin o' them wi' a string o' big red beads roond her neck.

'"Ye'll notice, Duffy," says I, "that though ye canna get ony drink here, ye can tak' a fine bead[8] onywye, but he didna see my joke.

'"Chaps me no'!" says he. "Whit did ye say the name o' this room was?"

'"The Room de Looks," I tellt him.

"'It'll likely be the Room de Good Looks," says he, lookin' at the waitress that cam' for oor order. "I'm for a pie and a bottle o' Broon Robin."

"'Ye'll get naething o' the kind. Ye'll jis tak' tea, and stretch yer hand like a Christian for ony pastry ye want," said I, and Duffy did it like a lamb. Oh! I had the better o' him; the puir sowl never saw onything fancy in his life afore since the time Glenroy's was shut in the New City Road, where the Zoo⁹ is. It was a rale divert. It was the first time ever he had a knife and fork to eat cookies wi', and he thocht his teaspoon was a' bashed oot o' its richt shape till I tellt him that was whit made it Art.

"'Art," says he, "whit the mischief's Art?"

"'I can easy tell ye whit Art is," says I, "for it cost me mony a penny. When I got mairried, Duffy, haircloth chairs was a' the go; the sofas had twa ends to them, and you had to hae six books wi' different coloured batters¹⁰ spread oot on the paurlor table, wi' the tap o' yer weddin'-cake under a gless globe in the middle. Wally dugs¹¹ on the mantelpiece, worsted things on the chair-backs, a picture o' John Knox ower the kist o' drawers, and 'Heaven Help Our Home' under the kitchen clock – that was whit Jinnet and me started wi'. There's mony a man in Gleska the day buyin' hand-done pictures and wearin' tile hats to their work that begun jist like that. When Art broke oot –"

"'I never took it yet," says Duffy.

"'I ken that," says I, "but it's ragin' a' ower the place; ye'll be a lucky man if ye're no' smit wi't cairryin' coals up thae new tenements they ca' mansions, for that's a hotbed o' Art. But as I say, when Art broke oot, Jinnet took it bad, though she didna ken the name o' the trouble, and the haircloth chairs had to go, and leather yins got, and the sofa wi' the twa ends had to be swapped for yin wi' an end cut aff and no' richt back. The wally dugs, and the worsted things, and the picture o' John Knox, were nae langer whit Jinnet ca' the fashion, and something else had to tak' their place. That was Art: it's a lingerin' disease; she has the dregs o't yet, and whiles buys shillin' things that's nae use for onything except for dustin'."

"'Oh! is that it?" says Duffy; "I wish I had a pie."

"'Ye'll get a pie then," I tellt him, "but ye canna expect it here; a pie's no' becomin' enough for the Room de Looks. Them's no' chairs for a coalman to sit on eatin' pies."

'We went doon the stair then, and I edged him into the solid meat department. There was a lassie sittin' at a desk wi' a wheen o' different coloured bools afore her, and when the waitresses cam' to her for an order for haricot mutton or roast beef or onything like that frae the kitchen, she puts yin o' the bools doon a pipe¹² into the kitchen, and the stuff comes up wi' naething said.

'"Whit dae ye ca' that game?" asks Duffy, lookin' at her pappin' doon the bools; "it's no' moshy, onywye."

'"No, nor moshy," I says to him. "That's Art. Ye can hae yer pie frae the kitchen withoot them yellin' doon a pipe for't and lettin' a' the ither customers ken whit ye want."

'When the pie cam' up, it was jist the shape o' an ordinary pie, wi' nae beads nor onything Art aboot it, and Duffy cheered up at that, and said he enjoyed his tea.'

'I hope the refining and elevating influence of Miss Cranston's beautiful rooms will have a permanent effect on Duffy's taste,' I said.

'Perhaps it will,' said Erchie; 'but we were nae sooner oot than he was wonderin where the nearest place wad be for a gless o' beer.'

NOTES

1. Erchie and Duffy are patronising the newly opened Willow Tea-Rooms in Glasow's Sauchiehall Street, designed by Charles Rennie Mackintosh for Kate Cranston.

2. Kate Cranston, temperance advocate and businesswoman, had opened a chain of successful tea-rooms across Glasgow, employing the best local architects and designers. 'Quite Kate Cranstonish!' became a local term of praise for something well-designed and stylish.

3. Three pound notes and a ten-shilling note (£3.50).

4. The shafts of a coal cart.

5. The Room de Luxe was the jewel of the Willow Tea-Rooms – the colours were silver grey and pink and Erchie's ironic description gives a fair account of the décor. The specially designed Mackintosh chairs appear to have caught his imagination: 'The chairs is no' like ony other chairs ever I clapped eyes on, but you could easy guess they were chairs'.

6. Erchie's 'purple leeks' are of course the classic art nouveau rose of the Glasgow style.

7. Glass balls as big as your fist. Glass and mirrored glass was a feature of the Willow Tea-Rooms.

8. To take 'a fine bead' is to take a good drink.

9. The Zoo referred to is Wombwell's Menagerie in New City Road.

10. The batters are the front and back covers of a book.

11. Wally dugs were the popular pairs of matching china dogs to be found on Edwardian mantepieces.

12. Orders were placed by coloured balls, each representing a menu item, being sent down a pipe to the kitchen. 'Moshy' is the children's game of marbles.

ERCHIE ON PROHIBITION

'What's a' this aboot shuttin' the pubs to sodgers?'[1] Duffy asked. 'What harm would the sodgers dae in a pub ony mair nor onybody else? I think at a time like this the sodgers should get a' encouragement, to cheer them on.'

Erchie looked at the coalman with humorous resignation. 'Man, Duffy!' he replied, 'ye're aye a week behind wi' your news the way ye are in takin' tuppence aff the bag when the coals come doon. It's no against the sodgers that they're gaun to shut the pubs; they're maybe gaun to shut them a'thegither.'[2]

Duffy was staggered, but incredulous. 'Nane o' your coddin', Erchie! Hoo could they refuse to serve ye if ye hae the money and nae signs o' drink aboot ye? They widna daur! They would lose thier licence!'

'Duffy,' said his friend, 'your education's painfully neglected; ye should have stayed another quarter in the night school. Ye've heard o' an Act o' Parliament? Wi' an Act o' Parliament they can dae onything. They could stop ye eatin' eggs or gettin' your hair cut. It used to tak' years to pass an Act o' Parliament, and even then a smert-like chap could march through the middle o't the same's it was a triumphal arch. But noo an Act o' Parliament taks less than twenty seconds; they dae't wi' a rubber stamp. If they took a notion to stop the sale o' coals the first ye would hear o't would be a telegram frae the Hoose o' Commons, sayin' that coals were contraband, and ony man found wi' a bunker in his hoose on and after Monday first would be put in jyle.'

'Somebody should write to the papers and expose them!' said Duffy, warmly, 'It shouldna be allo'ed! I'll never vote for onybody again! What sense is there in shuttin' pubs?'

'Oh, they're no' shut yet,' said Erchie; 'But a lot o' folk's got an awfu' start. I got a wee bit shake mysel'.'

The coalman gloomily stared at vacancy. 'My George! It's gettin' worse and worse!' he said despairingly at last. 'First it was Zeppelins, and then it was submarines, and noo it's pubs blockaded! It's perfectly redeeculous! What herm's a dacent pub if ye don't abuse it?'

'Ye don't understand,' said Erchie. 'It's military tactics; it's to get recruits. If ye want a people to win a war, ye must mak' them desperate. Look at the Russians and the French! The Russians, for ordinar', like to put past the time wi' a foreign drink called vodka because it jist tastes like that, and the French mak' a habit o' drinkin' absinthe, if there's ony left over when they're polishin' a chest o' drawers or a sideboard. When the war broke oot half the French kept on busy polishin' and the Russians moved that slow from the vodka shops to the fightin' line they ca'd them the steam-road-rollers.

'"If things go on like this," said the Czar to the President o' the French Republic, "the war'll last a lifetime. We'll need to tak' steps to mak' them move a little slippier."

'An Act was passed prohibitin' the sale o' vodka and absinthe till the war was settled, and the Russians and the French flocked to the Army determined to end the war at the earliest possible moment. Ye couldna stopped them goin' noo that there was naething to keep them at hame.'

'And what did the German dae?' asked Duffy.

'The Germans did the same in a different way. "If ye want good beer," says they to their sodgers, "there's plenty in Belgium and France is full o' champagne cellars." That made them breenge across the border, and they'll stay in Belgium and France as lang's there's a barrel or a bottle left.

'If they shut the pubs in Scotland, Duffy, it's because your king and country needs ye' quicker than ye come. Stayin' at hame and shirkin' must be made to lose its main attraction. When it's generally understood that the only place in Europe where ye can get a tot o' rum is in the trenches every high-spirited young man'll 'list.'

'It'll be gey hard on us that's no' that young,' said Duffy. 'Could they no' just mak' the Act apply to chaps that's under forty?'

'Na; na! if it comes at a' it'll come a' roond. The King himsel's teetotal[3] noo; no' a drop o' onything in the hoose for him but butter-milk, or maybe a bottle or two o' raspberry cordial. "What'll ye hae, your Majesty?" says his butler, bringin' in the tray at nicht. "I suppose there's naething for't but butter-milk as usual," says the King. "Right-o!" says the butler, and slaps him doon a jugful. It's a lesson to us a', Duffy. If ye want to get royal noo ye can get the whole concomitants o' a spree at the kitchen jawbox.'

'But still I canna picture the pubs a' shut in Gleska,' says Duffy. 'Everybody'll mak' a rush for Paisley.'

'Tuts! if they're shut in Gleska they'll be shut in Paisley too. But I'm like you – I canna figure to mysel' a total prohibeetion Scotland. Whaur would millionaires like you in the coal tred spend their money. A small limejuice and soda's a nice enough beverage in moderation, but ye canna spend a nicht wi't, and if there's nae pubs, a lot o' chaps, when their day's work's done 'll no' hae any place to go to but straight hame. They'll be driven to't!'

'And then,' continued Erchie, 'consider the effect on a' the associated industries! The peppermint and aromatic-lonzenge tred'll suffer dreadfully. The cultivation o' the clove'll stop, and the cork-screw manufactures may just as weel shut thir doors. It'll tell on the fishin' tred, for naebody'll go fishin'; ye canna keep the midges aff wi' eau-de-cologne or barley-water.'

'I simply *will not* stand it!' protested Duffy. 'I need a moderate refreshment noo and then to keep my strength up. You carry fifty hundredwechts o' coal –'

'Fifty bags ye mean,' corrected Erchie.

– 'Up them tenement stairs and ye'll find it canna be done on butter-milk!'

'Oh, ye'll get used to that,' said Erchie cheerfully. 'Drinkin's just a habit, like wearin' boots or sittin' in your shirt sleeves to your tea. There's days and days I never think o't, and if I was in a lichthoose I would clean forget that such a thing as drink existed. . . . My Jove! what would happen to Campbeltown?⁴ I would be vex't for Campbeltown!'

'Ye micht be vexed for yoursel',' suggested Duffy. 'There wouldna be the same demand for waiters.'

'Oh, just the same!' said Erchie. 'They canna stop folk eatin', except in Germany, where ye need to get a ticket before ye can cut a loaf. The only difference wi' us waiters would be that we would get hame sooner frae their public banquets; there wouldna be ony aifter-dinner oratory.'

'Ach! the thing's a' nonsense!' said Duffy. 'If ye met a chap ye kent at nicht, what could ye stand him?'

'Oh, ye would jist slip him an oranger or a tin o' Nestle's milk, and say "Here's to ye!". The springs o' human kindness needna be a'thegither dry because o' prohibeetion. At the worst ye would aye be at liberty to tak' a crony into Craig's or Cranston's,⁵ and fill him up wi' Russian tea, a drink that's fairly ragin' noo across the Blue Carpathian Mountains.'

'Tea's a' richt in its ain place,' admitted Duffy, 'but ye couldna be aye nip, nip, nippin' awa' at tea. It's maybe fine for folk that hae the time to spend on't, but it's no' for workin'men. If this calamity is railly gaun to happen us, I'll hae to lay in something in a press till the war blaws bye.'

NOTES

1. This story was published in the *News* in March 1915 at a period when concern was being expressed by the Government about the consumption of alcohol, particularly in the areas of war production.
2. While the public houses were not shut completely, in some areas the liquor trade was taken under Government control. The temperance movement was a powerful social force in the early twentieth century and legislation for local veto polls had been passed just before the outbreak of the War.
3. King George V and the Royal Household had renounced the use of alcoholic beverages for the duration of hostilities.

4. The Kintyre burgh of Campbeltown's prosperity was founded on whisky distilling with as many as 34 distilleries operating there at various times in the nineteenth and twentieth centuries.
5. Two of the famous Glasgow tea-rooms.

THE GRAND OLD MAN COMES DOWN[1]

With remarkable expedition, and unaccustomed cheerfulness, as if for once they were thoroughly enjoying their job, a gang of workmen had hoisted Gladstone[2] from his pedestal. Suspended by the neck in a most sinister manner, the grand old statesman swung at the end of the winch-chains, oscillating slowly. A fine, crisp, clear day, with the touch of Spring in it.

'Criftens!' exclaimed Duffy. 'Whit are they daein' here?'

'Fifteen feet o' a drap,' replied Erchie, solemnly. 'Ate a good breakfast o' bacon and eggs, and asked for a cigarette. Ellis[3] was assisted by William Johnson, a young shoemaker from Northampton, and before hurryin' back to England visited the Cathedral, havin' a keen interest in Gothic architecture and stained gless.'

'Awa and tak a runnin' jump at yersel!' said Duffy impatiently. 'Nane o' your cod, Erchie; whit are they ca'in' the Grand Auld Man aff his feet for?'

'They have every richt to dae't,' said Erchie; 'he's five-and-twenty years deid.'

'It's a statue that was daein' nae herm to onybody,' remarked the coalman with feeling. 'It's a hanged shame shiftin' it! I suppose it's Mr Dalrymple; he'll be gaun to bring his cars roond here. He has nae respect for onything.'

'It's no Mr Dalrymple this time, Duffy,' said Erchie, chuckling. 'It's the general consensus o' public opeenion that the time's come when public statuary and triumphal arches should be annually revised, and scrapped when necessary. In an electric age, wi' wireless and a' that, ye canna be bothered wi' them when they're the least oot o' date. To you and me, Gladstone was the greatest man o' his time; but by the growin' generation all that's kent aboot him is that he wrote "The Land o' the Leal"[4] and invented a portmanteau.'

'If it wasna' for him Ireland would never ha'e had Home Rule!' said Duffy with loyal admiration.

'Whisht!' warned Erchie, 'say naething aboot that. He meant it for the best.'

'There's far aulder monuments than Gladstone's here,' said Duffy; 'they should start wi' the auldest; it's only the other day they put up the Gladstone; I mind o't fine; there was a great furore and brass bands.'

'Just you wait and ye'll see the others shifted, too. Gladstone came first because, standin' aye there lookin' in at the front door o' the Municipal Buildin's he fair got on the nerves o' the Labour members. It spiled the Corona cigars for them. That's the way sae mony o' them went to London,[5] where a bronze Presbyterian conscience is no' aye glowerin' at ye. A' the time auld Willie has been standin' there he's seen a lot o' life.'

'But what are they flittin' him for?' asked Duffy, who never keeps abreast of local movements by reading newspapers.

'I've told ye already,' replied Erchie patiently. 'Statues nooadays are like comic songs; they go awfu' quick oot o' fashion. Naebody looks at them efter they're mair than a twelvemonth in position. The only yin in George Square that attracts attention noo is Mr Oswald[6] wi' the lum hat, for it has never occurred to onybody to put a lid on the hat to keep the boys frae pappin' stones in't.

'It's like this, Duffy – ye've seen yersel' wi' a grocer's calendar in the kitchen showin' The Genius of Scotland Findin' Burns at the Plough. For the first three months your eye was never aff it; a' the rest o' the year ye would never look at it unless the wife put it on the table in front o' ye on a plate. It's the same wi' statues – there's auld General Peel[7] at the other side o' the Square, naebody looks at him unless it's a polisman to see that there's naething chalked on the pedestal.

'Under the new movement for brightenin' up Gleska the authorities is gaun to put a' the statues on wheels and hurl them to different sites in the city twice a year. The priceless gift o' Art is to be brung hame to the toilers o' Brigton Cross and Maryhill. I wouldna say but ye'll have Watty Scott's monument sometime next winter clapped at the end o' Raeberry Street. Walk you roond it, Duffy, if ye're coming hame at nicht; mak' nae attempt to sclim' it.'

'Ye're aye tryin' to pull my leg,' said Duffy, impatiently. 'I wish you would talk sense.'

'I'm talkin' naething else. The perambulatin' statue is going to solve a lot o' civic problems: it's surprisin' they never went in for it wholesale sooner, seein' they had some experience wi' King William[8] at the Cross. They're goin' to shift him again. There's no' an equestrian statue in Europe that's done mair gallopin'. It's the only way to keep up wi' the urgent needs o' the greatest Corporation tramway system in modern times.

'Whit can be done wi' King William can be done wi' every monument in sicht as occasion requires; the only site for a memorial regarded as perpetual should be the Necropolis.

'Put them a' on wheels from the start, and hurl them where they're maist required from year to year. I wouldna destroy them althegither as lang's the memory o' the departed's green, but as soon as it's only folk frae the country on a trip that looks at them, I would send them to the stone-knappers and introduce a brand-new lot.'

NOTES

1. This story was published in the *News* in March 1923 as Glasgow's George Square was being rearranged to accommodate the monument to the dead of the First World War.
2. William Ewart Gladstone (1809–98) the Liberal statesman and Prime Minister – often referred to as the 'Grand Old Man'. His statue stood at the east end of George Square in the site where the Cenotaph was to be erected.
3. John Ellis, a Rochdale barber, was the public hangman between 1899 and 1924.
4. The Gladstone bag may preserve the statesman's name but 'The Land o' the Leal' is less clearly linked to Gladstone. It is a touching poem by Lady Nairne (1766–1845).
5. Many of the 'Red Clydesiders' elected to Parliament in the previous year's General Election had formerly been members of the City Council or other local public bodies such as education boards.
6. James Oswald was a Liberal politician and campaigner for the 1832 Reform Act. His statue has the reformer with an outstretched top hat in his hand – an obvious target for small boys to throw stones into. By a happy chance, a month after this story was published, Munro and the novelist Joseph Conrad were dining in the North British Hotel and afterwards came out into George Square, where Munro persuaded Conrad to throw a stone into Oswald's hat and thus become an honorary Glaswegian.
7. George Square has statues of Generals Moore and Campbell, but Erchie is probably referring to the statue to Robert Peel, Tory Prime Minister and Rector of Glasgow University.
8. The equestrian statue of King William III stood, until 1923, at Glasgow Cross but was removed to Cathedral Square because of road alterations.

'Para Handy' (1906, 1911, 1922)

INTRODUCTION

Since the retirement of Erchie *I have been fortnightly writing in the* Glasgow News *a series of somewhat analogous articles and stories round about the title* The Vital Spark. *They have caught on immensely in the West of Scotland; indeed in an infinitely greater measure than* Erchie *and I have not the slightest doubt that if you care to undertake their publication this Winter in the shilling form of* Erchie *they would exceed that gentleman's popularity.*

So wrote Munro to William Blackwood in October 1905. His assessment was accurate. The adventures of the crew of the puffer Vital Spark *had rapidly won a place in readers' hearts that they have never lost. The first story, 'Para Handy, Master Mariner', appeared in the* News *in January 1905 and by August 1905, when Glasgow was presented with an estate at Ardgoil, the* News *could run a cartoon entitled 'The Next Tramway Extension' showing a Corporation Tramcar mounted on the* Vital Spark *headed down-river for the new property. No explanation was necessary – the ship and its crew had become part of local folklore.*

The first collection of stories, The Vital Spark, *appeared in the spring of 1906 and Munro probably planned to leave matters there. However the characters were much too good to neglect, and in February 1908 the first story from what would become the second collection,* In Highland Harbours with Para Handy, *appeared in the* News.

Like Erchie *the 'Para Handy' tales were very often based on contemporary events and preoccupations. 'Pension Farms' is a typically topical story inspired by the introduction of Old Age Pensions by Chancellor of the Exchequer David Lloyd George in 1908.*

A third collection, Hurricane Jack of the Vital Spark, *appeared in 1923 but a number of stories were never included in the collections published in Munro's lifetime or in the 1931 Omnibus edition. One of these, the very last of the stories 'Wireless on the Vital Spark', dates from January 1924, and reflects Munro's interest in radio – an interest expressed in a number of 'Looker-On' columns as well as inspiring this final voyage for the* Vital Spark.

The American scholar Francis Russell Hart writes in The Scottish Novel from Smollett to Spark *(1978):*

... a combination of stateliness and shrewdness carries the captain through ... helping the helpless with charity and delicacy, perpetrating solemn pranks, managing minor extortions, dreaming of Hurricane Jack's gentility, boasting of the breadth of his experience and the supremacy of his boat, a humane and devious sage in whimsical mock-romance sailing on small waters.

Hart concludes: 'Para Handy is not out of place in the romantic, ironic world of Gilian the Dreamer, Ninian Campbell, and John Splendid'.

'Hugh Foulis' may have been the name on the title page but the spirit and the talent of Neil Munro clearly permeates these stories.

PARA HANDY, MASTER MARINER

A short, thick-set man, with a red beard, a hard round felt hat, ridiculously out of harmony with a blue pilot jacket and trousers and a seaman's jersey, his hands immersed deeply in those pockets our fathers (and the heroes of Rabelais) used to wear behind a front flap, he would have attracted my notice even if he had not, unaware of my presence so close behind him, been humming to himself the chorus of a song that used to be very popular on gabbarts[1], but is now gone out of date, like 'The Captain with the Whiskers took a Sly Glance at Me'. You may have heard it thirty years ago, before the steam puffer[2] came in to sweep the sailing smack from all the seas that lie between Bowling and Stornoway. It runs:

> Young Munro he took a notion
> For to sail across the sea,
> And he left his true love weeping,
> All alone on Greenock Quay.

And by that sign, and by his red beard, and by a curious gesture he had, as if he were now and then going to scratch his ear and only determined not to do it when his hand was up, I knew he was one of the Macfarlanes. There were ten Macfarlanes, all men, except one, and he was a valet, but the family did their best to conceal the fact, and said he was away on the yachts, and making that much money he had not time to write a scrape home.

'I think I ought to know you,' I said to the vocalist with the hard hat. 'You are a Macfarlane: either the Beekan, or Kail, or the Nipper, or Keep

Dark, or Para Handy –'

'As sure as daith,' said he, 'I'm chust Para Handy, and I ken your name fine, but I cannot chust mind your face.' He had turned round on the pawl[3] he sat on, without taking his hands from his pockets, and looked up at me where I stood beside him, watching a river steamer being warped into the pier.

'My goodness!' he said about ten minutes later, when he had wormed my whole history our of me; 'and you'll be writing things for the papers? Cot bless me! and do you tell me you can be makin' a living off that? I'm not asking you, mind, hoo mich you'll be makin' don't tell me; not a cheep! not a cheep! But I'll wudger it's more than Maclean the munister. But och! I'm not saying: it iss not my business. The munister has two hundred in the year and a coo's gress[4]; he iss aye the big man up yonder, but it iss me would like to show him he wass not so big a man as yourself. Eh? But not a cheep! not a cheep! A Macfarlane would never put his nose into another man's oar.'

'And where have you been this long while?' I asked, having let it sink into his mind that there was no chance to-day of his learning my exact income, expenditure, and how much I had in the bank.

'Me!' said he; 'I am going up and down like yon fellow in the Scruptures – what wass his name? Sampson – seeking what I may devour.[5] I am out of a chob. Chust that: out of a chob. You'll not be hearin' of anybody in your line that iss in want of a skipper?'

Skippers, I said, were in rare demand in my line of business. We hadn't used a skipper for years.

'Chust that! chust that! I only mentioned it in case. You are making things for newspapers, my Cot! what will they not do now for the penny? Well, that is it; I am out of a chob; chust putting bye the time. I'm not vexed for myself, so mich as for poor Dougie. Dougie wass mate, and I wass skipper. I don't know if you kent the *Fital Spark*?'

The *Vital Spark*, I confessed, was well known to me as the most uncertain puffer that ever kept the Old New-Year[6] in Upper Loch Fyne.

'That wass her!' said Macfarlane, almost weeping. 'There was never the bate of her, and I have sailed in her four years over twenty with my hert in my mooth for fear of her boiler. If you never saw the *Fital Spark*, she is aal hold, with the boiler behind, four men and a derrick, and a watter-butt and a pan loaf[7] in the fo'c'sle. Oh man! she wass the beauty! She was chust sublime! She should be carryin' nothing but gentry for passengers, or nice genteel luggage for the shooting-lodges, but there they would be spoilin' her and rubbin' all the pent off her with their coals, and sand, and whunstone, and oak bark, and timber, and trash like that.'

'I understood she had one weakness at least, that her boiler was apt to prime.'

'It's a — lie,' cried Macfarlane, quite furious; 'her boiler never primed more than wance a month, and that wass not with fair play. If Dougie wass here he would tell you.

'I wass ass prood of that boat ass the Duke of Argyll, ay, or Lord Breadalbane. If you would see me waalkin' aboot on her dake when we wass lyin' at the quay! There wasna the like of it in the West Hielan's. I wass chust sublime! She had a gold bead aboot her; it's no lie I am tellin' you, and I would be pentin' her oot of my own pocket every time we went to Arran for gravel. She drawled four feet forrit and nine aft, and she could go like the duvvle.'

'I have heard it put at five knots,' I said maliciously.

Macfarlane bounded from his seat. 'Five knots!' he cried. 'Show me the man that says five knots, and I will make him swallow the hatchet. Six knots, ass sure my name iss Macfarlane; many a time between the Skate and Otter.[8] If Dougie wass here he would tell you. But I am not braggin' abbot her sailin'; it wass her looks. Man, she was smert, smert! Every time she wass new pented I would be puttin' on my Sunday clothes. There wass a time yonder they would be callin' me Two-flag Peter in Loch Fyne. It wass wance the Queen had a jubilee, and we had but the wan flag, but a Macfarlane never wass bate, and I put up the wan flag and a regatta shirt and I'm telling you she looked chust sublime!'

'I forget who it was once told me she was very wet,' I cooed blandly; 'that with a head wind the *Vital Spark* nearly went out altogether. Of course, people will say nasty things about these hookers. They say she was very ill to trim, too.'

Macfarlane jumped up again, grinding his teeth, and his face purple. He could hardly speak with indignation. 'Trum!' he shouted. 'Did you say "trum"? You could trum her with the wan hand behind your back and you lookin' the other way. To the duvvle with your trum! And they would be sayin' she wass wet! If Dougie wass here he would tell you. She would not take in wan cup of watter unless it wass for synin'[9] oot the dishes. She wass that dry she would not wet a postage stamp unless we slung it over the side in a pail. She wass sublime, chust sublime!

'I am telling you there iss not many men following the sea that could sail the *Fital Spark* the way I could. There isss not a rock, no, nor a chuckie stone inside the Cumbrie Heid that I do not have a name for. I would ken them fine in the dark by the smell, and that iss not easy,

I'm telling you. And I am not wan of your dry-land sailors. I wass wance at Londonderry with her. We went at night, and did Dougie no' go away and forget oil, so that we had no lamps, and chust had to sail in the dark with our ears wide open. If Dougie wass here he would tell you. Now and then Dougie would be striking a match for fear of a collusion.'

'Where did he show it?' I asked innocently. 'Forward or aft?'

'Aft,' said the mariner suspiciously. 'What for would it be aft? Do you mean to say there could be a collusion aft? I am telling you she could do her six knots before she cracked her shaft. It wass in the bow, of course; Dougie had the matches. She wass chust sublime. A gold bead oot of my own pocket, four men and a derrick, and a watter-butt and a pan loaf in the fo'c'sle. My bonnie wee *Fital Spark*!'

He began to show symptoms of tears, and I hate to see an ancient mariner's tears, so I hurriedly asked him how he had lost the command.

'I will tell you that,' said he. 'It was Dougie's fault. We had yonder a cargo of coals for Tarbert, and we got doon the length of Greenock, going fine, fine. It wass the day after the New Year, and I wass in fine trum, and Dougie said, "Wull we stand in here for orders?" and so we went into Greenock for some marmalade, and did we no' stay three days? Dougie and me wass going about Greenock looking for signboards with Hielan' names on them, and every signboard we could see with Campbell, or Macintyre, on it, or Morrison, Dougie would go in and ask if the man came from Kilmartin or anyway roond aboot there, and if the man said no, Dougie would say, "It's a great peety, for I have cousins of the same name, but maybe you'll have time to come oot for a dram?"[10] Dougie was chust sublime!

'Every day we would be getting sixpenny telegrams from the man the coals was for at Tarbert, but och! we did not think he wass in such an aawful hurry, and then he came himself to Greenock with the *Grenadier*[11], and the only wans that wass not in the polis-office wass myself and the derrick. He bailed the laads out of the polis-office, and "Now," he said, "you will chust sail her up as fast as you can, like smert laads, for my customers iss waiting for their coals, and I will go over and see my good-sister[12] at Helensburgh, and go back to Tarbert the day efter to-morrow." "Hoo can we be going and us with no money?" said Dougie – man, he wass sublime! So the man gave me a paper pound of money, and went away to Helensburgh, and Dougie wass coilin' up a hawser forrit ready to start from the quay. When he wass away, Dougie said we would maybe chust be as weel to wait another tide, and I said I didna know, but what did he think, and he said, "Ach, of course!" and we went aal back into Greenock. "Let me see that pound!" said Dougie, and did I not give it to him? and then he rang the bell of the public hoose we were in, and asked for four tacks and a wee hammer. When he got the four tacks and the wee hammer he nailed the pound note on the door, and said to the man, "Chust come in with a dram every time we ring the bell till that's done!" If Dougie wass here he would tell you. Two days efter that the owner of the *Fital Spark* came doon from Gleska and five men with him, and they went away with her to Tarbert.'

'And so you lost the old command,' I said, preparing to go off. 'Well, I hope something will turn up soon.'

'There wass some talk aboot a dram,' said the mariner. 'I thought you said something aboot a dram, but och! there's no occasion!'

A week later, I am glad to say, the Captain and his old crew were reinstated on the *Vital Spark*.

NOTES

1. A shallow draft sailing vessel used in the Scottish coastal trade.
2. A small steam lighter. Puffers were extensively used as general cargo carriers along the Western seaboard of Scotland between the 1880s and the last decade of the twentieth century.
3. A mooring post.
4. The grazing for a cow – the parish minister's glebe.
5. Para Handy, though ready to quote Scripture, frequently gets things a little confused. Here, he is not quoting from the Old Testament story of Samson but from the New Testament: 1st Peter Ch.5 v.8: 'Be sober, be vigilant, because your adversary the devil, as a roaring lion, walketh about, seeking whom he may devour.'
6. New Year's Day according to the old or Julian calendar – still celebrated in parts of the Highlands and Islands.
7. A popular type of Scottish bread with a smooth crust, baked in a tin or pan.
8. A stretch of Loch Fyne.
9. Rinsing.
10. A small measure of liquid: hence a drink. Usually used of whisky, or, as Para Handy will frequently call it, 'British spirits'.
11. A paddle steamer built in 1885 for MacBraynes and used on their winter services to and from Loch Fyne.
12. Sister-in-law.

†

PENSION FARMS

The *Vital Spark* was making for Lochgoilhead, Dougie at the wheel, and the Captain straddled on a waterbreaker, humming Gaelic songs, because he felt magnificent after his weekly shave. The chug-chug-chug of the engines was the only other sound that broke the silence of the afternoon, and Sunny Jim deplored the fact that in the hurry of embarking early in the morning he had quite forgotten his melodeon – those peaceful days at sea hung heavy on his urban spirit.

'That's Ardgoil,' remarked Macphail, pointing with the stroup of an oil-can at the Glasgow promontory[1], and Para Handy gazed at the land with affected interest.

'So it iss, Macphail,' he said ironically. 'That wass it the last time we were here, and the time before, and the time before that again. You would think it would be shifted. It's wan of them guides for towerists you should be, Macphail, you're such a splendid hand for information. What way do you spell it?'

'Oh, shut up!' said the engineer with petulance; 'ye think ye're awfu' clever. I mind when that wee hoose at the p'int was a hen farm, and there's no' a road to't. Ye could only get near the place wi' a boat.'

'If that wass the way of it,' said Dougie, 'ducks would suit them better; they could swim. It's a fine thing a duck.'

'But a goose is more extraordinar',' said Macphail with meaning. 'Anyway it was hens, and mony a time I wished I had a ferm for hens.'

'You're better where you are,' said the Captain, 'oilin' engines like a chentleman. A hen ferm iss an aawful speculation, and you need your wuts aboot you if you start wan. All your relations expect their eggs for nothing, and the very time o' the year when eggs iss dearest, hens takes a tirrievee[2] and stop the layin'. Am I no' tellin' the truth, Dougie?'

'You are that!' said the mate agreeably; 'I have noticed it mysel'.'

'If ye didna get eggs ye could live aff the chickens,' suggested Sunny Jim. 'I think a hen ferm would be top, richt enough!'

'It's not the kind o' ferm I would have mysel whatever o't,' said Para Handy; 'there's far more chance o' a dacent livin' oot o' rearin' pensioners.'

'Rearin pensioners?' remarked Macphail; 'ye would lie oot o' your money a lang while rearin pensioners; ye micht as weel start growin' trees.'

'Not at aal! not at all!' said Para Handy; 'there's quick returns in pensioners if you put your mind to the thing and use a little caation. Up in the Islands, now, the folks iss givin' up their crofts[3] and makin' a kind o' ferm o' their aged relations. I have a cousin yonder oot in Gigha wi' a stock o' five fine healthy uncles – no' a man o' them under seventy. There's another frien' o' my own in Mull wi' thirteen heid o' chenuine old Macleans. He gaithered them aboot the islands wi' a boat whenever the rumours o' the pensions started.[4] Their frien's had no idea what he wanted wi' them, and were glad to get them off their hands. "It's chust a notion that I took," he said, "for company; they're great amusement on a winter night," and he got his pick o' the best o' them. It wassna every wan he would take; they must be aal Macleans, for the Mull Macleans never die till they're centurions, and he wouldna take a man that wass over five and seventy. They're yonder, noo, in Loch Scridain, kept like fightin' cocks; he puts them oot on the hill each day for exercise, and if wan o' them takes a cough they dry his clothes and give him something from a bottle.'

'Holy smoke!' said Dougie; 'where's the profits comin' from?'

'From the Government,' said Para Handy. 'Nothing simpler! He gets five shillings a heid in the week for them, and that's £169 in the year for the whole thirteen – enough to feed a regiment! Wan pensioner maybe wadna pay you, but if you have a herd like my frien' in Mull, there's money in it. He buys their meal in bulk from Oban, and they'll grow their own potatoes; the only thing he's vexed for iss that they havena wool, and he canna clip them. If he keeps his health himsel', and doesna lose his heid for a year or twa, he'll have the lergest pension ferm in Scotland, and be able to keep a gig. I'm no' a bit feared for Donald, though; he's a man o' business chust ass good ass you'll get on the streets o' Gleska.'

'Thirteen auld chaps like that aboot a hoose wad be an awfu' handful,' suggested Sunny Jim.

'Not if it's at Loch Scridain,' answered Para Handy; 'half the time they're on the gress, and there's any amount o' fanks[5]. They're quite delighted swappin' baurs wi' wan another aboot the way they could throw the hammer fifty years ago, and they feel they're more important noo than ever they were in a' their lives afore. When my frien' collected them, they hadna what you would caal an object for to live for except it wass their own funerals; noo they're daaft for almanacs, and makin' plans for living to a hundred, when the fermer tells them that he'll gie them each a medal and a uniform. Oh! a smert, smert laad, Donal'. Wan o' Brutain's hardy sons! Nobody could be kinder!'

'It's a fine way o' makin' a livin',' said Macphail. 'I hope they'll no' go wrang wi' him.'

'Fine enough,' said Para Handy, 'but the chob iss not withoot responsibilities. Yonder's my cousin in Gigha wi' his stock o' five, and a nice bit ground for them, and you wouldna believe what it needs in management. He got two of them pretty cheap in Salen, wan o' them over ninety, and the other eighty-six; you wouldna believe it, but they're worse to manage than the other three that's ten years younger. The wan over ninety's very cocky of his age, and thinks the other wans iss chust a lot o' boys. He says it's a scandal givin' them a pension; pensions should be kept for men that's up in years, and then it should be something sensible – something like a pound. The wan that iss eighty-six iss desperate dour, and if my cousin doesna please him, stays in his bed and says he'll die for spite.'

'That's gey mean, richt enough!' said Sunny Jim; 'efter your kizzen takin' a' that trouble!'

'But the worst o' the lot's an uncle that he got in Eigg; he's seventy-six, and talkin' aboot a wife!'

'Holy smoke!' said Dougie; 'isn't that chust desperate!'

'Ay; he hass a terrible conceity notion o' his five shillin's a-week; you would think he wass a millionaire. "I could keep a wife on it if she was young and strong," he tells my cousin, and it takes my cousin and the mustress aal their time to keep him oot o' the way o' likely girls. They don't ken the day they'll lose him.'

'Could they no put a brand on him?' asked Dougie.

'Ye daurna brand them,' said the Captain, 'nor keel[6] them either. The law'll no allo' it. So you see yersel's there's aye risk, and it needs a little capital. My cousin had a bit of a shop, and he gave it up to start the pension ferm; he'll be sayin' sometimes it wass a happier man he wass when he wass a merchant, but he's awfu' prood that noo he hass a chob, as you might say, wi' the Brutish Government.'

NOTES

1. The 9,500-acre Ardgoil Estate was presented to Glasgow in 1905 by Cameron Corbett, MP for Glasgow Tradeston.
2. A fit or tantrum.
3. A smallholding in the Highlands and Islands.
4. In 1908 David Lloyd George, as Chancellor of the Exchequer in Asquith's Liberal Government, introduced the first state old-age-pension scheme into Britain. This paid the sum of five shillings (25 pence) per week to single people aged 70 and over and seven shillings and sixpence (37 pence) per week to married couples.
5. Sheep pens.
6. To keel is to put a painted mark of ownership on a sheep.

WIRELESS ON THE *VITAL SPARK*: INTERCOURSE
WITH THE INFINITE[1]

When Macphail's bright young son, the apprentice engineer, came down to the *Vital Spark* at Bowling and fitted up an aerial, none of the crew save Macphail himself showed any great enthusiasm.

'What kind o' a contrivance is this?' Para Handy asked, when he came on board to discover the wires already stretched between the mast head and the funnel. As captain, he felt that the innovation, without any authority from him, verged a little too closely on the informal.

'Mind your feet!' said Macphail, irritably; 'you're standin' on the cat's whiskers,'[2] He was closely engrossed in the wiring up of the crystal set extemporised so ingeniously by Johnny, who had left an expansive blueprint showing the whole lay-out for his father's guidance.

'I can see its goin' to be a wild New Year this,' said the Captain, ominously. 'There's no' a cat on the whole horizon. The sooner we're at sea the better.'

Macphail paid no attention, but stuck a headphone over his ears, and assumed an intently listening aspect . . . Science! . . . The newest marvel of human discovery! . . . All made by Johnny from workshop scrap! A glow of pride went through the latest listener-in. For a little he heard nothing. Then came a faint pulsating sound of wheezing, curiously accompanied by an odour of beer. He screwed up his face and strained his ears with eager expectancy, while Dougie, the mate, bent over him in an effort at eavesdropping on this communion with the infinite.

'Confound you and your asthma!' indignantly cried the scientist, plucking off the 'phones. 'I thought I was on to the start o' a comic song frae Gleska!'[3]

It was the nearest approach to wireless intercourse they got that evening.

Para Handy, from the start, was dubious of the whole thing, though induced to countenance the aerial by its manifest adaptability for drying shirts. Too proud to ask Macphail for explanations, he consulted Dougie, who gave him a brief synopsis of the principles of wireless telephony, as gathered at first-hand from the engineer.

'The sounds comes through the air and hit the mast,' said the mate; 'then slide down the wire and into Macphail's wee box that catches them like a moose-trap.'

'Where do they come from?' asked the Captain in incredulous tones.

'From the air,' replied the mate; 'it's chock-a-block wi' music and news aboot the weather.'

'But who makes the noise?' inquired the Captain.

'There's men and women that's paid for't,' patiently explained Dougie. 'Most of the time they're in London⁴ and they speak into a great big trumpet. The sound travels at the rate o' a hundred and fifty miles a minute, and lands on a bit o' crystal.'

'Would Macphail no' be better wi' a lemonade bottle?' asked the Captain ironically. 'When does the concert start?'

'Start!' exclaimed Dougie. 'Man, it's goin' on aal the time! Stop you till Macphail gets his bits o' wires put right thegither, and ye'll think ye're at the Mull and Iona Soiree, Concert and Ball.⁵ They tell me it's wonderful.'

'Dougald,' said the Captain, putting his hand on the other's shoulder, 'don't you listen to Macphail's palavers. He's pullin' your leg for ye. If you're wantin' to study music, buy a pair o' bagpipes.'

Even Dougie's confidence in the engineer was shaken ultimately. Macphail spent all next evening in alternate tinkering with his set and futile listening. The others jeered at him.

'If we all sat round in a circle and joined hands,' suggested Para Handy, 'we might get a word or two from the Duke o' Wellington. Do you hear any spirits knockin', Mac? Maybe ye'll need to put oot the light, they're fearful timid.'

'I wouldna' say but your instrument's needin' oilin',' was Dougie's sardonic contribution to the criticism. 'Did ye oil it plenty?'

'A body might ass weel be readin' a book for aal the fun that's in this new diversion,' said the Captain. 'It's me that's vexed for poor Mrs Maphail! Gie them a shout, Mac; maybe they divna know ye're listenin'.'

'Would a gimlet be any use?' inquired Dougie helpfully. 'It's maybe fresh air that's wanted. Ye should surely be hearin' something or other, and it so close on Hogmanay! Never mind aboot Gleska or London, turn it on to Kinlochaline. There's bound to be gaiety of some kind on at Kinlochaline.'⁶

'I wish youse would shut up!' cried Macphail, exasperated. 'I canna hear an article wi' your bletherin'.'

'Isn't he the poor, deluded cratur!' sadly soliloquised the Captain, addressing nobody in particular. 'Good enough schoolin', too, and seen a lot o' trevel in foreign steamers. Never wass the same man since Hurricane Jeck hit him over the heid wi' a spanner!⁷ I wonder what would give him the notion he could hear anything wi' them things on his ears. He would be far better wi' a couple o' bungs and a bit o' marlin.'

'Stand aside and gie me a shot at it,' said Dougie at last. 'Ye were always dull o' hearin, Mac.'

He put the 'phones on his ears and listened a moment or two with increasing hopelessness. Suddenly he gaped; his eyes goggled.

'Dalmighty!' he exclaimed and pulled the 'phones off hurriedly, pale with apprehension.

'Are ye hearin' them?' inquired the Captain. 'What's the latest news from London?'

'Ass sure ass I'm livin' I heard a man sayin' "Hallo! hallo! hallo!" as plain ass anything,' panted Dougie. "A great big English chentleman wi' a whisker!'

'The Duke o' Wellington,' suggested Para Handy, still incredulous. 'Plug up your ears again and ye'll maybe hear him gie a stave o' a song. Ask him if he knows the Gaelic.'

'If ye don't believe me try't yoursel',' said Dougie, proffering the 'phones with some anxiety to get rid of them as soon as possible. 'Ye would think the man was standin' beside ye sayin' "hallo, hallo!" Sounds like a chentleman that would have a yacht. Where would he be speakin' from, Macphail?'

'Might be anywhere,' said Macphail, himself a little dubious of Dougie's bona-fides. 'London, Cardiff, or perhaps America.' He picked up the 'phones again and stuck them over his ears with no great expectation of hearing anything.

'America!' said the Captain with withering sarcasm. 'There's great blow-hards in America, but I never thought they could blow the length o' Bowlin'. Tell me when you're on to China.'

A look of ecstasy came over Macphail's countenance. His head sunk into his shoulders: every nerve and fibre of his being seemed all at once to concentrate on listening.

'As clear's a bell!' he exclaimed in a whisper. 'Good for Johnny! I kent that boy had talent.'

'Isn't this deplorable?' said the Captain, sadly. 'It's his own son Johnny he hass in the moose-trap noo. I never heard the like o't since Hurricane Jeck wass in the horrors. I'll go away ashore and get a bottle o' something from the druggist.'

'Wheesht!' implored the engineer with a hand up. 'It's a band, and they're playin' music. Reel and Strathspey – ye can hear them hoochin'! Just you listen to this, Dougie.'

'Is't from Kinlochaline?' inquired the mate. 'If it's not, I'm goin' ashore wi' the Captain.'

Two hours after, when Para Handy and his mate returned, they found Macphail had gone to bed.

'Did you really hear a chap cryin' oot "hallo"?' asked the Captain.

'I thocht I did,' said Dougie, 'but maybe it wass chust imagination.'

Para Handy put on the phones, and plucked them off in a minute or two impatiently.

'There iss no more music there than there iss in a blecknin'-bottle!' he declared; 'Macphail and you iss a bonny pair o' liars!'[8]

NOTES

1. This uncollected story appeared in the *News* on 7 January 1924. During the previous year Munro had written on a number of occasions about developments in radio in Britain and the USA and had reviewed a broadcast play in his column.
2. The popular term used for the fine wire used with the crystal detector in early radios.
3. The British Broadcasting Company's Glasgow station (call sign 5SC) had commenced broadcasting in November 1923.
4. National radio broadcasting from London (call sign 2LO) had started in November 1922.
5. The Mull and Iona Soiree, Concert and Ball, a Glasgow entertainment for exiled natives of those islands, had featured before in the Para Handy stories.
6. Unaccountably, Kinlochaline in Morvern, despite being the birthplace of Hurricane Jack, a former member of the crew of the *Vital Spark,* has still not been favoured with a BBC radio station.
7. A previously unrecorded incident.
8. It is very appropriate that this, the last of the Para Handy stories to appear in the *News* before Munro's final retirement, should look forward to the new and exciting world of radio. During the nineteen years in which these stories had delighted the newspaper's readers the world in which they were set had experienced many changes, changes which Munro had faithfully recorded through their impact on the crew of the *Vital Spark.* The stories reflect a wide range of contemporary events and concerns ranging from German spies to General Elections, from Old Age Pensions to the problems caused by the introduction of Summer Time. All of these were able to provide Para Handy and his crew with the raw material for an enjoyable 'baur' and it is fitting that this final tale, about the crew's 'Intercourse with the Infinite', should have been, in its day, equally topical.

Jimmy Swan, the Joy Traveller (1917)

INTRODUCTION

In May 1911 Munro created a new comic character for his News *column: Jimmy Swan, sales representative for the Glasgow wholesale drapery warehouse of Campbell & Macdonald. However in a 'Looker-On' column of February 1910, 'Knights of the Road', he had written of a thinly fictionalised John Swan, a draper's traveller for the real-life Glasgow firm of Stewart & Macdonald, who clearly provided something of the inspiration for his more famous namesake.*

In September 1913 Munro wrote to George W. Blackwood suggesting another one-shilling 'Hugh Foulis' volume: 'For some time back I have been running a series of humorous sketches in the Glasgow Evening News, *dealing with the character and road experiences of a pawky old commercial traveller, "Jimmy Swan".'*

Blackwoods were keen on the project but Munro delayed submitting his collected newspaper sketches because of a desire to provide a better selection. The outbreak of war in 1914 introduced further delays, and it was not until 1917 that Jimmy Swan set out in book form around the small-town drapers of Scotland on his mission to bring the latest Glasgow fashions and elastic corsets to the rural areas. Thirty stories of this 'ambassador of commerce' appeared in this collection and in the 1931 omnibus edition. Another seven Jimmy Swan tales were written for the News *and published for the first time in book form in the Birlinn edition.*

Jimmy Swan is socially a class above his contemporary, Erchie: he lives in the desirable suburb of Ibrox and goes out on the road with a Mazeppa cigar in his hand, a flower in his buttonhole and a pound a day for expenses. He is a gentler, quieter character than Erchie, with an attractive vein of sentimentality in his character. Jimmy is not only a commercial traveller, he is a universal provider for his rural communities, undertaking little commissions, ranging from the purchase of an engagement ring, or a piano, or a brass band, to the acquisition of a new minister.

'Stars to Push' introduces the Joy Traveller musing on how his sample case is filled with goods 'meant for comfort, consolation, the pleasure o' the eye, or the pride o' life'.

'A Spree' finds Jimmy at a loose end in one of the quiet country towns where so much of his life is spent, and joining in a choir practice. The joys of choral singing are splendidly portrayed in this unusual tale which offers

what is surely one of the best descriptions of the delights of music to the performer.

Glasgow in Munro's time saw three great exhibitions held at Kelvingrove in 1888, 1901 and 1911. Munro wrote often about these events but seldom more entertainingly than in an uncollected story 'The Adventures of a Country Customer'.

STARS TO PUSH

Mr Swan, the work of the day accomplished, stood smoking at the Buck's Head door, and the sky was all a-glee with twinkling stars which are quite irrelevant to the story, and are merely mentioned here to indicate that it was evening. And yet, when I come to think of it, the stars deserve this mention, for their shining, so serene, and cool, and joyous, had some influence both on Jimmy and the story. They set him wondering on the mystery of things and on the purpose of his being and his life.

Behind him, in the hall of the hotel, the Boots, old Willie, piled his sample-cases ready for the boat at six o'clock next morning. The billiard-room seemed full of villagers; the sound of chaff and laughter and the clink of tumblers came from it occasionally. But Jimmy scarcely heard it – wrapt in contemplation of the stars.

From out the billiard-room, at last, there came a man who seemed to have decided, not a moment too soon – indeed, unfortunately, too late – that it was time for home. He fumbled for his top-coat, hanging with a dozen others on a stand, and he was forced to stretch himself a little over Jimmy's cases, piled up very high about the stand by Willie.

'A fine night, Mr Sloan,' said Jimmy, who knew even recent incomers to Birrelton[1], and he helped him to put on his coat.

'There's naething wrang wi' the night,' said Mr Sloan, 'except for thae damn bags o' yours . . . Perf'ly rideec'lous! A body might as weel be on a steamer . . . Shouldn' be allowed!' He was at that particular stage of fermentation where the scum of personal temperament come bubbling to the top.

'Sorry they should be in your road,' said Jimmy, affably. 'They're often in my own. It's yin o' the chief drawbacks to bein' what the papers ca' an ambassador o' commerce[2].'

'Ambass'or o' commerce!' hiccoughed Mr Sloan. 'Nonsense! Jus' a common bagman[3]!' And two younger men who had joined him laughed at this brilliant sally.

'Right ye are!' said Jimmy. 'Just a common bagman! That's what I was thinkin', standin' here and takin' my bit smoke, and lookin' at the stars. Just a plain auld bagman sellin' silks and ribbons! I wish my line was traivellin' for stars. My jove! if I had stars to push, I could get orders! A line like that would gie me scope; I'm sometimes sick o' wastin' words on Shantungs⁴ and on down-quilt patterns.'

Mr Sloan was feeling nasty – distinctly nasty, having barked his shin on a sample case, and having an uneasy sense that he had forgotten something, and that he should have been home to his wife a good deal earlier. He wished to work himself into the proper spirit for a lively domestic altercation.

'What hae ye got in a' thae cases?' said he.

'Joy,' said Jimmy, rappin' out his pipe upon his palm, and pursing up his mouth.

'Oh to bleezes!' said the man, 'you're drunk.'

'Just touched a wee, perhaps, wi' drinkin' starlight,' said Jimmy. 'But still I'm tellin' ye, I'm a traiveller for joy, and there's my samples. If I was openin' up my bags to ye, it's likely ye would only see dry-goods. I saw them, last, mysel' as dry-goods when I packed them, but it just came on me here in lookin' at the stars I was mistaken; there's naething in my bags but human joy.'

The young men roared with laughter.

''Scuse me, Mr Swan,' said Mr Sloan, a little more agreeably, 'I've often seen ye gaun aboot, and thought ye were in the drapery line; how was I to ken ye were traivellin' for beer?'

'No,' said Jimmy, solemnly, 'not beer! Wholesome human joy. Glowerin' at the stars there, I was tryin' to find some excuse for my paltry and insignificant existence, and then I minded I was an essential bit o' the mechanism for providin' dresses for the lassies o' Birrelton for next month's Territorial ball. Do ye think ye grasp me, Mr Sloan?'

'But what aboot the joy?' said Mr Sloan.

'That's joy,' said Jimmy. 'Youth, and a new frock! I ran over a' my samples in my mind, and there's no' a one that's no' a swatch o' something meant for comfort, consolation, the pleasure o' the eye, or the pride o' life. What would life in Birrelton be withoot me, or the like o' me? Man! that's one o' my ties ye're wearin', Mr Sloan! I wish ye would learn to put a better knot on't and gie the stuff a chance.'

'Wha's tha' got to do wi' stars?' asked Mr Sloan, vaguely. 'You said ye were sellin' stars. Or was it beer? I forget which.'

'No,' said Jimmy. 'I'm not at present sellin' stars, though maybe that's in store for me if I could be a better man. I only mentioned stars because they set me wonderin' if an auld bagman was ony use at a' in that big scheme that put them twinklin' yonder . . . Good night, gentlemen! I'm aff to bed.'

When they were gone, he watched the stars a little longer, finishing his pipe, and then went to the stand to take his coat upstairs with him. Instead of it he found the errant Sloan's.

'By George, I must get my coat,' he said to Willie. 'I have a pair o' gloves and a box o' chocololates for the wife in't.'

Mr Sloan meandered home with that uneasy sense of something overlooked, forgotten and only recollected what it was when his anxiously awaiting wife asked him if he had the mutton.

'Mutton!' he exclaimed with a sudden sinking of the heart. 'What mutton?'

'Oh, John!' she said, 'didn't you promise me to be sure and get a gigot for to-morrow? You know that it's the holiday, and all the shops 'll be shut. What am I to do for dinner?'

'As sure as death I clean forgot it, talkin' with a chap aboot the stars,' said Mr Sloan, contritely, as she helped him to take off his coat.

She put a hand into his pockets and produced a pair of reindeer gloves and a box of chocolates. 'What in all the world is this?' she asked him, and he stared, himself, confounded.

'I don't have ony mind o' buying them,' said he; 'but that's a' right: I likely meant them for a peace offerin'.'

'You're just a dear!' she cried, delightedly; 'although you did forget the mutton,' and she put the gloves on, finding them a perfect size.

There was a ringing at the door.

'I'm very sorry to disturb you at this hour,' said Mr Swan, 'but there's been a slight mistake. I have a coat the very neighbour of your husband's, and we got them mixed between us at the hotel. This, I think, is his; I wouldn't trouble you, so late, but I have to leave by the early boat.'

'Oh!' she said, despairingly, 'I might have known!' and started pulling off the gloves. 'Then these are yours, and the box of chocolates?' The tears were in her eyes.

'No,' said Jimmy firmly. 'There was nothing in my pockets, Mrs Sloan: your husband must have bought them,' and got his coat restored to him by a delighted wife.

'Who is he that?' she asked, when he was gone.

'Old Swan,' said Mr Sloan, half sleeping.

'What is he?' she asked. 'I liked the look of him.'

'Travels for stars,' said Mr Sloan, vaguely; 'bags full of joy! Old Jimmy Swan! He's drunk!'

NOTES

1. Birrelton is a fictitious location used for many of the Jimmy Swan stories.
2. A somewhat pretentious term used for a commercial traveller.
3. A commercial traveller. So called because, like Jimmy Swan, they carried samples of their wares in bags and cases.
4. A soft silk fabric originating from the Chinese northern coastal province of the same name. Now more usually transliterated as Shandong.

A SPREE

Having finished high tea at the George Hotel, Jimmy Swan, a little wearied after a cross-country journey of five-and-twenty miles in a badly-sprung waggonette[1], sought out his usual bedroom, and searched his bag for slippers.

They weren't there!

The ready-flyped[2] extra socks were there; the shirts with the studs in them; the Cardigan waistcoat; the chest-protector he had never used in all his life; the little 'housewife' or bachelor's companion, with needles, thread, and button in it; the sticking-plaster; the bottle of fruit saline; the pokcet Bible and the Poems of Burns; but not a hint of carpet slippers.

'I doubt Bella's gettin' a bit auld, like mysel',' he meditated. 'It's the first time she forgot my slippers since we married. I'll hae to be awfu' angry wi' her when I get hame – if I can keep mind o't.'

He went down to the Commercial Room and rang the bell for the Boots.

'Have ye a pair o' slippers, Willie?' he inquired.

'There's no' such an article in the hoose, Mr Swan,' said the Boots, 'unless I got ye the lend o' the boss's.'

'Oh, don't bother!' said the traveller. 'I'll can dae withoot.'

'We used to hae a couple o' dozen pair for the use o' you commercial gentlemen,' said Willie, 'but nooadays naebody asks for them; I suppose it's this new sanitary and high-jinkic education.'

'The innkeepers made a great mistake when they stopped providin' slippers,' said Mr Swan. 'There was naething better for keepin' a customer in the hoose and no' stravaigin'[3] roon the toon wastin' his money in other premises. If ever I start an inn, I'll hae a pair o' slippers, a rockin-chair, and a copious free supply o' cake and speldrins[4] for every customer. What's the result o' me no' hae'in' slippers? I'm just goin' awa' ootbye for a walk to mysel', and there's no sayin' where I may forgaither wi' a frien' or twa. No man's hame for the nicht until he has aff his boots.'

He lit his pipe, and walked through the little town at the hour when the cows, that had been milked for the evening, were released from their byres and driven back to their common pasture. The Free Church bell was ringing for the Thursday prayer-meeting. The shops were shuttered. An odour of burning oak from the bakehouse, commingled with the curious redolence from the hot oven-sole, impregnated the atmosphere until he got so far as the smithy, where a little earlier sheep's heads had apparently been singeing. From what had once been the U.P. chapel[5], and was now a hall for the Parish kirk, came the sound of choral voices.

Jimmy stood in front of the hall and listened. The combined Established and U.F. choirs were practising for the Ancient Shepherds'[6] annual church parade, and at the moment singing Sullivan's 'Carrow':

My God, I thank Thee, who has made
  The earth so bright,
So full of splendour and of joy,
  Beauty and light;
So many glorious things are here,
  Noble and right.

Outside, on the pavement, he put in a restrained, but rich, resonant, and harmonious bass. A lifetime of encounter with bleak weather had not impaired his naturally mellifluent organ, and he counted no artistic joy so exquisite as the hearing of his own voice giving depth and body to the parts of a well-sung church tune. He knew all the words and harmonies of hundreds of hymns and psalms; they were ineradicable from his memory, which would never retain the words or air of a pantomime song for more than a week.

'That's Bob Fulton, my customer, puttin' them through their facin's for the Sabbath,' reflected Mr Swan. 'Good soprano, capital alto, bass no' sae bad, but tenor, as usual, no' worth a docken. Ye'll no' get a dacent tenor in Scotland out o' Gleska; it must be something emollient and demulcent in Italian ice-cream[7].'

A moment later, in a cessation of the singing, he put his head diffidently in at the hall door.

'Come awa' in, Mr Swan!' cheerfully invited the choir conductor. 'We'll be nane the waur o' an extra bass.'

'Oh, ye are daein' splendid, Mr Fulton!' said Jimmy, joining the musicians, with many of whom he was well acquainted. 'Good attack; fine balance; tempo tip-top! Wi' an organ ye would just be as good as oor ain Cathedral.'

But to his vexation, the practice was at an end. And he had just administered a peppermint lozenge to himself before entering, to get the proper atmosphere, and tone up the larynx!

'Hang it a'!' he said, 'the night's but young yet, and I was fair in the key for a spree o' Psalmondy.'

'The minister's for naething but the newer hymns on Sunday – except the Old Hundred[8] to begin wi',' said Mr Fulton, and the commercial traveller made a grimace.

'New hymns!' said he. 'New fiddlesticks! He'll be takin' to Anthems next, and a solo soprano cocked up in the gallery cravin' the Wings o' a Dove wi' her mind on a new pair o' wings for her bonnet. There hasna been half a dozen new hymn tunes made in my time I would tolerate at my funeral; there's only "Peace, Perfect Peace!", "St Margaret", "Lead, Kindly Light", "St Agnes", "Pax Dei", and "Carrow" – there's no' much more in their novelties to boast o'. I wouldna gie St George's, Edinburgh, for a' the rag-time stuff in Sankey.'[9]

'Let us have a try at St George's,' said the conductor; 'No. 141 in Carnie's Psalter – "Ye Gates Lift Up", and the choir, to show Mr Swan the traveller what it was equal to, proceeded to sing with astonishing vigour and address. The summer shades in zephyrs and in hosiery; new stripe and twill designs; the Mona Lisa (speciality of C. & M.), the slump in Bulloch's order, and the rumour of sequestration for Macbain might never have been in the mind of Jimmy Swan; he sang his bass like a soul transported high above the gross affairs of earth, and emulous of the cherubim. In the second part, where the voices of the males asked Who of Glory, no other bass infused the phrase with so emotional a sense of wonder, inquiry, and reverence; he might have been the warder Peter.

'Excellent!' he exclaimed, when they were finished. 'I liked particularly the lah-soh-fah-me o' the tenors; it's the only bit we can aye depend on tenors gettin' a proper grip o', but a' your tenor, Mr Fulton, 's capital – what there is of it. If I might suggest another Psalm, it would be the Old 124th – "Now Israel may say and that truly".'

And the Old 124th it was. The inspiring bass of the visitor was enjoyed as much by the choir as by himself, and when he took his upper Bs with a clarity no less assured than the sonorousness of his lower Gs, there was an ecstasy in Jimmy's soul he would not barter for a fortune. He got his choice of an hour of Psalmody – Selma and Kilmarnock, Coleshill and Torwood, and Dundee, 'Oh, Send Thy Light Forth' and 'By Babel's Streams'; and Robin Brant, the joiner, leading bass was put upon his metal. Himself a man in his prime, of six-feet-three, he was determined no grey-headed traveller from Glasgow, rather small in stature and slightly paunchy, should beat a voice that had been brought to its perfection by daily warblings, pitched in tone to the constant bizz of a circular saw. But Jimmy Swan was envious or emulous of no one, utterly delivered over to the art of harmony and the meaning of the lines. It would there and then have seemed but reasonable to him that the portion of the blest should be to sing eternal Psalms. The weariness of his journey was dispelled; sharing a Psalm-book with another chorister, he rarely needed to glance upon its pages, he was doing what had been familiar and inspiring for him to do ever since the day the crackle left his adolescent voice, and he found he was a singer.

The rosy face was lit with animation; the shrewd grey head just faintly moved in time to the wave of Fulton's pitchfork; when at 'Invocation' he said 'my harp, my harp, my harp I will employ', there was an absolutely luscious 'dying fall' in the opening notes for tenor and bass which gave the flexibility and colour of his voice magnificent exposition, and he knew it, for he glanced across at Fulton with the mute inquiry in his eye – 'Did ye hear me that time?'

'Ye're no' oot o' practice onyway, Mr Swan!' said Fulton. 'Where in a' the world do ye keep it up?'

'Maistly on slow trains, when I ha'e a carriage to mysel',' said Jimmy. 'Ye have no conception o' my compass on the N.B. Railway oot aboot Slamannan[10]. But to tell the truth, I'm no' much use at solos; I think I'm at my best when I swell the volume.'

He went home to his inn with a pleasing sense of having spent a profitable evening. He had not only helped the harmony, but from a copious lore about psalm-tunes and their history he had entertained the choir to an instructive, though unpremeditated lecturette; and pledged himself to Mr Fulton to give the same at greater length with the choir as illustrators at a public gathering when he next to next came round.

At the door of the George the innkeeper was standing speaking to Miss Bryce, the mantua-maker, one of Jimmy's customers.

'There you are, Mr Swan,' he said, 'I've been asking high and low for you; I found you a pair of slippers.'

'I've been employing my harp,' said Mr Swan, serenely blissful, 'and I've had a glorious night o't, Robert.

So many glorious things are here,
  Joyous and bright!

Man! it's a blessin' we're no' born dummies! Good evening, Miss Bryce; I'm just lookin' forward to seein' ye in the mornin'.'

'I hear from Mrs Clark you're going to favour us some day with a lecture on Psalmody. I hope ye'll tell us some o' your funny stories!' said the mantua-maker, who had the greatest admiration for his gifts as a raconteur, and the traveller looked ruefully at his host.

'She's a worthy body, Robert, but she doesna understand the grandeur o' solemnity, and the joy o' sacred song – if ye happen to be bass,' said Jimmy.

NOTES

1. An open, four-wheeled carriage with an inward-facing bench-seat along each side.
2. Turned inside out.
3. Wandering.
4. Dried fish, such as whiting or haddock.
5. The United Presbyterian was formed in 1847 from a union of the Secession and Relief Churches. In 1901 the U.P. Church merged with the Free Church to form the United Free Church. As a result this building was surplus to requirements and had become the Established Church of Scotland's Church Hall.
6. Not a reference to aged farmers. The Loyal Order of Ancient Shepherds was a popular friendly society. A Royal Commission in the 1870s had reported it to have 46,000 members organised in local lodges. The coming together of the Established and U.F. Church choirs to support the Shepherd's church parade is indicative of better relationships between the Presbyterian denominations at this time – a process which ended in the reunion of the two denominations in 1929.
7. At the end of the nineteenth century and in the early years of the twentieth century many Italians emigrated to Scotland. Large numbers of them entered the catering industry and came to dominate the two key areas of the fried-fish trade and the ice-cream parlour.
8. The 100th metrical Psalm 'All People that on Earth do dwell'. With its familiar tune 'Old 100th' taken from the Franco-Genevan Psalter of 1551, it was probably second only to the 23rd Psalm in the affections of Scottish worshippers.
9. The American evangelists, D. L. Moody and I. D. Sankey, published two collections of gospel hymns in the 1870s. These were highly popular, though obviously not with the traditionalist, Jimmy Swan.
10. The North British Railway's routes included a branch line through the Stirlingshire town of Slamannan.

✝

THE ADVENTURES OF A COUNTRY CUSTOMER[1]

Now that the Exhibition has the gravel nicely spread, and the voice of the cukoo is adding to the monotony of a rural life, there is going to be a large and immediate influx of soft-goods men from places like Borgue in Kincardineshire and Lochinver in the North. They will come into town on the Friday trains at Exhibition excursion rates; leave their leatherette Gladstone bags at Carmichael's Temperance Hotel or the Y.M.C.A. Club, have a wash-up for the sake of our fine soft Glasgow water; take a bite, perhaps, and sally forth to the Wholesale House of Campbell & MacDonald (Ltd.) ostensibly to see what can be done in cashmere hose, summer-weight underwear, and a large discount on the winter bill. Strictly speaking they know nothing about Campbell & MacDonald, having never seen them, even if they have any existence, which is doubtful; the party they are going to lean on is Mr Swan the traveller, who covers Lochinver and Borgue two or three times a year, and is all the Campbell & MacDonald that the rural merchants know.

Mr Swan came through our two former Exhibitions[2] with no apparent casualties beyond a slight chronic glow in the countenance and a chubby tendency in the space between the waistcoat pockets where he keeps his aromatic lozenges and little liver pills respectively. For an hour's convivial sprint through the various Scottish blends with a hurried customer in from Paisley, or a real sustained effort of four-and-twenty hours with a Perthshire man who is good for a £250 order, Mr Swan is still the most reliable man in Campbell & MacDonald's. He can hold his own even with big strong drapers from the distillery districts of the Spey; help them to take off their boots and wind their watches for them and yet turn up at the warehouse in the morning fresh as the ocean breeze, with an expenses bill of £3 10s. 4½d. which the manger will pass without the blink of an eyelash. The City of Glasgow, for the heads of the retail soft goods trade in Kirkudbrightshire and the North, is practically Jimmy Swan and a number of delightfully interesting streets radiating round him. In Borgue and Lochinver he has been recognised affectionately since the 'Groveries'[3] year as a Regular Corker and Only Official Guide to Glasgow, and no one knew better than himself when the turf was turned up again in Kelvingrove, just when the grass was taking root, that 1911 was going to be a strenuous year.

'I feel I'm getting a little too old for the game,' he said to his wife with a sigh.

'You ought to have got out of the rut long ago, Jimmy,' said Mrs Swan. 'It isn't good for your health.'

'A rut that's thirty years deep isn't a tramway rail, Bella,' he rejoined, 'and anyhow, I'm not in it for the fun of the thing, but mainly because I like to see you in a sealskin coat. But mark my words! this is going to be a naughty summer for your little Jimmy; every customer I have from Gretna to Thurso is going to have some excuse to be in Glasgow sometime when the Fairy Fountain's[4] on.'

The first of the important country customers turned up on Friday afternoon. He came from Galloway, and ran all the way from the station to the warehouse so as not to lose any time in seeing Mr Swan, who was just going out for a cup of tea. 'Why! Mr MacWatters! Delighted to see you!' said Jimmy, with a radiant smile kneading the customer's left arm all over as if he were feeling for a fracture. 'Come right in and see our manager! He was just saying yesterday, "We never see Mr MacWatters' own self," and I said: "No, Mr Simnpson, but I'll bet you see his cheques as prompt as the cheques of any man in Campbell & MacDonald's books!" I had him there, Mac, had him there!'

The manager was exceedingly affable to Mr MacWatters, but vexed that he had not sent a postcard to say he was coming. 'I should have liked,' he said, 'to take you out to the Exhibition, but unfortunately I have a Board meeting at three o'clock – of course I could have the meeting postponed.'

'Not at all! not on my account!' said the Galloway customer with genuine alarm and a wistful glance at Jimmy. 'I just want to look over some lines and leave an order, and then –'

'But my dear Mr MacWatters, you must see the Exhibition, and you must have a bit of dinner, and – Perhaps Mr Swan would take my place?'

'Delighted!' said Jimmy, heartily.

Mr MacWatters was introduced to some attractive lines in foulards, Ceylons, blouses, and the like, and said he would think it over and give Mr Swan his order at his leisure.

'Very good!' said the manager, shaking him by the hand at leaving. 'I'm sure you'll have a pleasant evening and enjoy the Exhibition. You will be immensely struck by the Historical section: it will show you what an intensely interesting past we have had; and I'll wager you'll be delighted with the picture gallery. Then there's Sir Henry Wood's[5] Orchestra – I wish I could be with you. But Mr Swan will show you everything; you can depend on Mr Swan.'

Five minutes later Jimmy and his country customer sat on tall stools in a lovely mahogany salon, and Jimmy was calling the country customer Bob, an affability which greatly pleased any man from Galloway. It was Bob's first experience of the mahogany salon; his business relations with the firm of Campbell & MacDonald didn't go back to the 'Groveries', and he had so far only the assurance of the soft-goods trade in Galloway that in Glasgow Jimmy was decidedly a good man to know.

In Galloway it is drunk out of a plain thick glass, with a little water, and it is always the same old stuff. In this mahogany salon, Jimmy appeared to control magical artesian wells from which the most beautiful ladies, with incredibly abundant hair, drew variegated and aromatic beverages into long thin glasses that tinkled melodiously when you brought them against your teeth. Jimmy gave his assurance that they were quite safe, and the very thing for an appetiser, and the man from Galloway said he never dreamt you could get the like of that anywhere except on the Continent. He added, reflectively, that he really must take home a small bottle. Pleased with his approval, Jimmy prescribed another kind called a Manhattan Cocktail[6], and the country customer enjoyed it so much that he started feeling his hip-pocket for his puse that he might buy another. But Jimmy said, 'On no account, old man! Leave this to me, it happens to be the centenary of the firm.' So the country customer carefully buttoned up his hip-pocket again, and consented to have another cocktail solely out of respect for the firm.

It was now decided by Jimmy that they could safely have a snack upstairs where the band was, and the country customer, being a corporal in the Territorials, walked upstairs carefully keeping time to the music, but somewhat chagrined that he had not divested himself, somewhere, of his yellow leggings.

They began with 'Hors d'oeuvres', which tasted exactly like sardines, then they had soup, of which the country customer had a second helping, after which he looked round for his cap and was preparing to go. But Jimmy laughingly said the thing was just starting, and a banquet followed which reminded the country customer of the one they had had at the Solway Arms Hotel in 1903 when the Grand Lodge deputation visited the local brethren.[7]

When the fish had passed, Jimmy picked up a List Price card or catalogue affair and said something about a bottle of 'buzz-water'. Concealing his disappointment, the country customer, who never had cared for lemonade, said he didn't mind. It turned out to be quite a large bottle with a gilt neck, and except for a singular tendency to go up the nose, it was the most pleasant kind of lemonade he had ever tasted. He was surprised that Jimmy hadn't ordered two bottles and said so, and Jimmy, begging his pardon, promptly did so.

This stage of the proceedings terminated with cups of black coffee and two absurdly minute glasses of a most soothing green syrup strongly recommended by Jimmy as an aid to digestion. There was also a large cigar.

'I think,' said Jimmy, in dulcet tones, with the flush of health upon his countenance, and a roguish eye, 'I think we will be getting a move on, and as one might say, divagating towards the Grove of Gladness.'

They had just one more, seeing it really was the centenary of the firm, and the country customer, as he walked downstairs, was struck by the beautiful convoluted design of the marble balustrade.

In the very next moment the country customer asked 'What is this?' and Jimmy responded, 'It is the Scenic Railway. Feel the refreshing breeze upon your brow!'[8] They were dashing with considerable celerity past a mountain tarn, and the country customer expressed a desire to stop for a moment that he might lave his fevered temples in the water. Far off a band was playing a dreamy waltz. A myriad lamps were shining in the night, and restlessly flitting from place to place. The air had a curious balminess that is not felt in Galloway. It was borne home to the country customer that he must there and then tell Mr Swan – good old Jimmy Swan! – about Jean Dykes in Girvan, and how he loved her and meant to marry her if he could get another extension of the lease of his shop at present terms, but before he could lead up to this subject with the necessary delicacy, he found himself on a balcony looking down on an enormous crescent of humanity, confronted by a bandstand and a tumbler.

'The firm,' Jimmy was saying solemnly, 'has always appreciated your custom. Our Mr Simpson says over and over again "Give me the Galloway men; they know what they want, and they always see that they get it!" he says, "Whatever you do, Mr Swan, pay particular attention to Mr MacWatters, and put him on bedrock prices." I have always done so, Galloway has been, as you might say, the guiding-star of my business life.'

The country customer, profoundly moved, shook Jimmy by the hand.

'Where are we now?' he asked and the balcony began to revolve rapidly. He steadied it with one hand, and tried to count the myriad lights with the other. They, too, were swinging round terrifically, and he realised that they must be stopped. He became cunning. He would pretend indifference to them as they swung round him, and then spring on them when they were off their guard. 'Where are we now?' he repeated.

'The Garden Club,' said the voice of Jimmy, coming out of the distance. 'Try and sit up and have this soda-water.'

Next morning, sharp at nine, Mr Swan came into the warehouse with a sparkling eye, a jaunty step, a voice as mellifluous as a silver bell and a camelia in his button-hole.

'Morning! Morning!' he cheerily said to the Ribbons Department, as he passed to the manager's room.

'Old Swan's looking pretty chirpy,' said the Ribbons enviously. 'He's been having a day at Turnberry[9] or the Coast.'

Jimmy laid a substantial order for autumn goods for Galloway and a bill of expenses for £3 9s. before the manager.

'Ah! just so!' said the manager. 'And how did Mr MacWatters like the Exhibition?'

'Immensely impressed!' said Jimmy.

'It is bound to have a great educative influence. Great! And such a noble object – Chair of History![10] What did Mr MacWatters think of the Art and Historical sections?'

'He was greatly pleased with them particularly,' said Jimmy. 'I have just seen him off in the train, and he said he would never forget it.'

The manager placed his initials at the foot of the expenses bill and handed it back to Jimmy who proceeded at once to the cashier's department.

'£3 9s.,' said the manager to himself. 'Art and History in Kelvingrove appear to come a little high, but it's a good order. And there's only one Jimmy Swan.'

NOTES

1. This previously uncollected story appeared in the *News* on 8 May 1911, just five days after the opening of the Scottish Exhibition of National History, Art and Industry – another example of Munro's topicality with many of these sketches.

2. Glasgow had held successful and popular exhibitions in Kelvingrove Park in 1881 and 1901. The first of these was intended to raise funds for a new Civic Art Gallery and Museum – the second was designed, in part, to inaugurate the new gallery.

3. 'The Groveries' was a popular, if unofficial, name for the first Kelvingrove Exhibition. However Munro thought little of this name and wrote in one of his columns 'On Saturday, 10th November, 1888, "The Groveries" – silly name for an International Exhibition – had closed.'

4. The Fairy Fountain – a large, central water feature illuminated by coloured electric light, was a focus for both the 1888 and 1911 exhibitions.

5. Sir Henry Wood (1869–1944) is of course otherwise best remembered as the originator of London's Promenade Concerts.

6. A Manhattan cocktail consists of bourbon or rye whiskey, vermouth and bitters.

7. One of a number of references to Freemasonry in these stories. Munro was himself a member of the Inveraray Masonic Lodge.

8. The mile-long Mountain Scenic Ride was one of the most popular features of the Exhibition.

9. A seaside resort in Ayrshire much frequented by golfers and the location of a luxury hotel.

10. The 1911 Exhibition had as one of its objects the raising of funds to endow a Chair of Scottish History at Glasgow University.

6

The Looker-On

Munro's career on the Glasgow Evening News *saw him move from reporter to chief reporter in 1888, then to a more literary and editorial role in which he was contributing gossip column items, reviews, leaders, special articles and interviews. In 1895 he took on the Thursday literary column 'Views and Reviews' in succession to J. N. Dunn and in 1897 he started a more general and discursive column 'The Looker-On' which appeared every Monday. When, in October of that year he left the office-staff of the* News *to concentrate on his fiction, he agreed to continue with these two columns. This commitment was both a financial safety-net and a useful way of keeping in touch with the paper and with contemporary events and preoccupations. Munro's diary for 4 October 1897 has the very human note: 'First day in the house as a Literary Man! Feel a little queer about it.'*

Munro would continue to write his two columns every week, with occasional interruptions, until he finally left the News *in 1927 and the variety and excellence of the over 2,000 columns that he contributed can only be hinted at in this anthology. A selection of this material, and some articles contributed as 'Mr Incognito' to the* Daily Record *between 1927 and his death, were gathered together by George Blake and published as* The Brave Days *(1931) and* The Looker-On *(1933).*

This selection uses fresh material that does not appear in Blake's two delightful volumes but underlines the same point that Blake makes, that only a fraction of the available riches have been harvested. Most of the pieces come from 'The Looker-On' but two characteristic pieces, reflecting Munro the poet and infuential critic, come from 'Views and Reviews'. One of these is a remarkable attack on Christopher Murray Grieve's 1920 collection of contemporary Scottish poetry, Northern Numbers, *a collection that was, by the way, dedicated to Munro himself. Munro, writing from the very thinly-veiled anonymity of his unattributed column, roundly condemns Grieve's presumption in placing John Buchan and himself in any Grieve-engineered group or poetic movement. To have 'a guid conceit o' one's self' has always been seen as a distinctive Scottish trait – but Munro's conclusion that:*

> ... *the truest poetry in* Northern Numbers *has come from the pen of him to whom the collection is dedicated. Mr Munro contributes five poems, brief, sombre, and moving, on themes apparently suggested by the names of bagpipe tunes. They have unique atmospheric quality; they 'tell' – inevitably, as it were: and though they are so distinctively 'Highland' in inspiration, they are, at the same time, the truest possible expression of the Scottish spirit*

does seem to take a proper self-confidence slightly beyond the bounds of modesty.

Munro's review of Northern Numbers *may be a partial explanation of why Grieve, who reinvented himself as Hugh MacDiarmid, became so critical of Munro, a process that culminated in his article in the* Scottish Educational Journal *of July 1925, an attack that concluded with the following paragraph:*

> *Neil Munro has also written a certain amount of verse. Most of it is no more. One little poem – a gem of its kind – is sure of life. This is 'John o' Lorn' already appearing in many anthologies. . . . It will serve better than anything else he has written, I think, to perpetuate its author's memory. His other poems are rhetorical, windy, empty for the most part and bear a curious vague impression of having been translated. Perhaps here we stumble upon a real clue. Had Neil Munro never learned English – and lived quietly in an entirely Gaelic-speaking community – he might have come to his true stature as an artist. Is the cardinal flaw that vitiates all his work, so easy to detect and so difficult to explain, really the product of a species of mental miscegenation?*

This remarkable attack is particularly curious coming from the man who, just five years earlier, had dedicated Northern Numbers *'with affection and pride to Neil Munro'. Munro's poetic style had not significantly altered in the intervening five years; indeed he wrote little in this period, so the difference may reasonably be sought in MacDiarmid rather than Munro.*

The other 'Views and Reviews' piece, 'Scottish Minstrelsy', reflects Munro's keen interest in all fields of poetry in Scotland, and in particular what might at first be thought of as an unusually keen interest in poetry in Scots. Munro, being from a Gaelic-speaking family and environment, himself bi-lingual, might not be expected to respond quite so keenly to lowland Scots. However, as has been pointed out by Ronnie Renton in his edition of The Lost Pibroch, *Munro's home area had taken on a large amount of Scots, as opposed to English, vocabulary. This was doubtless in* part due to economic links between mid-Argyll and the Clyde coast, and partly due to the planting of lowlanders in and around Inveraray by successive Campbell chiefs.

As has been seen when considering the comic short stories, published in book form under the pen-name of 'Hugh Foulis', most first appeared in the 'Looker-On' column. However, the more usual material in this column was non-fiction, and our selection indicates the range of subjects that proved to be grist to Munro's mill. The first, 'Braid Scots', reflects the linguistic interest that has already been touched on. Others such as 'Children of the Road' and 'Our Lost Arcady' demonstrate the vein of nostalgia and regret for a changing world that imbues much of Munro's writing. 'The Old Road' is one of many pieces which arise from Munro's deep interest in matters of Highland history. 'Music on Deck' is a light-hearted piece about Clyde steamer bands by a real man of the Clyde.

Comedy features largely in the non-fiction of the 'Looker-On' – his essay in praise of the school slate, 'The Jotter Age', alone would prove this. Highland folklore, Highland landscape and a gentle poking of fun at the English are combined in 'Ghosts in the Mountain', a witty, but finally thoughtful, reaction to the story of the 'Big Grey Man of Ben Macdhui'. The rather unlikely subject of fox-hunting provokes Munro to a fine tongue-in-cheek look at the hunt in 'The Sport Royal': an essay by a man who does not hesitate to write: 'I have never seen a fox, except the Highland kind we shoot (with all respect to the M.F.H. of Eglinton), without compunction'.

George Blake wrote in his introduction to The Brave Days:

> . . . a great deal of the most brilliant journalistic work of our times lies buried in the files of the Glasgow Evening News. It is no exaggeration to say that Neil Munro made that paper. . . . He was the master of a most enviable journalistic style: crisp, colourful, and yet gracious.

This selection from the News between 1899 and 1926 reveals the truth of Blake's judgement.

BRAID SCOTS

from 'The Looker-On', 13 February 1899

A column for Gaelic speakers and for Gaelic-and-English speakers has been included in the census schedules in at least two censuses. Much edification has, let us hope, been thereby given to all who interest themselves in the perpetuation of The Language; and a correspondent, who signs himself 'Seltown Terrace', writes, asking me to propose a Braid Scots census for the year 1901. I have no objection. There will be difficulties in the way, of course. It will be difficult for a good many respectable people to decide for themselves whether they speak Scots – or only Gleska, its most dreadful variant. A London paper the other day said the population of North Britain could be divided into two parts – 'those who speak Scots and are proud of it, and those who speak what they imagine is English and are not ashamed of it.' To that I would add that there is on the fringe of these two sections a not inconsiderable section, who are not worth counting perhaps, who speak English better than the real English do. They almost invariably become Auld Kirk ministers in Quoad-Sacra churches, or lead lingering deaths as process clerks in law offices.

But – one confesses the dreadful truth with reluctance – Braid Scots is a decaying tongue. It survives in the rural districts among the older people. In our own immediate neighbourhood a fine rich fruity Scots is still to be heard about East Kilbride; it has come over the moors (and yet has the tang of Burns) from Ayrshire. Paisley vaingloriously brags of speaking a fine brand of Scots, but I must confess I prefer it a little more dulcet than prevails in Seestu. Greenock also affects (I have heard it in her Town Council) a robust and classic vernacular, but I have studied her West Blackhall Street on a Saturday night, and will kindly draw a veil. No, the dire truth cannot be concealed; Mr Montgomerie-Fleming may tear his hair over it and bring out Doric Dictionaries if he likes, but in school, in church, in office, in warehouse, in the home and in the football field we are surrendering our proud Caledonian privilege of rolling our 'r's,' and prolonging our vowels, and multiplying our gutturals.

When the adult Scotsman in easy circumstances is not writing to the newspapers to prove that the theatre is unscriptural, or that Professor Cooper is a sort of Papist, or that the tramway cars go too fast or too slow for his taste, he is training his children to say 'porridge' instead of 'parritch', and the bitter lesson is fraught with many tears for the unfortunate victims of Anglomania. If they cannot pick up the true English inflection (as Ethole Gerdens understands it), they are sent to

Academies and boarding schools where the teachers are guaranteed products of Oxford or Cambridge. There was a time not very long ago when the very oldest and most eminent Scots families included worthy dames who gloried in their Doric, and even yet at long intervals one comes across the elderly representative of a 'lang pedigree' who has a wholesome and supreme contempt for English.

I dipped into a school-book the other day, published for the school children of Scotland by a Scottish firm of publishers. Apparently with regard for their 'genteel' clients, the publishers had, I found, excised as far as possible the Scots words, idioms, and phrases, of classic Scots prose and poetical extracts, and substituted English of the most commonplace and unsuitable character. The book, for instance, contains what pretends to be a poem entitled, 'Wee Willie Winkie', one of the classic nursery rhymes of our country, and one which fairly entitled its author, William Miller, to rank as the 'laureate of the nursery'! In this anglified version of a very expressive and beautiful song, 'rins' becomes 'runs', 'nicht' becomes 'night', and 'weans' is made children. In the original

– the wean's in a creel,
Wamblin' aff abody's knee like a verra eel,
Ruggin' at the cat's lug and ravelling a' her thrums,
Hey Willie Winkie – see there he comes!

but the conscientious Englishman who edited Miller makes the child 'pull at the cat's ear as she drowsy hums'. Even the 'waukrife laddie' is transmogrified into 'the wakeful little boy'. So is the budding intelligence of Sandy directed in proper channels, and his earliest vocabulary freed from the degraded and demoralising dialect of his rude forefathers.

It might have been imagined that a fear of the consequences which overtook Mr Henley for a less heinous offence would prevent sacrilegious hands from being laid on the phraseology of Burns, but such is not the case. 'Tam o' Shanter', as pointed out in this page the other day, has been Englished by a lady and printed in a booklet by a Glasgow firm of publishers. That was probably an experiment in the interest of English readers. What is to be said for another school-book in use in Scottish schools – not in many, I hope – wherein 'Auld Lang Syne' is Englished in all but the refrain. Only one example may be given from another poem in the same book to show how prim and proper the bard of Ayr may be made if a countryman with a fine discrimination cares to undertake the work. Although to the average Englishman the lines,

> Forejeskit sair, wi' weary legs,
> Rattlin' the corn out owre the rigs,
> Or dealing through among the naigs
>   Their ten hours' bite,

may be uncouth and obscure, they are intelligible, I hope, to any juvenile Caledonian of ordinary intellect. Yet in the volume before me this verse is transformed into –

> Fatigued with toil, with weary legs,
> Rattling the corn about the rigs,
> Or dealing through among the nags
>   Their ten hours bit.

At the schools in the Highlands less than a century ago, indeed, less than half a century ago, it was positively criminal for young Donald to indulge in his native tongue in the play-ground. He was not only whipped for such a lapse into primitive barbarism, but was subject to punishment which was much more drastic, and Evan MacColl, the well-known Gaelic bard, who died in Canada a few months ago, tells of nameless atrocities perpetrated on him by a teacher, who, like many others of his class and age in the Highlands, would do anything to secure the 'advancement' of his pupils in English by suppressing the Gaelic. What was done in the Highlands in the case of Gaelic fifty years ago (happily better ideas now prevail), is being done all over the Lowlands with regard to Scots. Teachers insist that the English of the school-book and of the school hours shall be carried into the play-ground, and a boy of ten in a Renfrewshire school tells me he was severely reprimanded a few weeks ago by his teacher for using the delightful word 'ettled' in his Sunday School class. The Sunday School teacher, a fastidious lady, had reported the lapse to the day school teacher and trouble ensued.

In the after moments of life we may indulge in Scots, but in serious business it is to be resolutely tabooed. The commercial traveller, while he is in the smoke room of his hotel, will tell his stories in unctuous Doric, but hear him tackle a customer at his own counter and you find that he has an accent that approximates as near as he can make it to that of Birmingham or London. Go to the Courts of Law, either the local Sheriff Courts, or the Supreme Courts of Edinburgh, and you will listen in vain for a hint of the vernacular. I think Lord Deas was the last of the old Lords who spoke with a speech racy of the soil; and Parliament House is far away now from Lord Braxfield, whose vigorous use (and sometimes abuse) of Scots, is so well suggested in *Weir of Hermiston*. In the Glasgow churches, I can think of no minister who has an honest Scots accent except the Rev. Robert Thomson, and in his case it needs the strong excitement of an anti-ritualistic boom to bring it forth. The learned doctor who presides over the St Columba's Church has an accent, undoubtedly, but it is not Scots.

Not only do the school-book publishers Anglify our poetry, the music publishers sometimes mutilate our songs, as a copy of 'The Lass o' Ballochmyle' I saw the other day proves. When the publishers do not do it, the singers often do it for them, and it is pathetic to hear a choir of red-headed Macs, with their native heather still growing out of their boots, harmoniously allude (as I experienced recently) to 'All the Arts the Wind Can Blow', as if they referred to something of the nature of an organ. And the evil becomes accentuated when it is apparent in a solo singer. Nevertheless patriotic Scotland has not yet revolted against the person who asserts that 'Willie Brewed a Peck of Malt' or peremptorily orders someone to 'Go Bring to Me a Pint of Wine'. The Scottish comedian of the music-halls, even, has begun to modify his vernacular and bring it up to date in order to escape the charge of vulgarity. All this portends that before many generations the only Scotsmen who speak their native tongue will be in London.

'OATMEAL'

from 'The Looker-On', 2 January 1905

Recent ethnological statistics, the authenticity of which are beyond question, comparing the average, height, weight and phrenological development of English, Scots, and Irish students show that the Scots stand easily first, the rest being 'nowhere'. It is a fact which I always reflect upon with a solace to myself when our 'Cockney Causeur', battening on roast beef, plum pudding and ale, writes his weekly hymn of thanks for the glory of being in England, and inferentially suggests (it is only his playful humour) that bleak life is here our portion and we are Boetians with nothing to live for. For if the Scot is bigger-boned, bigger-brained and bigger-brawned than his English or Irish fellow-subjects, it can only be credited to the past or present use of that homely cereal which the prejudiced and sarcastic English lexicographer (mainly invented by the Scotsman Boswell) described as the food of horses in England and of men in Scotland. Scotland still makes her breakfast or her supper, or both breakfast and supper, of oatmeal in the form of porridge, and has now infected the whole English-speaking world with her taste for oatmeal, which the Englishman and the American buy in cute little pasteboard pictorial boxes, wherein it costs a great deal more than we pay for it, buying it as frank oatmeal by the boll.

Possibly there was a time in the history of this country when even the Scot knew not the art of pounding out grain into meal, and baffling a healthy appetite with the result, but that is bordering on the primeval. Centuries ago oatmeal was almost altogether eaten raw by the Scot. He took it in the form of broses – delightful, sonorous and suggestive word! There were then, and there are still, kail-brose and brose, pure and simple. With kail-brose, which has unhappily gone out of fashion, even a pock-puddin' Englishman could put himself on good terms; for the benefit of Kelvinside it may be described as an elegant and eminently satisfying compound of oatmeal, bouillon, and green kail; a dish, on which according to the lyrist, Fergus, the first of our Scots kings, was wont to kill many foes. Brose – plain, or 'sojers brose', as they call it in some districts – would no more commend itself to the English palate than would sauerkraut. It is too appallingly simple, being composed solely of oatmeal, hot water and salt stirred about in a basin. It was upon that preparation that our forefathers raided and won their battles. But not one in a thousand in Glasgow ever tasted it. Somewhat of the same primitive quality is the Gaelic 'fuarag' or crowdy, a mixture of meal and any cold liquor that may be handy. 'The sweetest meal that ever I ate was fuarag stirred inside my shoe south of the Border,' said an old Highland raider.

The introduction of porridge or boiled meal marked an epoch in Scottish cuisine, it was the premonition of the dawn which culminated in the artistic triumphs of Megg Dods and the Glasgow Man with the Hundred Sandwiches. Porridge – for all you may hear to the contrary – is as truly the national dish of Scotland as roast beef is of England, or potatoes are of Ireland. Many evil practices have drifted north of the Tweed from England, including 'high teas', but Caledonia abides by her porridge. Its reek ascends from the thresholds of most Scottish homes like a natural incense. We are coerced into eating it in our foolish youth when we would much rather have coffee, bacon, and London buns; and when we are old we do not depart therefrom. Twenty years ago it was a form of food you could not get south of Carlisle but with the greatest difficulty; today there is no first-class hotel in the kingdom, in America, or Canada, where it is not on the bill-of-fare. Boiled oats, and flake oats, and oats of various kinds they call it; but 'tis simply our gritty friend made 'sliddery', and to the discriminating palate, less finely flavoured. On the Border, almost, a certain town has in the present generation, grown prosperous by the manufacture and sale of porridge oats in pictorial boxes.

Somewhat akin to porridge, of equal simplicity in its preparation, and much more exclusively Scots, is pease brose. Few English people have ever heard of it, it figures on no hotel menu, yet the appetising odour of it still wafts, more or less pungent, over the north of Britain. A handful of pea flour, a dash of salt, a lump of butter, a bowl of boiling water – and there you are! Seven miles out of Glasgow I know a one-time oatmeal mill that has for two decades maintained itself exclusively by the grinding of peasemeal. Afar you can perceive the odour of the roasting peas before they are fed into the hopper; upon its product men with their households at the coast in summer-time have extemporised a simple breakfast. Next to porridge come oatmeal cakes or bannocks, which the sarcastic Englishman objects to as being too rich for his blood. Simplicity in the art of baking could surely no further go than in the case of the 'farl' of meal and water fired on a girdle. Froissart tells that the ancient Scottish soldiers, when they took the field (and everything else portable they could lay hands on), carried a wallet of oatmeal and a girdle of iron to make cakes, and so the cakes are made until this day, though possibly the great bulk of those consumed are made in factories. There probably never was a time when oatcake was more popular than today, thanks to the facility with which it can be bought in shop packets, but the domestic Culross girdle has largely disappeared.

Nor even then have we exhausted the application of the bearded oat. To the Spaniard his 'olla', the Italian his 'macaroni', the Frenchman his 'vagont', and the Turk his 'pillau'; but the haggis, though it never commanded the panegyric of a Sala or a Brillat-Savarin, is as worthy of a song as when our poet gave it immortal lyric praise. Into the composition of Athole Brose, also, does oatmeal enter. Some days ago a writer denied that any such thing existed, and I must confess these eyes have never beheld a man who had partaken of that comestible. Perhaps it is the swansong of tipples, that men drink but once of it and then gladly die. It must have had a vogue at some time, or else the cookery books of old were liars, for they minutely describe the preparation of Athole Brose, with 'a cupful of heather honey, two cupfuls of whisky, the yolk of an egg, and a table spoonful of oatmeal beat together'. There might seem, to some tastes, an excess of solids in this preparation.

CHILDREN OF THE ROAD

from 'The Looker-On', 28 July 1919

The tinkers are with us just now. In the old quarry beyond the manse they have stretched their whale-backed tents and lit their fires. Ragged children are on that part of the road continually, and at night, rough men, not always sober, straggle about the fields and lanes. The women are at our doors several times in the day, a white pony wanders aimlessly to find sustenance on the burnt borders about the ditches, and the acrid smoke of burning wood drifts always down the village street.

We have them every year at this time. They come from the shire over the hill, stay with us a fortnight, then go mysteriously. One night we hear them singing or brawling among their pots; next morning the old quarry is empty, and only heaps of grey embers mark the place where their caravan has rested. A strange people.

But an interesting people forbye. In them is centred the last lingering traces of the old nomadic spirit that informed our fathers, with their destinies is the last of the clan spirit bound up. Already the tinkers feel the tug of modern ways. The Education Act – the real Education Act which preceded that of 1918 – chained them to the earth. The exigencies of war threw out the net of the Military Service Act to bring their young men in from the highways and byways.

But it was the Education Act that truly marred the perfection of tinkering as a profession. Its provisions demanded that the wandering folk should bide over the winter in towns, that their children might have schooling. So there was nothing for it but to hire lodgings in such places as Lochgilphead and Campbeltown, thole the long, eventless winters, and set forth on the roads again for the three months of summer. It says much for the stoutness of the tinker spirit and much for the depth of their nomadic instincts that tinker clans are to be met on the roads in this summer of 1919.

You will meet tinkers in every part of Scotland – a man and his wife and a draggled bairn perhaps – but only in the West are they found in large numbers, in proper clan formation. It seems that they have a fondness for the shire of Argyll, which is richer than most Highland shires, and is wonderfully free from the restrictions of metallic modernism. And in that county, in July, you will meet them on almost any road. The procession is headed by the old white pony and the broker's cart; behind it straggle swarthy men and fair-haired women and children, each one loaded in the tinker fashion. The men have their strange bundles of sticks and umbrellas, the children carry anything from gasaliers to baskets, and the women have their babies in the nooks of shawls on their backs. Last come the young, ruddy women, begging money in the characteristic tinker whine.

It is never exactly clear how the modern tinker makes a living. Not that he needs much; but he has to provide against the winter's lodging and feeding. So most of them are brokers now, with licences all in order and labels on their carts, proclaiming a profession and a domicile to all the world. Yet of trade on the Highland roads there can be little. No vast deals in 'marine stores' are to be made; cottars do not seek greatly to enrich themselves with the lumber brought by hawkers. The old trade of pot-repairing doubtless brings in a handful of shillings in the season, and it is notable that tinkers have taken, of recent years, to the sale and repair of baskets and basket-chairs.

But it is certainly not a rich life. Modern habits of thought do not encourage the encouragement of tinkers. 'Tinkers' is often a substitute for 'Trespassers' on Highland notice-boards; factors of estates are strong on the law of trespass; universal scarcity leaves no room for the open-handed giving of days before the war; and outlying farmers are too keenly alive to the market values of their products to lavish it on the tinkers as they once did fairly.

No, not a rich life. The tinkers – the last section of the population to do so, perhaps – have encountered the implacable forces of economics. It may be that the war, with its demands on the private purse and its opportunities of other activities for young men has passed sentence of extinction on the wanderers.

The war, at least, has wrought great changes in those friends of ours who are in the old quarry just now. Prior to 1914, odd as it may seem, the lads of the clan were Territorials. It may be that they were possessed of the old Celtic weakness for a red coat and a green kilt; but there it was. They put in their drills with the detachments throughout the shire, and went to camp with their urban comrades. In that black August they were mobilised, and went in their turn to France. Others enlisted in the course of that autumn, and the Military Service Act got the rest.

So the young men have come back with the spacious ideas that are born of travel. The vagrom life of the roads, perhaps, does not now satisfy their errant souls. They have acquired, it may be, the wage sense of the more sophisticated comrades with whom they fought. Some of them may even have elected to stay for ever in the low country, earning big money and trying to forget the bills. It is not by such that roving clans are carried on in romantic existence.

The effects of this modernisation are already plain. The lads flirt with our village girls in a fashion that would be looked upon as overbold in real Argyll. They play football in Branchal's fields. Their voices have lost much of native song, and have taken on the coarser ring of the Lowlands. And as I passed their camp the other night a gramophone was to be heard at its dark work; it reproduced a rendering of Tosti's 'Parted', according to Mr Hubert Eisdell.

So the world goes on. Civilisation gains territory by sacrificing the picturesque. Twenty years hence, the tinkers may only be a memory for the old ones among us.

I would not write sentimentally of this, for humanity is unfit to judge the processes of change it undergoes. But I may be permitted to deplore for one special reason the passing of the tinkers. This, my complaint, is: That the world cannot well afford to lose anything that presents a picturesque contrast to our drab enough existence, or anything that reminds us, by that very contrast, that a less sophisticated mode of life may yet be followed. The tinkers are drunken, perhaps dishonest, not over-clean, and their morality may not be that of Calvin. But they have what we worldlings have not. They have a magnificent, unconscious disregard for the stereotyped.

I am glad they are with us. When I return at night and have to light a mundane gas-jet, use the telephone, or wind-up my wristlet watch, it is a relief to know that there are others who take simply what nature gives them, and have, beyond nature, no thought of, or regard for oppressive powers that be.

✝

SCOTTISH MINSTRELSY
from 'Views and Reviews', 4 September 1919

In a dusty corner the other day I picked up a stoutly bound volume that was published in Glasgow about forty years ago, perhaps. *Recent and Living Scottish Poets* it was called, 'being a series of brief biographical sketches of Scottish poets, with illustrative selections from their writings'. The biographical sections were dull (though one remembers that the anthologist wrote of his contemporaries), but the illustrative sections were of profound interest. That prosy old book has reminded me once more that the truest artistic expression of Scottish sentiment came from people unknown to fame, and that the songs we regard as most truly national were piped on rustic lutes.

The little men – and a few women – created the minstrelsy of our land. Burns, of course, a big man, crowned the work and handed on the high tradition; but it was the honest, sentimental balladists of tavern and smiddy who tilled the soil for the reception of the crop that is so representative and racy of Scotland. They were at their best in dialect and at their worst in English. The dialect songs lived, were wedded to traditional airs, and co-operated wonderfully in the truest earnest of national art, the Scottish minstrelsy.

It is the modern fashion to ignore the old songs or even scorn them openly: a suicidal fashion. It is cursing the breed of which one was born. Let us have a great Scottish poet writing in the English convention before we throw out the little Doric treasure we do possess.

All good Scots, however, know the songs of Scotland without knowing or recognising authorship. So it occurred to me, as I read the old book, that this opportunity should be grasped to do some posthumous justice to the little men. *Recent and Living Scottish Poets* shall be robbed of its guarded treasure.

The first name I encounter is that of Sandy Rodger. The name does not suggest much. But Sandy did his bit: he wrote 'Robin Tamson's Smiddy', a work of the purest native humour. After Rodger comes William Miller, a name that suggests anything from a stonebreaker to a barber. But if I quote a quatrain about Wee Willie Winkie who rins through the toun, perhaps I shall suggest the greatness of one who was born in Glasgow in 1810, and who was happy enough to hit upon the title *Whistle Binkie*, for his first published volume.

After him comes Hew Ainslie, born in the parish of Dailly in 1792. Hew Ainslie . . . But let me quote:

> It's dowie in the hint o' hairst,
> At the wa-gang o' the swallow.
> When the wind grows cauld, and the burns grow bald,
> And the woods are hingin' yellow . . .

That, sirs, is poetry. Hew Anslie was at the heart of the matter. I should regard it as tragic if Scottish children were to forget that a poet of such worth was their kinsman. It is tragic enough that he had to emigrate to America, and wrote so poignantly of his native land, an exile – prosperous enough, but yet an exile.

So the record proceeds in the most interesting and revealing fashion. There is much in it we did not know, much that we ought to know.

Here is Hugh Macdonald, of Glasgow, with his 'bonnie wee well on the breist o' the brae, that skinkles sae cauld in the sweet smile o' day'; after him Alexander Anderson – 'Surfaceman' – fondly remembered for 'The bairnies cuddle doon at nicht'; then James Hyslop, of the 'Cameronians' Dream' – subject matter, by the bye, for one of the finest cantatas of Hamish McCunn of Greenock, the greatest composer ever produced by Scotland. The list could be extended, also, to include gems that are hidden here, their lustre forgotten.

There are, of course, reams of third-rate stuff. That monument of patriotic fatuity – 'Scotland Yet' – is included, though its companion piece of Victorian bombast – 'Draw the Sword, Scotland' – is not to the fore. And the failures are almost all written in classical English. Dr Joseph Roy offers us this contrast:-

A (in English)	In a dingy room in London's gloom,
	In the very heart of the nation,
	A woman lay on Christmas Day,
	Moaning of sheer starvation.
B (In Scots)	Since Adam fell frae Eden's bower
	And put things sair ajee,
	There's aye some weakness to look owre
	And folly to forgie.

Dr Roy should have known better than to write A.

That, however, is how native art comes into being, and finally passes into the speech of a nation. One is, at least, glad to find that the mid-Victorians not only were foolish in the 'Scotland Yet' manner, but did give us something worthy and lasting.

The path, however, was cut for them long ago, by Alan Ramsay and Burns, with the assistance of a remarkable group of women. Let us record one debt to the latter. We do not forget Joanna Baillie and her 'Woo'd and married and a'' and 'Saw ye Johnnie comin'?' nor Lady Ann Lindsay and 'Auld Robin Gray.' Then there was Mrs Grant of Laggan – she of the 'Letters from the Highlands' – with 'O where, tell me, where' and Mrs John Hunter, wife of the anatomist, who wrote (of all things) 'My mother bids me bind my hair', to which Haydn gave immortality, Greatest of all was Caroline Oliphant, Lady Nairne. 'The Land of the Leal', 'The Auld Hoose', 'Caller Herrin'', 'The Hundred Pipers', and many others are all of her creation.

Add the names of Hector MacNeill, Allan Cunningham, Robert Ferguson and Tannahill, and the strength of the tradition begins to be comprehended.

Where, then, do we stand to-day?

Few great names occur to us. Charles Murray and Mrs Violet Jacob seem to stand for the last of the great Doric school and we know that their dialect is, in the quite inoffensive sense, an affectation. That is, it does not spring from the earth-born spirit. Mr Murray is a South African Government official; Mrs Jacob is the daughter of a laird. Both are capable of writing just as finely in English, while Robert Sterling, killed in France, derived from purely English models, and would have been ill at ease in Doric.

But though the great may be few, the little are still many. Of the verses that reach Scottish newspaper offices from contributors outside more than half are in dialect – though it must be said that the influence of Sir Harry Lauder is more apparent than that of Burns. And there come to me continually for review the slender, locally-printed verses of rustic singers. They are seldom first-rate; they are often thoroughly bad: but they are always honest. Therefore I say with confidence, the spirit is living yet.

NORTHERN NUMBERS

from 'Views and Reviews' 23 December 1920

In this paper, some short time ago, there were reviewed at considerable length, three volumes of verse by living Scotsmen. It was pointed out in that article that something very like a revival in Scottish poetry is actually in movement at this time, and that a long-standing reproach to Northern men of letters was being wiped out by the poets of the day. With all the more interest, therefore, does one approach a volume called *Northern Numbers*, beautifully printed, and published by T.N. Foulis at 6s. net.

The title of the book is elaborated thus – 'Being Representative Selections from Certain Living Scottish Poets'; it is dedicated 'with affection and pride to Neil Munro'; and it possesses a 'Foreword', initialled C.M.G. Without more ado let me quote the first two paragraphs of this Foreword:

> This collection does not pretend to be in any sense an anthology of contemporary Scottish poetry. It merely consists of representative selections (chosen by the contributors themselves) from the – mainly current – works of certain Scottish poets of today – and tomorrow!
>
> Many contemporary writers of the highest merit, whose work will unquestionably be given a place in any future anthology of Scottish poetry embracing the output of the twentieth century, have not been invited to contribute to this volume. The chief reason for that lies in the fact that for the most part the contributors to this volume are close personal friends, and that this is rather an experiment in group publication than an anthology.

I shall return to discuss this declaration later. In the meantime, we can have a look at the fare offered for our consumption.

Eleven poets are represented. Their names are:- Neil Munro, John Buchan, Violet Jacob, Will Ogilvie, T.S. Cairncross, C.M. Grieve (presumably the C.M.G. of the Foreword), Joseph Lee, John Ferguson, A.G. Grieve, Donald A. Mackenzie, and Roderick Watson Kerr – hardly a homogeneous group if one may take the liberty of saying so. For some reason or other a brief biography of Donald A. Mackenzie is incorporated, though weightier names are left undocumented; and we are informed on page 104 that Mr John Ferguson's *Thyrea* has run into more editions than any other volume of distinguished modern verse – an ambiguous and hardly relevant statement.

Of the eleven, five have contributed verses of genuine distinction. Mr John Buchan can be depended on for an honest piece of poetry; his best in this collection is 'From the Pentlands', which, if inevitably reminiscent of Stevenson both in manner and subject has fine qualities of atmosphere and warmth. The excellence of Violet Jacob's songs in the doric of Angus is sustained in five characteristic numbers. Joseph Lee has a pungent gift; there are good examples here from *Workaday Warriors* and *Ballads of Battle*, but he gets the best effects in 'The Burial of the Bairn', a poignant thing in the true ballad style. The name of T.S. Cairncross may be unfamiliar to many readers, and I am glad to think that this volume will introduce his fine, unconventional, rugged work to a wider circle than he has, perhaps, previously entertained. 'The Martyr Graves' is great stuff!

Finally – and unmistakably – the truest poetry in *Northern Numbers* has come from the pen of him to whom the collection is dedicated. Mr Munro contributes five poems, brief, sombre, and moving, on themes apparently suggested by the names of bagpipe tunes. They have unique atmospheric quality; they 'tell' – inevitably, as it were: and though they are so distinctively 'Highland' in inspiration, they are, at the same time, the truest possible expression of the Scottish spirit.

And so I return to this 'Foreword' and quote another paragraph thereof:

> If this venture is sufficiently successful, subsequent volumes . . . will be published at convenient intervals. No new contributor will, however, be admitted without the approval of the majority of the present group.

This, you observe, carries the 'Group' idea still further – and this 'Group' business is precisely what I do not like about *Northern Numbers*. Indeed I find it difficult to believe that there is any such Group at all. That two of the foremost Scottish litterateurs of the day should be associated with a number of young poets of, at least, questionable promise is a state of affairs my imagination is incapable of conceiving. I cannot help regarding this 'Foreword' as misleading, unconsciously misleading, but still phrased in such a way as to create a wrong impression in the mind of the non-professional reader, who may be led to believe that Messrs Munro and Buchan are members of an ambitious coterie. My point is, that Messrs Munro and Buchan should not be graded quite as low.

But that by the way. The chief argument against a poetry Group is that it imposes limitations to which no free artist will ever submit. Just so is the *Northern Numbers* Group imperfect. It includes Munro and Buchan – it excludes Charles Murray. The 'Foreword' gives a sort of reason for omissions of this kind – 'that for the most part the contributors to this volume are close personal friends'. C.M.G. will have to find a better reason for the absence from his pages of the verses of the most distinguished Scottish poet of the day.

✝

THE OLD ROAD

from 'The Looker-On', 31 December 1923

In the past year, new light has been thrown upon the state of the Highlands in the Eighteenth Century, through the discovery of a series of manuscript maps which are now in the collection of the Royal Scottish Geographical Society. They were probably prepared for General Wade and his roadmakers, and the oldest of them, dated 1724–25, is dedicated to him. In July 1724, Wade began to reconnoitre the 'greatest and most uncivilised Parts of the Highlands of Scotland', and in December of that year submitted his first report to the King. In the following year he suggested 'mending the Roads between the Garrisons and Barracks, for the better Communication of His Majesty's troops' and in 1726 he began making roads out of what previously had been mere hill-tracks. A good many Highland highways now credited to Wade were neither designed nor executed till long after his appointment abroad in 1743. But they were made by soldiery, and in after years loosely attributed to him.

The manuscript maps, by soldiers and surveyors, indicate the routes followed by troops and Government officials in passing between Fort-William and the Forth and Clyde, which were at the time the 'rail-heads' of civilisation. Hill-tracks and drove-roads of the roughest description were fairly numerous, but by the time Wade's work was finished there were only three roads, in the modern sense of the word, in the Highlands. Two of these – in the Western Highlands – were founded on foot-tracks beaten through the glens by centuries of use.

It is not necessary to consult the Geographical Society's manuscript maps to learn what these two roads were; they will be found in a most interesting map published this week by Messrs Duncan Campbell and Son, St Vincent Street, from an original copy in the possession of that firm for over one hundred years. This map, dated 1734, was prepared by J. Cowley, and shows the Highlands from the Mull of Kintyre to the southmost point of Skye, and from the Outer Islands to Loch Laggan.

The greater part of it was prepared without actual survey, and was doubtless based upon pre-existing maps wherein the main topographical features of the country were shown graphically, but without any roads or tracks being indicated.

Cowley's map, which is not mentioned among those referred to in *The Lyon in Mourning* as accessible in the insurrection of 1745, is described as a 'Map of Such Part of His Grace the Duke of Argyle's Heritable Dukedom and Justiciary Territories, Islands, Superiorities and Jurisdictions as lye contiguous upon the western coast of North Britain within the now United

Shyres of Inveraray and Tarbat and these of Inverness and Dumbarton'.

In 1743, Government troops or officials desirous of going most conveniently and safely from Glasgow to Fort-William went by the riverside to Dumbarton, up the Garelochside and over Whistlefield to Portincaple, Loch Long, where they ferried into Loch Goil. From Lochgoilhead they went through Hell's Glen to St Catherine's and thence ferried Loch Fyne to Inveraray. Thence, going up Glenaray, they went to Port Sonachan, Loch Awe, ferried again, and went through Glen Nant to Bonawe.

They had here a choice of two routes – they could cross Loch Etive and go through Benderloch to Port-Appin, whence they must take the boat to Nether Lochaber, as no feasible road lay through the country of the Stewarts; or they could cross at the Bridge of Awe, make a long detour to the east through the Pass of Brander and Glen Lochy to Tyndrum, where they could join the road from Stirling. Thereafter their route was by the fringes of the Moor of Rannoch, to the east of Loch Tulla, past Achallader, down Glencoe and to the ferry at Callart in Nether Lochaber. Callart Ferry across Loch Leven had to be negotiated no matter what route was taken. Not till after the '45 was a so-called Wade's Road made over the Devil's Staircase in Glencoe into Kinlochleven to obviate this ferry.

Communication from Stirling was by Callendar, Balquhidder, and Loch Dochart to Tyndrum, and thence as indicated by travellers by the more western route.

There was no road by Loch Lomondside or up Glen Falloch, which would enormously have shortened the journey; nor were Arrochar and Glencoe convenient for anything but cattle. Travellers for Mid Argyll, Lorn, Mull, and Morvern went through Hell's Glen and Inveraray; in all the maps of the 18th century and in all manuscript notes regarding these routes, Inveraray figures as of the utmost strategic importance.

In Cowley's map there is no road shown anywhere near Loch Lomond, though there must have been the rough hill-track known as the Old Luss Road, between what is now Helensburgh and the Colquhoun village, and doubtless some kind of track along the west side of the loch. The advantage of a road from Dumbarton by the loch-side to Tarbert and so through to Arrochar and Glencoe to Loch Fyne, seemed to have dawned on the military only about 1745. Writing in 1748, Sir John Clerk of Penicuik, then living at Luss for the sake of its health-giving goat's whey, said, 'It was this year that the military corps, by command of the Government, began in good earnest to make the highway to Inveraray from Glasgow, or rather from the Town of Luss, along the side of Loch Lomond. This way was carried on by 50 or 100 men at a time, and before Winter they brought it to Loch Skeen [Loch Fyne?]'. However, there were several beginnings made to it, even in 1745, when the Rebels carried away some of the men prisoners.

One of the manuscript maps recently discovered, and drawn apparently between 1720 and 1730, by an officer of the Fort-William garrison who knew the country, confirms the correctness of Cowley's map, and adds the information that travellers to Inveraray sometimes took a boat for Bonawe through the Pass of Brander to Cladich in Lochawe, instead of going down Glen Nant. Another of the manuscript maps written about the same date as Cowley's by a surveyor has notes in which it is stated that the road by Bonawe and Appin is always good, and 'officers goe generally by this road'. The surveyor states further, that there is a good inn at Achallader.

Seen from the West Highland Railway today, Achallader would seem the last place on earth for an inn of any kind; Bridge of Orchy would appear the more obvious place for such a public convenience, but Achallader in the 17th and 18th centuries was a stronghold of Breadalbane, and here in 1691 he had that meeting with the Jacobite chiefs which led to the Massacre of Glencoe.

THE JOTTER AGE
from 'The Looker-On', 23 November 1925

Slates were condemned last week as useless and insanitary by the Glasgow Education Authority, in whose schools they will henceforth be abolished.

None of us alive, I am certain, ever used the Horn-book in our school days. Most of us indeed, are ignorant of what a Horn-book looked like. But the school slate is familiar to us all in Scotland. It was at one time or another, the best of playthings and the worst of tyrants for most of us. And now it is to be abolished. Another English innovation! Slates were never used, I fancy, in Eton or Harrow: instead good money was wasted on paper and pens or lead-pencils, and such extravagant ideas are spreading North.

I fear it will be a degenerate race that is brought up on the Jotter.

A brand-new sevenpenny slate, you remember, was a possession to take all the anguish out of resuming school after the summer holiday. It created envy in the breast of every other little boy who had to carry on with an old slate with a corner missing or perhaps without a frame of any kind.

But the pristine charm of the new slate vanished quickly. Too soon it lost the fresh enticing odour of the shop where it came from; its pleasant whitewood frame grew grimy, notched by knives and sadly dented in playground tumults. The slate itself – an immaculate blinding grey to begin with – horrible to write on with a stone pencil just as grey – in a week or two was toned down to a purplish hue through which, in spite of all your spittles, showed the ghosts of multiplication sums all wrong in the answers, the 'O's' of old games of noughts and crosses, and your first bold essays in the art of caricature.

Famous Scots artists, if you believed their written biographies, began their art careers in a School of Art, and were first inspired to delineate the human form in expensive life classes. All nonsense! They started in Standard I, with a slate, and the pity is that some of them ever went any further.

In the Slate School – not to be confused with the Slade School – almost every phase of Georgian art – impressionist, cubist, vorticist, Rotarian, expressionist, and emetic – was anticipated generations ago.

Art in general is an expression of emotion, communicable to others and evocative of delight. Ages before Cézanne, Matisse, and Roger Fry were heard of, we were, on our slates, conveying delight to each other by producing figure drawings of characters we least liked in what is now known as the Franz Cizek Free Expression Method. In its technique were very few conventions. The only one I can recall was handed on by the best draughtsman in Standard IV: 'Ye shouldn'a put two eyes on one side of a man's face, for a man's no' a flounder'.

For Art, for noughts and crosses, and for cooling the hands on after a brutal assault with the tawse, the slate was admirable. Unfortunately the teacher expected more from it than that. It was accessory to the most callous efforts on his part to interest us in the eccentricities of cisterns.

With what distaste for the task we would write on our slates the details of that loathsome cistern whose inlet pipe could fill it in half-an-hour, and whose outlet pipe could empty it in so many minutes, and proceed with throbbing temples to calculate how long it would take to fill! No slate on earth, I felt sure, was big enough to hold all the figuring necessary for a problem like that, and no human being had sufficient saliva to revise and correct with as one went on.

Those cistern sums must have been craftily suggested first of all by tailors; they played the very devil with your jacket cuffs, or with the handkerchiefs of the nauseating swells who used such things.

At that time, even the youngest boy from a family bereaved wore white muslin bands for a week or two on the cuff edges of his jacket; they were called 'weepers'.

'I canna' do the count, sir,' said one crying little boy to the teacher; 'I canna' clean the slate, for my granny's deid, and I'm wearing weepers.'

So sponges were introduced. Theoretically you fastened the sponge at the end of a piece of string to the slate, and used it instead of your coat-cuffs, but the absorbent quality of the sponge made terrific demands on the salivary glands. Unfortunate youths who had breakfasted on salt herrings were rendered desperate and had to demand assistance.

Slate pencils, which, henceforth, will probably never be seen outside of those incredibly trusting public-houses that figure in English novels, were not altogether unpleasant things except when used for writing and counting. There was a very jolly kind which had gay-coloured paper gummed round them, and had quite a holiday air. As the pencil wore shorter by usage, you sucked the paper off, and it had a faint taste of cough drops. Something of the same glad flavour can be got by similarly removing the paper from sticks of shaving soap.

Into the mystery of slate pencils nobody has penetrated. It is impossible to say where they came from, or how they were made. In all *Kelly's Directory of Great Britain* there is not a single slate-pencil maker mentioned. I would suspect the slate pencil of being a natural product, possibly from the Giants' Causeway; but for the nodules of iron, which must be inserted by hand, they are – or were, at least in my time – so ingeniously devised to break your heart by their screeching and scratching!

Yet what delight was to be got from a slate pencil intelligently used!

With a pocket-knife or a gimlet you bored a hole two inches deep on the edge of your desk. Above the inner end of the hole you bored a second hole communicating with the first. Therein was the germ idea of the cannon. Having scraped some inches of pencil into dust, you unostentatiously loaded the cannon, and later on induced some innocent child (from the country if possible) to apply his eye to the touch-hole to see what he should see.

At the moment of his intentest gaze you blew up the other hole, and when he, half-blinded, and weeping bitterly, was hauled up on the floor by the teacher for misbehaviour, you became rapt in your Latin book and the Second Declension.

And all this must end now from a silly deference to English notions of hygiene! Hereafter nothing for Scottish youth but the threepenny jotter.

✝

GHOSTS IN THE MOUNTAINS
from 'The Looker-On', 7 December 1925

Scottish alpine climbing is bound to get a great fillip from the disclosure of Professor Norman Collie last week that there are ghosts on the Cairngorms. I always took it for granted, myself, that such was the case, and have carefully avoided the Cairngorms after dark. Nothing would induce me to go up to the top of Ben Macdhui after sunset; I am content to look at it from a smoking-room window in the hotel at Aviemore.

Mr Seton Gordon, who for some years back has spent all his waking hours in skipping about these particular mountains, is never to be found in the Larig Ghru after nightfall. He has played the pipes too long to be indifferent to the menace of spectral ancient things that wheeple and moan in the gloaming. When he goes tramping up Glen Derry, and Coire Etchachan by way of the Ben, from Mar to Rothiemurchus, it is always in sunshine, never later than September, while thrift still blooms on Loch Etchachan's edges, and the tiny alpine willows have still the midsummer green.

We have always kept it dark about Macdhui's sinister reputation as the haunt of the night-blooming Fear-liath-mor – the fearsome Big Grey Man. He has scared generations of Rothiemurchus folk, who, in fear of him, no longer travel to the Linn of Dee with their eggs and poultry – or even for courting – through the most desolate pass, whose very name implies a shudder. We had no desire to attract the attention of the Psychical Research Society and have them litter the places with the paper of their luncheon wrappings. Above all we wanted no confounded sceptics who don't understand, not having learned the pipes nor sat in winter ceilidhs.

And here Professor Norman Collie, President of the Alpine Club – an Englishman, I fear, in spite of his name – has callously risked making Ben Macdhui a mere show place by telling the public about its ghost!

Very shortly, no doubt, we shall see the Railway Companies advertising something like this:

COME TO THE CAIRNGORMS
See Ben Macdhui, the New Brocken!

The only mountain peak in Britain with Authentic Ghosts as Guaranteed by Intrepid members of the Alpine Clubs. Here alone can the tourist depend on seeing the old-time Apparitions that make Scotland's fame, and get the delightful thrill of the Uncanny.

Fifteen hours after leaving Euston you may be on The Only Ben that today can boast of spectral revels; a night in the corries will make your flesh creep.

See the Fear-mor-liath, and feel that fine old Middle Ages frisson without the slightest danger!

————

Pullman Sleeping and Restaurant Cars

I fear Ben Macdhui is done for as a sanctuary for one of the most interesting as well as the most inoffensive of Highland phantoms. The Fear-liath-mor (whose name they can't even spell properly yet), is most unlikely to tolerate thermos flasks and flash-light photographers.

He is still on Ben Macdhui, as Seton Gordon and I know, though it is 30 years since Professor Collie saw him, or rather shivered to the sound of his footsteps. The Professor who is an LL.D. and an F.R.S., and holds a chair of Organic Chemistry, describes himself as walking on Ben Macdhui in a mist, and hearing the crunch of footsteps in the snow behind him, 'as if someone was walking after him, but taking steps three or four times the length of his own.' He said to himself, 'This is all nonsense,' but at last was seized by the most profound terror, though he had never before felt alarm at being alone on the hills.

'The uncanny something which he heard caused fear to seize him by the throat. He took to his heels and ran, staggering blindly among the boulders, for four or five miles, nearly down to the Forest of Rothiemurchus.'

Dr Kellas, it appeared, had a similar experience. He saw, under like circumstances, a human figure come out of the Larig Ghru, about midnight one month in June, and wander round the cairn on the top of Ben Macdhui. 'What surprised him was the man was practically the same height as the cairn, which was 10 feet high, and that it was not an ordinary thing for people to wander alone on the top of Ben Macdhui at midnight.'

I should think not! You don't get Seton Gordon or me on top of Ben Macdhui at midnight, at which hour we are usually to be found lower down beside a fire cursing the tyrannical demand for picturesque mountain 'copy'.

'There is something very queer about the top of Ben Macdhui,' says Professor Collie, 'and I will not go back there again by myself, I know.'

The natives, no way surprised at the experiences of Professor Collie and Dr Kellas, injudiciously let it out that the mysterious figure was the Fear-liath-mor. Curse the natives! Dirty dogs! We don't want everybody to know about our Fear-liath-mor.

It appears that Professor Collie, as an alpine climber, has been over the

Himalaya and Rocky Mountains, and has written about them in books. There is no indication in the books that he ever saw a single eerie thing in either the Indian or Canadian mountains. Though I know so little about the Himalayan Mountains that I never can spell them twice the same way, I have been in the Rockies, and climbed some of them much loftier than Ben Macdhui's 4,000 feet. They were, indisputably, grand, but always I missed something about them. Seen from Calgary, uplifting serried ranges to the sky, they thrilled, after weeks of the prairie, like a letter from home. But in their intimate presence was something lacking which spoiled them for me as an evocation of emotion and dreams – they had no Fear-liath-mor in them; they were not haunted. Nothing was there but a cold marmoreal grandeur of eternally untrodden glacier and snow. Old as the hills of home they might be, but they had no history, no human associations older than my own life-time, nor even names to them till men like Edward Whymper, who was with me, had christened them. It is the dead – ancestral story – a thousand years of human voices, that make haunted mountains. Only on the Cairngorms and the Grampians do fears take human shape.

THE SPORT ROYAL

from 'The Looker-On', 15 February 1926

The most invigorating, picturesque, romantic and dignified outdoor sport in the West of Scotland must be Hunting. When you write of Hunting with an initial capital, it means, of course, the fox – rabbiting and wild-duck shooting do not count. Yet, how little is made of Hunting, by the Saturday evening papers, and how few take part in it compared with the crowds who go to football, or the dancing palaces, or twirl the knobs of wireless instruments!

For some reason or other, Glasgow neglects the Hunt. For many years the Eglinton hounds and the Lanark and Renfrew, have been hunting, each winter, with the utmost enthusiasm on the very confines of the city almost, yet the public attendance is hardly greater than at a village tournament in dominoes.

Something really should be done to popularise this grand old sport if foxes are not to get the upper hand of us entirely and terrorise the milkboys of Hillhead and Pollokshields in the early mornings. The Meets should be regularly advertised. Let them start from George Square, and ride over Jamaica Bridge, winding their horns and tally-hoing. More should be made of the competitive spirit. There should be handsome prizes – a cup for smartest turn-out in hats and harness: a case of fish-knives, say, for the boldest rider through the pack and the first to score a hit on Reynard.

As it is, the sport of old John Peel is pursued in the West of Scotland almost surreptitiously. The same small group of ladies and gentlemen turns out on each occasion, as it were to a Repertory Theatre or a Monday morning in the Central Police Court.

The only handicap to Hunting as a Glasgow pastime is that it involves early rising in the morning and the hire of a horse. There is, too, a prescribed uniform – a pink coat, reinforced cord breeches, Wellington boots, a silk hat and a horseshoe tie-pin.

You have to be up as early as 8 a.m. if you want to see Glasgow huntsmen start for the chase by taking a railway ticket for Houston or Carstairs. They go forth furtively, jingling their spurs as little as possible and wrapped up in trench-coats to divert suspicion.

The Meet is usually on an extensive patch of gravel in front of a stately old mansion-house standing in its own grounds. An unforgettable scene! The hounds, baying loudly, and gambolling over the recently-planted beds of wall-flower; the huntsmen cracking their whips or playing a merry roundelay on their horns; selected villagers in the avenue singing some fine old hunting-songs in four-part harmony. Through vistas in the stately trees are delightful prospects of pastoral country, arable land, and fir plantations, all swarming with foxes.

Someone comes out with a tray and passes round a spot of the famous old Madeira and a bit of ginger cake, and the ladies, having dusted a final coat of powder on their noses, the Charge is sounded and the cavalcade streams out to draw the nearest covert.

I have never seen the Hunt myself, but I love to read about it every other day just now as described with accomplished pens by 'Knockjarder' and 'Tantivy', who seem in journalism to have got the most enviable job I know. They wake in me old memories of Mr Jorrocks, read about in boyhood; I listen again to the horn in Troutbeck; hear John Peel hallooing. Landscapes familiar to me by walking through them, or from a train or automobile, take on a fairy, wizard, old-world aspect. Georgetown becomes a place of becks and thickets, filled with canine music; the Fullwood Moss is no longer a dump for city refuse but a place enchanted.

It is, as I think then, always a tender gloaming there, with starlight and a touch of frost. Sweeter than Roland's horn 'on Fontarabian echoes borne', we have heard to-day the pack give tongue at Barochan, and now Diana and I ride home a little wearied, but bantering merrily.

Alas! I do not know the real Dianas, but always I figure them as young, and brave, and beautiful – the most glorious subjects for the paintings of Mr Furze or Mr Munnings, for the poetry of Mr Masefield.

Now, the strange thing is that I have never seen a fox, except the Highland kind we shoot (with all respect to the M.F.H. of Eglinton), without compunction. I have spent years in Renfrewshire and Lanarkshire, without seeing a single 'varmint' except an occasional stuffed one in a farmer's lobby – deliberately trapped, I fear, in his poultry-yard.

Yet the whole of the country south and south-west of Glasgow seems to be infested with Reynard, who apparently never comes into the open unless he is fascinated by a red coat or a cry of 'joicks!' There are days, it is true, when the Eglinton and Lanark and Renfrew draw blank, which are the days I like best, for then 'Tantivy' and 'Knockjarder' get a chance to be picturesque and poetic. But more frequently there seems to be a fox in every covert.

There is one in Dargavel Moss five minutes after the Madeira, and with a vigorous view halloa from Dickinson, the field pelts after him by Barngary Farm and Bishopton, through Glenshinnoch to Barochan Moss and the woods of Houston, where the scent is lost.

Never mind! There's another fox on North Brae willing to enter into the spirit of the game. He gives us a run across the hill past Barochan Mill, through a poultry yard, to near Corslie Hill, and onwards to Barnmore and the Drums covert, where he 'bites the dust' in the grand old phrase of venery.

The mask and brush are cut off and ceremoniously presented to young sports who do not yet suspect what a nuisance they may be to dust in after years. Experienced grim old riders who have balked at no fences, draw apart, I fancy, and lubricate the oesophagus from cute little silver hunting-flasks.

'Hoicks!' again, and there breaks from his lair in Knockmountain Bog a third fox, who goes steaming down the valley. The pack in full cry go chiming after him in a dappled wave over stubble pasture, plough and moorland. Intrepidity leaps its fences like a lifting plane; Caution trots along the road and looks for a gate to bunch at; the sheer poltroon dismounts and conceals himself in a spinney, hoping the scent will soon be lost.

In well-organised Meets, the last fox of the day, I gather, is usually permitted to escape into a culvert or unsuspected earth, having given the company a pleasant run as savoury to the menu.

And how magnificently the whole thing ends! I have almost the style of it – 'By this time the shades of evening were descending on the uplands. Lights began to twinkle in the farms. Hounds filled the bosky hollows round Auchentibbert with their eager cries as they quartered the woody dells, having come through the taint of wintering sheep and lost the varmint's scent near the Black Bull Inn. It was in a lovely night of stars we rode home after one of the best days of the season.'

On second thoughts, I declare it would be a pity to spoil it all by running char-a-bancs and motor-buses to the Meets. Dickinson wouldn't like it.

OUR LOST ARCADY

from 'The Looker-On', 16 August 1926

There is a loch-side road, sixty miles from Glasgow, where, till recently, one could walk for hours without encountering a human being. Ancient peace possessed it. At long intervals might pass a farmer's cart, the van of some enterprising baker, or, twice-a-day in summer, a four-in-hand with leisurely-stepping horses. The Arcadian quiet of the landscape was communicated even to the passengers, who seemed to travel in a dream.

The road for miles followed the sea-beach, in the odour of golden wrack fresh-bared by the tide; in the sound of wavelets beating on rock or hissing through shingle. Here and there were grouped the falchions of the water-flag – yellow iris – *seilisteir;* in spring the wayside banks spilled over with primroses; what looked a little way off, like pools reflecting the blue of sky, were patches of the hyacinth.

Ah! but you should be there in Autumn, when the hazels filled our pillow-slips with nuts! We would draw our little boat into a creek, and make a fire, be gypsies for a while, and then plunge through the hazel thickets, plucking the clusters to be kept till Hallowe'en. What a disturbing silence when our shouts were still! Flitting birds but no song. Scattered in the wood we would cry to each other to maintain our courage. Something was there, intangible, invisible, that sings through memory.

I walked on that road last Sunday, and could have wept to see the ruins of its ancient peace. There is no change that could be set down on a map; still are the nuts in Achnatra, and when evening falls no doubt the rabbits come out again. But the very devil now possesses the road itself in daylight. It is for ever spoiled for wayfaring folk and children, become a roaring gully filled with great machines that hoot and squirt, and belch foul odours as they plunge continuously over it, bearing multitudes who seem to find in speed alone something that compensates for the fact that they are missing almost all that makes the land worth visiting.

On Saturday and Sunday that peaceful road of a dozen years ago is practically closed to age and childhood, unless they be on wheels; to the leisurely pedestrian; to the lover and his lass. The nuts, nowadays, must rot there. Who that has a vagrant soul would picnic on the Thames Embankment or go nutting in Kelvingrove?

Every few minutes, walking on this road that was once safe even for a somnambulist or a mooning poet, you are yelped at now by imperious motor cars and charabancs from as far away as Southport or London, not to mention those from Glasgow, to which, as native to the country, a little reasonable impertinence may be conceded.

For every mile of walking you are a hundred times in the ditch, and even there is a chance of mudguards rasping you. For this road, like all the old-time beautiful roads in Scotland, has not an inch of pavement sanctuary to it.

It is the first time I have seen an honest rural road which I loved slaughtered in this way – except from a motor-car, where, as actor or art and part, one feels it is a great lark rather than a crime. It has horrified me! I can see twenty or thirty years ahead of us during which my dear road will be increasingly degraded and all nice natural living creatures driven off the face of it. In thirty years, perhaps, when no more charabancs, motor-cars, or motor-cycles can squeeze into it, it will occur to somebody that this road was never made for a racing track and the use of a whole nation's populace. Then they will think of opening a supplementary road for tramps, tinkers, ramblers, shepherds, lovers, children and all the wretched native people who at present have to bolt into the wood or make for the shore to make room for Paddy Hearn of London.

But a supplementary road will not restore to us Arcady. The sylvan deities have fled for ever. They have taken refuge up lonely little glens that are closed at the upper end and encourage no wheeled traffic; or in little isles of the sea that will always remain unspoiled by the sport of the flivver.

As the aesthetic sense awakens to influences more vital than the paintings of Augustus John or the music of Stravinsky I can see arise a great demand for islands and strictly private valleys on the part of the affluent and refined. 'Nearest motoring road, fifty miles' will be a significant intimation on a duke's notepaper.

The worst of it is that we have only a limited selection of suitable islands and cul-de-sac glens; a good many of us are going to be left behind in the rush for them. Mr Compton MacKenzie, with the shrewd Celtic judgment you would expect from a man of his name, has already acquired a sanctuary in the Shiant Isles. Dr Lauchlan Maclean Watt, of the Cathedral, with the same foresight, bought a discarded lighthouse. Lord Howard de Walden saw the trend of things and became the possessor of Shuna before the war. They ought now to be the happiest men in Britain, knowing that whatever happens they can keep the devil at a distance.

It can't be done now anywhere on the Western Highland seaboard. The grandeur of these deep-indented lochs attracts the demon petrol, though their roads are more easily destroyed than any others in the kingdom. We have, all round these lochs, only a very narrow raised sea-beach to make roads on; between storms, land-slides, and motor traffic they cannot be expected to last for ever, and short of terracing the hillsides and making Corniche Roads on them, I can think, at the moment, of nothing to take their place.

MUSIC ON DECK
from 'The Looker-On', 23 August 1926

The steamer has no sooner got all her train passengers on board and got under way than the Chief Engineer and two mates start wheeling a piano to the most sheltered part of the 'tween-decks, where the moneyed interests are most densely concentrated. All wrong, nautically! A Chief Engineer ought, at this moment, to be down among his engines lubricating the crank bearings and keeping his eye on the captain's telegraph. At any moment one of those little row-boats with which the bay is crowded – the 'Bella Ann' or 'Winifred', for example – may barge in right under our bows and scrape the paint off. The right place for a mate, too, is surely abaft the funnel making certain that the davits and falls are all in working order.

It breaks upon the observer, a moment later, that, after all, the seamen with the piano are not really members of the crew, though they wear navy-blue suits and deep-sea caps with white awnings. They are not tattooed, and two of them wear spectacles, contrary to all maritime practice and the strict regulations of the Board of Trade.

A sheaf of collapsible music-stands is produced from under a seat, and ranged round the piano. One of the men opens a case and reveals a Stradivarius violin. Another discloses suddenly a cornopean, and the trio is joined by a bass violin attended by a jolly-looking little man who manifestly belongs to it.

Sheet-music is distributed – good! It is going to be *Cavalleria*

Rusticana. The cornopean takes out all its valves and stoppers, blows through them carefully, and replaces them, then twiddles a few notes: the piano strikes quite a sound G; the violin picks it up perfunctorily, and the bass rasps out a full chord to show that basses are always in tune under any circumstances at sea.

Simultaneously with the first warning of the breakfast bell, the band breaks, with admirable attack, into 'Valencia'.

We have been sold again! A Clyde steamer band rarely plays from any score until it has exhausted a long repertory of items it knows by heart. If, on leaving Gourock or Fairlie, you make a special request for that bright little piece of Schumann's, the 'A Minor Scherzo', the bass alone will seem willing to have a go at it; the band as a whole very properly shows a determined preference for old sea traditions which, this season, make 'Valencia' to breakfast almost compulsory.

After all, I am glad it is not *Cavalleria Rusticana*; the 'intermezzo' is too poignantly sad an air with which to start a trip to Campbeltown. I like 'Valencia', and it is sad enough for me. It pretends to be a merry air, though drenched in melancholy, and so much danced to by youth, on whom its undertones of disillusion and frustration and regret are lost.

But all melodies, played at sea, are sad, are they not? One remembers the despondency of sea music as played in its most primitive form on the old Lochgoilhead steamers by a single fiddler or a blind concertina performer. The tunes might have the merriest titles and associations – 'The Wind that Shakes the Barley', 'A Bicycle Built for Two', or the 'Blue Danube' waltz – there were always disengaged from it moods not altogether unpleasingly disconsolate.

It must be something in salt water or navigable water of any kind that adds the pensive element to ukuleles heard in moonshine on Loch Lomond, or steamboat bands upon the Firth.

At one time it seemed not unreasonable to attribute to this the frequency with which an earlier generation of down-the-water passengers went 'down to look at the engines'. The stewards kept an excellent antidote for *melancolie-de-mer*.

Yet it is now apparent that the more accomplished the music, the less is the business done at the bar. I am assured that the liquor consumption by passengers on the river steamers now is trivial compared with what it used to be. Just when special bars became features of Clyde craft that previously had no such discreet alternatives to the open saloon for drinking in, the public interest in the study of enginry became languid. Even the Glasgow Fair but little disturbs the peaceful solitude of the steamer smoke-room and bar.

If the passenger of today feels to dejected about 'Annie Laurie' or the poor lady who was 'Far From the Land' where her young hero slept, he buys himself a lunch or tea-ticket, and uplifts his spirits with an excellent meal. A person more unfit to keep up the ancient reputation of the Clyde for boisterous joviality can hardly be imagined: he is getting as keen on mere food as an Englishman.

It is a lovely day, the Firth resplendent after a night of torrential rain, and the sea-sadness of jazz itself (a mercifully mitigated jazz through the absence of drums, banjos and saxophones), is not enough to drive us off the deck. From time to time a change in our angle to the wind is followed by a transference of the passengers to other parts of the ship for shelter. The band picks up its graith, puts the piano on wheels again and takes up a new position so that we may miss nothing of the rollicking 'Tea for Two'.

Rather sad looking themselves, these marine musicians! All except the fellow attached to the bass, who has a humorous countenance and seems thoroughly to enjoy his own contribution to the harmony, as I should do myself in his place, for the bass (perhaps fallaciously) looks an instrument that is not so exacting as the others.

To all passengers, the Clyde steamer's wholly British band remains the mystery it was in the beginning when it was mainly German. Does it count as part of the 'crew' on the ship's certificate? Is it engaged and paid by the steamboat owners or does it depend entirely on the collections made from time to time by the cornopean?

Where do steamer bands go in the winter? I have not seen them on the Riviera. For that part of it, where does it go at night now, when the evening cruise is finished? It vanishes unaccountably from the deck, between two piers, without so much as a farewell National Anthem. Nobody ever sees a bass violin or a piano landed. Perhaps the quartette stays on board and employs its leisure hours in rehearsal till the morning when 'Valencia' begins again.

The Clyde: River and Firth (1907)

INTRODUCTION

†

Munro, for most of his literary career, was regularly published by William Blackwood & Sons, both in serial form in Maga *and in book form. He was tempted away by the London firm of Isbister & Co. for his 1899 novel,* Gilian the Dreamer, *and the 1901 novel,* Shoes of Fortune, *and twice collaborated on illustrated books for A. & C. Black.*

The first of these ventures was The Clyde: River and Firth, *a handsome volume in Black's series of full-colour travel guides – their 'Twenty-Shilling' series. These were remarkably expensive works for the period, costing about four times as much as a new hardback novel, but they were popular and did much to introduce colour printing to a general audience.*

Munro took second billing on the title page after the two artists, Mary Y. Hunter and J. Young Hunter, who contributed the sixty-seven pleasant, if slightly insipid, illustrations. It is, however, hard to think of a contemporary writer who could have done more justice to the theme. Munro throughout his life was very much a man of the Clyde and its attendant sea-lochs.

The Clyde: River and Firth *describes the great river from its source in the hills of southern Lanarkshire to its meeting with the sea. There are fascinating echoes of Munro's other work, especially in the section dealing with the docks and harbours of Glasgow. In a splendid passage in the chapter 'Harbour Life' Munro writes:*

> *Nor even then can one rightly comprehend the harbour who has not brooded beside sheer-leg and crane-jib that are mightily moving enormous weights as if they had been toys; swallowed the coal-dust of the docks, dodged traction engines, eaten Irish stew for breakfast in the Sailors' Home, watched George Geddes trawl for corpses, sat in the fo'c'sles of 'tramps', stood in a fog by the pilot on the bridge, heard the sorrows of a Shore Superintendent and the loyal lies of witnesses in a Board of Trade examination, who feel bound to 'stick by the owners' and swear their engines backed ten minutes before the accident; or sat on a cask in the Prince's Dock on peaceful Sabbath mornings when the shipping seemed asleep, or an unseen concertina played some sailor's jig for canticle.*

For a student of Munro's Para Handy stories there are many resonances in this passage. Sunny Jim claims to have been the '... best wee soomer Geordie Geddes dragged by the hair o' the heid frae the Clyde...' ('To Campbeltown by Sea' – No. 46 in the Birlinn edition) the 'loyal lies of witnesses' irresistably call to mind the crew of the Vital Spark's *evidence in the case of 'The* Vital Spark's *Collision' (No. 82 in the Birlinn edition) and the closing image of the unseen concertina recalls the musically inclined Sunny Jim once more. This is all hardly surprising, for, however much we try to put Munro's writing into categories (a process which he started with his assumption of the 'Hugh Foulis' persona) it was all written by one man, and a man who did not forget his novelist's art when he entered the* Evening News *office, or let his journalistic training and instincts atrophy when engaged on more 'literary' ventures.*

Our selections from this charming work of topography are: 'Down the Water – Summer', its companion piece 'Winter on the Firth', and an account of Munro's own native parts in 'Loch Fyne'.

The first of these is an evocation of what is now a long-vanished phenomenon – mass holidays at the Clyde coast. Munro points out that the habit of the middle classes moving to the coast and building marine villas was brought about by the advent of the steamboat. Until the Second World War commuting to Glasgow from a wide range of locations served by the Clyde's numerous piers and her competing steamer services was popular and practical, at least as a summer activity. The Clyde was of course also the place of resort for the working classes and the annual holiday 'doon the watter' was the delight of many of Glasgow's population.

The very different atmosphere in winter, when the crack steamers were laid up safe from the ravages of the winter's gales and the more economical, workaday vessels maintained the lifeline of Clyde sailings, is caught in the second piece. The notion that you could not really know a Clyde resort if you only knew it in the summer is one that obviously intrigued Munro and is one that he returned to on a number of occasions. He starts one of his Para Handy stories ('Para Handy's Piper' – No. 14 in the Birlinn edition) with the observation: 'If you haven't been at your favourite coast resort except at the time of summer holidays, you don't know much about it. At other seasons of the year it looks different, smells different, and sounds different – that is, when there's any sound in it at all.'

And in one of his 'Looker-On' pieces, collected by George Blake, he writes of the last trip of the season for one of the 'summer-only' steamers like the Lord of the Isles: *'It is the closing trip of the season; on Monday the steamer goes to sleep in Bowling; the shores of the Firth will see her no more till April.'*

The third chapter on Loch Fyne touches on that most mysterious fish – the herring, and the once-vast Loch Fyne herring fishery, now much reduced from the days of which Munro writes when at night hundreds of boats would be out and give 'the mid-channel all the aspect of a town'. Para Handy described this industry in even more colourful terms: 'The herrin' wass that thick in Loch Fyne in them days, that you sometimes couldna get your anchor to the ground, and the quality wass chust sublime.' ('Herring – a Gossip' – No. 45 in the Birlinn Edition)

The three chapters together reflect Munro's passion for Scotland's west coast and its ships and seafarers. In one of his pieces contributed to the Daily Record *under the pen-name of 'Mr Incognito', and collected in* The Brave Days *by George Blake, he wrote of that most famous of West Coast shipping companies, MacBrayne:*

> *Along the western sea-board, from Tarbert, Loch Fyne, to Lochinver, and throughout the Inner and Outer Isles from Port Ellen in Islay to Stornoway in the Lews, generations of young Highlanders have grown up with the idea that their very existence was more or less dependent on MacBrayne. But for MacBrayne, most of them would never have seen bananas or the white loaf of the lowlands, might still be brining coalfish oil in cruisies, and getting no more than sixpence a dozen for their eggs.*

He went on to recollect his exploration of the west coast:

> *The farther I wandered from home and into the Western Ocean the more it was obvious to me that MacBrayne meant all the Mercantile Marine in sight. You could not stick your nose round a headland without seeing a red-funnelled steamer coming up to starboard with a cloud of gulls about her, nor land at a quay but across red-painted gangways.*

From his birth in Inveraray on Loch Fyne to his death at Helensburgh on the north bank, Munro's life had revolved around the Clyde and his affection for the area comes across very clearly. As he wrote in his introduction: 'For such as have eyes and their own imaginations, independent of the guidance of poet or novelist, the Clyde is, none the less, the most astonishing, beautiful and inspiring of Scottish waterways.'

†

DOWN THE WATER – SUMMER

It was our grandfathers who found out what joys the Firth could hold for a holiday spirit – our grandfathers who worked till all hours in Glasgow shops, assured that that was life, and compelled to make the most of an annual week of playtime. Once they used to walk to Govan where the eggs were fresh and salmon was not expensive, and they thought a casual picnic there on the grass was as much of nature's rapture as mortal man need look for. Their noisier and more common pleasure took the form of 'high jinks' round the booths, 'geggies' and taverns of Glasgow Fair, and anywhere west of Kelvin was the wilds, to which one never went from the cosy city unless his health was poorly or his bills were to collect.

When Henry Bell had the *Comet* built for him in 1812, and she gallantly stood away to Helensburgh with a square-sail on her funnel, she was an oddity that might make us laugh to-day, but none-the-less she was a mighty portent, and not the least of her influences was the change she was to bring on Glasgow's notion of a holiday. She had the key to the hillls and glens; she had the secret of the lochs and our now beloved western Archipelago. Behind her, still unrealised, merely draughts as it were in the drawing shops of Destiny, steamed a noble fleet of pleasure vessels bearing the city's millions to the shores that have become their playground. Govan, Camlachie and Stra'ven were to satisfy the roving cit no longer; he was into the age of Saturday-to-Monday travelling-bags and hazardous delights with rowing-boats at sixpence an hour. As Glasgow's vigour largely came from the West, either as food or men from the neighbouring Highlands, to the West she has ever looked with a wistful holiday eye, too much grime and a different people being to the east of her; so the Firth continues her especial Paradise. She cannot get there too often or too fast. Our grandfathers went by fly-boats – that must have got the name on the principle of *lucus a non lucendo*, since they took twelve hours to go from Broomielaw to Greenock under the most favourable circumstances; we could reach it now by paddle in less than two if we did not prefer the train to Gourock or Wemyss Bay, where we smell sea-wrack and hear the tide on the beaches forty minutes after leaving Glasgow.

It is perhaps the stranger's only fault with the Firth of Clyde that Glasgow has too palpably usurped it. He finds the shores interminably fringed by villas that have 'suburb' written large on every feature from the name-plate and the aurucaria in front to the outhouse in the rear to which the owners retire when their home is let in the season. Such of these seaside dwellings as are not hired by the month by Glasgow families are the property of Glasgow men, their country houses; the Firth would have a poor existence wanting the approval and patronage of the city, thirty, forty, or fifty miles away. The month of May has no sooner lit the hills at night with fires of burning heather, brought the daffodil to the city parks, and made the terrors of the coming Whitsun term loom over the merchant's pillow like a nightmare than he yearns to escape to a place where he may briefly forget and sleep. Straightway his coast house – elsewhere in the East we should call it bungalow – is aired and opened, his wife and family – if the latter are not at school – go down to the sea, and he becomes a daily traveller. From Kilcreggan, Dunoon, Lochgoil, Rothesay, Millport, Largs, Arran, or the Kyles, he rises to a hurried breakfast, dashes to the quay to reach his city shop or office about nine o'clock, feeling like one who for a pearl quits the sunshine and the bouneous air to dive breathless in unpleasant and murky deeps. In the early evening he returns laden monstrously with groceries, or garden tools, or a pile of books from the Western Library. The natives know him as a man whose name is often in the newspapers, a pillar of the Second City; for four or five months he dwells among them, sharing humbly their interest in the signs of weather and the local kirk affairs, but they vaguely feel some sense of transiency in his presence; though with them he is not of them, even on the golf course; he is unmistakeably and hopelessly 'a Gleska man'.

Possibly he may not for more than a few weeks in midsummer be able to quit the desk or counter save from Saturday-to-Monday; then his dull brown business hours are shot with moments of sunny dream, the thoughts of the coming holiday when town may be absolutely forgotten and the hard hat of a blameless life in commerce may be discarded for a cap or Panama. There is probably no other city in the world where such brief interregnums in a life of toil among the middle-classes are more universally the custom or more wholesomely utilised. It is the knowledge of the Firth at our back door, as it were, and of the happiness it proffers that makes Glasgow, for all its disabilities, a pleasant enough place wherein to strive for fortune.

But not to the upper and middle-class alone is the Firth of Clyde a sample of Paradise; there is no working-man, milliner, or seamstress in the city, who does not keep some dreams of happy days along its shores. Once a year Glasgow, tired, insurgent against toil, throws off her chains, damps down her furnaces, and hies her to the sea. It is her Fair. And over all the Firth there settles down in mid-July a swarm of citizens. In these days Glasgow's pall of smoke rolls back, and one may, from her eminences, see her from end to end, and the bastions of her protecting hills; the air alters and grows clean; a curious silence falls on streets for ordinary loud with footsteps and beseeching cries. The tide of life has ebbed and beats upon the distant estuary. Let us go to the Broomielaw in that too brief season and we shall find the quays packed dreadfully with people for the steamers which will take them down the river for a shilling; let us go by train to Greenock, Gourock, or Wemyss Bay, and we find ourselves swept onward still in the rush of holidaymakers bound for the favourite coast resorts yet further down. To sail in a Clyde passenger steamer at this time is so cheap a joy – it is cheap indeed at any season – that the national thrift compels us not to stay at home. In that one week in July, the Clyde coast towns, it must be owned, are no places for the contemplative pilgrim, the sensitive poetic soul. The great god Pan himself must takle affright and skulk in the hill ravines; dryad and nymph must flee for a space to other scenes before the onset of St Mungo's children, who come as an army with banners, to command the erstwhile quiet little towns, to bring the perfumes of the Trongate to the esplanades, to render lanes and fields and country roads untenable by their numbers and their pranks, to affront the moon with their uncouth gambols and the strains of their melodeons. There is no escape from them. The Glasgow accent – peculiar, indescribable, part Scots part Irish, to the stranger wholly unmusical – everywhere prevails; the Glasgow sportsmen stalk the whelk and cockle or cull edible seaweeds on all the more insanitary beaches, or row with incredible lack of skill in small boats round the bays, a source of constant horror to the captains of the hurrying steamboats.

Who can grudge these children of the streets their week of manumission by the purifying sea or on the hillsides whence so many of them came originally to lose their simple rustic airs and acquire a dubious urban cleverness? If the Firth be theirs for a week in July, all Summer is for luckier folk. I have written too hastily, perhaps, of the interminable fringe of villas – in truth the term is applicable only to the Cowal shore, and even there the Villa sometimes has as much of dignity as on Bellagio. There are massive dwellings, not inelegant, with lawns, tennis-courts, great gardens, vineries – summer homes of men retired from business, or of merchant princes, who have moorings out in the bay, and, nodding at them, white steam yachts that you may see in Autumn on the Baltic, or in Norwegian fiords, or in winter in the blue of the Mediterranean. All round the seashore go roads of the finest character, not so much the prey of the motor car as they might be in England, in Bute and Arran almost wholly free from its insistent hoot, its dust and swooping menace. Behind are peaceful lonely little glens, backwaters of life in a hurrying age, woods, hill-slopes purple with heather, and the spacious moors.

It is significant of Glasgow's close association with the coast that the very names of the steamers that daily ply there are dear to her, and their achievements in the way of speed or cheap teas are topics of universal and abiding interest. It might be natural that the city should take pride in the vessels that start at morning from the Broomielaw and cant at evening there, having still about them some air of holiday and adventure among fairer scenes, so that homesick Highlanders go down to the harbour and find pleasure in the sight of the *Columba* or the *Lord of the Isles*; but there are steamers which Glasgow sees only when she is on holiday, and these she knows and loves almost as well – those of the railway companies whose sailings start at the end of a train journey to Greenock, Gourock or Craigendoran. There is no pleasure fleet in the world that offers so much for so small a cost. We know the captains by their Christian names; when pursuers defalcate and disappear, as pursers will at times despite their haughty splendour, we feel a personal sense of shame or grievance, since we had come to look on them as intimates like our own domestics, with the prospect of being more permanent in office. Should you hear the names of Scott's heroes and heroines, or of Scottish nobles, or of Scottish scenes in any West of Scotland conversation, be sure it is not of literature, Burke's Peerage, or actual strath or glen the folk are speaking, but of some favourite river steamer, for the nomenclature of the fleet has always run in settled national lines.

If the Glasgow citizen in summer cannot spare the time for a more protracted outing on the Firth, he will go on an evening cruise after business hours, and he may even venture down the water on a Sunday, though there he gets small encouragement, either from popular sentiment or from railway or steamboat companies. A certain obloquy hangs about the 'Sunday breakers', as the Sunday boats are called, and there are at present only two, which conduct their traffic on teetotal principles and on lines more decorous than their predecessors of some generations ago, for the Sunday breaker is no modern innovation, having often tried and failed. When the present Summer Sunday service was established a few years ago, Dunoon, remembering and alarmed at the prospect of rowdy Sabbaths, bolted the gates of her pier and refused the passengers admittance, but wiser counsels now prevail, and so far as can be seen, Dunoon at least is none the worse.

To be 'down the water' on the Clyde in recent years was mightily different from being at an English watering-place – a Blackpool or a Margate. Great sandy beaches are unknown there; the shores descend too rocky and precipitate to retain any surface less than shingle; we gain by better drainage, but we lack a feature that the stranger, thinking of other coasts, might naturally expect. To bask or bathe from rocks, to fish and boat in the bays, were the only recreations of a purely marine character we could, till lately, offer. Now, places like Gourock, Dunoon, and Rothesay, pride themselves on their esplanades, where the pierrot, the minstrel, and the band have come to give our coast in the season something of an English aspect which may please the young but rouses mingled feelings in the middle-aged and elderly who remember more natural, less giddy times.

WINTER ON THE FIRTH

The time to see the Firth most profitably, if it is not simply a sunburned face you want, but an exaltation of the mind, is not in summer, but in winter, when the black squall flies. It is good at all times – except when fogs possess it – but in January are charms unknown to travel there in July. There are, for instance, no bands upon the steamers, Hack-enschmidts and Madralis of cornopian and concertina wrestling with Scotch airs that come badly mauled through the encounter, and you may venture into a saloon without the risk of finding little Maudie there before you playing the first part of the latest pantomine air on the public piano. I delight in the winter steamer to go down into the fore saloon as dusk comes on, and see the glowing stove with dusky forms about it, and hear men talk in the accents of Ardrishaig about hoggs and herrings, or catch the timid whisperings of the girl going south to her first situation. I like to mix with unaffected, healthy-looking fellow-creatures wearing top-boots and leggings – not in an ornamental affectation, as the young city man does in summer in a pathetic attempt thus to 'get back to nature', and look very fit and rural, but because top-boots and leggings are essential to their business. I like to stand in the warm lee of the funnels, with men covered up in oilskins, and other men with thick, inartistic-coloured blunt-cut clothes and squashy hats – farmers and the like – not 'redolent of R. L. S.', as a lady once said to me of Edinburgh, but mildly of sheep-dip, whisky, and plug tobacco, and hear the wind whistle in the cordage, and see through the blurr of rain the winking of the lights of Toward, Cloch, and the Gantocks. Then there is something compact, friendly, communal, about a Clyde steamer; the very purser, no longer gold braid from clew to earing, as the sailor says, but human, wet, and unaffected, as oilskin clad he bears a hand at a rope; the captain so much on a plane with all of us that

we feel we may, without offence, call him Duncan and be done with it. A
Clyde steamer in July is like a section of Sauchiehall Street cut out and
sharpened at each end, with engines in the middle to go down and look at;
but at this time of the year it is pure Highland, a thing apart, as dignified
as a mountain, and as full of real 'characters' as a clachan.

We leave Gourock, say, this winter day, in a south-west gale, in the
Duchess of Montrose, her saloon windows shuttered against the seas, and
make for the mouth of the Holy Loch. I never cared much for the Holy
Loch; its mud and shingle come too quickly, so I am glad we are not going
in there. Hunter's Quay receives us, and here you have the first idea of
winter days at the coast. A deserted pier, but for two men in oilskins to
catch the ropes; paraffin oil casks piled against the railings; flag-pole
halyards flap-flapping in the winds; villas, sombre and black with rain,
standing in gardens of glistening shrubbery; thin brown woods behind
the village; in front a rain fog hiding the other side of the Firth. Not much
doing at Hunter's Quay. A man with a brown-paper parcel gets off the
steamer reluctantly, his coat-collar high on his ears, and bending to the
wind, stands a moment to watch the ropes cast off, and looks after the
steamer as she proceeds on her way. He is sorry he came. Any other day
might have done, perhaps. He looks over his shoulder at the village, and
once more at the wake of the steamer, and then he slowly goes up the pier.
At Kirn, where we stop next, the red tiles and gilt of the waiting-room
suggest that somebody has got a part of the old Glasgow Exhibition
down for wintering – a piece of frivolity belated, and quite out of keeping
with its surroundings. More paraffin oil casks in profusion – plainly the
chief import of the coast town at this season is paraffin oil. Not much
doing at Kirn either. A gentleman with a tall silk hat comes on board. He
has evidently eluded the vigilance of the local hotels, and made his escape,
for when the steamer resumes her way he stands beside the paddle-box,
his silk hat – which looks as appropriate to the situation and the season as
a Spanish mantilla would do – clutched firmly by both hands, and thows
a look of relief upon Kirn as the rain-blur wipes it out behind us.

And then Dunoon. Where is Winnie? or Marion? or Agnes? or whatever her name was, who, with her comrades, stood so persistently on this
pier in August, and waved studiously graceful adieux after her friends
bound for the city? On that spray-swept wharf there ought to be the
wraith of the Summer Girl in muslin and chiffon, the Tam o' Shanter on
her glorious head, the walking-stick in her hand, the happy consciousness
in her heart that, even if the wind does blow, her shoes are of the neatest.
Summer Girl! Summer Girl! In wintry gales today I think of you, so
dainty and so sweet, the fairest flower of the summer gardens, so fresh, so

tanned, so rosy with the wholesome air of the sea. I loved you, Summer Girl; I loved you, one and all; many a time we walked and talked together, but you never knew it, 'twas but an old man's ghost! Today not even your wraith haunts the pier of Dunoon. My heart will not go out to Highland Mary on her pedestal. I never liked her – there; but much less loveable than usual does Highland Mary look in the drenching rain, wind buffeted. She is no ethereal spirit of the hills; her very existence there shows that in Scotland we do not understand. The poet's Mary was a Mary of the mind – the winds of spring were her breathing; her voice was the sound of water in tiny glens; her eyes were the remote and unfathomable stars. She died – it was always so; he never married her – and so it was bound to be, that a memory and unattainable, she should rise for ever before him, the virgin bride of fancy. Little doing in Dunoon, only a clammy, inefficient statue of a dream. And a policeman, monstrous in his cape. More casks of paraffin, too; bathing places deserted, gardens sodden, rows of villas silent and dead, hills behind menacing. No; we will not go ashore at Dunoon. Into the teeth of a stiffer wind we proceed towards Innellan, to see the Bullwood houses snuggling in their hollows, to speculate upon what is at the other end of the gaps of glens in the hillsides, to discover the burns roaring down in hundred-feet falls, and snow-white.

At Innellan more paraffin oil and a yellow dog; a woman struggling with an umbrella blown outside in; but positively nothing doing except the landing of some groceries and weekly papers. Before us lies Toward, that in this grey gale might be the end of everything, for beyond the point is nothing visible. Through the steamer goes the wrenching sound of struggle; the engines pant and heave distressed in the midst of her, wild gusts blow in alley-ways, tarpaulins flap, the funnel whoops with wind. We cannot make Craigmore, but land at Rothesay. One solitary badge porter – last of all his tribe – stands on the pier and points his finger at us. Do we look like folk that come with baggage to stay at the 'Madeira' in days like these? 'faith, no, we have homes! But in truth Rothesay always seems to me a more habitable and desirable place in winter than when Wull the Glasgow larrikin possesses the pier, and the minstrels are on the esplanade. It is the ideal size of a winter town – big enough for warmth, and a sort of self-contained society, not big enough to catch the music-hall disease or to have an unpleasant number of strangers coming about. It seems to shrink in the rain; its sea front to be only half as long as when Glasgow crowds the pavements and the esplanade; the hotels have lost a good deal of their importance with the taking down of their flags. We walk a lonely road to Ascog, in front of which the sea is white with spindrift; but this is too like going into the wilds, and we return hastily to

Rothesay, and its shops, and its tramway cars, that look as real as anything, and run with frequency, as if in weather like this there were actually people who wanted to get to Port-Bannatyne.

Before we are halfway back to the mainland the night is almost come. It is then that a one-and-nine-penny trip in a river steamer has the faint suggestion of adventure double the money cannot buy when you go in summer sunshine by the *Columba*, the *Lord of the Isles*, or the turbines. Night, and a gale, and flying spray, and the ship heaving; the land out of sight, and the red-hot stove in the saloon, and slightly odorous paraffin lamps swinging responsive to the roll of the waves; a smell of brine and tarpaulin, a thumping of doors, a clanging of shovels down below, the muffled tread of sea-boots, and the flap of oilskins. No band, no Maudie at the piano, no excursion party at the bows singing 'Rolling Home to Bonnie Scotland', no sense of holiday, but a feeling that everybody is here on the business of his life. Far before us a star shines on a dim promontory for a moment, and then dies out, to be revealed again and again. It is the light of the Cloch, and closer, but less ardent-white, begins to wink the light on the skerry called the Gantocks.

LOCH FYNE

Of the Clyde sea-arms, Loch Fyne, which now we come to, has doubtlessly figured most importantly in the earlier periods of Scottish history, though we must judge of that more by deduction than by surviving story. Its immensely greater expanse than that of the other lochs; its deeper penetration into the country; its situation and its natural resources gave it prior claims on the invader and the settler, and the early establishment near its head of a great feudal family, the Campbells, brought it more prominently into relation with the lowland world. It was the Mediterranean Sea of the Dalriadic Celts who came from Ireland; Magnus Barefoot knew its shores and coves, and claimed no small part of them for Norway by a stratagem of a character not uncommon among Celts and Scandinavians if all folk tales be true. The law ran, more or less limpingly, on Loch Fyneside, and a certain security of domestic peace was there while as yet Loch Long, Loch Lomond and the Gareloch were open to the excursions and alarms of petty clans and the depredations of gentlemen like Rob Roy.

With the greater part of Loch Fyneside for generations under the hand of the Argylls and their cadets, it had the position of an *imperium in imperio*, and prosperous internal states of the kind knit together by the ties of blood and common interest are not lightly to be meddled with by envious or resentful peoples outside the pale. Thus, singularly few attacks of any moment were made on the integrity of Loch Fyne, considering the temptations it must have offered; it was ill to get at with an adequate force of footmen, for the passes to it were hard to traverse and easy to guard, and there is no record of 'spulzie' by ships. Montrose made its shores the objective of a demonstration in force by his lieutenant Colkitto in 1644, and the men of Athole, with hordes of clansmen from further north, plundered both sides of it in 1685, but it was, save on these occasions, exempt from the more serious manifestations of Highland strife. Even Rob Roy, when he borrowed the potent name of Campbell and came to the head waters of the Shira to a cot whose ruins still look over Loch Fyne, had to comport himself like an honest man.

Whether the 'guile of the Campbells' differed in anything more than degreee from the guile of any other powerful family of the feudal days it would ill become a tenant of the Campbells to expatiate on, but at least the clan's diplomacy always led to desirable results in civilization even if the methods might have been open to criticism. The old Dalriada or Earaghaidheal was early in the seventeenth century a tolerable enough place for lowland merchants and mechanics to settle in, secure of Argyll's protection, and up till 1745 the good government of the greater part of the Highlands, the restraint of the Jacobite clans particularly, depended upon that portion of Clan Campbell territory that borders Loch Fyne and has its focus in the now declining and somnolent Royal Burgh of Inveraray. It was to the Duke of Argyll – the MacCailen Mor – and his vassals the government of the eighteenth century looked for the proper subjection of his turbulent neighbours on the west – the Stewarts, Camerons, Macdonalds and others of the old régime. According to an official report submitted to the government in 1750 the Duke and his clan, including Breadalbane, could raise if necessary 10,000 men able to bear arms. The bulk of them must have been found between the shores of Loch Fyne and Loch Awe: single glens of Loch Fyne could turn out over two hundred swords; now they are desolate, though there were none of the wholesale clearances that dispeopled many other parts of the Highlands.

It is, however, in a purely commercial connection that Loch Fyne is known to our day – as the source of a surprisingly succulent variety of herring. Its fame for herring is hundreds of years old; Frenchmen used to barter wine for herring at a point called Rudha nan Fraingeach, a few miles out of Inveraray, and many generations of Loch Fyneside men have followed a vocation which has much of the uncertainty of backing horses without so much amusement. Towns like Inveraray, Lochgilphead, and

Tarbert grew up, as it were, round the fishing smacks that in old days ran
into their bays for shelter, and Minard, Crarae, Lochgair, Castle Lachlan,
Strachur, and other villages on either side of the loch depend to some
extent for their existence on the silver harvest of the sea. A fish whose
migratory movements still baffle the scientist, the herring is elusive and
erratic, and seasons of success are divided by recurring periods when the
shoals appear to go elsewhere. The means of capture are netting, either
with the drift net kept on or near the surface by buoys and stretched out
to great lengths to intercept the shoals, or with the seine net, here called
the 'trawl,' in which two skiffs combine to run a net round the shoal or
'eye' of fish wherever it is observed. Sailing up Loch Fyne in daytime
when the fishing skiffs are in the harbours, the loch vacant of active life, it
is difficult to conceive that the same great empty stretch of water may at
midnight be busy with hundreds of boats, when the cry of the fishers as
they 'hale' their nets, the lights of their flares as they summon the
steamers to carry their takes to the Clyde, give the mid-channel all the
aspect of a town.

The loch is about forty miles long and one to five miles broad, with its
portals opening at Skipness and Ardlamont; hills enfold it, that, except at
the head, have not the same sublimity as those of Arran looming near the
entrance. The Knapdale hills on the left indeed are tame; the Cowal hills
on the other shore are suave in parts to monotomy. Only in the upper
reaches is there any multitude of trees; there the Argyll estate is clothed
with ancient forest, which Dr Johnson must have gone through with his
eyes shut. But some reclusive charm is in these hills and bays that is not
elsewhere; you have left the changing lowland world behind you at
Ardlamont, and breathe a more romantic air. Tarbert, coyly hiding itself
in a winding, lake-like inlet, fretted by rocky promontory and isle, is a
fishing village, crouched at the feet of a ruined keep which Robert Bruce
inhabited. Quarter of a century ago it was the St Ives of the Scottish
painter; to-day the taste for yellow wrack and fishing-skiffs is somewhat
in abeyance, but the same spirit, pensive mystery, and expectation haunt
the place as Colin Hunter found in his 'Trawlers waiting for Darkness'. It
is only a narrow neck of land that keeps Loch Fyne from the appealing
arms of the Atlantic. Magnus Barefoot, reading lawyer-wise the treaty by
which King Malcolm of Scotland ceded all the islands 'between which
and the mainland he could pass in a vessel with its rudder shipped',
landed at West Loch Tarbert, according to the *Orkneyinga Saga*, and had
a boat drawn across the isthmus to Loch Fyne, himself holding the
rudder, so that he secured for the Norse the whole of the Kintyre
peninsula, 'which is better than the best island of the Sudreyar, except

Man'. Hakon later in like wise evaded the rough, long passage round the Mull of Kintyre, and, forty years after Hakon, Robert the Bruce portaged it also, since which time a canal or shipway has been Tarbert's great ambition.

But the canal to the Atlantic is already made elsewhere – ten miles further up the loch, no great thing as canals go, though picturesque, fit only to float a tiny passenger steamer or a cutter yacht. Ardrishaig is its entrepot, at the mouth of Loch Gilp, at the head of which is a quiet and pleasant township, left at low tides to the rueful contemplation of an unattractive stretch of muddy shore. A curious sand spit and a group of rocks almost bar the passage up Loch Fyne at Otter; a little further north of them fishermen dry their nets, and surely fairies dwell in the green creek of Lochgair. Still further north, on the left, are the manorial lands of Minard, with a handsome modern castle, and the great whin quarries of Furnace and Crarae. The village of Strachur, on the right, is the terminus of the route which David Napier opened from Kilmun by Loch Eck; twenty minutes' sailing brings us to the county town of Inveraray, which stands on a promontory, under wooded hills, whose foliage renders more distant and austere the myriad peaks that culminate in Cruachan, by Loch Awe. Six miles further inland, Loch Fyne, having narrowed quickly from the point where stands the ruined sixteenth-century castle of the MacNaughtons of Dunderave, ends in the brackish pools of the river Fyne.

It is the north end of Loch Fyne that, till recent years, travellers have seen most of, since, before the coming of the steamer, the road by Arrochar, Glen Croe, and Inveraray was the highway from the lowlands to the west coast and the isles. This way came Faugas de Saint Fond in 1784, to find French spoken at the dinner table of Inveraray Castle 'with as much purity as in the most polished circles of Paris'; this way came Robert Burns, to find the very antithesis of that 'Highland welcome' he declared could not be bettered over Acheron; this way, too, came Keats to Inveraray to have his first experience of the bagpipe, as sole orchestra at a performance of Kotzebue's 'Stranger' in the ducal barn. Dorothy Wordsworth and her brother had come the same road fifteen years before, and though Inveraray on a closer inspection scarce approved itself to the tidy dame, her first impression was that it looked as pretty as a raree show – 'or pictures of foreign places – Venice, for example – painted on the scene of a play-house'. Dr Johnson and Boswell found in its inn, which remains unchanged, 'as good a room and bed as at an English inn'; the Doctor called for a gill of whisky, to taste what 'makes a Scotchman happy', and Bozzy drank the dregs of his idol's glass. Turner painted the bays, woods, and hills of the neighbourhood with an artistic ecstasy that soared above all considerations of topographical accuracy.

On a summer day, if you be fortunate, you may sail from end to end of Loch Fyne on a surface without a ripple, in a silence undisturbed save by the cry of birds. Flocks of divers scatter and sink before your bows, the porpoise wheels in the sunshine; you may even see a whale roll out of Kilfinan Bay, leisurely chasing herring, lord of the fiord, huge, in love with himself and the heat of the day, and the sting of salt on his hide and the taste of fish. You may see the gannet fly, too, high in heaven, and plunge like an arrow from the height. The very cottages on the hillsides are transfigured then, and seem more habitable than palaces. Even winter brings its own stern beauty to Loch Fyne, when the peaks of snow are mirrored on its surface, or the ice-floe roars at high tide on its beaches. The stones of Inveraray Castle were brought from the opposite side of the loch on sledges, and twenty-seven years ago skaters disported themselves, miles from its head, as on an artificial pond.

8
Ayrshire Idylls (1912)

INTRODUCTION

✝

In 1910 the publishing house of A. & C. Black commissioned Munro and the talented Ayrshire-born artist George Houston (1869–1947) to collaborate on a colour-plate book devoted to Ayrshire landscape and characters. Houston was already well known to Munro, and was indeed a friend of Munro's. The two men were both members of the Glasgow Art Club and shared an interest in angling and other country sports.

Houston was very much a rising figure in the Scottish artistic world and was recognised as one of the best Scottish landscape painters of the day. His individual and distinctive style set him apart from movements such as the slightly older Glasgow Boys, or the slightly younger Scottish Colourists. Houston had been elected an Associate of the Royal Scottish Academy in 1909 and would become a full Academician in 1925.

Munro was later to tell G. W. Blackwood that the original concept for the book was for a: 'kind of artistic itinerary of Ayrshire, but I found the guide-book sort of thing impossible to me, and wandered off into story-telling instead'.

The result was undoubtedly an attractive book, but one in which the text bears little relation to the twenty colour illustrations and not very much more to the twenty black and white drawings which appear at the beginning and end of each of the ten 'idylls' which Munro eventually produced.

The Glasgow Herald, *in enthusiastically welcoming the publication of* Ayrshire Idylls, *observed:*

> *. . . the writer and the artist were not intent on gathering archaeological and topographical detail, after the manner of industrious delvers; their purpose was to express the character and temperament of the county, to reveal something of its soul.*

Munro's approach to the soul of Ayrshire was to write about some of the county's people rather than simply describe its topography. In fact this technique does allow quite a strong feeling for the landscape to come through as a by-product.

Two of the idylls deal with little-known figures, in two others Ayrshire's seventeenth-century covenanting history is explored, and in a fifth the Irvine-born nineteenth-century novelist, John Galt, forms the centre of attention.

Our selection consists of the opening story, 'Ursa Major', which entertainingly retells the story of the visit paid in 1773 by James Boswell and Samuel Johnson, at the conclusion of their famous tour to the Hebrides, to Boswell's family home, and disapproving father, at Auchinleck. Munro attributes the Boswellian notion of writing his epic Life of Johnson *to this visit – as Boswell tells his father, Lord Auchinleck: '. . . a dwarf on the shoulders of a giant can see a good deal further than the giant. Believe me, papa, he'll make a splendid book.'*

Our other choice from this entertaining but lesser-known Munro work is a group of four idylls about Ayrshire's most famous son, Robert Burns. They depict Burns at four stages in his career and are among the earliest fictional treatments of Burns' life. 'Mossgiel Rab', set around 1784, finds the young poet as joint tenant of Mossgiel Farm with his brother Gilbert and kicking against the restrictions of the farmer's life. 'Burns and Clarinda' is set in Edinburgh in December 1787 with Burns, having published the Kilmarnock Edition of his poems in the previous year, and having become the darling of literary Edinburgh, meeting Mrs Maclehose, with whom he was to conduct the long romantic correspondence between himself as Sylvander and Nancy Maclehose as Clarinda. 'The Making of Tam o' Shanter' is a fascinating study of the process of artistic creation, set at Ellisland, near Dumfries, in November 1790 with Burns married to Jean Armour. The final piece, 'The Democrat', has Burns as a gauger, a customs officer, and walking the lonely streets of Dumfries, an unpopular supporter of the French Revolution – at least up to the point – in January 1793, when the French Republic declared war on Britain.

Munro's depiction of Burns at four periods of his life and at four phases of his artistic development is interesting and perceptive and makes one wish that he had been able to write a more extended piece of fiction based on the life of the poet. Munro's interest in Burns was significant – his poem 'The Immortal Memory' appears in the poetry section of this anthology, and he became Honorary President of the Greenock Burns Club, a body of more than local significance.

Munro's texts, some of which had previously been published in other places, stand securely enough by themselves to be enjoyable and neatly-crafted miniatures, and the collection was indeed reprinted by Blackwood in 1923 in a 'text-only' version. Munro himself thought well of the book, even though he had mainly taken on the contract as a gesture of friendship to Houston; indeed he wrote to G. W. Blackwood, 'I must add that I think some of them are as good as I've done.'

URSA MAJOR

At every reputable tavern on the road from Glasgow, Boswell stopped the chaise, professing a humane anxiety about the horses, and while Johnson lurched round the rude, grey, rough-cast houses, peering at them curiously with his single efficient eye, as if they had been kraals or crannogs, his companion drank claret, chucked waiting-maids under the chin, debated points of politics or faith in Scots with strappers, and felt awake within him the joy of being in a countryside where he was as much respected as in Corsica or the Lews. In London he seldom thought of this land of Ayr, and never with any degree of longing; yet once in the bailiwick of Cunningham, and something in the weather, the landscape, or the folk, restored a sense of self-sufficiency and confidence that were never wholly at his command in the Metropolis, however valiantly he cleared his throat and thrust his chest out in the coffee-houses.

He was known, at every stopping-place, to be the son of Auchinleck; in truth, where his identity was not suspected, he dropped a crafty hint to landlady or landlord which immediately ensured a flattering gush of new civility; but the character of his fat companion baffled them.

'Dr Samuel Johnson,' whispered Boswell once or twice, impressively, with an open hand against his nose. 'The Englishman who made the Dictionary; the talk of London! Amazing! What a brain!'

'He'd be a d——d sight better makin' sangs,' said the irreverent host of the change-house at Dalry. 'Any idiot could make a dictionary, and by the bulk o' him, this ane must hae swallowed his,' but that was to his wife when Mr Boswell had departed. 'I'll wager Mr Jamie has the size o' him!' he added, looking at the chaise go lumbering down the brae. 'Ye could see by the kyte o' yon one he was English.'

There is a certain kind of autumn day in Ayrshire when in parts, to a not too exigent eye, it has a look of England. Something of Surrey is in those lush well-cultivated plains of Cunningham and Kyle; compared with the Hebrides, whence he had just retreated – those islands wholly void of trees, untracked and desert-melancholy – this landscape seemed familiarly benign and opulent to Johnson. The little towns they passed through might be squalid, but the highway led among delicious fields of vivid green where cattle pastured, or by stubble-land on which wrought peasants, singing as they carted home the sheaves. There were English hedges, garrulous English rooks; below Kilwinning he once got a glimpse of red-tiled roofs uprising over sycamores, and they roused an interest in roofs and tiles he had never felt before; they gladdened his eye that had now grown tired of looking upon grey Caledonian slates. But for the absence of oasts, and smocks, and hop-poles, and the presence of wind-warped pines upon a distant eminence, he could beguile himself with the idea that he travelled among southern wolds.

At Eglinton he found himself in a lordly park, planted with giant secular trees, and mentally amended an impression that the sylvan deities had no harbourage in Scotland.

'H'm!' he purled approvingly. 'Not so bad at all, sir! Not so bad! Beeches. Oaks. Fallow deer. H'm! Quite creditable! Even an Englishman might here enjoy the soft vicissitudes of pleasure and repose, attended by all that is calculated to delight, and gratified with the most that elegance and taste in rural beauty may command.'

He was charmed with the Countess, who was to be their hostess for the evening. She was elderly, but had the nicest sense of his importance. While Boswell gave assiduous attention to a good old Hock, the great man fixed his disconcerting eye upon her ladyship and boomed opinions, articles of faith, emphatic dogmas, in the papal manner so efficacious with Mrs Thrale. She agreed with him in everything; her principles in Church and State, he found, were singularly sagacious, being, in every particular, his own; and as he took his candle at midnight through the corridor on his way to bed, he remarked to Boswell, 'Sir, her ladyship has a grace which I always thought peculiarly fine in a woman – she is a good listener. It is the one virtue which embellishes and strengthens social intercourse. I confess I had not looked to find it in these wilds; 'tis primarily a civic quality and an essential principle in what we justly call urbanity. When we see in the works of Cicero and others, particularly in Quintilian, the care, the trouble, the continued application which went to form the great men and women of antiquity, we are astonished that there are not more of them. Bolingbroke has remarked –'

'Good night, sir, God blesh you!' said Boswell fervently, wringing his hand, and disappearing to a couch for which the exertions of the day and the influence of the excellent Hock had made him ready some hours earlier than usual.

The great man sought his own bed-chamber, and before engaging in the nightly struggle with his boots, reversed his candle for a moment to secure a better light. He paid no heed to the grease that guttered on the carpet. He had a soothing sense of having spent some profitable hours.

'I think,' he said to himself, 'I was particularly happy in my allusions to Ariosto.'

As the chaise was about to set off in the morning, the Countess took the great man's friend aside. 'There are two things sadly lacking in your lion,' she remarked, '– a sense of humour, and a family. It took me all my time to keep my countenance when he was lecturing me upon how to bring up children. An amazing man, Mr Boswell, but I never slept a wink last night for a headache!'

Johnson would have appeared to have slept but poorly too, for he dozed in his corner till they reached Dundonald Castle. Perched high on its isolated knoll, it recalled to him some ruined stronghold he had seen in the Isle of Skye, and seemed wholly inharmonious with surroundings tame and pastoral. They got out of the chaise more closely to examine it, and he roared and laughed till the ruins rang at the homely accommodation of the Sovereign whom he playfully called 'King Bob', and who had been born, and died there, with some animated hours between.

'It is strange,' he remarked, as they resumed their journey, 'that nothing architectural in Scotland seems to be more than a century old except those gloomy fortalices, and the shrines of the Middle Ages. I have perceived no ancient dwellings of the common people; no grange or manor, hamlet, thorp, inn or cottage with a roof-tree older than the holly bushes at its gate. Sir, did all Scots of the past reside in caves, except the barons and ecclesiastics?'

Boswell, both chins sunk profoundly in his black cravat, and rosy at the gills, gave a conciliatory chuckle. 'Plenty of stones, sir!' he suggested. 'As easy to build a new house as to repair an old one.'

'Sir,' said his companion, whose punctilio of address appeared grotesque to Boswell when they were in Scotland, though somehow natural in the Mitre tavern; 'Sir, I surmise the reason is not so flattering to the racial self-esteem, and has some relation to the conveniency of clay and wattle. Where indigence is national and prolonged through centuries, the affections never root with any depth in soil that poorly rewards the travail of the husbandman, and has no charm of actual possession as with the English yeoman. I begin to see why your countrymen have always been great travellers; strictly speaking, they had never any home except the shadow of the feudal keep. The Scottish pine, the first and hardiest of woodland growths, has no tap-root, but a superficial foundation, and is the easiest of all umbrageous things to sever from its native mould.'

'By heavens, sir, you are right! You are always right!' said Mr Boswell, and in the shadow of the chaise he grimaced to himself.

'Nay, sir, not exactly always,' said the Doctor, with that precisian firmness which made him a delight at supper parties. 'Omniscience is an attribute of the Deity alone, and on more than one occasion in the course of my life I may perhaps have fallen slightly into error.'

'Not at all, sir! Not at all!' protested Boswell, with the utmost gravity, and his companion, crossing his hands complacently on his waistcoat, seemed for the first time to be shaken in conviction.

It was late in the afternoon when they came to Auchinleck, for Boswell had a score of plausible excuses to prolong the journey through a region where his family importance had ever more eloquent recognition the nearer they approached to Lugar Water. There were villages to show to Johnson – Tarbolton of the Beltane hill; Mauchline with its machicolated castle walls and crow-step gables; the wreck of Fail, whose friars

>   made guid kail
> On Fridays when they fasted,
> And never wanted gear enough,
> So long as their neighbours' lasted.

Montgomery woods; the river Ayr at Ballochmyle, loud-roaring through deep chasms overhung with foliage and moss – these the nominal occasions for innumerable divagations which were in truth more influenced by Boswell's sentimental interest in some scene reminiscent of youthful dalliance, or his vanity to show himself at mansion-houses with the famous lexicographer.

'One thing, sir, I should like to warn you of,' he said to Johnson as they drove to the front of what now, with an unconscious lapse into the custom of the country, he called Place Affleck – 'My father, as you know, is a Whig and a Presbyterian, and it were well to avoid discussion either on politics or the Church.'

'I shall certainly not be disquisitionary on topics disagreeable to a gentleman in whose house I shelter; especially I shall not be so to your father,' answered Johnson, with the finest condescension. 'Fortunately there are innumerable other themes on which I hope I may consider myself qualified with edification to dilate.'

Lord Auchinleck, though only a few years older than his guest, appeared in no way overawed by a visitation so momentous; on the contrary, he looked with a depreciatory eye and a grim pursed mouth of disapproval on the corpulent gentleman who had been taking James away from business, and who now rolled ox-like through the hall, already booming erudite opinions upon Scottish weather.

As he disappeard upstairs to repair his toilet, his hosts uneasily regarded one another.

'I wonder if he has his tawse with him?' said Lord Auchinleck. 'I think sometimes, Jamie, ye're gane gyte! First it was yon land-loupin' Corsican Paoli ye were traikin' after, and now it's ower the hills ayont Dunblane wi' this auld dominie that keepit a schule and ca'd it an academy. Your frien', I can see already, is just a hectorin', conceited schulemaister, still drum-majorin' bairns.'

And in spite of Mr Boswell's warning, the altercation came to pass. Five days' incessant rain, which amply justified the stranger's estimate of Scottish weather, held him prisoner in the house among the classic folios of Auchinleck. His ponderous figure seemed, to the eyes of his host, to swell and make the library smaller every day, as if he got unhallowed sustenance there between the common meals, a flatulent vampire diet from the mildewed tomes. There was a blink of sunshine on the Sabbath and the Boswells went to the kirk, but lofty Anglican disdain for what he called a chapel made the Doctor stay at home. Magnificently and immovably disposed in an easy-chair, over the edge of which his ampler parts seemed to roll like something viscous, he surveyed mankind from China to Peru, set everybody right on everything, and boomed – and boomed – and boomed. Lord Auchinleck, no trivial dialectician, and a man who had seen the world, not through the smoke of a coffee-room or the skylight window of an attic in Bolt Court, was early worsted in the fray, with a voice incapable of shouting down a man, as he said despairingly, 'that has been bellowin' a' his days, and would keep up practice on a grosset bush if he couldna get a human audience.' That the onerous task of entertaining such a guest should be shared by somebody, he invited guests to dinner; Dr Johnson found in one of them, the minister, Mr Dun, a sounding-board for loud prelections on the Druids, the Chaldeans, Gymnosophists of Ethiopia, Turditanes of Spain, Augurs of Rome, Apollo's priests in Greece, Phoebades and Phythonissae, their oracles and phantasms, but above all others that iniquitous high priest of Rome.

' 'Twixt Roman pope and English prelacy I never could see a chink ye could stick a knife in,' said Lord Auchinleck abruptly, and the fat was in the fire.

The war-horse snorted and let out a couple of buttons. '*Dum vitant stulti vitia in contraria currunt*,' he retorted. 'When fools avoid one vice they run into another of an opposite character, and your Covenanters in their zeal to abolish ritual have abolished beauty.'

'The graves of Peden and Cameron are there on the hills behind us, sir!' cried Auchinleck; 'and their death was beauteous as the rose.'

'The Presbyterian Church, sir, has not produced by the hands of its divines a single work of letters,' said Johnson.

'It is plain, sir, you have not read Durham on Galatians,' retorted Auchinleck.

'I have not, sir,' answered Johnson. 'Have you?' and got his answer in Lord Auchinleck's confusion. 'I should as soon read Cromwell on Terpsichore.'

'Praise God for Cromwell!' cried his lordship.

'What good did Cromwell ever do?' Dr Johnson asked.

'I'll tell ye that, man,' answered Auchinleck. 'He gart kings ken they had a lith in their necks. Pass up the bottle, James, and we'll drink to the confusion of all Jacobites.'

The post-chaise started off for Edinburgh in the morning. 'There's nae cure for the disease o' bein' a dominie,' said Lord Auchinleck to his son as they watched the servants packing the baggage. 'Your wife is right to be vexed at seein' ye dance at the end of a string in the hands o' yon big bear. Call yersel' a Boswell! It was wiser-like ye were attendin' to your proper business.'

James Boswell chuckled, gave a wink implying superhuman subtlety, and replied, 'That's all right, papa; he's really a splendid fellow if you once get used to him, and I see my way to make him into a book.'

'A book!' cried Auchinleck. 'Leviathan on a hook! The man's a giant, Jamie, and you're but a wee bit dwarf.'

'Just so, papa,' said Boswell, 'but a dwarf on the shoulders of a giant can see a good deal farther than the giant. Believe me, papa, he'll make a splendid book!'

MOSSGIEL RAB

Gilbert, in his shirt-sleeves, read a book – *The Life of Hannibal* – more to improve that douce mind of his than for amusement, seemingly, since he yawned at the turning of every page; and Blane, the ploughboy, mended harness. A north wind whooped in the spacious chimney, where a pot hung boiling low on the swee, and the trees, that sheltered Mossgiel steading, cried piteously as for entrance, rapping at the white-harled gable.

On such nights, Gilbert's brother felt, more poignantly than usual, his passion for the wild, his fierce impatience with the humdrum tenor of their peasant home. It was the fire that mainly lit the kitchen; a tallow candle guttering on the brace but gave to the wholesome glow of peat a wan complexion, a hint of the artficial, and to the poet a discontented thought of other chambers read about or seen through unshuttered windows momentarily, where numberless candles shone against sconces on the walls of the well-to-do. He cast a curious glance about him as he sat in a swither with his fingers on the laces of his shoes – at the low, stained rafters, the planked enclosures of the beds, the dresser of chipped blue delf, the sleeping collie, the bubbling pot, the studious brother, the industrious Blane; and the thought in his bosom came to his lips with no restraining – 'Gibbie! is this – is this, can ye tell me, our eternal doom?'

Gilbert, straightened his stooped back, and turned his fire-freckled face on Robert.

'What's the time?' said he.

Burns drew a watch from the fob of his breeches, glanced at the dial, snapped the words 'half-nine,' and strode to the pot that swung on the chimney chain. He lifted the lid, peered at the contents – tomorrow's dinner – and shut them from his view again with an iron clatter.

'Offal!' said he. 'Is that Hannibal yet ye're at? Was he fed, Gibbie, do ye think, on offal?'

'I would ca' nae guid meat offal, Rab,' said Gilbert. 'And if it had been offal at Capua it wad hae been better for Hannibal and his men. Half-nine? It's time we were bedded.'

The eyes of Burns fired deeply under their cliff of brow, the flambeaux of revolt; he grimaced and shrugged his shoulders. 'Half-nine,' said he, 'and bed! What's in the veins o' ye, Gib? – is't buttermilk? In mine, thank God! it's blood. I'm for nae stupor on a caff mattress in a loft at half-nine on a nicht like this so lang's there's men to be met at Poosie Nancy's. Here's you and General Hannibal, every line of him wide awake and thrang wi' tramping sodgers, and ye're ganting for your bed; and here's

Jock Blane cobbling brechams, content himsel' in the trams o' the dung-cart o' destiny – a kind o' patient cuddy! Please yersels, but I'm neither for bed nor brechams! Three-score years and ten's the allotted span; I misdoubt I'll see but the half o't, and six-and-twenty's gane. The lave o' my years are no' that lang that I'm ready to gae to bed at nine and lie like an auld maid chitterin' and listenin' to the win' – do ye hear't, Gibbie? Do ye here't, Jock? It's got the deil's own spite at puir Mossgiel, and we're in a bit box, buried under snaw, three nameless bodies, and twa wi' the disease o' dull contentment. As for me, I'm choking, and I'm aff to Mauchline!'

He threw a plaid about him, scrugged down his bonnet on his brow, and made for the door.

'Poosie Nancy's, I suppose?' said Gilbert. 'It's no' the best o' company ye'll get there.'

'At least,' said Burns, 'they're no ganting for their beds or cloutin' brechams for their ain necks, and they'll no' be buried before their time!' and he slammed the door behind him.

'Faith! he's in a droll key, Rab, the nicht,' said Blane, the ploughboy.

'It's pride,' said Gilbert helplessly; 'fair upsettin' vanity! Wealth's the warld's curse! He's awa' wi' his half-year's pay in his pouches – three pun' ten!'

Mossgiel lay high on the breast of the brae and Burns for a moment stood at the door of it to look on Kyle below him, blanched to a cold reclusive beauty by the snow. The sky was held by racing clouds, and the moon, at the full, fell giddily from space through the hurrying vapours, chased as in terror by her sweet young infant stars. Old treees overhung the dwelling, the tall haw-bushes made a hedge to shelter it; among them went the wind, that seemed to sweep the shire of Ayr of all its chilly elements and pile them, drift-white, in the wide quadrangle of the steading. Some sparks from the fire that Blane was banking for the night came up through the low chimney, and lived a moment – red aspiring little stars, that gave to the poet a fancy of his own and all men's sad futility; his heart played thud in his breast and he gasped with an emotion such as poets feel from things that may seem trivial to the world, but to the gifted have the import of a cataclysm. There was some spirit in the scene and hour – cold, pure, austere, remonstrant – that made him swither on the threshold, for he knew already that in the tavern he would find no higher uplift to his soul than came this moment from communion with the cleansed night. But still – but still, the sober face of the virtuous Gilbert ready for sleep, and the silence of the assiduous Blane, came back to him, and the sordid pot of tripe and thairm, and the dreary prospect of those waukrife hours in bed, with all his thoughts insurgent against slumber, and by comparison the barmy smells of Poosie Nancy's tavern, the feel of a pewter can, the gluck of poured ale, the loud dispute of hinds, and the admiration for his gifts of wit and clinking song-stuff, proffered an alternative that could not be resisted. He summoned the memory of other carousing nights to his weakening inclination for the ploy; stepped over the frozen duck-dub in the lane, and down between the mantled fields to the lighted village.

Upon these boozing peasants he made, in truth, but a rare intrusion. They felt half pleased and half disquieted, for though his presence was a kind of compliment, they had the start of him by several chappins, and they knew him for a man too apt to keep the crack on a level above the long-continued stretch of their ale-mused brains. His was the table-head, the fir-wood lug-chair; his the next round, his as many rounds as he cared to pay for; and the room of Poosie Nancy rang with a Bacchic symphony.

Before him, for a little, snow-white Kyle, the surging cloud and the moon intruded; in pauses of the trumpery conversation came across his mind that glance to the heart of things, that second's ecstasy he had found before the house on the brae, so that he almost rued the disposition that had brought him among this noisy crew. But one man had a story – not for parlours, witty, human, wicked, rich with the arterial blood of passion and grotesque of circumstance such as men heard then in Ayrshire even between the kirks; and another had a novel air with a ranting and resistless chorus, and the moon – the calm, clean, sovran moon – went down behind the clouds of vile tobacco, and over the remembered vision of the pure white fields was a mantle drawn, and the sound of the wind in the trees around Mossgiel was drowned in foolish chatter.

And yet he sought, as he sat among it, for those revelations of his loftier self; he drank with a deliberate purpose – not wholly for the warm sense of equality with these, his fellow-victims in the joke of Fate; for that rare elation, that confidence, that content, of which at times he had found the barley-fields possessed the magic key. Once he found it – in a thought that tore him from company, a thought that only briefly kept a concrete form in the brain of him, then broke in a thousand irridescent pieces, each as precious as the whole, never to be brought together into something rational – a joyous, heady gambol through centuries of sun and storm; song, women, and the old lost fields of the youth he had never properly known; a sense of warmth, well-being, and perfection.

They had sung, among them, these dear hinds, his brothers, whom so well he understood, and pitied, one of his own songs, and this was his happy hour! A fiddle jigged in his brain, and Poosie Nancy's reeking chamber was transfigured.

Only for a space. The hour was late, right well had they scourged the gantrys for their ale; the morning hurried towards the fields of Ayr, and a woman stood beseeching for her husband, or his wages, at the door.

The man, the very boon companion who had started Burns's song. hung his head, and the shrill high voice of the vintner could be heard behind the wife's pathetic figure, proclaiming the respectability of her house, and her helplessness to quench the drouth of any man with the fate to belong to Tarbolton.

'Vive la bagatelle! hae ye no' the money, Will?' said Robert Burns; and the man said, 'No' a doit!'

'That's bad!' said Burns, with his fingers combing back the dank black locks from his burning brow; 'ay, man, that's damn bad! If I was a married man' – he laughed a little bitterly – 'if I was a married man, I would likely still be Rabbie Burns; here, wife, it's a' that's left; it's aff-and-on thirty shillings; your man's a bonny singer, and I'm for hame.'

It was dawn when he came to the farm-house door, and Blane, the plough-boy, beat his arms across his breast ere he turned to mucking the byre. Kyle fell away below in billows of grey, and the cocks were crowing. The smoke of a green fire floated from the chimney-head, and the countenance of Gilbert, blameful and questioning, filled the door of the trance.

'Ye've had a nicht of it, Rab!' said he.

'I've had that, Gib!' said his brother peaceably.

'And what did it cost ye?' asked the keeper of the frugal conscience of Mossgiel.

'It cost me exactly three pun' ten, and cheap at the money,' said the poet.

'On drink!' said Gilbert, horrified.

'Sae be't!' said Robert; 'whether or no', I'll get the name o't.'

BURNS AND CLARINDA

The light of the afternoon came flooding through the windows; bathed Miss Nimmo's parlour in a golden radiance, and gave a mellow, pensive tone even to the poet's reverie. He sat with his face in the shadow, for he had not yet got rid of his rustic fears of these fine Edinburgh ladies, the very elegance of whose apartments contributed to his uneasiness. With any man living he could hold his own, but these unusual women – calm, confident, unabashed before the fervour of his eye; moving like swans, conversing like schoolmasters upon abstract things, witty, prone to mocking smiles – they were the very devil! He feared yet he adored them, since they had for him abundantly the one thing dear to poets and lovers – Mystery.

'A penny for your thoughts, Mr Burns,' said the charming Mrs Maclehose, showing her drift-white teeth in a smile that seven or eight years ago had done terrific execution among the bucks at Edinburgh balls.

'A poet's thoughts are surely worth more than that, Nancy,' said Miss Nimmo.

'It all depends,' said Mrs Maclehose archly; 'he might be thinking us very uninteresting after meeting such sublime examples of our sex as the Duchess of Gordon.'

'A fine woman!' said Burns with some enthusiasm. 'In her company I forget that she's a duchess and feel myself a duke.'

'It'll likely be her awccent,' drawled Mrs Maclehose, in a clever imitation of the Duchess's uncompromising Scots, and the charming mimic fell a little in his estimation; he liked his women, above all things, kind.

'It's an accent that some of the greatest in the land have respected from the lips of the Duchess of Gordon,' said Burns, with a curious tension of the jaw and a flash of the eyes. 'I'm a Scot myself.'

'The very greatest!' said Mrs Maclehose, grasping the generous widths of her gown and dropping him a courtesy, half ironic.

She was a lovely woman, Mrs Maclehose, and Burns, with the sense of sex as keen as his poetic vision, regarded her in this playful mood with his old illusion that here might be the long-desired Ideal – the woman of whom one could never weary. She was short in stature, just the right height for the head to fit in the nook of his shoulder; with hands and feet small and delicate; fair complexion; flushed with health, with dancing eyes and a soft vivacious utterance. An air of elegance, refinement, grace, seemed to respire from her presence, and she could rise like a bird, and instantly, to the loftiest, most poetic fancy he cared to express. They did not breed that kind of woman in the shire of Ayr; at all events, he had never had the chance to meet them.

And she admired him – that with Burns, as with all sons of art, was the main thing! He knew she did, and what was better still, he knew it was not wholly for his poetry, of which she generally preferred what shrewder judgment would have told her were the poorest stanzas. She admired him for his fame and for his story, and most of all she plainly admired him as a Man. So far as women were concerned, the poet would sooner be loved for his legs than for his lyrics.

She admired him so much that he would have been quite at his ease with her, were it not for the presence of their hostess, Miss Nimmo, who too obviously realised the situation, and was amused at something.

'What are you smiling at?' asked Burns, when the visitor was gone in a rustle of silk, leaving a wake of lavender perfume, and for the poet a sense of deprivation. Miss Nimmo had come from the door with that sly and merry aspect which women assume when they mean to betray the weaknesses or follies of their sex.

'Nancy has asked me to take you to a dish of tea at her house on Thursday,' she replied primly.

'I'll go!' said Burns emphatically.

'Of course, of course!' said the quiet little lady; 'I kent you would go, and I said as much. Nancy's raptures were surely not to be altogether thrown away on you! You must be the proud man to excite such sudden adoration in our impressionable sex.'

'A fine woman!' said Burns fervently.

'H'm! So's the Duchess of Gordon,' was the reply of Miss Nimmo. 'Do you know, I think, so far as women are concerned, you're gey and easy pleased,' and she smiled up at him with her shrewd, pawky, plain little face, sadly disconcerting him, for he was not used to the subtleties of women who knew the game.

'What do you mean?' he asked suspiciously.

'I was thinking,' said the old lady, 'of a girl called Jean Armour,' and she looked at him with penetrating and unflinching eyes.

'Easy pleased,' said he, with a flush appearing on his pallid countenance. 'Madam, if you knew Jean Armour ——'

'My rural swain,' said the lady, rapping him on the fingers with her fan, 'you'll maybe can write braw poetry, but there are things you do not understand. When I talked about your being easily pleased, I was not passing judgment on the girl I name, whom I have never had the honour to see, but thinking of what is due to her, and of the way that you forget, and of your readiness to interest yourself in any other bonny face that comes the way. It's wonderful to me, who ken women, how you clever men can be glamoured by a little flattery from any designing creature with a languishing eye –'

'You are hardly fair to your friend or loyal to your sex,' said the poet, relieved and laughing.

'I like my friend in spite of her failings,' said Miss Nimmo, taking snuff. 'I have plenty of my own; and she was made by nature for the beguiling of silly men-bodies like yourself. And I am so loyal to my sex that I cannot think but with compassion of the lassie Jean, in Ayr.'

'I can think of her mysel',' said Burns, abruptly and uneasily. 'I hope you haven't mentioned her to Mrs Maclehose?'

'It wouldna make muckle odds if I did – to Mrs Maclehose.'

'Who is she? What is she?' eagerly pursued the poet.

'An honest married woman who has had a family of four,' replied Miss Nimmo, with a faint malicious smile, and the face of the poet fell a little – a family of four was something of a staggerer!

'A widow?' he asked indifferently, remembering there had been no mention of a Mr Maclehose.

'In a fashion,' said Miss Nimmo. 'Grass. Her husband is in the Indies, and she hopes he'll bide there. Meantime it is plain she wants to keep herself in practice at the gallivanting. I'm touched at her raptures over your book; she must have raced through it unco fast, for she borrowed my copy at nine o'clock last night when she heard there was a chance she might see you here.'

'She's clever enough to understand even my poor book at a gallop,' said Burns, pulling down his embroidered waistcoat. 'What time did you say was her tea?'

Miss Nimmo sighed. 'Hech, sirs! and this is genius!' said she. 'My Nancy's got a head like a fizzy drink, and a tongue like the clatter-bane o' a duck, and the Bard o' Caledon, forgettin' the "true pathos and sublime" he writes so bonnily about, is just as easily made dizzy wi' her arts as if he were a writer's clerk. Ye read French?'

'Yes,' said the bard; and she plucked a volume from the table and directed his attention to Voltaire's counsel to the Duchess of Richelieu:

> Ne vous aimez pas trop; c'est moi qui vous en prie,
> C'est le plus sûr moyen de vous aimer toujours.
> Il faut mieux être amis tout le temps de la vie
> Que d'être amants pour quelques jours.

'Quite so!' said the poet; 'it's long since I learned that philosophy for mysel', but what o'clock did ye say was the lady's tea?'

An injured knee kept Burns to his lodgings for some days after this, and he missed the chance of drinking tea with Mrs Maclehose, on whose charms of person and mind he had the better opportunity for musing. One evening, after a succession of blythe and roystering visitors, in a state of pleasant exaltation he wrote the lady a letter, drafting it carefully first in the very best style of *The Elegant Letter Writer*, on which he and Gilbert had one time modelled their correspondence:

> I do love you, if possible, still better for having so fine a taste and turn in poesy [he wrote]. I have again gone wrong in my usual unguarded way, but you may erase the word, and put esteem, respect, or any other tame Dutch expression you please in its place. I believe there is no holding converse or carrying on correspondence with an amiable woman – much less a gloriously amiable fine woman, without some mixture of that delicious passion whose most devoted slave I have more than once had the honour of being.

'That's the style for Mistress Blue-stocking!' he exclaimed complacently, as he read it over. 'It wouldna be muckle use wi' Jean,' and then, resuming his pen, he wrote these memorable words:

> Oh Clarinda! shall we not meet in a state, some yet unknown state of being where the lavish hand of plenty shall minister to the highest wish of benevolence, and where the chill north wind of prudence shall never blow over the flowery fields of enjoyment! If we do not, man is made in vain.

'By the Lord!' said he, 'that's genius!' and taking another toddy went well pleased with himself to bed.

Next morning he read the still-unposted letter, and laughed. 'Oh, Robin! Robin! whatna Machiavelli!' he exclaimed. 'And whatna dulcet key! "Lavish hand of plenty", by Gad! "North wind of prudence"! "Flowery fields of enjoyment"! Keep us! what transparent sophistry! It would make even Jean laugh, and Miss Nimmo, if she saw it, would be unco nippy. Oh, Rab! ye write a bonny letter!'

He took a penny from his pocket and tossed it.

'Heads,' said he when it fell. 'The letter goes, with north winds and flowery fields and a' the rest o't; I wouldna say but it's just the thing for Nancy Maclehose.'

And so began the Clarinda correspondence.

✝

THE MAKING OF TAM O' SHANTER

It was a dirty day in mid-November. The roads of Nithsdale, after weeks of rain, were fetlock-deep with mire, and the gauger's pony, ten parishes and two hundred miles of roads like these to her credit for the week, was very weary. If she smelt her oats at Ellisland, she did not show it in the usual way by the quickened pace and the eager shudder of the withers; she had fallen from a canter to a trot, from a trot to a walk. The steam rose from her flanks, and the flakes of froth were washed from off her neck by the rain that fell continuously; her head hung low. On treeless slopes, seen dimly against vague horizons on that weeping afternoon, or rising over sky-lines thinly fringed with starved, wild, haggard pines; or again in the scanty winter woods, the pony and her rider might have seemed to an observer, had there been one, like the last survivors of some hopeless sally in the endless fight of man against unconquerable wilds. Sometimes she turned a sad complaining eye upon her master when she felt his heel.

He was weary himself – sick-tired to the very soul! It was not altogether the weariness of the flesh, for once that day, for a too brief hour, he had been mighty. Back beyond Dunscore, he had had the idea for a song at the sight of a girl who smiled upon him from a wayside steading, and suddenly he had felt the old fond rapture; wakened and transported – not by the girl, for she was soon forgotten, but by that heady gush of song creation that tore through his brain at times, and made him feel eternal and gigantic. He had not found the words for the song beyond 'Ae fond kiss and then we sever', but he had the sweet low wail of it somewhere in his head, and was content to give every pulse of his heart to the emotion that he knew from experience he should easily find the words for later on.

There and then he was not weary. There and then was he invincible, for to him without research had come the true divine elation, that exaltation of the soul he sometimes sought for in the bottom of a glass with old companions, only to find a coarser substitute. 'Twas then he knew he would not die, he could not die; that he was older than the hills, and would outlast them; that he had been admitted to the Secret; that he partook of God's delight in that ancient hour when He was happy, and in one evening filled the empty space with shining stars! The rare joy of his senses went to his very blood and bone, so that his limbs became like iron; he could have split the oak with Cyclop fingers, or hurled the boulders of the Nith over the Lowther Hills!

Now, in this miry afternoon, home-coming, an utter weariness possessed him, holding him in body less than in his spirit. Round him was a landscape that in summer and in sunshine always filled his mornings with a gladness to contemplate, but was now become most gloomy and portentous. The dripping little woods were full of creaking boughs and lawless shadows; the mist-wrapped braes, appearing so inimical and strange; the river so inhuman and so out of key with any mood of conflict, helpless, swirling to the Solway just because it must, without volition, as men swirl giddily through space and time – these fed the stark rebellion of his soul at the fate that mastered him. And he was come in sight of Ellisland, his farm. The place brought to his soul a pang as if the memory of an ancient sin had stung him. There it was, its steading bowered in trees, near the verge of the gravelly precipice that sank to the river's side, a poet's farm, God help him! – a visionary's choice, as if a man could harvest crops of shilfy-song or winnow a rent from evening sunshine!

Clarke, his ploughman, came ganting – suspicious sign! – from the barn to take in his horse. Burns put the reins in his hands and looked at him for a moment like a man that burst with tidings.

'Did ye ever hear tell o' Sisyphus, Will?' said he, and the ploughman stared at his master.

'Man!' said he, 'I think there used to be an auld packman wi' that by-name that gaed aboot Kirkmahoe when I was there –'

'Na, na, Will, that wasna my Sisyphus,' said Burns. 'Ye can aye let down a pack, and a pack's something wiselike, but Sisyphus was a king in Corinth, and now he is in Hell, for doom to push a bowlder o' stane for ever up a hill where it winna bide. There's a lot mair joyous recreations I could think o' for a king, that ance was happy, and can mind, that still has all his faculties about him, and beholds, at his labour, the accursed truth. My God! My God!' The cry burst from him like a cry of Calvary, and over his fields he looked, his sodden cauldrife fields, so helplessly unprofitable, and at his cottage with its dripping thatch already rotting, and at his fowls that sheltered in the byre door. In his eyes flamed wild rebellion.

'The Globe at Dumfries again!' thought the ploughman, turning to lead in the mare.

Burns held him for a moment with his hand upon his sleeve. 'Tell me this, Will,' he demanded. 'Are ye a contented man? Do ye sleep sound at nicht? Do ye mind auld things? Do ye ever think ye micht be better? Do ye see yoursel' the actual man ye are? Do ye meet wi' mony folk that understand ye? Have ye ever had but a glimpse o' a' the possible joys o' life, and seen them gaun by ye like Nith down there, wi' you stuck helpless on the bank?'

The questions poured forth from him in a spate; he stood with his plaid half-loosened, as eager in his manner as if his fate were in the answer.

'O, I'm no complainin',' said the ploughman, whose mind had grasped but little of this fierce, bewildering catechism. 'I'm no' complainin', I aye tak' my meat, and sleep like a peerie.'

Burns looked in the broad red face with envy, his own pallid and drawn with inward pain.

'Ye're the lucky man!' said he, and then he started, for from the cottage came an infant's cry – piteous, pathetic, the protest of the soul that is torn from heaven for a space of years to suffer trial. A myriad fresh emotions shook the gauger as he listened, and last of all a gush of tenderness.

'In wi' the meare!' he said, and slapped her kindly on the shoulders.

Next day was Saturday. He stayed at home.

'What Sisyphus was this ye were haiverin' to Will Clarke about last nicht, Rab?' asked his wife. 'He's been at Sisyphus a' this mornin', and jalousin' it's some new sang ye are makin'. I tell't him I never heard tell o' Sisyphus.'

'And I wish to the Lord I had never heard tell o' him either, Jean,' said Burns. 'He's just a chiel in a book, that had a gey ill task to do, and did the best he could, but could never get it done, and kent he couldna.'

'Are ye sure it was a man, Rab?' asked Jean Armour. 'It's liker to have been his wife,' and she started to rock the cradle, humming a country air.

Burns wrapped his plaid about him, for the day, though dry, was bitter cold. He went down before the house on a path that wound to a slip of holm, and walked by the river's bank, here overhung by trees. The melancholy of the night before was gone completely; the irrevocable past and Ellisland's cold, clammy acres – 'the riddlings of the world' – were no longer like a black dog on his back; he was even in a mood to rejoice that after all he had made a poet's choice, if not a farmer's, when he picked on Ellisland. To his mind came a promise he had made to Grose the week before that he should write a poem about the Carrick witches.

Now, it was the way of Burns, when he would spur emotion to give truth and passion to his lines, to seek, not through his later years for the inspiration, but in those golden irrecoverable hours that seemed to have concluded with abruptness, when he turned his back upon the land of Ayr. Never in youth had he been, strictly speaking, happy; sordid needs and fierce rebellions; shame, ambition, inability, and pride, made, in these early times, the texture of his being, and weighing now with then, his intellect would have convinced him that his present state was vastly more enjoyable. But the heart, and not the head, was ever his adjudicator, and his heart invested certain transient hours by Doon with incommunicable grandeur, for no other reason than that there and then he had been innocent and young. All Kyle, in such reflections, was invested with a fond and pensive charm for whose surrender the most princely future could not make amends. He loved her very stones!

From Edinburgh parlours, Highland and Border wanderings, communion with his social and intellectual betters, he had nothing learned that was not his already when he walked behind the plough, and all the fervours, all the sweet illusions and enchantments which he gave a voice in song were harvested in Ayrshire.

Babbling river! – babbling Nith! – a fonder cry, a sweeter chuckle on the stones was in old Doon whereto this water of Dumfries recalled him. As on many a night, awake, an exile, and remembering, he followed her again through all her courses, from the great dark muirland reservoir, by deep ravines and Castle Downan's fairy dells, down into Alloway and the bay of Ayr. It was the sound of distant waters, and estranged, that sang through his imaginative ear this afternoon; the river Ayr herself swept through his retrospect – how blest was he to have been born upon her banks!

Old homes, each with a ghost of him yet tenanting its silence, still were standing where he left them, faithful to the streams he had deserted – Mount Oliphant, Lochlie, Mossgiel; and folk he knew who had been young with him, still breathed the native air.

Thus wrapped in the essential sentiment of youth and home from which the vivifying spirit of his music always came, he turned his inward gaze upon the earliest scene that had impressed his childhood eerilie – the ruin of Kirk Alloway, and in a flash beheld its possibilities for the thing he sought.

The old Kirkoswald legend, and the man of Shanter Farm! The story cried for more of fantasy and fun than it ever got in Mauchline taverns, and Douglas Graham was manifestly designed by Heaven to be its chief protagonist.

The sun, as it were in benediction on his essay, burst through the surf of clouds and poured illumination. Burns paced beside the river, muttering,

When chapmen billies leave the street,
And drouthy neebors, neebors meet,
As market days are wearing late –

'By God! I have it! It's the night and it's the weather, and the right lilt for a body startin' on an unco journey wi' nae convoy except a wheen o' witches. Mirk lanes and dreepin' thickets; glaur underfoot; an angry wife at hame; an awfu' lowe in the aisle of Alloway; the Brig o' Doon to cross, and Shanter seven miles awa!

– market days are wearing late,
And folks begin to tak' the gate.
And we sit –

'And we sit, and we sit – now what would we be sittin' daein'? Are ye
there, Shanter? Ay, there ye are, auld Truepenny! What would ye be sittin'
late for? Bowsing, of course!

And we sit bowsing at the nappy,
And getting fou and unco happy –

'Rab, man! ye rascal, ye're fair started! If gaugin' was as easy!'
For hours he paced the sheltered holm attended by the shapes of men
and fantasy created by his will. Below, the Nith went rushing to the
Solway, in ignorance of the appointed end, but fearless. Green plovers
wheeled and cried above his fields; when the sun was whelmed in clouds,
the air was cold. But not for Burns, who, for his fever, loosed the grey
plaid and gave his bosom to the wind. Tears came to him, and laughter; he
fell on each fancy like a prize and clutched it till it took a shape in cadence
and in rhyme; more often better blessed as are the noblest artists, thought
and words were born together in his brain.
A hundred times he went back on the lines completed, sometimes to
enrich or chasten, but his aim was rather to maintain the whole in tone, as
clouds are, and the forests, the colours of bays and ships, the sounds of
storm, the choiring of the cherubim. And his imagination the more surely
mastered him at every repetition, so that he shivered when

The wind blew as 'twould blawn its last,
The rattling showers rose on the blast,
The speedy gleams the darkness swallowed;
Loud, deep and lang, the thunder bellowed.

He wept at his image of brevity of pleasure that

– like the snaw, falls in the river,
A moment white then lost for ever.

He saw before him

– Doon pour all its floods,

and only for a moment woke to see that it was the Nith that thundered at
the bend.

The sun was setting on the distant hills when the poet was done; a
rookery went clanging home, and to his bosom flew content. To his mind
came that great ease, that satisfaction which attends on inspiration met
with open arms, not shunned for fear or indolence, nor for a second set
aside until the work is done. 'Twas done! 'Twas good! He felt himself a
king, and this was his golden hour. From the stuff of dreams, from the
impalpable air, he had fashioned human characters, had made a little
world of Scottish people with all their whims and humours, mystery and
fears. Oh! he loved them, drunk or sober – he, their creator, he that
wrought the miracle and brought them from the void. But more he joyed
that he had, in their making, maintained the deeper, greater, more abiding
thing – the Symbol, the essential soul that makes all that is great in the art
of man a microcosm, a miniature of the world – the world that cries with
vast night-deep and interstellar tragedies, and stuns to think on, yet is no
bigger than a nut! Ellisland's cold bankrupt acres? – Bah! How little did
they matter! The glimpses of what had seemed a Paradise – Edinburgh
and Clarinda, and the parlours lost? – a fig for them! The narrow ways,
the hard, poor years in front, the shrinking store of money? – what
matter if he died a beggar, he had lived this hour!

He went back by the river side, and in where the cradle rocked.

'Jean,' he said, 'I have made a poem.'

THE DEMOCRAT

The stores and arms of the smuggler's brig which the gauger Burns had boarded, sword in hand, on the previous day in the shallows of the Solway were being sold by auction in Dumfries. Cutlasses and brandy-kegs, muskets and marlin-spikes, were rapidly knocked down to peaceable burgesses who did not very much want them, but were rendered recklessly acquisitive by the humorous sallies of Jock Pender the auctioneer, who was using the smuggler skipper's pistol for a gavel, and kept a couple of men from Taylor's inn going briskly round the crowd with copious supplies of spirits, ale, and cake.

'And now, gentlemen,' said the auctioneer, 'we come at last to the bulky stuff; thae four cannon – genuine Carron; see the mark o' the foundry on them for yoursel's. For a nice bit decoration to a house wi' a plot o' grun in front, there's naething beats a pair o' cannon. They're a' the vogue the now in London. There they are – thirty-two-pounders, scoops, sponges, rammers; mounted a' complete! I've never had a finer lot o' stuff gae through my hands. They're worth twenty pounds apiece if they're worth a penny, but I'll no' ask that for them; wha bids five?'

'Shillin's,' cried Willie Armstrong the persistent humorist, and Pender turned upon him with derision.

'Man, Will,' he said, 'they're worth that just to look at; what *you* want's a pen-gun and a wheen peas to pap sparrows wi'. Come awa' wi' a wise-like offer.'

'What the deil would I dae wi' them?' asked Armstrong, munching cake.

'Ye could stick them down before your door to frighten aff your creditors,' suggested the auctioneer, and the humorist withdrew discomfited to solace himself with draughts of eleemosynary ale.

Burns, who had never been to bed since he left the boarding party on the previous day, stood by the carronades with a foot upon the trunnion; a man with the heart to gush with tenderness for mouse or daisy ruined by his coulter, he yet had a love of arms, and kept upon his desk in the little closet in the Vennel the dirk of Balmerino. Arms were to him not cruel things for slaughtering, but the tools of valour, instruments of liberty, accoutrements of romance. Here they were, the carronades, grotesquely out of place in Pender's yard; squat, dumpy, silent, gaping with open throats for the breath of war. Nobody made an offer. He searched the faces round him for a sign that any one experienced his feelings at the sight of the degraded guns – not beautiful in themselves, but for him evocative of a sentiment as keen as he could get from morions and hauberks; he saw indifference; the good folk of Dumfries looked on this ordnance as so much useless junk.

'Three pounds for the lot,' he rapped out, slapping his hand upon a muzzle.

'Thank ye, Mr Burns!' said the auctioneer. 'Three pounds I'm offered for the lot; ony advance on three pounds? Going – going – gone!' And he brought the pistol down on the head of a harness cask.

'Oh, the devil!' said Burns, taken aback to have his impetuous bid so soon accepted. 'What am I to dae wi' a battery in the Vennel?'

'Ye can gie them to the French,' suggested the auctioneer, and the face of the poet lightened.

'Faith I can!' said he. 'Vive la Révolution! I'll pack them aff the morn's morn,' and he met the astonished and reproachful gaze of Bailie M'Kie with amused defiance.

The sale went on; the Bailie sidled up to Burns on the outskirts of the crowd and set about a delicate remonstrance. He was perhaps the only man within the burgh qualified to do it without offence, for he came from Ayr, was old enough to have been once the poet's father's friend, and the poet and he, at many a Sunday skailin' of the kirk, cracked fondly about Carrick, both convinced it was the bonniest region in the realm of Scotland.

'I havena seen ye for a fortnight gane, Robert,' he began, scooping up a pinch of snuff with a tiny ivory ladle. 'I hear that besides chasin' the runners, ye've been at Mossgiel wi' your brother Gilbert. How's the mother?'

'Gettin' gey frail,' said Burns sadly. 'I went up ane's errand just to see her. Ye wouldna ken her, Bailie – crined awa to a shadow! But still the pride o' life and the vanity o' the eye in her, thank God! As particular about the piping o' her mutches as she ever was. Man, I wish I had her spunk!'

'Ah, dear me!' said the Bailie pensively. 'I mind o' Agnes on her marriage day; she was a dashing one! H'm! we're a' gettin' on in years. And what way's Gilbert? Is he keepin' fine?'

'Oh, Gilbert's strugglin' at it! Ye ken yoursel' what Mossgiel is? – a gey cauld clarty hole; there's nae fineness in't for ony tenant, no, nor in ony place in Ayrshire but for landlords.'

'Yes, yes, I understand,' said Bailie M'Kie. 'Too true, Robert! Too true! But the market's risin'. And cauld and clarty, or no' cauld and clarty, I must say mysel' I aye liked Mossgiel.'

'I'm like that myself about it,' said the poet. 'It broke my heart, God d——n it! but in these days I was free, and no' a slave o' Geordie's, rummaging auld women's cellars. Besides that, it was Ayrshire, and no' so many gutsy money-bags gaun on the Mauchline plainstanes as in this Dumfries. Did ye ever see a town wi' mair respect for Mammon or mair terror o' a man reputed to hae Whiggish sentiments? They're beginnin' to think that I have horns! Ye're magistrate o' a bonny toon, Bailie!'

Bailie M'Kie snuffed nervously. 'About thae cannons, Robert,' he remarked. 'It's none o' my affair perhaps, but I kent your folk and I have a great respect for ye, so I hope ye're no' in earnest about sendin' thae things to the French. The Supervisor would be sure to hear o't.'

Burns shrugged his shoulders. 'Bailie,' said he, 'I have nae doubt that he will; there's a lot o' sneck-drawers about Dumfries to clype a' my political indiscretions to Corbet, but I canna help it, I could never be discreet. I abominate the very word; it has a Hanoverian smell. I ken fine a' the Corbies o'Dumfries are down on me because they understand I'm Jacobin, because I said George Washington was a better man that Pitt – and so he is, a thousand times! – and because I read the "Gazetteer".'

'Whisht! that's a' right!' whispered the Bailie, with a timid glance around to see that they were not overheard. 'I whiles read the "Gazetteer" mysel', and ye ken I'm as Whig as onything – in reason, Robert, in reason! but you're in the excise, drawin' your seventy pounds a year frae Geordie; ye should keep a calm sough and let independent men like Dr Maxwell or John Syme rant sedition. Think what ye like, man, but keep your mouth steeked; that's my advice to you, Robert!' and again he drenched himself with maccabaw, and turned away with apprehension that some gentry from the outskirts of the burgh were regarding them suspiciously.

Burns seized him by the shoulder. 'That's the real sneck-drawin' policy, Bailie,' he said, 'and I'm no' fit for it. The guns are gaun to France the morn's mornin':

> Heard ye o' the Tree o' France,
>   And wot ye what's the name o't?
> Around it a' the patriots dance,
>   Weel Europe kens the fame o't.
> It stands where ance the Bastille stood –
>   A prison built by kings, man,
> When Superstition's hellish brood
>   Kept France in leading-strings, man.

He clung to the arm of the affrighted magistrate while he hummed the unholy verse, then released him with a laugh and went home for dinner.

Sure enough, the cannons went next morning with a letter from the poet to the French Convention. The fact was bruited round the town before the twelve-hours' dram. The merchant folk were dubious that the prank was rather daring even for a harum-scarum poet; the gentry of the burgh were disgusted. He felt that week a polar rigour in the air; his closest friends were desperately busy; they were not to be found even of an evening at the Globe. 'It's silly! Downricht silly!' said M'Kie one evening to him, having risked a first-rate civic reputation, even the prospect of the Provost's chain, by sneaking in the dusk to the poet's domicile. 'I warned ye it was rank sedition and worse than that, it was throwin' awa guid money, for it's no to be expected that the French 'll get the guns.'

'That's what I told him!' said Jean Armour. 'Three pounds thrown awa on silly nonsense! But Rab's sae heidstrong!'

'Ye've made an awfu' hash o't, Robert,' said the Bailie, 'and ye're bound to hae Collector Mitchell down upon ye. Everybody's talkin' o' your rebel principles and sayin' ye're a dangerous man, prepared to see even Britain go to wreck and ruin. I ken better, bein' a Mauchline man, and what I thought was that ye might come up tomorrow night to the Masons' meetin' and set things right sae far as possible wi' a stave o' the patriotic.'

'What kind o' stave?' the poet asked, smiling.

'Oh, ony kind o' trumpet stuff would serve for the occasion; ye could slap a couple o' stanzas up in half a jiffy; I would get them printed aff and circulated round.'

'I daresay that!' said Burns. 'Most kind of you! But I'm no' gaun to buy the gudewill o' Dumfries wi' patriotic stanzas made to order, Bailie, and your dainty bit plan would mak' me angry if it hadna got its comic side.'

'Well, tak' my word for't, Robert,' said the disappointed Bailie, 'ye've made a bonny hash o' things, and may say "fareweel" to the Friars Carse folk, Craigdarroch, Lawrie, and the ladies o' Woodley Park.'

'Farewell and fair-good-e'en to them if that be so!' said Burns with a flashing eye; 'I may doff my hat to them at times but no' my politics.'

Bailie M'Kie was right too; only the tradesmen and artisans – Pyats as they onetime called them – could remain his friends. As in defiance, his political demeanour grew more boldly individual as time went on, and one night in the theatre when 'God save the King' was played he sat and kept his hat on. 'Turn him out!' 'Shame, Burns!' cried the loyal citizens. Next day he walked the street alone, shunned by all but a few reckless revolutionaries, regarded with eyes askance.

He clearly realised the situation; now the air was worse than polar, having a sepulchral chill. Men who were proud to be seen walking with him some months ago transparently jinked now into quite inappropriate shops when they saw him coming. The most illuminating evidence of the state of things was to be seen in the ridiculous alarm of Brown, the saddler, who, coming hurriedly out of his shop with his brattie on to seek refreshment in a tavern across the way, turned and fled back like a startled hen at the very sight of Burns, whom he had so often joined in a post-meridian dram.

'Brown, too!' said the poet to himself with bitterness. 'Well, poor soul! he has to think of his Dalswinton customers! And I should hae a bell about my neck – a leper's bell to let a' respectable, canny merchant-bodies ken that I'm on the street.'

One man crossed and spoke to him – young Grierson, whom once he had befriended in a smuggling affair, a fellow with no character to lose. 'Ye're takin' the air, Mr Burns?' he said politely, and the poet smiled a little ruefully.

'Ye see I'm welcome to as much of it as can be got on this side of the street,' he said; 'there's none of my fine friends over there inclined to share it.' The ladies of Woodley Park and half a dozen lairds had that moment crossed the causeway to the other side with the obvious intention to avoid him.

'I thought ye were maybe makin' a sang,' said Grierson sympathetically.

Burns shrugged his shoulders. 'I got the drift o' ane to an auld air just now,' he answered:–

Policy parts good company.

The honest folk o' Dumfries are a' content to tak' the shady side o' the street because a Republican rogue tak's the liberty o' strollin' in the sun.'

'It's thae d——n guns o' yours!' explained young Grierson impetuously. 'What way do ye no' deny ye ever sent them?'

'It would be a lee if I did,' said Burns. 'I have lee'd wi' a glass, and lee'd – God help me! – wi' a lass, but I canna, drunk or sober, lee about my heart's convictions. Well, *vogue la galère!* – and that's French for ye, Jamie – come on and hae a dram!'

'Over to the Inn?' said Grierson agreeably.

'Nay, nay, young James! nae inns for us to-day! Too many o' my friends are there. Do ye ken Grizzel Baillie's ballad? –

His bonnet stood ance fu' fair on his brow,
His auld ane looked better than mony ane's new;
But now he lets't wear ony way it will hing,
And casts himself dowie upon the corn bing.

O were we young, as we ance hae been,
We sud hae been galloping doun on yon green,
And linking it ower the lily-white lea, –
And werena my heart light I wad dee!

'Only my heart's no' light, James; that's where the ditty fails me. . . . Where in a' the world are thae folk crowdin'?'

'Then ye havena heard the news!' cried Grierson, astonished. 'We're gaun to war wi' France; she threatens to invade us, and these are Volunteers. I joined mysel' an hour ago!'

When Burns got home to his house in the Vennel, Jean, his wife, was baking scones.

'What's that on your hat?' said she; it had a bow of coloured ribbons.

'Great news!' he cried, elated. 'The French are goin' to fight us, and I've joined the Volunteers. I wish to the Lord I had back my cannons!'

'Three pounds! And the children needin' boots! Ye're a braw poet, but there's whiles ye're awfu' stupid, Robert!' said Jean Armour. 'And the French are goin' to fight us, are they? When are the puir deluded bodies goin' to start?'

'The sooner the better so far as I'm concerned,' said Burns. 'I'll be better wi' a gun than at the gaugin'. But the idiots up the toon imagine' – and he laughed – 'that I'm no patriot!'

'If that's the case,' said his wife as she cut the scones upon the griddle, 'they canna hae read a great deal o' your poetry.'

9
Jaunty Jock and Other Stories (1918)

INTRODUCTION

†

Munro's first literary reputation was made as a short-story writer with 'The Lost Pibroch' and the short-story form engaged him throughout much of his career. In March 1918 he wrote to Blackwoods asking if they were interested in publishing a volume of short stories which he described as:

> *... real Munroesque Highland and Lowland romantic yarns which in the past 12 years or so I have published fugitively. I have not yet decided on a general title, but one of the tales is called 'Jaunty Jock' and that might, in the present circumstances, be an irresistible title.*

The present circumstances being, of course, the war and the public focus on Scottish soldiers – the 'Jocks'.

The eleven stories that make up the collection date from at least 1902. Munro's diary records that in one week in July 1902 he wrote two of the stories in the collection 'The Silver Drum' and 'Copenhagen'. Similarly 'The Silver Cup' and 'The Scottish Pompadour' are recorded in the diary as each occupying him for three days in 1910. In view of other suggestions about the painstaking slowness of Munro's fictional creativity these stories seem to have been swiftly produced.

When the collection was published in November 1918 it was greeted with enthusiasm. The reviewer in the Glasgow Herald *observed:*

> *'Jaunty Jock' is a model of compression. Mr Munro in these stories seems to employ the method of the pointillist painter: there are many colours in the detail, splashes of humour and grimness; and every stroke tells, every detail has its essential place in the structure.*

After commenting on the individual stories the reviewer concluded: '"Jaunty Jock", like his first literary adventure, "The Lost Pibroch", reveals Mr Munro as a master of the short story.'

Munro's friend, R. B. Cunninghame Graham, wrote to him in December 1918 with warm praise, particularly for the story 'Young Pennymore', which he described as 'very fine and tragic'.

We have selected from this collection the title story, 'Jaunty Jock', and Cunninghame Graham's favourite, 'Young Pennynore'.

'Jaunty Jock' renews Munro's interest in a genuine eighteenth-century historical character, Coll Macdonell of Barisdale (1698–1750). Coll Barisdale appears in The New Road *where he is presented as a bullying, blustering, unscrupulous commander of a Highland Watch company, making use of his official position to feather his own nest. His meeting with Barisdale gives Æneas, the young hero of the novel, one of his first insights into the false nature of much of traditional Highland life. Barisdale enters his room in his usual brash and pompous fashion brandishing a sword:*

> *. . . a tremendous sword that would have given Æneas qualms if he had not seen that the man who bore it was, for all of his bellowing, and devouring eye, as hollow as a drum. All at once it came upon him that his glamoured notion of the North was just a kind of poetry in himself, it vexed him to reflect that, the heroes of the ceilidh tales – the chiefs and caterans – were, like enough, but men of wind as this one seemed.*

Barisdale, a protection racketeer and ruffian in the Highlands, and an accomplished gentleman of breeding and manners in the Lowlands, intrigued many Scottish writers. Munro, in one of his 'Looker-On' columns, noted that Andrew Lang had supplied Stevenson with material on Barisdale with a view to Stevenson writing a novel about this very Highland rogue. In this short story he is removed from the Highlands to a society ball in Edinburgh but is shown in very little better light. For some reason Munro has used the Macdonald spelling for his surname – rather than the Macdonell or Macdonnell spelling favoured by Coll's kin – the Glengarry branch of Clan Donald.

'Young Pennymore' returns Munro to his native Argyll (Pennymore is about eight kilometres south of Inveraray) and a dark, classically tragic story set in the post-1745 era. John Clerk of Pennymore is the last man in the county to be tried and sentenced for a crime linked to the Jacobite Rising. Set in September 1752 it reflects the popular confusion caused by the change then from the Julian to the Gregorian calendar – a confusion which caused mobs to rally around the cry of 'Give us back our eleven days!' However beyond the naïve belief in a dies non *lies a short, grim but extremely skilfully told tale of betrayal, love, revenge and destiny.*

†

JAUNTY JOCK
CHAPTER 1: The West Bow Ball

The last of the West Bow balls before Lady Charlotte ran away with her dancing-master was on a dirty evening in November. Edinburgh was all day wrapped in haar, and now came rain that made the gutters run like mountain burns and overflow into the closes, to fall in shallow cataracts to the plain below. There was a lively trade in the taverns. 'Lord! there's a sneezer for ye!' said the customers ordering in their ale, not really minding the weather much, for it was usual and gave a good excuse for more assiduous scourging of the nine-gallon tree; but their wives, spanging awkwardly on pattens through the mud on their way to the fishwife at the Luckenbooths for the supper haddocks, had such a breeze in their petticoats and plaids they were in a terror that they should be blown away upon the blasts that came up the gulleys between the towering 'lands', and daring slates and chimney-pots, and the hazards of emptied vessels from the flats above, kept close to the wall as luggers scrape the shore of Fife when the gale's nor'-west.

Lady Charlotte was director of the dance – a creature most majestic, who ballooned about the room as if not her feet but her big hooped petticoat conveyed her, the only woman without a mask; that in her office would be useless. All the other women kept theirs on, with silken cords bit between the teeth (except when a favourite partner caused a titter). Below the velvet, when it tilted up, they showed the cheeks of youth and beauty, sometimes a little high in the bone for classic taste, and a patch on the chin just at the point where to a resolute lad it looked like a defiance. The flute, the hautbois, and the 'cello gave body to the melody of the harpsichord, somewhat flat the whole of them, for the place was sweltering, and the stuccoed ceiling sweated, and the walls.

A gentleman, conspicuous from the fact that he wore no wig, stood in the dusk at the foot of the room, away from the guttering candelabra, and put up his hand to hide a yawn. The minuet was beyond him, and seemed to him who came from the wilds, where the languid had no place in merriment, a somewhat insipid affair. In the cardroom, where old dowagers played cards till their girls should be ready to go home, and the young ones sat with their chosen gallants, sipping tea in the latest manner, he had ventured a harmless remark to a lady neither too young nor too lovely to resent a politeness at a masque assembly, and she had fled to her friends as if he were an ogre.

He was neither surprised nor vexed; he was accustomed to have the fair avoid him, though scarcely with such obvious fastidiousness as tonight. It was one of the things to be expected by a man with a crooked nose and the plainness of his other features in conformity with that one, even if he had not happened to be there incognito.

'To the devil!' said he to himself. 'I cannot expect them to be civil to any casual Jo at a two-and-sixpenny ball.' And he yawned again, impatient for the coming away of his cousin, whose gallantries to a lady at the other end of the room seemed unending. From that cousin he neither expected the ordinary courtesies of life nor desired them. They were usually as cool to each other as if they had sprung from different clans, and it was only the accident of a law plea affecting the family in its various branches that brought them privately to the capital and to the same lodgings from widely different parts of their native shire, and from widely different ways of life.

Whatever the cousin had to say to madam, she was pretty merry on the head of it, and seemed entranced with her gallant. He was such a coxcomb surely as never before came off the heather, with his Genoa velvet coat, his sky-blue breeches, and a waistcoat of the tartan of his clan, a thin, delicate, lady-like sword at his haunch that better knew the swing of the claymore.

'A rogue, Jock! and a tongue to wile the bird off the tree,' thought the man with the crooked nose, in no envy at all, but just in a distaste at nature's perversity; and he saw that his cousin and the lady looked at him as if he were the object of their conversation.

To his astonishment, the lady, at the forming of the next quadrille, was brought to him by Lady Charlotte. 'You see, if the mountain'll not come to Mahomet, Mahomet maun just come to the mountain,' said the directress airily. 'Here's a leddy I'm determined shall not miss her quadrille, and you are very lucky, Mr – Mr –'

'Macdonald,' said he, with a bow and a glance of shrewdness at the young lady, who had plainly made the arrangements herself for the introduction.

'Mr Macdonald – just so! a rale decent clan,' said Lady Charlotte, who prided herself upon the quality of her Scots. 'I mind you had the tickets from Lord Duthie; you're lucky to have the chance of the bonniest partner in the room.'

'I'll take your word for it,' said he, with another glance at a very soothfast mask that came down on as sweet a pair of lips as ever man took craving for.

At a quadrille he was not amiss if one could get over the crook in his nose and the rugged plainness of his countenance generally. When he was done and brought the lady to a seat, she was good enough to say he danced divinely. She had herself the carriage of a swan, her voice was of a ravishing and caressing quality, with none of the harsh, high-pitched, East-country accent that would have grated on Macdonald's ears, and yet there was something shallow in her phrase and sentiment.

'You are very good to say so, ma'am. I rarely dance, and I have seldom danced less at an assembly than I have done to-night,' said he, taking the compliment at its real value, for his dancing was a point on which he had no illusions.

The lady toyed with her fan; her eyes, mischievous and profound as wells and of the hue of plums, sparkled through the holes in her mask.

'Oh la! and you divine at it, I declare! Our Edinburgh belles, then, do not tempt you, Mr Macdonald? But I daresay you will think them quite good enough for our Edinburgh beaux; now, did you ever in your life see such gawks?'

Macdonald rubbed his chin. 'On the contrary,' said he, 'I was just thinking them uncommon spruce and handsome.'

'You are very tolerant; have you any other virtues to be aired?' said the lady with a smile that puzzled him. 'There's still another dance, I see; her ladyship is fairly in the key to-night; you'll have time to tell me all of them seriatim, missing out the lesser ones *brevitatis causa.*'

'H'm!' thought he; 'her father's in the law,' and wondered who she was. 'I could tell you all of them in the time it would take to dance a step of the Highland Fling,' said he.

'Faith, there's modesty! Item, Mr Macdonald?' and she sat back in her chair, her hoops bulged out in front of her like the bastion of a fort.

He counted them on his fingers humorously. 'Item, the tolerance you have given me credit for, though you have no example of it as yet, madam; items, an honest liking for my fellows, even the scamps of them; item, a habit of aye paying my way; item –' his forefinger hovered dubiously over the other hand, but never lighted on another virtue. 'I declare to you I have got to the end of my list and the man has not yet finished the tuning of his fiddle,' he said, laughing in a way so pleasant it almost made amends for his unhappy nose.

He had taken a seat beside her, she tapped him with her fan upon the knees with an air of the superior that struck him as a little droll, and, looking straight in his face, said in an affected Scots, as if to take the sting from the words: 'A' very fine, Maister Macdonald, a' very fine! What have ye given me here but twa-three virtues that come – except maybe the last – so easy to maist folk they're nae mair to your credit than that you should sup kail wi' a spoon?'

'A poor show, I confess it, ma'am; if you want a list of more brilliant virtues, you should try my worthy cousin, your last partner,' he replied.

'Do you tell me that – Barrisdale?' said the lady, burring her 'r's' with a gusto to make him certain she had no dubiety regarding his identity.

He could not hide a little start of surprise, for he thought the secret of his cousin and himself being in Edinburgh was known to but two men there, Lord Duthie and Mackee.

'You're the daughter of Lord Duthie,' said he, remembering her law Latinity.

She was confused at so shrewd a guess, but admitted he was right. 'It has long been my wish,' said she, 'to have a crack with a Highland rob –, with a Highland person of your experience; and I must confess I asked Lady Charlotte for the introduction, though you may not think it modest. Let me tell you that I'm disappointed; it ill becomes a gentleman of Barrisdale's reputation to be claiming such paltry common virtues as those you have named to charm the ear of an unknown lady in a mask. They credit ye with Latin and French, and say ye cut a dash whiles in London – oh la! a wonnerfu' man entirely! – but upon my word, I never thought to get a catechist in my Hielan cateran.'

'Here's a comedy,' thought he, looking across the room to his cousin, 'How in the world did you discover me?' he asked her; 'did my cousin –'

'He did,' said she, 'and he told me not to mention it; but you see, I take the privilege of my sex.'

'I cannot but be flattered at your interest, ma'am, I'm sure, and I hope you will not let the thing go further so long as I'm in Edinburgh. Now that I'm discovered, I'm wae to be back to my ruffian gang,' said he, with a quizzing air. 'I must have a most tremendous reputation, and I would not wonder if you could go over all my history.'

'I daresay I know the worst of it.'

'Do you? Faith! it's more than I do myself; might I ask you to be jogging my memory?'

'When I come to think of it,' said she, 'the very virtues that you claim are what in the rough bounds of the Hielans may well manifest themselves in fashions that hereabouts in lalland towns we clap men into jyle for.'

'Indeed, I should not wonder, ma'am,' said he; 'what's counted a crime in one parish, even in the Hielans, is often looked on as a Christian act in others not a glen removed.'

'You talk of tolerance. Barrisdale; was it that made you hide in Ben Alder for a twelvemonth the man that shot Breadalbane's factor?'

'He was a very old man, the factor, Miss Duthie,' said he glibly. 'He would have died in another winter, anyway, by all appearances, and not half so handsomely as with a bullet. And the poor fellow who shot him – you would not have us send a man with a wife and ten of a family to the gallows?'

'Lord!' cried the lady, affecting to be out of patience. 'You are a rebel too, my father tells me, and all for having back those Papist Stuarts and putting the dear King away out of the country. Is that a sample of your love for your fellow-men?'

'Logic,' thought Macdonald, 'is not a branch that's taught with the virginals and tambouring in lawyers' families.' 'Well, ma'am,' said he, 'could you blame me? I have been in France a while myself, and I ken the kind of drink they have to drink there; I would not poison dogs with it. I would have Jamie back for no other reason than to save what relics of his stomach may be to the fore. What's that but love for my fellows?'

'Was it that made you fight with the London gentleman and send him – poor soul – to his Maker at five o'clock on a cold winter morning?'

'It's a small world. Who would have thought the gossip of that trivial affair would have travelled to an Edinburgh assembly? Sure you would not have had me put off the occasion till the summer weather; we were both warm enough at the time, I assure you, or that black folly they call a duel had never been engaged in.'

'You have the name of – of – I hate to mention it,' said the lady, now grown eager and biting her under lip.

'Oh, out with it! out with it! Crown Counsel should never be blate, ma'am; on my word, the talent for cross-examination would seem to run in the family.'

'Blackmail and –' said she in a whisper.

'One at a time!' said Macdonald. 'That's the prose way of putting it; up north we put it differently. You call it robbery; we call it rent. Some charge the rent by the penny-land or the acre; we charge it by the sound night's sleep, and the man who rents immunity for his cattle from Barrisdale gets as good value for his money as the man who rents some acres of dirt from Appin.'

Madam worked her fan industriously – now she was on his heels, and could not spare so plain a mercenary. 'You steal cattle,' was her next charge.

'Steal! ma'am,' said Barrisdale, with a frown. 'It is not the bonniest word; up north we call it *togail* – lifting. It is an odd world, mistress, and every man of us had to do some sort of lifting for a living – if not in the glen, then in the market-place, where the act is covered in a fine confusion. If we lift a *creach* now and then in Barrisdale there are other clans that lift from us, and at the season's end no one is much the worse, and there has been much frolic and diversion.'

'On the same reasoning, then, you would justify the attempt at abducting Glen Nant's rich daughter?' said the lady.

'Do you happen to have seen her?'

'I have,' said the lady, and could not for her life have kept from smiling. 'It was the sight of her spoiled what small romantics I had about the Hielan cateran.'

'Are you sure there are none to the fore yet?'

'Not a morsel!' said the lady, looking point-blank at his nose.

'*Mo thruagh!*' said Macdonald tragically; 'then are we indeed forsaken.'

'You made a shabby flight, by all accounts, from the lady's brother.'

'Humph!' said he, for the first time disconcerted; indeed, it was a story no way creditable to Clan Macdonald. 'I think,' said he, 'we'll better let that flea stick to the wall,' and looked across the room to where his cousin sat glowering in a manifest anxiety.

'Oh, Barrisdale, Barrisdale, can ye no' be a good man?' said Miss Duthie, in a petty lady-like concern, and unable to keep her eyes from that unlucky nose.

He put up his hand and covered it. She flushed to the neck that he should so easily have divined her, and he laughed.

'It's no use trying, ma'am,' said he. 'Let me be as good as gold and I would never get credit for it from your sex, that must always fancy that a handsome face never goes but with a handsome heart.'

She rose with an air of vexation to leave him, very red below her mask; the last dance was on the point of ending, the dowagers were coming in with their Paisley plaids on their shoulders. 'I would never hurt any person's feelings by allusion to his personal appearance,' she said, as she was turning away.

'I am sure of it, ma'am,' said he; 'you are most considerate.'

CHAPTER 2: The Fire

Macdonald and his cousin Jock walked to their lodging in Halkerston's Wynd without a lanthorn. The watch cried, 'Twal o'clock, twal o'clock, and a perishin' cauld nicht'; they could hear the splash of his shoes in the puddles of the lane although they could not see him. The town now rose above the haar that brooded in the swampy hollow underneath the citadel; the rain was gone, the stars were clear, the wind moaned in the lanes and whistled on the steep. It was like as they were in some wizard fortress cut from rock, walking in mirk ravines, the enormous houses dizzy overhanging them, the closes running to the plains on either hand in sombre gashes. Before them went sedans and swinging lanterns and flambeaux that left in their wake an odour of tow and rosin not in its way unpleasant.

'Yon was a dubious prank upon the lady,' said Macdonald, and his cousin laughed uproariously.

'Upon my word, Donald,' said he, 'I could not for the life of me resist it. I declare it was better than a play; I have paid good money for worse at a play.'

'And still and on a roguish thing,' said Macdonald, hastening his step. 'You were aye the rogue, Jaunty Jock.'

'And you were aye the dullard, Dismal Dan,' retored the other in no bad humour at the accusation. 'To be dull is, maybe, worse. You had the opportunity – I risked that – to betray me if you liked.'

'You knew very well I would not do that.'

'Well, I thought not, and if you did not take the chance to clear yourself when you got it, there's no one but yourself to blame. Here was madam – quite romantical about the Highlands, as I found at our first country dance, and languishing to see this Barrisdale that she has heard from some one – (who the devil knows? that beats me) – was to be at Lady Charlotte's ball. "I'm sorry to say he's my own cousin," says I – "a Hielan cousin, it does not count when rogues are in the family." "You must point him out to me," said she. I gave her three guesses to pick out the likeliest in the room, and she took you at the first shot.'

'A most discerning young person!' said Macdonald.

'She knew your history like a sennachie, lad, and rogue as she made you, I believe she would have forgiven you all but for that nose of yours.'

'Oh, damn my nose!' cried Macdonald. 'It's not so very different from the common type of noses.'

'Just that! just that! not very different, but still a little skew. Lord! man, you cannot expect to have all the graces as well as all the virtues. Madam picked you out at all events, and I was not in the key to contradict her. She paid you (or was it me?) the compliment of saying you were not at all like her idea of a man with the repute of Barrisdale.'

'Very likely! Indeed, I could guess she was more put out at that than at finding herself speaking to a scamp who laughed at his own misdeeds. You made a false move; Jock, had you admitted you were the man, she would not have been greatly mortified. In any case, she thought to improve the occasion with advice. She told me to be good!'

Barrisdale could hardly speak for laughing. 'You kept up the play at any rate,' said he, 'for when I saw her to her chair, "Yon's an awful man, your cousin," said she. What do you think of her?'

'Something of a simpleton, something of a sentimentalist, and a very bonny face forbye to judge by her chin – that was all of it I saw.'

'She kept too tight a mask for even me to see her face. Man, ye've missed her chief charm – she has twa thousand a year of her own. I had it from herself, so you see I'm pretty far ben. With half a chance I could make a runaway match of it; I'm sure I took her fancy.'

'Tuts! Jock. I thought you had enough of runaway matches; take care she has not got a brother,' said Macdonald.

Jaunty Jock scowled in the dark, but made no answer.

Their lodging was in a land deep down in the Wynd. Flat on flat it rose for fourteen stories, poverty in its dunnies (as they called its cellars), poverty in its attics, and between the two extremes the wonderfullest variety of households bien or wealthy – the homes of writers, clerks, ministers, shopkeepers, tradesmen, gentlemen reduced, a countess, and a judge – for there, though the Macdonalds did not know, dwelt Lord Duthie with his daughter. In daytime the traffic of the steep scale stair went like the road to a fair, at night the passages were black and still as vaults. 'A fine place the town, no doubt,' said Jaunty Jock, 'but, lord, give me the hills for it!'

They slept in different rooms. The morning was still young when one of them was wakened by the most appalling uproar on the stair. He rose and saw his window glowing; he looked from it, and over on the gables of the farther land he saw the dance of light from a fire. He wakened Jaunty Jock. 'Get up,' said he, 'the tenement's in blazes.' They dressed in a hurry, and found that every one in the house but themselves had fled already. The door stood open; on the landing crushed the tenants from the flats above, men and women in a state of horror, fighting like brutes for their safety. The staircase rang with cries – the sobbing of women, the whimper of bairns, and at the foot a doorway jammed. Frantic to find themselves caught like rats, and the sound of the crackling fire behind them, the trapped ones elbowed and tore for escape, and only the narrowness of the passage kept the weaker ones from being trampled underfoot. All this Macdonald could define only by the evidence of his ears, for the stair was wholly in pitch darkness.

'By God! we'll burn alive!' said Jaunty Jock, every shred of his manhood gone, and trembling like a leaf. Their door was in a lobby recessed from the landing – an eddy wherein some folk almost naked drifted weeping to find themselves helpless of getting farther. 'Where's the fire?' asked Macdonald from one of them, and had to shake him before he got an answer.

'Two landings farther up,' said the fellow, 'in Lord Duthie's flat.'

'Lord Duthie's flat!' cried Macdonald; 'and is he safe?'

'He's never hame yet; at least, I never heard him skliffin' on the stair, but his dochter cam' back hersel' frae the assembly.'

'Is she safe?' asked Macdonald.

'Wha' kens that?' replied the man, and threw himself into the stair, the more able now to fight beause of his rest in the eddy.

'It looks gey bad for your runaway match, Jock,' said Macdonald. 'Here's a parcel of the most arrant cowards. My God, what a thin skin of custom lies between the burgess and the brute beast. That poor lass! It's for you and me, Jock, to go up and see that she's in no greater danger than the rest of us.'

He spoke to deaf ears, for Jock was already fighting for his place among the crowd. His cousin did the same, but with another purpose: his object was to scale the stair. He pushed against the pressure of the panic, mountains were on his shoulders, and his ribs were squeezed into his body as if with falling rocks. His clothes were torn from his back, he lost his shoes, and a frantic woman struck him on the face with the heavy key of her door that with a housewife's carefulness she treasured even when the door it was meant for was burned, and the blood streamed into his eyes.

He was still in the dark of the stair; the fire at least was not close enough to stop his mounting, so up he felt his way in a hurry till he reached Lord Duthie's flat. A lobby that led to the left from the landing roared with flame that scorched him; a lobby on the right was still untouched. He hammered at the only shut door but got no answer, plied the risp as well with the same result, then threw it in with a drive of the shoulders. He gave a cry in the entrance and, getting no response, started to go through the rooms. At the third the lady sat up in her bed and cried at the intruder. 'The land's on fire, ma'am,' said he quietly in the dark.

'Fire!' she cried in horror. 'Oh, what shall I do? Who are you?'

'Barrisdale,' said he, remembering his rôle and determined to make this his last appearance in it. 'You have plenty of time to dress, and I'll wait for you on the landing.'

He went out with a sudden project in his mind, ran down the stair with its litter of rags and footwear and found it almost vacant, the obstruction at the bottom being cleared. 'Take your time, my friends,' said he, 'there's not the slightest danger; the fire will not get this length for half an hour yet.'

His cousin came back from the crush. 'As sure's death, I'm glad to see you and sorry I never bided,' said he. 'You never came on her; I knew very well she must have got out at the outset.'

'Indeed!' said Barrisdale. 'As it happens, she's yonder yet, and I had the honour to wake her; I fancy she's taking her hair from the curl-papers at this moment. You never had a better chance of getting credit for a fine action very cheaply. It was in the dark I wakened her; I told her I was Barrisdale and would return when she was dressed. You may go back to her.'

'Man, I wouldn't mind,' said the cousin; 'but what's the object?' he added suspiciously.

'Only that I'm tired of being Barrisdale to suit you. If you like to be Barrisdale and carry your own reputation, you'll have the name of saving her life – one thing at least to your credit that'll maybe make her forget the rest. With a creature so romantical, I would not wonder if it came to the runaway match after all.'

'Faith, I'll risk it,' said Jaunty Jock, and ran up the stair. He came down with the lady on his arm, and took her to a neighbour's.

'And did you confess to your identity?' asked his cousin when they met again.

'I did,' he answered gloomily.

'Surely she did not boggle at the Barrisdale; I was certain it would make little odds to a lady of her character.'

'Oh, she was willing enough, but it's not a match,' said Jaunty Jock. 'After this, I'll always see the mask off first; she had a worse nose than yourself!'

YOUNG PENNYMORE

Of the half-dozen men of Mid-Argyll condemned on one account or another for their part in the Rebellion, the last, and the least deserving of so scurvy a fate, was young John Clerk of Pennymore. He had been out in the affair more for the fun of the thing than from any high passion of politics; he would have fought as readily for the Duke as for the Young Pretender if the Duke had appealed to him first; he was a likeable lad to all who knew him, and the apple of his mother's eye.

The hanging of young John Clerk seemed at the time all the more harsh a measure since he was not charged directly with rebellion, but with being actor or art and part in the death of the Captain of Clonary, who was shot on his way from Culloden by a gang of lurking Jacobites of whom the lad was one, and maybe innocent. The murderers scattered to the mist and to the sea. For six years Clerk sequestered in the land of France, and was caught at last in a tender filial hour when he had ventured home to see his folk. A squad of the Campbells found him skulking in the wood of Pennymore on the very afternoon of his return; he had not even had the time to see his people, and the trinkets and sweetmeats he had meant for his mother were strewn from his pockets among the bracken as he was being dragged before the Lords.

They looked at him – these dour and exigent gentlemen – with eyes that held no pity, not men at all for the nonce, but bowelless, inexorable legal mechanism; and Elchies, squeaking like a showman at a fair, sentenced him to the gallows.

'John Clerk,' he said, 'you have had an impartial trial; you have been defended by an able advocate, who has made the most of a wretched cause; the jury has found you guilty as libelled, and it only rests with this court to pronounce sentence accordingly. You may yet, during the brief period you have to live, best serve your country and your friends by warning them against those pernicious principles which have brought you to this untimely end, and may the Lord have mercy on your soul!'

Then the doomster declared doom – that young John Clerk be handed over to the Sheriff-Depute, hanged by the neck on the burgh gibbet at Creag-nan-caoraich on the 5th September, and thereafter left for a time in chains.

The lad made a bow to his judges, gave a last quick, eager glance about the court to assure himself his parents were not there, and then he was hurried down the trap-door to the cells.

There was still a month to go before the day of execution, and the Clerks of Pennymore – the proud and bitter dame and her pious husband – scoured the shire in search of sympathetic gentlemen of influence, and forswore sleep itself in their efforts to secure reprieve. They seemed, poor souls! miraculous in their great endurance, singly or together tramping here and there on a quest no neighbour dared to share, tragic to see upon the highway, horrible to hear at midnight when their cart went rumbling through the sleeping clachans. Sympathy was plentiful, but influence was shy, and the hopes of Pennymore were narrowed at last to Campbell of Lochgair, a lawyer himself, with the ear of His Grace and the Crown authorities.

Lochgair, more, as it strangely seemed, for the sake of the peevish dame than for her husband's, promised his active interest, and almost guaranteed release, and in the latter days of August went to Edinburgh to wait on the Lord Advocate, who was Prestongrange. It was the year of the stunted corn – 1752 – and never in the memory of man had been such inclement weather. The seas would seem to have forgotten the ways of peace; the glens were flooded, and the Highlands for a space were cut off from the Lowland world, and in a dreary privacy of storm. So the days passed – for most folk as if Time itself were bogged among the mire – for the man and wife in Pennymore as the flap of wings. They longed each evening for the morrow since it might bring welcome news, and yet they grudged the night and looked with terror on the dawn, since it brought the horrid hour a vigil closer.

And there were no tidings from Lochgair!

'I might have known! I might have known! – a traitor ever, like his clan!' cried the mother, all her patience drained to the bitter dregs, wringing her hands till the blood came to the knuckles. 'Lochgair will see the laddie hanged, and never jee his beaver. Too well I know his promises! We're here forgot, the pair of us, and all the world sleeping sound, no way put about at the thought of young John Clerk. Deserted of men! deserted of men!' and her cry rose like a dirge in their lonely dwelling.

'But not of God and His grace,' said her husband, shrinking before the fury of her eye. 'I have trusted Lochgair in this with all my heart, and he cannot betray us. He knows that his breath is all that lies between our laddie and eternity.'

'Oh, trust!' she hissed. 'I ken the man; but I have trusted too, this fortnight, till my very heart is rent, yet God Himself cannot put off the 5th September.'

'Yea, even that, if it be His will; our times are in His hands,' said the pious husband, and turned him again to his Bible. But the woman's doubts were justified, and on the morning of the day before their son should perish, they yoked the horse and drove in the cart to the burgh town to see him for the first time in the cell he had shared with some doomed sheep-stealers.

Six miles lay betwen their home and the tolbooth gates, and yet it was in pitch-black night they came to the confines of the burgh, for they dreaded the pitying eyes of men and women. And all the way the woman fondled something in her plaid. They saw, afar, and few, and melancholy, wan lights in the burgh lands, blurred by the weeping rain; and at this spectacle – which told them the world went on its ordinary way and thought of breakfast, while their lad sat counting the hours, and they were engaged with misery – the man put his hand on the woman's shoulder with a grip of steel, and she gave the last sob that was ever heard from her. For ever after she was a woman made of stone. The horse, as if it shared their feeling, stopped on the highway, reared itself in terror of something unseen, and snapped its belly-band, and the cart stood still under heaving beeches whose windy branches filled the dark with noise and cried down the very waves which roared on Creag-nan-caoraich.

The man jumped from the cart and fumbled with the harness, to find that further progress, wanting a girth, was not to be contemplated.

'I will walk into the town,' he said, 'and get a rope, if you sit here till I return. You will not mind my leaving you, Margaret?'

'Mind!' she exclaimed with bitterness; 'I have learned my lesson, and there is no more to mind.' But she fondled the thing concealed in her plaid, and her man walked quickly towards the wan lights of the tenements, leaving her all alone.

For a moment only she heard his footsteps, the sound of them soon lost in the din of nature – the uproar of the forest trees, whose ponderous branches creaked; the wind, canorous, blowing between the mountains; the booming crepitation of the sea upon the rocks. And yet no sense of solitude depressed her, for her mind was occupied by one triumphant thought – that young John Clerk should at least be spared the horror and shame of a public execution.

She had drawn, at first, the drenched plaid over her head to shield her and shut her in from the noise of tempest; but her hands in a little while were so busily engaged with her secret possession that the tartan screen at last rolled back on her shoulders, and she was aware of another sound than those of nature – the near, faint clang of chains. it was scarcely audible, but unmistakable – the beat of a loose end of iron links against wood, somewhere above her head, as she sat in the cart by the side of Creag-nan-caoraich. She stared up into the darkness and saw nothing, then stood to her feet and felt above her with trembling hand.

Her fingers searchd along a beam with a rope attached to it, whose meaning flooded to her brain with a gush that stunned; she touched a dead man's feet! and the pitless clouds that had swept all night across the heavens heaved for a moment from the face of the reeling moon, and she saw the wretch upon the gibbet!

'My son! my son!' she screamed till the rocks and trees gave back the echo, and yet the distant lights of the burgh town glowed on with unconcern.

Her cries had ceased; she was sunk in a listless torpor in the bottom of the cart when her man returned in a state as wretched as her own, running with stumbling feet along the rutted highway.

'My God! my God!' said he, 'I have learned of something dreadful!'

'I have learned it for myself,' said his wife. 'You're a day behind the fair.'

'Not one day, but eleven of them,' said her husband, hardly taking her meaning. 'It is the fifteenth of September, and I'm so fearful of the worst. I dared not rap at a door in the town and ask.'

'The fifteenth of September,' she repeated dully; 'we have not slept so sound this month back that we could miss a fortnight. Have you lost your reason?'

'I have seen a placard put up on the mercat cross,' said her husband, with his brow upon the horse's back. 'I read it in the light of the tolbooth windows, and it tells that the Government have decreed that the day after September 2nd should be September 14th. Eleven days are dropped; it is called – it is called the Gregorian Calendar, and I have forgotten about the rope.'

The woman harshly laughed.

'Are you hearing me, Margaret?' he cried, putting up his arms to seize her, feeling some fresh terror.

'Gregorian here, Gregorian there!' she exclaimed. 'Whose Calendar but the cursed Campbells', who have bonnily diddled me of my son! Our times are in God's hands, you said; you are witness now they are in the devil's!'

'But it may be I was right, and that this is our Father's miracle; John could not be – could not die but on the day appointed, and no such day, it seems, was on the Calendar. But I dared not ask, I dared not ask; I was dumfounded and ran to you, and here I am even without the rope.'

Again the woman harshly laughed.

'You need not fash about the rope, goodman,' said she; 'at your very hand is plenty for your purpose, for there my son is, young John Clerk, and he hangs upon the tree.'

The woman would not put a hand upon the body. Without her aid her husband lowered the burden from the gibbet, laid it in the cart and covered it with his plaid; and when a girth for the horse had been improvised from a part of the shameful halter, the two of them turned for home, walking side by side through the dawn that now was coming, slow and ashen, to the east.

The man was dumb, and walked without volition, wrestling with satanic doubts of a Holy Purpose that had robbed him of his son with such unnecessary and ghastly mockery; the woman cuddled her cold secret in her bosom, stared glassily at the coming day, and for a time let fury and despair whirl through her brain like poison vapours.

'I will never rest,' she cried at last, 'till Lochgair has paid the penalty for this trick upon us. My laddie's death is at his door!'

Her man said nothing, leading the horse.

'At his door!' she cried more vehemently. 'Are you hearing me? He has slain my son in this shameful way as surely as if he had tied the rope himself.'

Her husband made no answer; he found in her words but the thought of one for the time demented, and he walked appalled at the chaos into which the precious edifice of his faith had tumbled. Rudely she plucked his arm and screamed in his ear –

'What will you do to Campbell?'

'To Campbell?' he repeated vaguely. 'God forgive him his false hopes and negligence, but it was not he who condemned our son.'

'But for him,' said the woman, 'my son would have died like a gentleman, and not like a common thief.'

'I do not understand,' said her husband blankly.

'No, you never understand,' she sneered, 'that was ever your failing. Do you think that if I had not the promise of Lochgair, I should let my laddie die upon the gallows? The first of his race! the first of his race! I had brought with me his pistol that he might save himself the scandal of the doomster's hand,' and she took the weapon from her bosom.

Her husband looked at it, grasped at once the Spartan spirit of her scheme, and swithered between chagrin that it had been foiled, and shame that the sin of self-slaughter should for a moment seem desirable.

'Oh, Margaret!' he cried, 'you terrify me. Throw that dreadful weapon in the sea,' and he made to take it from her, but she restored it to her plaid.

'No, no,' she cried, 'there may be use for it –'

'Use for it!' he repeated, and she poured into his ear the torrent of her hatred of Lochgair. 'He could have won my laddie off,' she said; 'we had his own assurance. And if we had not put our trust in him, we would have gone to others – Asknish or Stonefield, or the Duke himself – the Duke would have had some pity on a mother.'

'Lochgair may have sore deceived us,' said her husband, 'yet he was but an instrument; our laddie's doom was a thing appointed from the start of Time.'

'Then from the start of Time you were doomed to slay Lochgair.'

'What! I?' quo' he.

'One or other of us. We are, it seems by your religion, all in the hands of fate and cannot help ourselves. Stand up like a man to this filthy Campbell, and give him the bullet that was meant for a better man.'

'You are mad, goodwife,' said her husband; 'I would shed no man's blood.'

'I speak not of men,' said she, 'but of that false fiend Lochgair who has kept us on the rack, and robbed Time itself of a fortnight to make his clan diversion. Oh, man! man! are you a coward? Challenge him to the moor; remember that at the worst my son who lies in the cart there could have died in decency and not at the doomster's hand if Lochgair had not misled us –'

'Woman!' cried her husband, 'get behind me!' and took refuge in a gust of mumbled prayer.

They were now upon the Kenmore shore where the sea came deep against the rocks; no living soul had met them on their passage down the coast with their disgraceful burden, and alarmed at the prospect of encounter with any curious wayfarer, they drew the cart behind a thicket, to let an approaching horseman pass without his observation. Far off they heard the clatter of his horse's hoofs, and while yet he was a good way distant the questing eye of the woman saw he wore a beaver hat, and a familiar coat with silver buttons!

'Look! look!' she cried, 'here comes the very man, delivered to our hands.'

'I will not touch him! I will not touch him!' said her husband, cowering behind the bushes.

'Then will I!' said she, and drew the pistol from her breast, and her husband wrestled with her for the weapon.

Lochgair in a furious haste came galloping, his vision engaged on the road before him, and would have swept on his way unnoticing the cart, its burden, or attendants, but for the altercation in the thicket. He checked his horse, turned round on the saddle, and peered among the branches, where the husband, breathing hard, had got possession of the weapon.

'He has slain my son, but I will spare him,' said the husband, and the woman put her mouth against his ear.

'No son of yours,' she whispered, 'that is the curse of it! – but his own!'

'My God!' cried her husband and fired at the horseman's breast. He fell like a sack of oats on the roadway, and his horse flew off among the brackens.

For a while the world seemed in a swound. In a swound the waves lapped up against the rocks; in a swound the leafage moved; in a swound the sea-birds cried, and the man and woman, desperate, sought to hide the evidence of their crime. They turned the dead man over on his back, emptied his pouches, filled his clothes with stones, then threw him, with the pistol, in the sea.

'Home! home!' the wife commanded, placing the dead man's papers in her plaid, and she walked, without remorse, by the side of her whimpering man, to Pennymore. She stirred the embers of the fire, and one by one destroyed the dead man's documents, until the very last, and that she glanced at horror-stricken, for it was her son's reprieve!

With a scream she rushed outside and turned her husband's plaid from the face of the dead man in the cart – and it was not young John Clerk!

10

The Poetry

INTRODUCTION

†

John Buchan, who edited the posthumous collection of Neil Munro's poetry which was published by William Blackwood & Sons in 1931, wrote in his preface that Munro's 'prose seems to me more strictly poetic than his verse'. Which may be one of the less encouraging editorial remarks to appear in the introduction to an author's collected verse – but which may also be true. Much of Munro's verse arguably stays at the level of the routine and commonplace but there are also, to be fair, a number of poems which rise to significantly greater heights.

Munro's poetic output does not at first seem large. The volume of collected verse includes only thirty poems, but the slimness of the Buchan edition is deceptive and it should be remembered that Munro had written poetry all his life. Indeed his first, unsuccessful, submission to Blackwood's Magazine, *as a young man of twenty-three, had been a poem, and just three months before Munro's death George W. Blackwood's last letter to him was enquiring about the prospects of some more 'Bagpipe Ballads'. One of his poems, 'Sergeant of Pikes', was written for inclusion (in a longer form) in his 1898 novel* John Splendid, *and other poems were composed for particular occasions.*

Munro was an inveterate reviser of his poetry – and perhaps not always to its advantage. Our first choice is one of his best known poems, 'The Heather'. This first appeared in Blackwood's Magazine *in October 1896 but when it appeared in a collection published by the Glasgow Ballad Club in 1898 it had been quite substantially revised and underwent further slight changes for its appearance in 1910 in W. Macneile Dixon's* Edinburgh Book of Scottish Verse. *Yet more revisions must have been undertaken by the author, because, when Buchan printed it in 1931 there are marked changes from the 1910 version. For example, verse 1 line 3, which formerly read 'And my castles lay in scores along the wine-land', becomes 'Were my castles grey and scowling o'er the wine-land'. This particular change has the effect of darkening the mood of the poem but some of the other changes are less felicitous. Buchan noted in his edition that he had 'tried to embody his [Munro's] pencilled corrections'. Buchan tells us that Munro had planned a volume of his poems and these pencilled corrections presumably date from quite late in his life – and thus indicate a process of revision extending over perhaps a quarter of a century.*

While the Collected Verse *is quite a slender volume Munro also contributed verse to the* Glasgow Evening News. *Much of this has been lost sight of and has only recently been recovered. Three poems from 1894 represent this strand in Munro's work and reflect his intellectual interests. When Robert Louis Stevenson died Munro wrote 'R.L.S.' as a tribute for the* News. *This poem was written in some haste: it appeared on Tuesday 18 December, the day after news of Stevenson's death in Samoa had reached the British press. Munro later revised this poem as 'The Story Teller', in which form it is included in Buchan's edition of the collected verse. In the* News *it appeared over the signature 'M'. The same signature was used on 25 January for a poem 'The Immortal Memory', which reflects Munro's serious interest in Burns. He became Honorary President of the Greenock Burns Club and, of course, his four stories about Burns form the core of* Ayrshire Idylls. *A very different tone is apparent in 'The New Woman in Art', which appeared, again over the signature 'M', in the* News *of 13 November. Inspired by the exhibition of posters by Frances and Margaret Macdonald at the Glasgow Institute of Fine Art Exhibition, this squib reflects something of the outcry which the 'hag-like' portrayal of women by the Macdonald sisters, two of the leading 'Glasgow Girls', had provoked. Their art was evidently not much to Munro's taste, and his general view of women artists can perhaps be inferred from the comments of Erchie MacPherson in stories such as 'Among the Pictures'.*

'Nettles' is a poem of loss. The Glen Aora [the home of Munro's mother] of line 1 is the more accurate rendition of what is more generally spelled as Glen Aray – Gaelic not using the letter 'Y' in its alphabet. The common stinging nettle (Urtica dioica) *is, of course, a prime indicator of former human habitation, flourishing in areas where the soil has been disturbed and nitrogenous waste deposited. 'Nettles' is yet another of Munro's works which take for their theme the process of change in the Highlands – in this case depopulation. He wrote of the changes in his native Argyll in* The Clyde: River and Firth:

> *. . . in 1750 the Duke and his clan, including Breadalbane, could raise if necessary 10,000 men able to bear arms. The bulk of them must have been found between the shores of Loch Fyne and Loch Awe: single glens of Loch Fyne could turn out over two hundred swords; now they are desolate, though there were none of the wholesale clearances that dispeopled many other parts of the Highlands.*

'John o' Lorn' also evokes the loss of the exile driven from 'the green glens, the fine glens we knew'. The immediate occasion for this exile is politics,

presumably the Jacobite cause, but the poem could also be read equally well as an elegy for the Highlanders cleared to make way for sheep, or the economic migrant from the Highlands forced to leave home to seek his fortune in the Lowlands or furth of Scotland as part of 'an auld Hielan' story'. Munro himself left Inveraray in June 1881, and a safe if boring job in a lawyer's office, to make his way in Glasgow.

'Lament for Macleod of Raasay' is one of Munro's wartime poems, but of a more deeply emotional and elegiac nature than many. Munro's son Hugh, a medical student at Glasgow University, had joined a Territorial battalion of the Argyll & Sutherland Highlanders and was killed in action on the Western Front in September 1915, and the abiding pain of this loss would seem to have its echoes in this moving poem first published in 1917.

One readily available poem which Buchan did not include in his collection of Munro's verse is a work inspired by the tragedy of the Iolaire. *The* Iolaire *was a steam yacht taken into Admiralty service during the First World War. On New Year's Day 1919, the War almost two months over, she was approaching Stornoway harbour crowded with returning Lewis servicemen. A fatal miscalculation of the approach to the harbour caused the* Iolaire *to run on the rocks known as the 'Beasts of Holm' and over two hundred island men, who had survived years of war, died in sight of home. Munro's response to this bitter tragedy was 'Prologue of Lament by Players' which appeared in a collection of contemporary Scottish poetry:* Holyrood, a Garland of Modern Scots Poems *published in 1929.*

THE HEATHER

If I were King of France, that noble fine land,
And my gold was elbow-deep in the iron chests;
Were my castles grey and scowling o'er the wine-land,
With towers as high as where the eagle nests;
If harpers sweet, and swordsmen stout and vaunting,
My history sang, my stainless tartan wore,
Was not my fortune poor with one thing wanting,
    The heather at my door?

My galleys might be sailing every ocean,
Robbing the isles and sacking hold and keep,
My chevaliers go prancing at my notion,
To bring me back of cattle, horse and sheep;
Fond arms be round my neck, the youngheart's tether,

And true love-kisses all the night might fill,
But oh! *mochree*, if I had not the heather,
 Before me on the hill!

A hunter's fare is all I would be craving,
A shepherd's plaiding and a beggar's pay,
If I might earn them where the heather, waving,
Gave grandeur to the day.
The stars might see me, homeless one and weary,
Without a roof to fend me from the dew,
And still content, I'd find a bedding cheery
 Where'er the heather grew!

THE IMMORTAL MEMORY
(25th January)
from the Glasgow Evening News, *25 January 1894*

Cauld Janwar' win', ye hanselled in
 Dear Rab, auld Scotland's bard,
And, by my sang, it wad be wrang
 To ca' ye dour and hard.
Yer braggart roar, yer hail and hoar,
 We'll tak' in right guid part:
Ye blew ower Ayr when first beat there
 Oor bardie's gentle heart.

Had Simmer breeze, 'mang Southron trees,
 Its warmth owre Rabbie flung,
We dinna ken but aiblins then
 His sang had ne'er been sung:
Or else his lay had been gey wae,
 And little worth, a tune
O' jasmine floo'ers and dallying oors,
 Or maunderin's 'bout the mune!

For Scotland stern dear Rab, was born,
 No' for some saft Sooth land,
That puirtith cauld and pride sae bauld
 Thegether, couldna' understand.
His harp, sae clear, for Scottish ear

Was tuned on nature's key;
He plucked the strings and gave the wings
  To mair than mortal harmony.

The ruined hoose o' shiverin' moose
  Brought his saft heart a pang;
The humblest floo'er amang the stour
  Was worth his boniest sang.
We feel the fire o' War's desire
  Quick lichted by his lay,
Or launch wi' joy at simple ploy,
  Tauld in his pawkie way.

Ae single glass aroon' we'll pass
  (Be't either wine or water;
Sae lang's the heart is in the part
  It disna' muckle matter).
Confusion to the blackguard crew
  That fain wad black his fame!
May guid luck fa' on each an' a'
  Wha still upholds his name!

                      – M.

THE NEW WOMAN IN ART

from the Glasgow Evening News, *13 November 1894*

Many of the pictures exhibited by ladies at the Exhibition of School of Art Work in the Fine Art Institute are fearfully, wonderfully and weirdly 'new'. Their impressions of the female form, particularly, are startling.

                      – *Art Gossip*

Would you witness a conception
Of the Woman really New,
Without the least deception
From the artist's point of view?
See the Art School Exhibition
In the Rue de Sauchiehall;
They don't charge you for admission
(For they haven't got the gall).

As painted by her sister
Who affects the realm of Art,
The Woman New's a twister
To give nervous men a start.
She is calculated chiefly
To make him really think
That he's got 'em, and that, briefly,
It's the dire result of drink.

For if Caliban was mated
With a feminine gorilla,
Who in her youth had dissipated
O'er the Book yclept the Yellow,
The daughters of the wedding
Would be something such as these –
Sadly scant of fleshly padding
And ground-spavined at the knees.

But the dodge is very easy,
If of conscience you're devoid;
Take a supper – if it please you –
Of roast pork and liver fried,
From the nightmares that will follow,
Paint impressions in pale green
Of the hags who sought your pillow,
Spectral, hideous, and lean.

Let them waltz across your paper
In a weird Macabre dance,
Or perform some fiendish caper
With the Beardsley leering glance.
Let their slim limbs sprawl erratic,
And eschew all kinds of dress;
If the whole thing's idiotic,
Then your picture's a success!

If you're asked for explanations,
Talk vaguely of design;
Or adopt a few evasions
About temperament in line.
But if nothing save confession
Of your real intent will do,
Say the hags are your impression
Of the Women who are New.

– M.

R.L.S.

from the Glasgow Evening News, *18 December 1894*

Before the firelight, in the sober gloaming,
The one far-wandered readily will tell
The brave memorials of his weary roaming,
Until he holds us in a warlock spell.
And, sudden, at the lozen comes a rapping –
'Oh, Sennachie, I'd speak wi' ye, my son!'
The wanderer for the cold night must be happing
Ere yet his latest tale is half-way done.

And where the door is snecked behind the rover,
Who went with yon Convoy we dare not name,
We tell again his curious stories over,
The thought in every heart the same, the same –
'Oh these were fine, the stories he narrated,
But there were others that he had in store;
Ours was the gain, indeed, could he have waited,
But now our ears are vain for evermore.'

So you are happed and gone, and there you're lying,
Deep down the world, upon the slope of seas;
Upon the lonely peak where clouds are flying
No sounds of homeland on the feverish breeze.
We need not keep the peat and cruisie glowing,
The good-wife may put bye her ale and bread,
For you, that kept the crack so blythly going,
Have learned the dour, dull silence of the dead.

Far, far away, where Taca saw day waning,
On bossy isles that stud the dreary main,
Did you expect, your eager vision straining,
To catch a blink of Scotland's lights again?
To hear the laverock's pipe, the kirk bell's clanging,
Come on some errant breeze across the waves,
Or smell the sweetness of the birches hanging
Above the unforgotten martyrs' graves?

Snell winter's here, the mists like wool are trailing,
The busy rain-smirr rots the fallen leaf;
Among the glens old Ossian's ghosts are wailing
As if they guessed at something of our grief.
But one last sprig of Highland heather's growing
Upon the hills of home that well you knew.
And it (oh! tell him, wind that's south'ard blowing)
My wanderer, my Sennachie, 's for you.

– M.

NETTLES

O sad for me Glen Aora,
 Where I have friends no more,
For lowly lie the rafters,
 And the lintels of the door.
The friends are all departed,
 The hearth-stone's black and cold,
And sturdy grows the nettle
 On the place beloved of old.

O! black might be that ruin
 Where my fathers dwelt so long,
And nothing hide the shame of it,
 The ugliness and wrong;
The cabar and the corner-stone
 Might bleach in wind and rains,
But for the gentle nettle
 That took such a courtier's pains.

Here's one who has no quarrel
  With the nettle thick and tall,
That hides the cheerless hearthstone
  And screens the humble wall,
That clusters on the footpath
  Where the children used to play,
And guards a household's sepulchre
  From all who come the way.

There's deer upon the mountain,
  There's sheep along the glen,
The forests hum with feather,
  But where are now the men?
Here's but my mother's garden
  Where soft the footsteps fall,
My folks are quite forgotten,
  But the nettle's over all.

JOHN O' LORN

My plaid is on my shoulder and my boat is on the shore,
  And it's all bye wi' auld days and you;
Here's a health and here's a heartbreak, for it's hame, my dear, no more,
  To the green glens, the fine glens we knew!

'Twas for the sake o' glory, but oh! wae upon the wars,
  That brought my father's son to sic a day;
I'd rather be a craven, wi' nor name, nor fame, nor scars,
  Than turn a wanderer's heel on Moidart Bay.

And you, in the day-time, you'll be here, and in the mirk,
  Wi' the kind heart, the open hand, and free;
And far awa' in foreign France, in town or camp or kirk,
  I'll be wondering if you keep a thought for me.

But nevermore the heather nor the bracken at my knees,
  I'm poor John o' Lorn, a broken man;
For an auld Hielan' story I must sail the swinging seas,
  A chief without a castle or a clan.

My plaid is on my shoulder and my boat is on the shore,
  And it's all bye wi' auld days and you;

Here's a health and here's a heartbreak, for it's hame, my dear, no more,
    To the green glens, the fine glens we knew!

LAMENT FOR MACLEOD OF RAASAY

Allan Ian Òg Macleod of Raasay,
    Treasure of mine, lies yonder dead in Loos,
His body unadorned by Highland raiment,
    Trammelled, for glorious hours, in Saxon trews.
Never man before of all his kindred
    Went so apparelled to the burial knowe,
But with the pleated tartan for his shrouding,
    The bonnet on his brow.

My grief! that Allan should depart so sadly,
    When no wild mountain pipe his bosom wrung,
With no one of his race beside his shoulder
    Who knew his history and spoke his tongue!
Ah! lonely death and drear for darling Allan!
    Before his ghost had taken wings and gone,
Loud would he cry in Gaelic to his gallants,
    'Children of storm, press on!'

Beside him, when he fell there in his beauty,
    Macleods of all the islands should have died;
Brave hearts his English! – but they could not fathom
    To what old deeps the voice of Allan cried;
When in that strange French country-side war-battered,
    Far from the creeks of home and hills of heath,
A boy, he kept the old tryst of his people
    With the dark girl Death.

Oh Allan Ian Òg! Oh Allan aluinn!
    Sore is my heart remembering the past,
And you of Raasay's ancient gentle children
    The farthest-wandered, kindliest and last!
It should have been the brave dead of the islands
    That heard ring o'er their tombs your battle cry,
To shake them from their sleep again, and quicken
    Peaks of Torridon and Skye.

Gone in the mist the brave Macleods of Raasay,
  Far furth from fortune, sundered from their lands,
And now the last grey stone of Castle Raasay,
  Lies desolate and levelled with the sands.
But pluck the old isle from its roots deep-planted
  Where tides cry coronach round the Hebrides,
And it will bleed of the Macleods lamented,
  Their loves and memories!

†

PROLOGUE OF LAMENT BY PLAYERS

April has come to the Isles again blythe as a lover,
  Shaking out bird-song and sunshine, and soothing the tides:
April has come to the Hebrides, filled them with frolic,
  Only in Lewis of sorrow, bleak winter abides.
Always they went to the battles, the people of Lewis,
  And always they fell, in the wars of a thousand years;
Peace never to Lewis brought Springtime of joy or of season,
  The wars might be won, but her women were fated to tears!

That is, today, why in Lewis the lark sings unheeded,
  The sparkle of waves in the sea-creeks gladdens no eye;
No dance to the pipe in the croft, and no mirth in the sheiling,
  Waebegone, weary, the hours of the Spring go by.
They had lit up their windows for beacons, the women of Lewis,
  The peat-fires were glowing a welcome, the table was spread;
The sea brought their sons back from war, and the long years of tumult,
  And cast them ashore, on the cliffs of their boyhood, dead!

We are but players in motley, brief moths of a season,
  Mimicking passion and laughter, and loving and grief;
But yet are we kin to all souls that are sad and enduring,
  Acquainted with sorrow ourselves, we would bring them relief.
Far, far is the cry to the Lews and its storm-bitten beaches,
  To the Isle of lamenting, that lies on the sea like a gem;
If aught be of feeling profound in this place of our playing,
  'Tis because we remember the women, our thoughts are with them!

11

The Man of Letters

INTRODUCTION

Neil Munro was a major figure in the Scottish literary scene and, indeed, beyond Scotland, with a noteworthy influence both as a creative writer and a critic. He was in considerable demand for occasional contributions to various publications. Much of this material has now almost totally vanished from sight, and some of it, for example his perceptive article on Joseph Conrad, was never widely available in Britain, appearing as it did in a limited memorial edition of Conrad's work, published by Doubleday in the United States.

Our choice of material in this section spans most of Munro's literary career. The earliest piece, dating from 1899, is an essay on Rudyard Kipling which appeared in Good Words. *Munro's novel* Gilian the Dreamer *had appeared in this very popular London-based literary magazine in the previous year. As we have noted in 'Some Contemporaries' Munro had reservations about Kipling in his 'Technical Dictionary' mode but freely recognised Kipling's overall merits: 'the marvel is that a writer so profuse and versatile should have made mistakes so few'. Munro had read Kipling as his works appeared: in his diary for April 1890 he recorded that he had read* Soldiers Three *and rated it 'very good'. However, five months later* Plain Tales from the Hills *was described as being only 'middling'.*

Munro makes an interesting comparison between Kipling and Scott. Kipling, he suggests, had made the life of the British soldier and the work of the Indian Empire become real and actual to the domestic reader for the first time: '. . . we were in a new world, where, luckily, people, as in the days of Scott, were doing things eternally, and not simply whining at existence.'

Scott is fairly credited with the invention of the genre of the historical novel, a genre whose justification lies in the fact that although the past is different it has also got lessons to teach the present. Munro suggests that Kipling, as poet and novelist of the Empire, not only brought India into the expanded consciousness of the British reader but also created a new and vibrant literary genre dealing with the Imperial experience. While

Munro seems uneasy with aspects of Kipling's imperialism he recognises the human sympathy he displays for 'Tommy Atkins' and his personification in Kipling's fiction – Terence Mulvaney, the hero of Soldiers Three.

In 1909 Munro contributed 'Carlyle's Last Sitting to Whistler' to The Odd Volume, *an annual publication produced in aid of the funds of the National Book Trade Provident Society. The subject, a witty and imaginative account of the final portrait sitting of Thomas Carlyle, the great Scottish historian, philosopher and sage, for James McNeill Whistler, was an intriguing and appropriate one which makes effective use of the idiosyncrasies of both men's natures. Whistler's portrait was painted in 1872/3 when the subject was in his seventy-seventh year. Munro, as an art critic and experienced observer of the Scottish artistic scene, well understood the influence that Whistler had exercised over the Glasgow Boys, like Walton, Guthrie, Melville, Hornel and Henry. It was due to E. A. Walton and James Guthrie's efforts that Whistler's iconic portrait,* Arrangement in Grey and Black, No. 2: Thomas Carlyle, *was acquired for the Glasgow municipal collection in 1891. Carlyle died in 1881 and Whistler in 1903.*

'The Celestial Bookshop', which appeared in The Odd Volume *in 1910, is a brief fantasy on some of the great unwritten works of literature. Of particular note is Stevenson's* Barrisdale, a Romance – *a novel about the Colonel Barrisdale who features in* The New Road *and is the central figure in the short story 'Jaunty Jock'.*

The Odd Volume for 1915 is the source for 'Wotherspoon's Windfall', a humorous account of what happens when a rural postman inherits £50,000 from a brother in Canada. Munro had been on a journalistic trip to Canada in 1903 as part of a promotional effort by the Canadian authorities, and this perhaps provided some of the background.

The short story 'Old Brand' probably owes something to an autobiographical source. Munro's first staff job in journalism was on the Greenock Advertiser *in early 1884. He then worked for the* Glasgow News, *a morning daily paper, not the same title as the later* Glasgow Evening News *with which he was so long associated, and then was a reporter for the* Falkirk Herald *between November 1885 and April 1887. This little tale of a young reporter, an old editor and the ticklish problems of obituary writing, or 'doing the stiffs', on a local newspaper was Munro's contribution to* The Queen's Gift Book, *a charitable publication produced in 1915 in aid of convalescent hospitals for limbless servicemen. Quite which paper from Munro's past provided the inspiration for 'Old Brand' is unclear. There unfortunately was not a 'Courier' in either Greenock or Falkirk and while the rival paper referred to, the* Telegraph, *does suggests*

Greenock, where a daily of that title still flourishes, the feel of the piece perhaps rather suggests Falkirk.

'Call of the Pipes to Scotland' appeared in Country Life *in December, 1916. Topical, in its relation to the on-going war, it also reflects Munro's interest in the bagpipes – an interest which had found expression before the war in his taking lessons on the instrument; his diary recording a first trial lesson in 1894. The music of the pipes inspired much of his wartime poetry – what Munro called his 'Bagpipe Ballads' – works like 'Hey Jock!' and 'Pipes in Arras'. After the War this interest would continue with a contribution to Sir Bruce Seton's book* The Bagpipe in War.

'Ballantrae' originally appeared in Munro's 'Views and Reviews' column and, very slightly altered, was offered as his contribution to Atalanta's Garland, *a 1926 volume published in aid of the Edinburgh University Women's Union. The origins of this essay, inspired by Stevenson's novel* The Master of Ballantrae *and a walking tour that Stevenson had made in Carrick and Galloway, may well have been as material for the original concept of* Ayrshire Idylls – *when that volume was designed to be a 'kind of artistic itinerary of Ayrshire'. In any event it combines topographical and literary interest in an attractive fashion and represents the type of general literary journalism which Munro combined with reviews of new books and topical gossip about literature and the book world in his Thursday 'Views and Reviews' columns.*

Stevenson and Munro, although they never met, have many significant interconnections. Munro's masterpiece, The New Road, *has often been compared with Stevenson's* Kidnapped – *although it could be argued that Munro's novel is in some respects the more complex and rewarding work because the clash of personalities and backgrounds, which Stevenson engineers by bringing together the Lowlander, David Balfour, and the Highlander, Alan Breck Stewart, is managed by Munro with an exclusively Highland cast. Munro visited Stevenson's friend and collaborator, W. E. Henley while travelling in England in 1893. Henley, then editing the* National Observer, *had published 'Red Hand', a story that later formed part of the* Lost Pibroch *collection, a few months earlier. Henley, by then editing the* New Review, *published Munro's short story 'Jus Primæ Noctis' in 1897. On Stevenson's death in December 1894 Munro wrote a poem 'R.L.S.' as a memorial piece for the* Evening News. *He later altered this poem and it appears as 'The Story Teller' in the posthumous volume of Munro's collected verse. In its original form it appears elsewhere in this anthology. On Munro's own death it became a commonplace of tributes to describe him as the successor to Stevenson. The* Glasgow Herald *wrote that although he had written little in the latter years of his life: '. . . he had already accomplished his life work – of taking up and wearing the mantle of RLS with a personal grace until the next writer might come . . .'*

'Robert Bontine Cunninghame Graham' is another 'Views and Reviews' column, this time dating from February, 1905. Cunninghame Graham was an admirer of Munro's work and wrote to him in characteristically enthusiastic style in December 1898 on reading John Splendid *and again a few days later about the short story, 'Jus Primæ Noctis' which had been rejected by Blackwoods for* The Lost Pibroch *on the grounds of its sexual subject matter. Cunninghame Graham, nicknamed 'Don Roberto' from his South American adventures, came from an ancient Scottish aristocratic lineage. The Ardoch referred to in Munro's article was the Cunninghame Graham house near Dumbarton on the Clyde. The reference to Graham as 'the old Trafalgar Square warhorse' refers to his involvement in the Bloody Sunday riots of 13 November 1887 when socialist, radical and Irish demonstrators were violently dispersed by troops and police after a demonstration in London's Trafalgar Square. Cunninghame Graham was at the time a Liberal MP on the radical wing of that party and was one of those imprisoned after the Trafalgar Square demonstration. Cunninghame Graham's socialism and later move to Scottish nationalism (he became a founder of the National Party of Scotland in 1928) might have been at odds with Munro's mainstream Toryism, but each recognised in the other a literary craftsman of individuality and talent.*

Cunninghame Graham in an obituary of Munro for the Evening News *wrote: 'Perhaps he was our finest Scottish writer: that is for Scots, for most Scottish writers write for the English public, limning a snivelling, sentimental Scots . . .'*

He also noted Munro's poetic vein and his 'sly Celtic humour' and observed that in all Munro wrote, journalism included:

> *. . . there was a literary tang. And why for not, as some of his own characters might have said, for much of journalism is as good literature as the greater part of epoch-making novels, that come out today as modern, and almost before they are ready for their bourne, the dust-heap, have become antiquated*

When he spoke in 1935 at the unveiling of the monument to Neil Munro, Graham described Munro as 'the apostolic successor of Sir Walter Scott' and predicted immortality for him.

Munro, Cunninghame Graham and Conrad, although circumstances dictated that they did not often meet, enjoyed a close friendship and a reciprocal admiration of each others' work. As we have suggested elsewhere in this anthology Munro was an early and consistent advocate of Conrad's work.

Munro's appreciation of Conrad was given an international stage when he was asked to provide an article on Conrad for the fourteenth edition of the Encyclopaedia Britannica *published in 1929. When Conrad's American publishers, Doubleday, Page & Co., brought out a limited memorial edition of Conrad's complete works in 1925 they invited Munro to contribute an essay on Conrad for inclusion in* The Nigger of the Narcissus.

This appreciation of Conrad was based on a warm relationship between the two men which had continued from their first meeting in 1898. Munro had described The Nigger of the Narcissus *in his* Evening News *column as 'unquestionably one of the best half-dozen novels written in England in the present generation'. Conrad reciprocated this esteem; writing to William Blackwood, whose* Blackwood's Magazine *regularly published both men's works, he said: 'I am most sincerely glad to see Munro's book in its 4th edition. Munro is an artist – besides being an excellent fellow with a pretty weakness for my work.'*

Doubleday asked Conrad to come across to the United States in 1923 to help promote his works. A reluctant Conrad insisted on travelling from the Clyde on a Glasgow ship and meeting some Glasgow friends before he went. Conrad and Munro met for dinner in Glasgow's North British Hotel in April 1923 and, according to the account by Munro's friend and protégé, the novelist George Blake, after dinner the two distinguished novelists went into George Square where Munro persuaded Conrad that he could become an honorary Glaswegian by throwing a stone into the outstretched top hat of the statue of James Oswald MP, which graces the north-east corner of the Square.

When Conrad and Munro had first met in 1898 they had spent a long night together, first of all at a dinner in the home of the pioneer radiologist Dr John McIntyre. In a letter Conrad wrote:

> *What we wanted (apparently) was more whisky. We got it. Mrs McIntyre went to bed. At one o'clock Munro and I went out into the street. We talked. I had read up* The Lost Pibroch *which I do think wonderful in a way. We foregathered very much indeed and I believe Munro didn't get home till five in the morning.*

'Foregathered' is a fine and useful addition to our list of euphemisms.

A degree of 'foregathering' had clearly gone on in the North British Hotel in April 1923 to send the fifty-nine year old Munro and the sixty-five year old Conrad out into the Glasgow night to throw stones, like naughty schoolboys, at James Oswald's inoffensive statue.

MR RUDYARD KIPLING

The past month has seen oceans of ink spilled in the recountment of Mr Kipling's achievements, yet of the myriad commentators who made the novelists's sick-bed inspire their laudatory pens no one seems to have attempted an analysis of the man, and what, in our indispensable phrase, we call his message. It has been iterated to weariness that he writes with the star-gemmed quill of genius and the fiery exaltation of the patriot. These are the more obvious of his qualities, the abstract impressions created by his work, that would of themselves perhaps have left us cold because of their very commonness, for Providence flicks a brain-patch a little out of the normal in one or two skulls in every English Board School (with a double allowance for North Britain), and reverence for the Old Rag, the zest of the glory of going on and of being an Englishman, is thrust, with gas-pipe drill and the manual exercise, into multitudinous Boys' Brigades till pride of country exudes from every pore. The clanging patriotic note we have heard so much about in the past few weeks is, at least in its more arrogant note of Imperialism, by no means the most universally esteemed of Mr Kipling's characteristics, nor is it new with him. Did not Campbell trumpet to our hearts in the sonorous call that finds its last lingering haunting note in the name of Elsinore; and did not Tennyson and Doyle and Swinburne, eminently among others, strike lustily on Britain's brass-bossed shield generations more or less before the refrains of Atkins and the Adventurers hummed through the century end?

And yet the application of the spectroscope to a star so new and dazzling is no trivial business, for directly of the star itself we have seen but little. We have biographical glimpses of an infant in Bombay, a schoolboy at Westward Ho, a reporter and sub-editor in India, but no intimate details of what went to the making of a personality matured marvellously at the age of twenty-one, and destined to become the most potent influence in English letters in his own generation, so far as it has gone. What we know of Mr Kipling must be gathered from his work: him the interviewer has followed vainly, and the personal paragrapher has had to dish up for his patrons disappointing and more or less apocryphal scraps. We find revealed in those works a singular physical and mental vitality, 'a very strong man', as he has said himself of Tommy Atkins, with a great and exuberant zest in every aspect of life, with huge self-confidence, humour, irony, curiosity, and stoicism in a wonderful degree. That ever-apparent delight he has in the terminology of crafts, trades, and callings obviously outwith his direct experience, may be accepted as indicative not only of the common artistic appreciation for out-of-the-way and pregnant words or phrases, but of a real love for the teeming interests, the human activities they express. For generations our poets and romancers have cherished the old mechanical plant of their ancestors – loves, seasons, scenery, and (to a lamentable and indecent extent of late) the internals. Mr Kipling, thrown by the caprice of fortune into a career oscillating between two worlds, began the business of his life by surrendering most of the old conventional inspirations and locutions, and used his eyes to look abroad upon the marvel of the modern world. Cortes and his men (or, more correctly, Balboa) saw from their peak in Darien but an empty, wind-blown ocean; Kipling had a greater cause for wild surmise as perhaps the very first – Whitman out of count – to behold the Seven Seas thrid by the traffic of man, so infinitely romantic, so infinitely eloquent of the irrepressible valour of the race. Lesser men it has left unmoved – unless they were underwriters – him it touched to great emotional issues. It has been so with him on land too. Tommy Atkins and Britain's pioneer work on vexed frontiers have inspired him, not primarily because he was an Englishman, but because he was a man moved profoundly by the persistence of his fellows in a world whose pathos and oft futility he has obviously at the same time understood. Man the artificer, 'the disease of the agglutinate dust, lifting alternate feet', Mr Kipling has seen in the light of comprehensive humanity and brotherhood. Ships threshing the seas triumphant, armies combating ague, fever, heathendom, and bloody death; railways roaring over continents, hunters boldly venturing upon trails mysterious and forlorn, outposts of progress in raw new lands – the terrific yet magnificent significance of these human enterprises has impressed him. And all that he has observed he has seen with the philosophic eye, he has enveloped his every picture, his every sentiment with stoic calm, that, now we have emerged from the experiments of the problem – novelists and the didactic poets, is essentially the mood in which the century shall go out.

About a dozen books – a book a year for the years of his activity – provide us with the scope of Mr Kipling's genius. If he wrote no more they were sufficient to establish his reputation as a man marking an epoch in English letters. We could indeed sacrifice some of his work without detracting in the smallest degree from his permanent reputation, though the loss might mean the surrender of many light and cheerful hours. 'Under the Deodars', for instance, that exposure in youthful sarcasm of domestic eccentricities in Anglo-Indian life, so often superficially flippant and smart, reveals nothing of the mature, reflecting Kipling; another generation will probably confess that it would part without a pang with these and other stories where the Hauksbee flourishes. 'Brugglesmith' and 'Badalia Herodsfoot', 'My Sunday at Home', and a few other caprices of his prose muse might also pass into the limbo unwept, unhousel'd, unanel'd. The marvel is that a writer so profuse and versatile should have made mistakes so few. The perfect remainder, speaking comparatively, charm by their novelty, their vitality, their indubitable genius, but most of all because of the man they reveal, as must be the case in all great works of literary art, Mr Browning's doctrine of reticence to the contrary. In them we find the human affection that inspires good literature, the essential, but not too prominent, touch of pathos, the tolerance that says the charitable word for the weakling, yet bows the head to just punishment, for man is master of his fate. It may be that Mr Kipling has sought after the artist's impartiality in limning such a portrait as that of Terence Mulvaney, surely one of the most permanent and lovable characters in fiction, but despite himself his personal predilections emerge in the portrait. We have in that erratic representative of our red-coat rule in India the most familiar type of his creator's heroes. Mulvaney borrows some of the blackguardism of D'Artagnan; he is a little of the bully, of the drunkard, the barrack-room Don Juan, with few claims upon our respect as sober Christians and decent citizens. Yet how humorous are his lovable attributes; his cameraderie shines on him like a cuirass, his response to his better man is frequent and convincing. Savagely surrounded, savagely descended, the bitter circumstances of his life conspiring always to show the worst of him, we must be prizing, as his painter does, the occasions when he defies his destiny and laboriously acts the man. What sins are we not half ready to condone in a hero so speckled when, in 'With the Main Draft', having kept his heat-tortured comrades amused through the sleepless night with his story,

' "Oh, Terence," I said, "it's you that have the tongue." '

'He looked at me wearily, his eyes were sunk in his head, and his face was drawn and white. "Ey, ey," said he, "I've blandandhared thim through the night somehow, but can thim that hilps others hilp thimselves? Answer me that, sorr." '

Mulvaney is the composite Kipling hero. Unlike the musketeer of Louis XIII, he moves in an atmosphere, not a vacuum tube; we know not only what he is, but why he is what he is; he is a living person, not a marionette. This realism and this atmospheric envelopment distinguish all the best of Mr Kipling's creations. His women, whether they be camp heroines, dubious ladies of the married quarters, creatures of Simla intrigue, or common wives and mothers, stand upon their legs, move and have their being in their appropriate and native air, a phrase here and there, let slip as if it had no great relation to the matter at issue, telling all the history and ancestry which the new novelist of heredity must have numerous chapters, doleful and melancholy chapters, to lay bare. Mrs Hauksbee is not a heroine except to the tolerant artistic eye that beholds her wonderfully human and true to a life that has contradictions and complexities utterly beyond our unravelling. I have said we might part with her without a pang, and yet I doubt if we could; rather I should have said we could let go her attendant train of vapid and caddish followers, and forget the social life of which she is the centre. She herself is Mr Kipling's strongest female character. He knows her past, he reveals all the ignominy of her present, but, carrying his tolerance further in her than in any other, he betrays what seems an admiration for her powerful personality.

In his first few books Mr Kipling, with heroes and heroines more or less variant of the two named, made more populous the world about us of unforgettable men and women of the imagination. 'Plain Tales from the Hills', and the half-dozen booklets published first by Wheeler of Allahabad, in grey paper covers that yet to look upon is to experience a sense of boon friendships – these contain the work that he will find it difficult to improve upon. There we were made acquaint for the first time with the Terentian philosophy –

> For to admire and for to see,
> For to be'old this world so wide;

the British soldier became for the first time something more than a Surrey-side melodramatic tinpot hero; our little wars with Pathan and Dacoit jumped into actuality, and were no longer occult suggestions, remote, far-off, incomprehensible in the brief telegraphic news of the morning papers. India itself, with its name redolent of romance from the days of Virgil, found its exponent for the modern man, and we became of a sudden familiar with a country where nothing had ever happened before but famines and mutinies; with its heats, its rains, its colour, its vast spaces, its commingling odours. The hot savage soil on the fringe of barbarian blackness turned up red to the coulter of civilisation. Whitechapel and the English areas where zymotic disease abounds wrestled for our glory with savage Orientals; we were in a new world, where, luckily, people, as in the days of Scott, were doing things eternally, and not simply whining at existence.

'The Drums of the Fore and Aft' and 'The Man Who Would Be King', these notably among the early essays in a new method of fiction stirred us by the vivid illusion they conveyed, by the vista they suggested of space and action, by the romance with which they were informed in every image, the wholesome manliness that throbbed in every sentiment. It is in the genre of which they are the best examples that Mr Kipling is pre-eminent. In the superficial elements of many of his other stories there is much imitable though novel and ingenious, in those named and in the horror of 'The Mark of the Beast' and 'The End of the Passage', there is inspiration of a much more rare and elusive kind, a quality that cannot be repeated by any other writer.

The gods were extravagantly good to Mr Kipling, for with his gift of dramatic tale and a career to equip him for its expression, they gave him the gift of poetry, lacking which prose narrative is soulless and evanescent. It is the poetic insight that over and over again redeems brutal and even vulgar passages in his tales from our indifference or contempt; there he would have shown the poet if 'Departmental Ditties', 'Barrack-room Ballads', and 'The Seven Seas' had never been written. But he has in his works of verse justified himself as the laureate of English endeavour. A brain-weary people, sick of abstruse sermons played upon dulcimers, have hailed with gladness a song and chorus accompanied by the banjo. Some of the strenuous young gentlemen who sing in pestilently unmusical and jerky measure of life, time, and early demise have an equipment Mr Kipling cannot or does not boast of. They rejoice in vocabularies extensive and precious; they have a fastidiousness that keeps them clear of the cheap tune, the vulgar hero, the sentiment of the Lion Comique, the dialect that is unheard in drawing-rooms. They can write much that Mr Kipling could not write to save his soul, but they cannot write so as to be read or listened to, which, cant aside, has been the first ambition of every ballad-maker since the days when Homer smote his lyre. Literature in prose or poetry is saved from eternal perdition by fresh starts; just when the material of conventional verse has been spread out thin to invisibility, and sheer intellect is going to upset our apple-cart, a lark soars into the heavens with a simple song for lesson, a man sheds the cerements of convention, steps back from the choir, and gives his natural voice a trial unafraid. Then, no matter what he sings – weariness and fret, the joy of life, passion, Spring or stars, if a robust individuality, a clean nature, a lyric lilt and cadence be his, we must be listening. His are the airs that the people find haunting; they may be even only temporary in appeal, but permanence is not, in spite of all we say to the contrary, the first and greatest essential of poetry. Wharton boasted that with 'Lillibulero' he had whistled a king out of three kingdoms; we have to-day forgotten that air that Uncle Toby so constantly dwelt on, but in the final balancing of things that have influenced, who can say that the forgotten 'Lillibulero' is not more weighty than studious measures in classic mould a few rare exclusive souls have sung for centuries?

With material entirely new, with a method novel, Kipling, in 'Barrack-room Ballads' and 'The Seven Seas', has captured the general ear and touched the general heart. That, it may be retorted, was done aforetime by the Muse of Mr Sims. Yet in this instance there is a great difference, though it seems sacrilege to hint the necessity of differentiation. It is not the music-hall audience alone that is impressed by the weird terror of 'Danny Deever', the sentiment of the majestic 'Ballad of East and West', the *élan* of the 'Sons of the Widow', and the cadence and wistfulness of 'Mandalay'. In these measures artists have found the lyric note no way abased. Good as 'Barrack-room Ballads' were, the more reent 'Seven Seas' was better. There we found Mr Kipling still with 'the best words in the best order', as Coleridge defined poetry, but more profound in the hearts of man. A wider sweep of interests, a more mature valuation of the phenomena of life, a more opulent and canorous note peals in his lines, the man behind the instrument is more finely revealed. Any claim by any other living man than the author of 'A Song of the English' to be considered the laureate by divine right of English peoples would be ridiculous. But the Imperialism of the book is only one of its impressive features. The age of steam and telegraph, Hotchkiss guns and Saratoga trunks has found its balladist there, and he has found nothing common or unclean. The soldiers of the later military ballads, too, betray an ageing creator; they are still strumming on the banjo, but their songs have lost some of the shallow inspiration of the 'Alls; they lean upon homing bulwarks and reflect upon the sweet futilities that have stayed them here and there upon the sides of 'the 'appy roads that take you o'er the world'. And the seas cry in his work for the first time, not the played-out oceans of dhow and galley and picturesque but unwieldy three-deckers, but of the darting cruiser, the liner spurning leagues a day in every weather, the buffeting of the elements, and the engineer.

There are other works of Mr Kipling than those I have named. The 'Jungle Books' delight by their insight, almost magic, of the untamed wilds and all their residents; *Captains Courageous*, less felicitously inspired but yet original and unique, *Many Inventions*, and *The Day's Work, Life's Handicap, The Light that Failed*, and *The Naulakha* have material fresh and strong. Taking either his prose or poetry in separate parts, testing by ordinary canons, it will happen that the writing seems often to be on a lower plane than the imaginative inspiration, and a sense of something wanting may ensue. But surveying the work of Mr Kipling as a whole, the most fastidious must be impressed by the greatness of its genius, the scope and variety it displays, the essentially wholesome influence it creates.

✝

CARLYLE'S LAST SITTING TO WHISTLER

The afternoon light was fast disappearing, and the painter darted to and from his picture in a final fury of inspiration, deepening a shadow here, breaking a line there, but most often poised on tiptoe, some yards from the easel, his brush and palette held up like a rapier and shield, his eyes swinging from the canvas to the silent figure of the man sunk in thought.

A dapper, dandified little man, with a flowing scarf escaping at the neck of the painter's blouse he wore, his hair in disorder, one white splash among its dark array. He had at one stage of his work hummed a French 'chanson' somewhat out of tune, but now was utterly silent in the ecstatic moment of fulfilment.

'Mon dieu! C'est epatant!' he said to himself once in a fervour of admiration at his own work; but that was all; the same 'By God, that's genius!' of Thackeray when he wrote of the breaking of the swords in *Esmond*, and the sitter, far off in a dream, broke up for a moment the brooding sadness, the weariness of his visage, and with a quick return to his surroundings just said, 'Beg paurdon, did ye speak?' He got no answer from the abstracted artist, and quickly sank again into those deeps of pensive thought from which the ejaculations of the latter had withdrawn him.

It was an uncomfortable enough posture the old man occupied – at first against his own protestations; for the slim, rush-bottomed Morris chair was pushed sideways up against the wall, as close as it was possible to place it without too seriously hampering his right arm, and he sat on it sideways to the wall, as men never do in the real life, which Art often hates, his legs crossed at the knees in a fashion that had given him 'pins and needles' a score of times in the course of his half-dozen séances with the painter. The artist himself – incarnate spirit of unrest – could not have so sat for ten minutes, but hard wood-bottomed chairs in Annandale and evening worship there in youth, on his knee on stone-flagged floors, had made the old man able to suffer the martyrdom of immovability under the present circumstances without complaint. He would have preferred to be more comfortable, but he had early given up hope of understanding why the artist insisted on a pose so eccentric; he had, indeed, given up the hope of understanding the artist himself, who was the most extraordinary being he had come across since daft Will Dyce, of Ecclefechan. So he sat each day as instructed with a plaid over his knees, and his worst hat – as selected by the artist – cocked quaintly before him, and, having thrust from his mind by a strong effort of will the disquieting thought that he was made to look ridiculous by adopting such an attitude and wasting so much of God's good time on a kind of mountebank performance, he lapsed as speedily as he could into the dream state. Now and then his lips moved quickly as if he spoke to himself, and this afternoon as the last touches were being put on his presentment (though he did not know it) he came with a start out of his abstraction, and said, 'Mr Whustler'.

'Yes, yes,' said the artist, feverishly fumbling among his sheaf of brushes for an essential one.

'Mr Whustler,' proceeded the old man very slowly and earnestly, 'there is a consideration in my mind that has been whirling round and round in it this hour or more like a piece of stick in the eddy of what in the North we call a burn, into my Annihilation of Self, my "Selbsttodtung", as the Germans say, some –'

'D——n!' said the artist, emphatically, to himself. 'Here's another speech; he's going to harrow me with more rococo utterance; I loathe your rococo rhetoricians.' And then, aloud, 'Just one moment, Mr Carlyle; don't move your – your jaw. I'm finishing the upper lip. Ha! ha! Just a second, s'il vous plait,' and he concealed himself from the sage by going right up to the canvas, where he grimaced comically as his hand hovered over the wet surface seeking a last imperfect spot on which to light. There was none. The work was done. He scrutinised it carefully close at hand and from the centre of the studio, then sighed a long sigh, half regret, half relief, threw his palette and brushes with a clatter on a table smeared with paints, and turned on his sitter with a radiant smile.

'Congratulate me, Mr Carlyle,' he said. 'The picture is done.'

'Done,' repeated Carlyle, dubiously, for he had never yet been asked to open up his coat and show his watch-chain.

'Done,' said Whistler. 'It is exquisite; it is perfect; it is worthy even of me. I congratulate you, Mr Carlyle, on my work. You will live, sir, yes, by heavens! you will live, and you will be remembered and adored on the canvas centuries after the mortuary celebrities who go to Bushey Park or St John's Wood for their portraits are dead as Diogones – burned in their own bitumen.'

'It's a gra-a-nd and comfortin' thought,' said Carlyle, looking askance at the perky figure of the artist now almost waltzing up and down the floor. He rose suddenly from the chair which in the stupid way of half-guinea, rush-bottomed Morrisses fell on its back behind him; threw the plaid and the hat that had cumbered his knees on to a sofa and produced from the pocket of his frock coat a clean clay pipe. He never glanced at his own portrait.

'What I was going to say, Mr Whustler,' he remarked, 'was that there was whirling and birling round in my mind in the midst of those

Penelope operations of thine – of yours I mean – an exposition of smoke. "Divine tobacco that from East to West cheers the tar's labours and the Turkman's rest".'

'Ah! have a cigarette,' said the artist, dancing towards an open bureau littered with old accounts, sketch books, and visiting cards, from among which he fished out a box.

'No,' said Carlyle, emphatically, and lighting his pipe, 'to the cigarette or the cigar I have ever said an Everlasting No. Methinks paper was made for some Diviner Purpose – some nobler end than to be incinerated under the moustachios of puppies, or inhaled by the lungs of foolish men. I can but thank ye, Mr Whustler; I am, as you know, a Pipe Man,' and relapsing into a chair with his back to the portrait, of whose existence he was apparently oblivious, he puffed voluminous clouds, and stared at vacancy.

Whistler spent ten minutes more in elaborating his own butterfly signature on the canvas and cleansing his brushes, and there was even yet no sign of interest on the part of Carlyle. But the circumstance never struck the artist; so far as he was concerned there was only himself and his picture in the room. At that moment he felt the room too small, too abominably mean for such a noble picture; miraculously to him it seemed to extend beyond the walls and fill the whole world, a vast and magnificent thing in whose shadow great men crept like mice. It sang angelically, like a celestial oratorio; to him it shone so that it did not matter a curse if the sun now disappearing over the chimney cans of Chelsea ever came up again. Ah he felt good, good!

'James,' he said to himself clapping himself on the shoulder. 'James, this is *the stuff*, by God! Poor old National Gallery! Poor old Rembrandt! Poor old Velasquez! Now, let me think; who the devil was Velasquez? Well – I'm sorry for them, but it is every man for himself. What shall I call it?'

He nervously picked up cigarettes after cigarette, to throw them away after a puff or two; his eyes never left the canvas; he surveyed it with his head first on one side and then on another, through hollowed hands, through a paper tube, in the reflection of a mirror. A million noble military bands went crashing through his blood; he trod on air; he wholly forgot the dull old silent man smoking a clay pipe. What he wanted was wine – wine – wine; and two or three who would listen for hours while he explained – ah, that was all that was needed to make the night a rapture!

'The Masterpiece!' he told himself – 'the veritable Masterpiece. And there are still people who dare to address me as Jimmy!'

'Mr Whustler,' said a voice that startled him; and he turned hastily to find an old man smoking in a chair. Who the dickens was this old man?

What was his name? His model. Yes, yes, of course – his model, a most useful and almost indispensable thing. Ta-ra-ra-ra, tum-ti-ti-ta-ra-ra.'

He suddenly remembered and was disgusted that Carlyle should not have shown the slightest sign of interest in his portrait. Over to him he skipped and 'Heavens!' he cried, 'you have actually not seen it yet! And life so brief!'

Carlyle tapped out the ashes from his pipe and rose.

'Oh, the bit picture,' he said – I forgot.'

'Forgot!' cried Whistler, tearing his hair.

'It's a humblin' sight,' said Carlyle with a deep sigh as he looked for a moment on his own effigy, then ran a finger along the mouldings of the frame.

'It is! it is!' said the artist joyously; 'the whole Academy will abrade themselves with shards and sit in their own studio stove cinders for pity of themselves when they see it.'

'What is it Worth now, this Work of thine; this pregnant Device?' said Carlyle. 'From some Idea, some exercitation the ganglia doubtless it did first of all take beginnings; some Thought of Value must it have in that Hierarchy of which they tell me thou art not the meanest.'

'Value?' repeated Whistler, bewildered.

– 'In dross – in dirt – in that stuff that jaundices the earth's rocks, that universal Touchstone men call gelt or gold?'

'Not a farthing less than £3000 – £5000 – no, £20,000 so help –. Well, at least £1000,' said the artist, 'a paltry thousand, which is to say half the value of the most infinite brush mark on it.'

'A thousand pounds – English,' said Carlyle, aghast. 'Prodigious! And all Eternity before thee! They will perchance give thee £1000 for this simulacrum made with gross earths and pigment oils; hast thou not a Brain, furnishable with glimmerings of Light and fingers to hold reputable tools withal? Man, man, why shouldn't thou not Work?'

'Once more the old man grows rococo,' thought Whistler, and lit another cigarette in silence. Several of the brass bands still played in his blood.

Carlyle went up close to the canvas again and peered as its details. 'Ach Gott!' he said, 'to lighten more and more into the Day the Chaotic Night that threatens to engulf him in its hindrances and its horrors were properly the only Grandeur in the history of the Artist. What –'

'What do you think of it?' asked Whistler hurriedly.

'I cannot understand,' said Carlyle, dropping into a manner less reminiscent of Sartor Resartus; 'I cannot understand why the beltings round your walls should be so high, and the pictures as depicted on this canvas should be so low. Are men monkeys that they should go upon their Hunkers to scan pictures? And this – this saucer, or scutcheon, plate, or ashet which is represented hanging behind my back, what symboliseth it?'

'That,' said Whistler, 'is my signature – the famous butterfly.'

'Poor soul! poor soul!' mused the Seer. 'How Will Dyce, of Ecclefechan, that was an honest enough man, would have loved thy whimsies. But Mr Whustler, let me ask ye, as man to man, when you mean to give up this pigment trade and work? To do something that will ennoble and cheer, that were worthy of a man.'

'Now the old gentleman's rococo again, and hopeless' thought Whistler and had no word to say. His sitter departed; the artist lit all the lights of his studio and stood long before the canvas, and the million military bands returned and crashed with songs triumphant through every artery.

FROM THE CELESTIAL BOOKSHOP

On Christmas Eve there came a wonderful box of books from the Celestial Publisher. It was better than an unexpected brace of pheasants, five hundred cigars, and payment of an old debt, cancelled 'bad'. A psychologist, writing recently in some paper, maintained there was no sense of exhilaration more intense than that you got from the knowledge that at night you were going to the theatre. He must have been a poor psychologist, of restricted experience and never had to write notices of the plays for newspapers, for the sublimest sense of afternoon gaiety, well-being and anticipation, has little to do with the theatre (unless, indeed, you belong to the country, and have still a thrill left for *East Lynne* or *The Span of Life*): it is to be gained only by the sudden possession of a fine new book. Not necessarily a great book, perhaps not even a very wise book, but a book by a man who has hitherto never bored you. As you make for the homeward car with that new book wrapped up in brown paper, you feel glad the night is wet, and that Brown's party has been postponed through the unfortunate loss of his maternal aunt. You feel like a boy going for three days' summer holiday at a farm where there is an old gun in the loft, and they let one ride the cart-horses; you feel like a young man going to meet a girl whom as yet he only half understands, but who has such sympathetic eyes; you feel like the gentleman (not Cortez) in Darien when he neared the peak that was to reveal to him the Pacific; you feel like a man with a cheese pudding to dinner. What delightful people are your fellow passengers in the car! What a nice comfortable car! What a pleasant 'ting' the bell-punch of the guard has! And the brown paper parcel at your side might be your first baby.

Conceive, then, the joy of a whole box of books from the Celestial Publisher! I knew instinctively that though the box looked like any other box of books from a circulating library it was a magic box. There was, for one thing, the way the man from the railway station put it down in the hall. It was Christmas Eve, yet he just put it down softly and went away without a moment's hesitation. I cried him back, thinking that at least he ought to have his eightpence freight, but he waved his hand, and said it was of no account, that his name was Tom Scrooge Cheeryble Pinch, and that he wished me a Merry Christmas for self and the directors of the railway company. A preposterous porter! A fine, stout, intelligent fellow! I made up my mind that in the morning I should get his name and address, and send a goose, or perhaps a rabbit, to his wife and family. And then I made to open the box. There, again, the magic of it was revealed. No screw nails, no turning and twisting, and wrenching of the lid required – I had just to touch it with the stem of my pipe, and behold it smiled! Smiled, I declare, is the only word. One of those broad, generous, impulsive smiles like what you get from a cabman at Christmas when you ask him if he would care to step in and have something, as the night is so cold. When it smiled thus – that is to say, when the lid rose of itself, revealing the contents, I had the third proof that it was a magic box. It was not only that the books were all spotlessly clean, and that their pages were cut, and that they were just the right size, but there was on the very top a neatly typewritten list of the contents, with an intimation from the publisher that the volumes were not for review on any account, but were meant as a testimony to his appreciation of my qualities as a man and a poet. 'You need not trouble to return the empty box,' he said – a final touch of generosity that moved me to tears. Two steps of the saraband did I straightway dance, round the magic box, with incredible agility, and then I read the list.

I ask any one who has ever spent four-and-sixpence on a book, and walked home as if floating on air, to try and imagine my feelings when I found the books in the box were as follows:

Lady Charlotte, a Tale of the Advocate's Close, by Walter Scott.
Wilkins Micawber, Senator, by Charles Dickens.
Cider Cellar Nights, by W. Makepeace Thackeray.
Barrisdale, a Romance, by R. L. Stevenson.
Ellisland, Being the Later Lyrics of Robert Burns.
Verses from Avilion, by W. E. Henley.
Memoirs of T. Mulvaney, by Rudyard Kipling.

A Return to Arcady, by Thomas Hardy.
The Astounding Duchess, by George Meredith.
Life and Letters of Benjamin D'Israeli.
Songs from Tennyson's 'Lotus Isle.'
A Son of the Manse, by J. M. Barrie.
The Derelict Brigantine, by Joseph Conrad.
Whistler Intime, by A Syndicate.

I rang the bell. 'Mrs Grant,' I said to my housekeeper, 'I hope you will take that roast bird for your own supper. All I want is some coffee, six or seven candles, and the fire replenished in my bedroom. And do not waken me in the morning, no matter how late I sleep. I have just been thinking, by the way, that a rise in your wages is long overdue; count on an increase of five pounds after this date.' With a fol-diddle-dol-diddle fol-di-die-day! And then I read my books. Fancy Scott in the happiest manner of *The Antiquary*! I found 'Lady Charlotte' the most vivid and enthralling account of 'high jinks' in old Edinburgh I had ever read, displaying in every chapter the Master's miraculous grasp of character, observation the most intent, humour the kindliest, adventure the most breathless. And who that has read that last letter of Micawber's in *David Copperfield* has not longed to learn of his after-career in Australia? From Mr Dickens' new book I found that Micawber had stayed but briefly in Australia, and had later removed to the United States. Micawber the oil magnate of Oleaginous City, Pa., Micawber the inventor of the New Patent Cocoa-Nut Milk Churn, Micawber's newspaper, *The Oleaginous City Siren and Public Ameliorator*; Micawber's famous lecture on 'System in Business', Micawber's work on 'Double Entry on a New Method' – our old friend lived again in Dickens' wondrous pages, and kept me laughing till I took a pain in my side. Perhaps the happiest passage in the book was that in which, after the Fourth of July adventure with the six Senators, we had Micawber's assurance that we should hear from him again, when he and 'the partner of his joys, the sweetener of his domestic cup, who was dear to him while Memory held her seat – in short, the amiable and inestimable Mrs Micawber,' should return from their trip to California.

The latest Thackeray proved no less fascinating; in *Barrisdale* Stevenson had taken one of the most talented and engaging scamps in all Highland history through the glens of Albyn and the gaieties of London and Paris, and discovered for us a character as immortal as Alan Breck. It was good to see the old hand had not lost its cunning, that back in his scenes among his own people the creator of Hermiston and Catriona could yet compel our smiles and tears. And that these matchless songs of Burns should have been so long undiscovered seemed a caprice of fate, intended only to add to the zest with which I was able to peruse them. I reflected that hundreds of Burns Clubs throughout Scotland on the next January 25 would listen breathless and almost incredulously to recitations of his hitherto unknown 'Lanrick Lasses', or the singing of his 'Charming Tibbie Cameron', 'At Mirk I Mourned the Morning Joys', 'Drimmindoo', or 'Mary I Vow'. It was almost reluctantly that I turned from Burns to Mr Kipling's indubitable masterpiece, *The Memoirs of T. Mulvaney*. At last we had Mr Kipling with all the stops of his genius out. No other long novel that he had written approached these remarkable confessions of the Black Tyrone soldier in intensity of interest, in excellence of technique. It was the 'Don Quixote' of English letters. Had there been any passage in all the literature of romance finer than 'How I bate the Band-sergeant and had Money left?'

I confess it was with some apprehension I turned to Mr Hardy's new novel, but my gratification may be imagined on discovering that *A Return to Arcady* was a novel in the earlier manner of the novelist, ere he had permitted despair to settle permanently on his shoulders. It was the Hardy of *The Woodlanders* or *Far From the Maddening Crowd*, only more matured, and with a genial spirit. As for Meredith's *Astounding Duchess*, it seemed to me the most brilliant of his work, though (to tell the truth) I got only half through it, leaving the rest until I should dip into the *Life and Letters of Benjamin D'Israeli*. What a life! What a marvellous new light upon the inner workings of parties and statesmen! Byron's Letters, I realised at once, must hereafter take second place to those of Beaconsfield. I followed D'Israeli with the Tennyson lyrics. Ah! the almost painful, haunting sweetness of them! Over and over again I read particularly 'The Lost Garden' and 'The Grandeur Wakes', the former likely to rank for all time coming as Tennyson's loveliest song. Then to Mr Barrie's *Son of the Manse* – surely the most quaint and beautiful and yet tragic work the novelist has given us. In *A Son of the Manse* we have the true Scotland, with none of the ultra-sentimentalism of one class of Scottish novelists, none of the Balzac brutality of another class. Conrad's new story, Henley's poems, and the Whistler papers occupied the rest of my time till my last candle was done, and then I went to bed.

The magic box and its contents were gone in the morning, when Mrs Grant, in spite of my injunctions, wakened me for breakfast. She declared she had never seen them.

WOTHERSPOON'S WINDFALL

I

Five years ago the Scottish newspapers kindled an unholy envy in millions of hearts by giving prominence to the dramatic experience of Samuel Wotherspoon, who went to bed one night a rural postman earning eighteen shillings a week, and awoke next morning quite unchanged in any respect, save that he needed shaving worse than ever, and was the owner of £50,000. 'Great Windfall to a Stirlingshire Letter-Carrier', the sensational news was headed. Samuel Wotherspoon, a bachelor, fifty-seven years of age, who for quarter of a century had been delivering letters in a sparsely populated district nine miles long, this fateful morning got a letter himel, which intimated that his brother George had died in Canada leaving him sole executor and assignee to a fortune of the figure mentioned, all in Dominion Industrial Bonds, bearing 6 per cent interest. He had never seen his brother for half a century; of his brother's wealth he had never had suspicion.

To innumerable Scottish householders upon that day, when the letter-carrier's windfall was reported to the world, the rank injustice of Providence was poignantly brought home. Why should it be this particular man who had a brother die in Canada and leave him £50,000? Why should hundreds of thousands of brothers who could well be spared not have gone to Canada and made fortunes like this, and died bequeathing them in the obvious and proper quarters? Why should some people not have the luck to be left so little as the price of a mourning-ring by anybody? Why should work be so beastly, and wages so small, and life so hard?

That morning, brothers were distinctly unpopular. You could not but feel that your elder brother Alick had behaved in the most scurvy manner to you by not going away to Manitoba in 1879 and dying a bachelor worth £50,000, instead of remaining at home to be an inconspicuous joiner with a wife and half a dozen children.

All Scotland, with one accord, made a hasty calculation with a pencil on the margin of its newspaper, and felt the most profound chagrin to find that it meant £3000 per annum. For a letter-carrier! More than £57 a week! More than £8 a day! What could not an intelligent man do with £8 a day?

Samuel Wotherspoon, a quite inoffensive creature, was, on this particular day, regarded with something approaching hatred and disgust by millions of people who had never set eyes on him.

Now I happen to know Samuel Wotherspoon, and I am in a position to state exactly how this windfall was to affect what remained of his destiny.

He was quite incapable of realising what £50,000 meant. A concrete image of one hundred one pound bank-notes all spread out upon the floor was, with an effort, within the grasp of his imagination, but beyond the hundred his head went giddy. The little Slamannan lawyer he was prevailed upon by the minister to consult did his best by means of diagrams to show that £50,000 was five hundred times a hundred pound notes spread out upon the floor, but he might as well have described in poetry the distance of Sirius from the earth for all that this conveyed to the legatee. What Samuel wanted to know was how much it was a week.

'It's not anything a week,' said the lawyer patiently, 'but it's exactly £50,000 a minute – this very minute that I'm talking to you. It's yours now! You've got it! You've got the £50,000 all in a lump. You can look upon it, if you like, as £50,000 for this one week.'

'And dae I only get it the one week?' said Samuel Wotherspoon in accents of disillusion. 'Lord! I daurna gie up my job, if Geordie's money is only for one week! I'm gettin' my 18s. a week frae the Post Office.'

'But this £50,000 is yours for ever, Mr Wotherspoon,' said the lawyer, 'at least as long's you're living, to do what you like with!'

'Ye said jist this meenute it was only for a week,' said Samuel.

'I mean by that that you get it only once, and for all; you surely don't expect to get £50,000 every Saturday?'

'I get 18s. frae the Post Office,' said Samuel. 'Every Saturday,' he added, in the tone of one who has never ceased to be amazed at the strict fidelity and promptness of the Government.

'Oh, hang the Post Office and its 18s. a week!' said the lawyer; 'what's 18s. a week to you now?'

'It's my livin',' said Samuel earnestly. 'A bonny-like habble I would be in withoot it! Man, I pay £6 o' rent!'

'But my goodness! Mr Wotherspoon,' said the lawyer, 'can you not understand that you have this £50,000 now, for altogether, to do what you like with? You can build a bigger house than Keir o' Kinslaps, keep half a dozen servants, run a motor-car, smoke sixpenny cigars all day, drink champagne, put a new steeple on the kirk, wear a different suit of clothes every day, travel on the Continent, keep a yacht –'

'Whit would be the guid o' that only for the one week?' interrupted Samuel. 'I'm faur better wi' my 18s. sure.'

'Man, ye couldn't spend it all in a week!' exclaimed the exasperated legal gentleman. 'Even if ye turned the fifty thousand into half-sovereigns and papped hens wi' them!'

Samuel reflected deeply, and shook his head, incredulous.

'There's some quirk in it!' said he. 'Unless ye're sure o' a certainty every week, ye canna depend on onything.'

'Look here!' said the lawyer; 'you see that potato-barrel? Suppose it holds £1000 in gold. That's ten times £100. You can see that if you took £100 out of the barrel every month to spend, the gold in the barrel would only be finished at the end of ten months.'

'There's something in that!' admitted Samuel, having turned it carefully over in his mind. 'Oh, ay! I'll admit there's something in that!'

'Well,' proceeded the lawyer hurriedly, eager to fan this flicker of intelligence into a flame; 'suppose, instead of one barrel, you have fifty barrels, all holding £1000 each –'

'The room wouldna hauld them!' said Samuel, looking round his tiny bachelor kitchen. ''Where in a' the warld could ye put them?''

'Never mind that!' cried the lawyer petulently. 'Just imagine there's room for fifty barrels, and that they're all there, and every one of them containing £1000. Do you not see that if every barrel lasted ten months, you drawing £100 a month from it, you would have enough gold in the fifty barrels to last you fifty times ten months, and that's five hundred months.'

'That's no' very lang,' said Samuel. 'A month soon slips awa'.'

'But five hundred months are over forty years!' shouted the lawyer, stamping his feet in his exasperation. 'You're surely not expecting to live for ever!'

Samuel shook his head. 'I get 18s. a week the way I am,' he said, 'as regular as the clock. Mr Rose, the postmaster, puts it in my hand.'

'But hang it all, man, your brother Geordie's putting more than 18s. a week in your hand; he's putting £50,000 in your hand; or, if it's plainer to you this way, he's going to give you £2000 a year for twenty-five years if you live that length of time, and that's supposing you didn't even invest, but spent the capital.'

'What would that be a week?' asked Samuel, having vainly tried to get some tangible idea of what £2000 a year was. The lawyer hurriedly made a calculation.

'It's more than £38 a week,' he intimated. 'Never mind the odd shillings.'

'Oh, but I aye mind the shillin's!' said Samuel shrewdly. 'A man has to be gey careful o' the odd shillin's.'

'You can surely afford to leave them out of account when you're getting £38 a week,' said the lawyer.

Samuel pondered upon this till he perspired.

'There's something in that!' he admitted grudgingly, and then he looked round the kitchen. 'But where can I put a' they barrels?' he inquired.

'Good heavens!' cried the lawyer. 'It's not going to come in barrels!'

'Ye said barrels – fifty barrels!' retorted Samuel.

'But that was only for an illustration. They were only imaginary barrels. Of course you don't get the £50,000 in barrels. You don't get it, strictly speaking, at all. You don't see the money, and you don't need to. But it's there right enough –'

'Where?' asked Samuel.

'Dominion Industrial Bonds at 6 per cent,' said the lawyer. 'Sound stock! Your brother was a cute business man, and you'll be well advised to leave that money where he put it.'

'Where did he put it?' Samuel asked.

'Cotton companies, lumber companies, paint companies – half a dozen first-rate Canadian concerns.'

'And I'm to leave it there?' asked the astonished Samuel.

'If you're wise you will.'

'I knew all along there was a quirk in it!' said Samuel. 'If I had been a fool and ta'en the minister's advice I would hae given up my job as rural carrier.'

With infinite patience the lawyer explained the mysteries of investment, and the sweet simplicity of Bonds; how the £50,000 of capital could remain perpetually intact and Samuel yet enjoy an income of £3000 a year, or £57 a week, with no more trouble than was involved in going every quarter to the bank with certain coupons.

'But ye said £38 and some odd shillin's a week a meenute ago,' Samuel pointed out.

'Yes, yes!' said the lawyer, 'but that was supposing you simply lived upon the £50,000 as your brother left it. Money makes money, and by leaving the £50,000 where it is, you make £57 a week.'

'That's mair nor Geordie left me.'

'Not at all!'

'But it is!' protested Samuel. 'Ye said yoursel' it would run to £38 a week – though I think mysel' that's fair rïdeeculous. And noo ye say that if I never see Geordie's money but leave it oot in Canada, I can mak' £57 a week. I kent there was a quirk in't! Na, na, Mr Grant; I'm better sure o' my 18s.'

But he was soon to learn a little better.

II

We all expected some wonderful change would be apparent in Samuel Wotherspoon whenever he became possessed of his windfall of £50,000. Possibly he would leave the district, where he had spent so many years in frugal humbleness; take up house in a swagger way in Glasgow or in

Edinburgh and live at heck and manger. At fifty-seven years of age he was not too old to marry even; at the very least he must shift to a house more fitting for a man with all that money than the but-and-ben he occupied alone, dispensing with all female ministration.

But three months passed; the flitting-term went by, and it became apparent that Samuel was, in all respects, exactly the same as he used to be. He would not even have given up his job as letter-carrier at 18s. a week, and was indignant when the postmaster appointed another man more needful of the money. Samuel stayed on in the but-and-ben, bought half a dozen cows, and leased a park for them; we spoke of him ironically as the gentleman-farmer, and speculated on the prospect of his coming out some day in knickerbockers.

Not till the first quarter-day came round and he went, at his lawyer's instigation, to the bank with the coupons on his Canadian bonds, did Samuel quite implicitly believe in his good fortune.

He went home that day with his pockets stuffed with notes to the value of nearly £600, nowise elated as one might expect, but on the contrary beset by hitherto unknown anxieties. The newspapers were full of stories of robberies of lonely men who were known to be possessed of money. If the village knew he had all that money in the shottle of his kist, the life would be pestered out of him by needy old acquaintances; the minister already had been on his track for a subscription to the building fund. The minister had even indicated £50 as the appropriate figure for a gentleman in Mr Wotherspoon's position. Good gracious! – £50! The price of four good calving queys!

He went immediately to his lawyer.

'Whit am I to dae wi' a' yon money?' he inquired.

'Spend it,' said the lawyer promptly. 'That's what money's made for.'

'Whit on?' asked Samuel. 'I'm no' needin' onything except a bit o' a bass for the lobby.'

'Then just invest it,' said the lawyer; 'I can put it into something for you.'

'I daursay that!' said Samuel dryly. 'But I was thinkin' would it no' be better in the bank. The bank's aye there, ye see, and onytime I wanted to be sure they had the money, I would only hae to ask for't.'

'Very well then!' said the lawyer. 'Please yourself! You'll only get two per cent on a deposit, and I could easily get you four. But it's better in the bank than in your kist. You should never lift the money the way you did; just put it back every quarter in the bank, and live on the interest of your dividends.'

'How much would that be?' Samuel asked; by this time he had grasped the golden axiom of finance that 'money makes money'.

'Oh, something over a pound to week to start with,' said the lawyer.

'That's the very ticket!' Samuel exclaimed. 'And it saves an awfu' lot o' bother.'

Samuel put all the money back in bank, save the fractional part required to keep him till next quarter-day came round, and a little extra which he had decided to disburse on three things he had had a longing for many years to own, but never could afford – a telescope, a set of bagpipes, and a web of shepherd-tartan cloth. A shepherd-tartan suit had always seemed to him the very height of splendour, incapable of tiring the eye, so he bought several webs while he was at it, enough to keep him in shepherd-tartan suits for the remainder of his life. The telescope was for astronomical purposes; he was always dubious about these mountains in the moon; the bagpipes seemed, to his ingenuous mind, an instrument that any one could play without the study of music. Some months later he sold both telescope and bagpipes at a profit, but all the rest of his days he was immutably in shepherd-tartan checks.

In his own mind, it seemed, he had nothing more than an income, sure, of about £1 a week, as the cow-keeping was rather a loss than otherwise. It was true he had the name of having £50,000, but he had only seen £600 of it, and that but briefly; hereafter he was never to see even so much as that again.

As the guaranteed dividends on his bonds became payable to him each quarter, he added them to what he had on deposit receipt, and the only actual cash he ever handled was the annual interest on the deposit receipt, which interest, to his bewilderment at first, grew larger every year, with nothing, so far as he could see, to account for it.

Yet, with a pound or two a week, he began to realise in a while that he was better off than he had been as a rural messenger. He had unwonted generous impulses which in a cautious fashion he indulged. On a Saturday afternoon he would invite an old friend or two into the Black Bull bar, and plunging deeply into the antique pocket of his shepherd-tartan trousers, he would stand them a schooner of beer with an air of some munifence.

But he was always disappointed if they, in their turn, did not stand another schooner. He had a sincere sense of democratic equality.

'You're the weel-aff man, Sam!' they would say to him enviously. 'Plenty o' money and naething to bother ye!'

'Oh! I'm no complainin' the way I'm left,' he would admit. 'But that's no' to say I havena ony bother . . . Thae women!' he suggested craftily. 'Ye understand? Because I hae the name o' haein' a pickle by me, they're never aff my face.'

Rightly or wrongly, it was his conviction that every unmarried woman in the parish, from the youngest girl in her teens to the oldest widow, was eager to change her name to Wotherspoon. The sight of a skirt five hundred yards along the road would send him scurrying across the fields.

So far, it might seem that Samuel Wotherspoon was a fool, and I confess that for years that was my own impression. We all of us felt for him contemptuous pity. We looked upon him as a miser greedily hoarding up and adding to a vast accumulation of wealth which in the course of nature he must by and by relinquish, leaving it perhaps to distant relatives who would take full advantage of its potentiality for luxury and pleasure.

Being simple folk, we thought of Samuel's hoard as so much money idle in a stocking – gold tarnished, notes mildewed.

We did him, there, a great injustice. He was not a fool, despite his early ignorance of what was meant by £50,000, the mysteries of investment, and the sweet simplicity of bonds. Nor was he a miser like to Daniel Dancer, Harpagon, or Gaspard. He never desired to see his money; the sight of more than a pound or two week would have genuinely distressed him.

In our appraisement of all his qualities, moral, domestic, and intellectual, we had quite overlooked the possibility that he might be philosophical.

So far as I was concerned, the first hint of this feature in his character came from the Slamannan lawyer. 'Wotherspoon's not so daft as you might think,' said he, one day. 'I'm sometimes half inclined to think he's wiser than myself. For one thing, he has pumped me dry of all I happen to know, or can find out, about these industries in Canada, where his brother George's money is invested; about joint-stock companies generally, and all the processes of high finance. You may think that's just his parsimony, but if you get a chance to tackle him you'll change your mind. I thought myself, at first, he was simply an idiotic miser, but I have had the opportunity of peeping once or twice into the depths of him, and there I saw Renunciation. It's not a businesslike quality, I admit, but it's made a lot of in the Holy Scriptures. Everybody here thinks Samuel should spend his money with a bang; they would think it natural and proper that he should surround himself with all sorts of costly self-indulgences –'

'– With the greater privilege,' said I, 'of helping those who needed.'

'I knew you would say that,' remarked the lawyer. 'But speak yourself to Samuel, and he'll maybe show how the greatest and the silliest of self-indulgences is helping other folk – with money.'

It was not long after when I came, one day, on the richest man in the parish standing at his byre door.

'You're worth between fifty and sixty thousand pounds,' said I; 'and there you are like a scarecrow, mucking byres!'

He leaned upon the handle of his graip and puckered up his face astringently a moment, then he chuckled.

'I'm worth, at the best,' said he, 'nae mair than £1 a week, and I get it, wi' a little over.'

'Yes, yes!' I said; 'that's what you spend, but for every pound you spend you might be spending hundreds.'

'What on?' he asked abruptly, and there, for the first time, I realised that spending is not the simple thing it seems, especially spending on ourselves. I thought of a hundred things on which it would be appropriate and beneficial to spend money for myself – a house with a bigger library, a vinery, a motor-car, a trip round the world – but manifestly it would be grotesque folly for Samuel to treat himself to these things. He had not the training to appreciate them or benefit from them, and at the age of sixty he was too late of starting.

My confusion was quite obvious to him, and he slyly laughed. 'It's no' sae very easy, ye see! I couldna spend mair than a pound or twa a week sensibly on myself if I tried; the thing's an art, and it needs an education. Noo I was never educated further than Bills o' Parcels and the Chief Mountain Heights, and as shair as daith I canna mind them! I have all I want; I have all that's guid for me!'

I fell back cravenly again upon the obvious, which is so often the erroneous.

'Consider,' I said, 'the good you might be doing – the debt on the church and manse; the need for a Cottage Hospital; a new piano for the Hall; prizes for the school children; winter coals for the poor –'

'What poor?' he interrupted.

'The like of Wully Scott and his wife,' said I.

'Wully Scott!' he cried. 'Man, I gied him yince a perfectly guid blanket, and he went and pawned it up in Fa'kirk, drank the proceeds, and went hame and bleckened her e'e. Na, na! Spending money in a wise-like way on other folk needs even mair education than to spend it on yoursel'! It's maybe the worst o' luxuries – worse than gemblin'. I've seen ower mony puir folk spoiled wi' gettin' mair nor whit was guid for them, and I like them a' ower weel to risk it. and it's no' for the like o' me to pay kirk debts, and build hospitals, and tak' the privilege oot o' the hands o' other dacent folk that understand thae things better than I dae.'

'Then what good is your money to you?' I demanded warmly.

'It's no my money at all!' he cried. 'I look on it as Geordie's, and he kent whit was best to dae wi't. He had an education; he was on as far as Algebra and Latin, and look at the money he made! I micht, if I was greedy, put a lot o't in my belly, and waste it riotously in a way to spoil my health and mak' the public laugh; but I have mair regard for Christian principle, and I ken my place. Geordie didna waste his money on himsel' or onybody else; he put it oot to work! And oot at work it is. It's runnin' spinnin'-mills, and railways, cuttin' doon the forests, paintin' toons, makin' guid wages for thoosands o' men – maybe faur better men than me. Let it bide there!'

'But the dividends in the bank?' I suggested, I fear, maliciously.

'It's a' the same,' said he; 'they're no' in a kist in the bank blue-mouldin' the way I used to think; the money I deposit's oot in the world and buildin' businesses and payin' wages. Whaur better could it be?'

There was probably some very effective answer to this question, but for the life of me I could not think of it.

OLD BRAND

When I was on the *Courier* first (and which particular *Courier* it was may as well remain unmentioned), it had an editor whose pride was in the fact that no other provincial paper in the country gave such prompt, copious, and well-informed obituaries as his. The breath was hardly out of a J.P., or even a local police-constable, when a neat and comprehensive biography was being set up in the case-room. Nothing was overlooked – the unfailing geniality of the deceased, his kindness to the poor, his renown as a pansy-grower, or his relationship to a procurator-fiscal. Invariably his demise 'cast a gloom over the whole community'. The promptness and the profoundly sympathetic spirit of our obituaries divested death of no small part of its terror. We depended for our circulation less upon football than upon the bereaved. An obituary of ours was always couched in language which made the surviving members of the family our friends and subscribers for life. The study of the obituaries in our files for twenty years would suggest that nobody ever died in the district except people of the most angelic character.

Old Brand, the editor, of course, got all the popular credit for this, and many a bag of potatoes. When any of the neighbouring farmers fell into the decline of years, or was in extremity as a result of some accident with a gig driving home at night at the end of too prolonged a sitting in the Blue Bell Inn on a market day, the family would take anticipatory steps to secure his posthumous reputation by sending a couple of ducks or a middle of pork to the editor of the *Courier*. You never saw a fatter man; for twenty years he battened on bereavement. On the wall above his desk he had pasted a list of words and phrases appropriate to these sad occasions – 'release', 'gone to his rest', 'pay the debt to nature', 'the way of all flesh', 'joined the great majority', 'long home', 'gathered to his fathers', 'retained all his faculties to the last', 'we shall never look upon his like again', 'sorrowing relatives', 'the Reaper has been busy this week', and so on. It was the days before half-tone picture-blocks were in the newspapers, but Old Brand anticipated all the artistic pleasure of the editor of today, on those weeks when a more than usually important demise justified turned rules for mourning borders.

'Poor Bailie Webster!' he would say. 'He's gone at last; but I think we have a very satisfactory notice of him. Fancy the *Telegraph* with only a quarter-a-column!' And he would generously drench himself with snuff – his way of handing himself a bouquet in acknowledgement of his efficiency as editor.

But the fact was that Old Brand got the glory and the ducks that by rights belonged to me and my predecessors as reporters of the *Courier*. Any expedition or any literary art that might be manifest in the production of obituaries were due to us. It was I who added 'Charon's ferry', and 'crossed to the Stygian shore', to Old Brand's mortuary thesaurus; I can prove it by the files. Brand, to be quite frank about it, had no sense of Style; a good enough man in many ways, and able, with the aid of the *Scotsman*, *Herald*, and *Daily News*, to turn out a quite plausible leading article, but with not a gleam of inspiration when thrown upon his own resources. When I introduced 'the blind Fury with the abhorred shears' (a rather neat thing of Milton's) into an obituary notice of a local tailor, Old Brand cut it out of my copy as being rather personal. Any touch like that, with what I considered literary grace and the charm of novelty, he would smother remorselessly. 'Just stick to the facks, James,' he would say; 'and don't be flimboyant. Facks! That's the mainstay of the *Courier*. Facks, and a kindly tolerant spirit when it comes to obituaries.'

In a press behind a discarded Eagle bill-machine we had what we called our Mortuary. There, alphabetically arranged pigeon-holes accommodated some fifteen or sixteen hundred obituaries of eminent local men who had yet to qualify for editorial treatment. Every man with a villa, a farm, a shop that advertised, or a reputation for fancy dogs and poultry, had his career and his achievements duly chronicled. When nothing else was doing, Brand expected me to bring these memoirs up to date, a task succinctly marked down in the reporter's book as 'Stiffs'. The solemn archives had been growing for many years; some of the pigeon-holes were tightly crammed; it was a heartbreak to Old Brand that the "M's'" appeared to be immortal. 'Aren't the deevils dour!' he would explain, peering into the Mortuary through his great gold-rimmed spectacles.

To prepare a man's obituary for a newspaper has often been observed to postpone indefinitely a dissolution that appeared imminent. The favourite practical joke of Providence is to catch the newspapers unprepared, and very often, when the doctors had given up a patient whose record in our Mortuary was somewhat out of date, I had only to skirmish around for fresh details and add some lines about his having won the black-faced wedder medal in 1886, and the patient was sure of a miraculous recovery. This was, I am certain, the reason why Old Brand always instructed me to make my inquiries with caution and delicacy. I fancy he had an idea that Providence could be outwitted.

When Willie Young, of the Driepps, the famous Clydesdale breeder, was *in extremis*, and I hurriedly gathered the later facts which were to make his obituary in the *Courier* consolatory to his family, he, of course, recovered immediately, to the professional chagrin of Brand, who used to play whist with him every Saturday.

'You must have gone about splairgin' at large for your facks, James,' said my editor. 'Amn't I aye tellin' you to be judicious? Mr Young was as good as deid when I spoke to you in the mornin'.'

He could not take a walk along the street at any time without encountering healthy-looking men whom secretly he regarded as enemies of the *Courier*; they had turned the corner and jinked Atropos after the editor had been at the pains to add with his own hand the final eulogistic phrases to their memoirs as prepared by his reporters.

On one occasion Providence caught us badly unprepared with the facts to do justice to the memory of a prominent townsman who had only recently come to the place, and the *Telegraph* beat us by about a column. The circumstances were all the more vexatious since the deceased was a man well stricken in years, whose failing condition had been commented on for weeks.

'Oh, James!' wailed Mr Brand. 'You saw the man at the Cattle Show on Wednesday; you might have had the common sense to see he would soon be needin' our attention! Tchk! Tchk! Tchk! Isn't it deplorable! There you were on Saturday, wastin' your time wi' the notice of Ninian Taylor, and him away, as cocky as you like, to Callander Hydropathic on the Monday!'

This bad break revolutionised Old Brand's ideas of how I was to attend to the Mortuary. Henceforth, instead of sitting in the office systematically going through the alphabet and patching up the memoirs of folk who seemed to have an unconscionable repugnance to dying, I was to daunder along the street and keep a shrewd look-out for elderly citizens showing signs of breaking up. If their identity was unknown to me I was to follow them up, discover where they stayed, and thereafter push judicious inquiries. More than once, on the track of some tottering old gentleman at dusk, who little suspected the honour I proposed to do him, I was suspected of designs upon his purse.

It was an extraordinary town for tottering old gentlemen, though I had never observed the fact before. The shortcomings of our Mortuary were lamentably disclosed; my predecessors had failed to secure the memoirs of hundreds of men who, in the ordinary course of nature, might require the alleviatory attentions of the *Courier* at any moment. The "M's'" in the Mortuary overflowed into the 'Q' recess. I acquired the furtive, speculative eye of an undertaker.

Nevertheless, Old Brand had rarely a worse year so far as concerned the Mortuary. It seemed as if I had only to cast my speculative eye upon any wreck of a man to endow him with something like the sprightliness and health of youth. 'You're the most unlucky reporter we ever had, James,' said Old Brand. 'There you are, slavin' away at the Mortuary, and I haven't had the chance to put the finish on a body for nearly a month!'

So desperate did he become about the situation that he led me once into an awkward fix. He came in one morning to the office with a brisk, exhilarated manner, and the news that Watty Rigg, the Cattle Auctioneer, was gone. 'Slipped away at eight o'clock this morning, I hear,' said the editor; 'and, with no ill-will to Watty, I regard it as most considerate – most considerate! It's seldom they do me the justice to wait for the day we go to press. It's eighteen years since your predecessor, Cameron, had him snodded off in the Mortuary. Watty was not exactly a Prince in Israel, but I never saw a bonnier curler, and we'll have to do the best we can to gratify his widow. You'll slip over to The Holm and get a few particulars about his Christian resignation. Now be sure and go about the thing with delicacy and caution.'

I would appear not to have gone about the thing with sufficient delicacy and caution to outwit Providence, for when I went to The Holm, and intimated to Mrs Rigg the object of my mission, I discovered that her husband was alive! What was worse, hearing who the visitor was, and surmising the occasion of his call, Watty Rigg insisted that I should be taken in to see him!

'Ye're the lad frae the *Courier*,' he said, propped up in bed, with weeping folk about him. 'I aye tak' oot your paper, thought it's no' worth a d——n for fat-stock prices. Ye'll be wantin' a few tit-bits. Tell Mr Brand I'm no' for nane o' his maudlin' sentiment. I was jist Watty Rigg the cattleman. Put that doon! I – I never gied naebody naething unless I got the value o't, and there's nae use tellin' ony lies aboot it. I was just an ordinar' business man, and I had a family to provide for. I never was a pattern to onybody, and I didna try. Mind this – I never had ony fancy relatives wi' a grand poseetion; I left the schule when I was ten, and I never could write my name, but I built a business! – a business! Put that doon! There was nane o' the gentle Jeremiah aboot the late Walter Rigg; he was a gey hard nut, and he found a lot o' hard yins biddin' against him. He wasna a model father, nor ony great catch as a husband, and don't you, for your life, say that he was! But at the worst he never was a hypocrite. And this is a thing ye'll have to tak' a note o' – he didna die in Christan resignation like a' the other peelywally folk that figure in the *Courier*; he died as dour as a brock, but he didna go to his Judge wi' false pretences!'

When I returned to Old Brand with this remarkable story, he almost wept. 'Still lingerin' on!' said he, despairingly. 'Isn't he the frightened coward! I doubt, James, you have been splairgin' noisily, as usual, in your inquiries.'

I am glad to say Watty Rigg, apparently relieved by his confidence to me, made a wonderful recovery, and, as far as I know, lives till this day.

But Old Brand himself is now, as he would have put it, 'beyond these voices'. My speculative eye discerned one day that he, too, was a tottering old gentleman, and, to put Providence off the trail of one I loved despite his literary disabilities, I carefully prepared his obituary in my lodgings. It was affection, not my taste, that made me load the notice with the hackneyed phrases he had used, himself, so often. For weeks I kept it in my desk. 'How goes the Mortuary, James?' he one day asked me wearily. 'I hope you're keepin' it up; we must always send them off like gentlemen,' and he read no menace in my furtive eye.

But Providence, for once, was not stalled off at the sight of a complete obituary in readiness; a few days later we had to turn the leads for Old Brand's memoir in the *Courier*.

CALL OF THE PIPES TO SCOTLAND

If the martial spirit be a good thing to perpetuate – and, meanwhile at least, the point admits of no controversy – Scotland, when war broke out, was fortunate in being closer to the martial traditions of the past than any other part of the British Empire. The last battle fought in these islands was a hundred and seventy years ago on that melancholy moor that lies between the foothills of the Grampians and the Moray Firth. The rising of the clans was not so essentially a response to the summons of Charles Edward as a last acknowledgement of the hereditary power of the Chiefs who ordered it, but it was, till now, the final manifestation in Britain of compulsory military service. The men of the clans were vitually conscripts – willing perhaps, but conscripts none the less, their tenures of the lands they occupied being conditional on their readiness to draw the sword. They still had their weapons and a rough kind of military policy and organisation, while the rest of Britain had put down the sword for good, as it thought, and taken up the ell-wand. One natural consequence of Scotland's tardy entrance into the modern life of ell-wands, manufactures and a seemingly settled peace was that in the mountains, and in the Hebrides at all events, military service under the Crown was not, when the present war began, repugnant to a people whose tribal and family histories got all the lustre they had from not very remote deeds of war. How much the British arms during the Napoleonic campaigns owed to this smouldering element of militarism in the Scottish nation has never been adequately acknowledged; the records of the Highland regiments have never brought out sufficiently the truth that their personnel, though largely recruited in Lowland districts, was, in the main, made up of men of the hills and isles who had found the life of the towns as uncongenial to them as the new atmosphere that came to their native Highlands after Culloden.

The call to war in August, 1914, found no more immediate response than in the North. In the more densely populated parts of the Highlands the possibility of war had never, as elsewhere, been regarded as unthinkable. Not only had every household a soldier in its proudest genealogy; the greater number of such households had never ceased to contribute to the manhood of the Naval Reserve and the Army. Waterloo and the Peninsula, with all their memories kept alive at cottage fires, made the profession of arms dignified and worthy to the Highlanders whose people had been there, and the industrial conditions of the Highlands and the Hebrides made it possible for an enormous number of young men to combine in their lives the arts of peace and war; they filled, for months each year, the ships of the

Naval Reserve and the ranks of the old Militia battalions. A very large number of the combatant officers and chaplains of our present Army in the field had served in the ranks of the third-line regiments; they had often found the price of their education in the annual dole of the paymaster.

There is no more shining and significant evidence of the Highlands' contribution to the present struggle than is to be found in such district Rolls of Honour as that of the Isle of Lewis, where, a few months after war broke out, young men were nearly as scarce as trees.

In the flux of modern Scotland, however, nearly all the old lines of demarcation between Saxon and Gael have broken down, and the never wholly quenched martial tradition and fire of the clan countries have, for a century back, been shared in more or less degree by Scots of all descents, down to the English border. The blend of intermarriage for at least three hundred years made this inevitable. Yet it has been to the kilted corps that Scots, Lowland as well as Highland, most eagerly flocked; our Scots Colonial contigents insist on the philabeg, and the typical 'Jock' of our Army, for the Hun as for ourselves, is a man bare-kneed. It is a tribute to the power of romance. For the Lowland Scots regiments, it cannot be too much insisted on, have records at least as long and brilliant as any of those that wear the tartan. Their origins and their contributions to national history will, on the whole, evoke more unqualified gratitude from the unprejudiced patriot.

But glamour and romance are nowhere more potent than in military affairs; modern Scottish art in song and story has ever been so admiringly preoccupied with the Celtic element in the national history of the eighteenth and nineteenth centuries that a foreigner might well imagine the picturesque and gallant characteristics of the race were confined to wearers of the kilt and players of the bagpipes. If the Lowlanders feel aggrieved at this, they must lay the blame with men of genius of their own race – Scott and Stevenson and Hogg, and many others who gave romantic mystery, poetic idealism, and all the old primitive graces to the Celts they wrote about, while endowing their Lowlands characters too generally with but the humdrum qualities of pawkiness and the moral virtues. High-hearted youth was never yet intrigued with pawkiness nor much inspired by the contemplation of meek kailyard attributes, and for a hundred years all that has been young and ardent and truly national in the Scottish race as a whole has felt some magic uplift in the sound of the mountain pipe, and its heart 'warm to the tartan'. Whether we are Highland or Lowland, the pipes – the only instrument of music carried through the battle charges of a world at war – speak to us out of our past, stir in us, whether we live in glens or cities, feelings strange and deep, ancestral ecstasies. It was probably the instrument of the Scottish plains long before it found acceptance among the mountaineers, who abandoned their native harps to make it theirs peculiarly, because of its wild and haunting cadences as of winds in mountain passes, its frenzy and its sadness, as if the passions of a bygone race were there articulate, its far-off faery influence, as though the distant vale were wakening to the song of some Celtic Pan.

Some degree of fervour in writing about the pipes is justified, since they are incontestably at the moment a symbol and an inspiration. They, and all they connote of picturesque garb and old tradition and renown, express the very spirit needed for a nation at war. It was well for Scotland, well for the Empire, that this romance of pipe and tartan and martial emprise survived to be the leavening which should raise a whole people. We have no 'Marseillaise' nor 'Brabançonne' nor 'Watch on the Rhine' to lift tired Scots feet on the muddy roads of war, for 'Scots wha hae' in its sentiment ill befits the moment, and is an anthem, not a march; but in those pipes, that have all the lure of Hamelin's wizard and lead Lowland and Highland corps alike even to the jaws of death, we have the past of Scotland rendered vocal, and an emotional stimulus no mere words could supply.

They have called, those magic pipes, through the sleep of men of our race in every part of the world and brought them Home. Many thousands of them, among the bravest and best, from Canada, Australasia, Africa and the outmost gates of Empire, had no thought of these isles as Home till the pipes commanded or implored; it was their fathers' Home they saw, for the first time, rising grey and old through the mist across the troopship's bows. But whoso answers the call of the pipes has ties with Scotland that reach through generations, even of exile, and cannot be unloosed. Tonight, while the waves crash on our darkened shores and the winds lament through valleys bereft of their youth, those children of the breed from distant lands, with all our native best, our dearest, hear, in brief lulls of the storm of shot and shell along the battling frontiers of the world, sing through the murk the pipes of Scotland.

✝

BALLANTRAE

Doubtless most good people who come into Ballantrae for the first time remember the name of Stevenson's novel, and give a glance about for some ancient mansion-house that may have been a prototype of Durrisdeer. But Ballantrae was merely a name picked up by the novelist in the by-going; the landscape of his story borrowed nothing from this fishing hamlet, and his House of Durrisdeer, the scene of Ephraim Mackellar's fidelities and the Master's sinister appearances, was (even in the fiction) far away from Ballantrae – 'near St Bride's on the Solway Shore'. Neither at Ballantrae nor on the Solway, however, will you find a scrap of building or of history that could have given inspiration to the story. And yet *The Master of Ballantrae* had some germ of inspiration from this neighbourhood; probably the scene of the story would not have been pitched exactly where it was but for a rambling tour which Stevenson made in 1876, of all seasons in the year, in the second week of January. A partly finished account of this 'Winter's Walk in Carrick and Galloway' is to be found in the complete editions of his works. He started out from Ayr through a snowy landscape by Dunure, Maybole, and Girvan to Ballantrae, where he spent a night. Doubtless he went further on, for his title speaks of Galloway, but the fragmentary record stops abruptly at Girvan, which is described as 'one of the most characteristic districts in Scotland'. 'It has, as we shall see,' say the essayist's concluding words, 'a sort of remnant of provincial costume, and it has the handsomest population in the Lowlands.' Unhappily he never fulfilled the promise of that sentence; I am mightily curious to know what kind of costume he referred to and why he should have singled out the folk of Girvan for their good looks.

The month of January, and particularly soon after the New Year, is no sane time for making the acquaintance of Ayrshire, and Stevenson's impressions of the country were rather bitter. I will not repeat what he said of Maybole, which, at the time, was spiritually distracted with revivalism and drunk. Near Culzean, he met 'three compatriots of Burns' in a cart. 'They were all drunk, and asked me jeeringly if this was the way to Dunure. I told them it was; and my answer was received with unfeigned merriment. One gentleman was so much tickled he nearly fell out of the cart; indeed, he was only saved by a companion, who either had not so fine a sense of humour or had drunken less.' I wonder if any of the three roysterers survive, and if any of them ever discovered that they figured so ingloriously in print. No inn at Girvan, where he stopped a while (like Keats, who wrote his ode to Ailsa Craig there), nor at Ballantrae, retains a memory of the unreasonable young pedestrian of 1876.

He lunched at Dunure in a public-house room, where four carters came in and drank eight quarts of ale between them in a jiffy, and the ruins of Dunure Castle were almost the only work of man throughout the recorded journey to engage his pen, as it does to the extent of a chilly paragraph. 'You never saw a place more desolate from a distance, nor one that less belied its promise near at hand. . . . The whole world, as it looked from a loophole, was cold, wretched, and out-at-elbows. If you had been a wicked baron and compelled to stay there all the afternoon, you would have had a rare fit of remorse. I think it would come to homicide before evening – if it were only for the pleasure of seeing something red!' At this stage, obviously, the young gentleman's feet were getting sore, and the beautiful bleak scenery of the coast was not to a taste confessedly inclined to prefer the lush, the trim, the woody. He has nothing to say of the finest ruins of all at Crossraguel Abbey, half fane, half old baronial keep, which the Earl of Cassilis and his servants in 1570 extorted from poor 'Commendatour' Stewart by the fine old mediaeval torture of roasting him in the vault of Dunure Castle. A squad of whistling masons upon scaffolding today are busy on the Abbey walls and plastering up its chinks.

It is a pity that Stevenson should have cut off the account of his itinerary where he did, for it is south of Girvan, whose length is surely a challenge to Kirkcaldy, that the coast is at its grandest, and might naturally have aroused some sympathy to relieve the spirit of disillusion in his narrative as it stands. For fifteen miles or so the road lies by the shore, or high on rocky terraces; in tiny coves below are clustered, as at Lendal-Foot and the Fishery, small hamlets that appear to be in the spray of south-west winds; when you reach the top of Bennan Hill you are among cliff scenery which Murchison has declared as picturesque as is to be found anywhere else in Scotland. It may have been a stiff walk for shanks' mare, which was the resort of Stevenson, and the cyclist may find an inconvenient amount of walking on it, but for the automobile there is no more fascinating coast road on the West of Scotland. Ballantrae itself could have proffered no hints to the romancer on a casual visitation; its smuggling atmosphere has long since dissipated, and its folk have tamed their taste for stimulants, to judge from the Italian ice-cream vendor's barrow which we met on its outskirts, making back for Girvan, empty.

Beyond Ballantrae the cliffs round Downan Point are apparently as majestic as those of the Bennan Head, but he wisely elects who diverges from the sea a little here, and for a change goes through the valley of the App – warm, wooded, sheltered from the sea winds, brilliant with wild flowers. Glen App should have charmed Stevenson if he saw it, for it is none of those 'wild and inhospitable places' he said once he was rarely able to visit in the proper spirit, 'being happier always with the tame and fertile, and not readily pleased without trees.' No traveller in Ballantrae should fail to see Glen App. It is the happiest of entrances to Galloway, and one emerging from it on Loch Ryan's shores finds that the whole coast scenery has changed in the brief period occupied by the divagation. Cliffs have given place to grey shelving beaches that may contribute to the pleasure of the gourmet from their oyster beds, but lack the broken shore lines, rocks, and creeks one looks for in a sea-loch, and the gorgeous hues of wrack.

ROBERT BONTINE CUNNINGHAME GRAHAM

Two qualities uncommon in present-day writing distinguish the work of Mr Cunninghame Graham – his own special philosophy and his style, which is mainly the natural, naïve expression of a whimsical, unconventional mind and is partly influenced by a host of Spanish examples of which Cervantes is the most obvious to a critic who knows no original Spanish. The philosophy of Mr Graham, who would himself hesitate to use the word, is of an early, one may even say a primitive type, the philosophy of the Arab, of the Gaucho, of all rude, out-of-doors men; it is mainly a philosophy of *laissez faire* – which is paradoxical enough, coming from the pen of a Socialist.

In certain moods, Mr Graham recognises pitfully that the things he hates – shoddy factory, drummer, chromo-lithograph, Offenbach, the missionary, and the corrugated iron colonial store, are kismet, are as inevitable as the stink of his beloved deserts. It is then he most commends himself. But ever and anon the old Trafalgar Square war-horse sniffs battle and begins to say, 'Ha, ha!' among the trumpets. Then he kicks at kismet, and particularly we hear him condemn success and progress, the success of commerce, war, and art, the progress of 'civilisation' – that civilisation which alone makes possible his own delightful books, which gives him his steamer to Tangier or Rio, his understanding of Wagner, and, say, the possibility of a pianola at Ardoch. It is then he seems less convincing. He captures our heart, for we all detest the factory and the corrugated iron roof, and admire, afar off, the 'friendly and flowing savage', who cries, 'No soap, till the powder runs out at the heels of his boots. But our head remains uncapitulating. There are more inconsistencies to the chapter in Mr Cunninghame Graham than in any writer I know. That perhaps enhances his interest, for 'a foolish consistency is the hobgoblin of little minds.'

The style of Mr Cunninghame Graham, who is one of the most distinctive and attractive writers of his generation, is another proof of the fact that to write fresh, bold, unhackneyed English, to ring frank and true, to make the soul cry out on the printed page, it is necessary to browse upon the early English masters or to know intimately another language. The English of modern life and modern letters often appals you by its flatness and insincerity; it is a mosaic of phrases, ready-made, and as the phrase comes to the writer's mind before the thought, it is, consequently, a mosaic of worn-out thoughts. A writer steeped in early English may escape the domination of the phrase, but more certainly can one escape it is who knows and loves another language than the one he uses. It is not enough to know it as the teacher instils it – by looks or on the Berlitz system; it must be a language you can think in, a language whose every idiom gives access to the inner life of the generations of people who have used it. Any language will do that has passion and poetry in it, but preferable is a language that has not known the blight of 'progress' as English has done, and best of all is the language that – like Spanish – retains its ancient spirit and enshrines a little – not too much – noble literature. Spanish has not rendered Mr Cunningham Graham immune against some solecisms in English grammar, for he falls to the temptation of the 'and which', or 'presently' for 'at present', or the 'like he did', but these are trivial offences only to the ear and eye of the supersensitive; they are to be looked over, because in all else he writes he has rhythm, art, and a happy unexpectedness due to his ability to bring his Spanish half of him to his assistance.

Many repeated devices of Mr Cunninghame Graham's sketches always freshly charm me, with a power to open up romantic vistas and immerse the spirit in that sweet melancholy, 'compounded of many simples, extracted from many objects, and, indeed, the sundry contemplation of my travels, in which my own rumination wraps me in a most humorous sadness'. I may refer particularly to his style in concluding scenes and incidents, of which I find examples in all his books – *Mogreb El Acksa, Father Arch Angel, Success, Notes on Menteith*, or *Progress*. This, from *La Tapera*, in the last-named book, is characteristic: 'Then, slowly saddling up, they used to mount, and strike into a little trot until they came to a slow-running stream, where, after watering their horses, and exchanging salutations, they would separate and sink into the plain, as birds sink out of sight into the sky.' Or this, from *His Return*: – 'With a last look at the sleeping tents, he mounted silently, and, settling his haik, touched his horse with his spur, and vanished noiselessly into the night, upon the road to Fez.' Or this, from *Un Infelix*: – 'I called and waved my hand, but he went upwards towards the huts without once turning, and when I looked again, the bent, grey, moving figure had disappeared among the stones.' I have learned to look for these conclusions in the minor key with expectancy. They may seem, quoted in this detached way, of no importance, but in their place they move one curiously, and seem to give the key to the real Cunninghame Graham who disguises himself so often in his attacks on that same 'stand o' black', Scotland, the Free Kirk, and our passion for *aqua vitae*. If the moods of wonder and pity, and this conviction that we are as dust and wind-blown through the streets could be sustained, and all his fictitious cynicism held in check, Mr Cunningham Graham would be always magnificent.

It may seem absurd to say so of a Graham of Gartmore, but I once doubted if he knew Scotsmen, and felt the conviction that he had taken many of his most pronounced views of Scotsmen, not from real life, but from bookish conventions. He works even yet unceasingly two types of Scotsmen only – one a Celt, the other Lowland; the former always admirable, touched with the old-time graces and courtesies, a brave gentleman who commends himself naturally to Mr Graham by his tradition of lawlessness, his fights in foolish and pathetic causes, his deer-skin mocassins; the other the Lowlander, a religious bigot, prone to ardent waters. I should be the last to deny that the Celt is other than Mr Graham imagines, but I think his Scotsman generally is old-fashioned, not quite so old-fashioned as Mr Graham used to make him, but still apt to be purely traditional. All that he thinks of the Scot of today is out of date except that we still assuage the arid œsophagus with too much whisky.

Mr Graham thinks our marine engineers quote Latin and the Bible in their intervals of blasphemy – the convention of Conrad, Kipling, and other modern sea-writers. That sort of engineer is not typical of Scotland, and never was. Mr Graham also thinks that the fear of hell is yet a potent influence in Scotland, and he makes one of his characters in *Progress*, the Rev. Archibald Macrae, missionary on the West Coast of Africa, think and speak as if he were a contemporary of John Knox. Scotsmen are not made like that now. Mr Graham might with advantage study them at a football match. The attitude to religion has greatly altered in the past two or three generations, in some respects for the better, in many for the worse.

A braw new Bible has been bocht
Revised to clink wi' Modern Thocht;
A braw new beadle has been socht,
   Soople and snod;
And this new Herd, himsel' has wrocht
   A braw new God.

A God wha widna fricht the craws;
A God wha never lifts the taws;
Wha never heard o' Moses' laws,
    On stane or paper,
A kind o' thowless Great First Cause,
    Skinklin' through vapour.

The auld blue Hell he thinks a haiver;
The auld black Deil a kintry claver;
And what is Sin, but saut to savour
    Mankind's wersh luggies;
While Saunts, if ye'd believe the shaver,
    Are Kirk-gaun puggies!

'A Scotch Presbyterian exceeds the strictest Nonconformist of the South in pitch of snuffle and intensity of whine,' says Mr Graham, and 'wax fruit and feather flowers, and humming-birds stuck upon the mantelpieces covered with glass shades' are in his description of a shipowner's house at Bearsden. The whine survives no more than the wax fruit; they have not existed in Scotland for some generations back, and it is about time they were disappearing from imaginative literature.

But though he still has a few curiously belated ideas of the humble Scot, Mr Graham, now that he is most of the time 'furth of Scotland', has developed (as every sentimental man will under similar circumstances) an affection for the people among whom for a length of time he has spent what may have been a sort of exile. It is the pensive, romantic, profounder Scot in Mr Graham who writes one half of the book, *Progress*. Scots sketches like 'A Traveller', 'The Laroch', 'A Convert', 'Snow in Menteith', and 'Pollybaglan', are among the most artistic and impressive things he has written; they show that though somehow he may occasionally have missed the character of the modern Scot, he has a quick remembering eye for Scotland herself, for that Scotland which he has written so much against in good-humoured satire, but plainly cannot stay long away from, to judge from his return to Clydeside as at least a summer resident and sort of bonnet laird. Absence seems to have made his heart grow fonder – even to the Scot, who, he admits, 'has the saving grace of humour which far surpasses wit, as whisky beer', and adds that, 'rising superior to climate and the terrors of the Calvinistic faith', this humour 'has made North Britons kindly in their hardness, and rendered them easier of indulgence to foreigners in spite of their angularities than the majestic and pure-blooded cis-Tweedian Celto-

Saxon'. 'Kindly, old-world, humorous' – that is the Laird of Ardoch's latest summing-up about us; he grows mellow with his years; here is distinct Progress.

JOSEPH CONRAD

A few years after his retirement from the sea, and his settling down, as it seemed for good, to the life of a literary man at Pent Farm, Hythe, Conrad had a period of utter disillusionment with his new calling. To the surprise and disquietude of his friends, he decided to abandon his desk and take up again the broken strands of his career as a sailor. To this end he went north to the Clyde in search of a command, and for three days went round the Glasgow shipping offices.

On a Clyde-built, Clyde-owned iron clipper, the *Loch-Etive*, his training as a seaman had been completed. At the age of twenty-three he had sailed as third mate on the *Loch-Etive*, to Sydney, signing on as 'J. Korzeniowski', his baptismal name. The ship was one of a famous line, commanded by a clipper captain of exceptional renown for quick passages, William Stuart of Peterhead, to whom Conrad makes affectionate allusion in his *The Mirror of the Sea*. Clyde sailing ships remained, for ever after, Conrad's ideal of sea-going craft, and the deluding thought so many of us have that, given the old familiar things of youth, we can again be young and happy, no doubt dictated his selection of the Clyde as port to sail from in his second period of sea-wandering.

Fortunately for himself and English letters, no command was forthcoming. 'The fact that I'm suspected of writing novels is a handicap on the Clyde, I fear,' he said a little ruefully, but probably that had nothing to do with his failure to get a ship. As yet his stories seemed of interest only to a few discerning critics, and for men in the Clyde shipping trade, Clark Russell and Frank Bullen were probably regarded as the supreme spinners of sound sea yarns.

Almayer's Folly and *The Outcast of the Islands* might be too deliberate in action, too strange in atmosphere, too remote from the conventional tale of adventure, to be in much demand at the libraries, but *The Nigger of the Narcissus* appeared to some of us not only the best sea-tale ever written, but possessed of qualities that would make it irresistible to the humblest reader. It was staggering to learn from the author himself that in two years its sales had been trivial, and that he found the bookshops rarely stocked any of his work. This discouraging trait of bookshops sooner or later vexes most authors, but Conrad's case seemed exceptional and unaccountable, and he was in the doldrums of depression.

Upon the reception of *The Nigger* he had built high hopes. It was, as he said at the time, and wrote long after, the story by which as a creative artist he would stand or fall; 'at any rate no one else could have written it.'

'And now,' he said, 'I sit for a whole day at my desk, and at the end I have produced only two or three sentences. My invention seems paralysed; I must get back to sea.' While W. E. Henley, Blackwood, Cunninghame Graham, Edward Garnett, Galsworthy, Quiller-Couch, and a few other critically fastidious people cheered him by their approval, others whose opinions he was bound to respect were indifferent to his work, or disconcerted him by their advice, which was contrary to theories and convictions on the art of fiction which he had thrashed out for himself through years of concentrated, lonely thought at sea. It seemed to us incredible that perhaps the best-known critic of his time should frankly express a dislike for *The Nigger*, and that another novelist in whose work we had delight should counsel the cutting out of the final passages of the story as it appeared in serial form – that superb and moving 'envoi' – the description of the crew's dispersion which in its feeling, its philosophy, its noble sadness, the cadence and beauty of its language, expresses Conrad in his loftiest inspiration. All Conrad still appears articulate in that final paragraph:

> A gone shipmate, like any other man, is gone for ever; and I never met one of them again. But at times the spring-flood of memory sets with force up the dark River of the Nine Bends. Then on the waters of the forlorn stream drifts a ship – a shadowy ship manned by a crew of Shades. They pass and make a sign, in a shadowy hail. Haven't we, together and upon the immortal sea, wrung out a meaning from our sinful lives? Good-bye, brothers! You were a good crowd. As good a crowd as ever fisted with wild cries the beating canvas of a heavy foresail; or tossing aloft, invisible in the night, gave back yell for yell to a westerly gale.

Though *The Nigger of the Narcissus* seemed to have sailed into the fog and been lost for ever when Conrad thought of leaving a farmhouse to go back to sea, she really carried his fortunes and made a good landfull at last. No sensible person reading the book and coming under the spell of its epic fury, its glorious language, could fail to be, thereafter, a zealous Conradian. He recaptured its magic twice – in *Youth* and *Typhoon*. I can still see him beat out, in a quarter-deck walk back and forward behind his chair, the story of *Youth*, a real and personal experience in which, as printed, only the vessel's name is imaginary. It was at the century's end.

He looked like his old profession – a ship's officer in his shore clothes, a wiry figure about five feet nine, with a black beard trimmed to a point, a tanned complexion; high cheek-bones, bushy eyebrows, dark brown penetrative eyes that glinted, and an aquiline nose; speaking English so perfectly that it was difficult to believe he was a Pole who did not know our language when he first set foot in this country in 1878. Not only was his English idiom impeccable – so far as a Scot may judge – but his mental attitude seemed wholly English; all that betrayed the foreigner was a gesture of the hands.

Conrad's *Tales of Unrest* shared equally with Maurice Hewlett's *The Forest Lovers* and Mr Sidney Lee's *A Life of William Shakespeare* the award of 150 guineas (about $750) offered by the London *Academy* for the three best books published in 1898. 'No one was more surprised than myself,' he wrote to me. 'Even yet (when the cash is spent and gone) I feel like an imposter and a thief. . . . Who am I? – I who accidentally write a sentence a day? Now and then for a moment or so the spell is removed from me – to the end that I might the better taste the despair of thought without expression, of the wandering soul without a body.'

Those blank, unable days came to him frequently throughout the remainder of his life, and he would declare the very thought of writing hateful to him, the process itself a torture. So have felt about it many of the most renowned and delightful writers. In Conrad's case, the parturition pains of artistic creation had a real physical origin; Congo fever, years before, had left some poisonous acids in his system; by and by to hold a pen in his hand became an agony, and finally, with gout and neuritis, he was compelled in the years of his popularity and prosperity to use an amanuensis.

In the spring of 1923 he revisited the Clyde for the last time, on his way to America. He was now in his sixty-sixth year at which period sea captains generally are in a lusty Indian summer. Five-and-twenty years before – but yesterday as it seemed – he was rising like a star from the sea, all the skyey space of fame to travel; still with the fire of youth in his breast and the brine of tempest in his blood; master of his body, unobserved and unharassed by men. Inspiring, enviable figure! And now he was an aged and stricken man, his cruel body whipping him with achings, indigestion, asthma.

Strangest thing of all, and most significant, was to find he had become less English. His accent, his gestures, his courtesies, his tenderness of sentiment, visible in tears, were foreign. Too big a man at any time for vanity or pose, he had become pathetically humble. His ancestry was in command of him – that sinister phase of one's latter years.

Inevitably one thought of the end of his story, 'Youth':

'And this is all that is left of it! Only a moment; a moment of strength, of romance, of glamour – of youth! ... A flick of sunshine upon a strange shore, the time to remember, the time for a sigh, and – good-bye! – Night – Good-bye ... !'

... And we all nodded at him ... over the polished table that like a still sheet of brown water reflected our faces, ... marked by toil, by deceptions, by success, by love; our weary eyes looking still, looking always, looking anxiously for something out of life, that while it is expected is already gone – has passed unseen, in a sigh, in a flash – together with the youth, with the strength, with the romance of illusions.

12

The Search

INTRODUCTION

When Neil Munro published The New Road *in June 1914 he had the pleasurable experience of finding his novel, set in the period between the two Jacobite risings, greeted with enthusiastic approval by the leading critics of the day. John Buchan, writing a signed review in the* Glasgow Evening News, *opened his comments with these words: 'It is a privilege to be allowed to express my humble admiration of what seems to me one of the finest romances written in our time.'*

Buchan singled out for praise the character of Ninian Macgregor Campbell, the beachdar *or scout or intelligence officer in the service of the Duke of Argyll and thus of the government. Despite the existence of the romantic leading character, Æneas, Buchan pointed out that Ninian was the 'true picaresque hero, kin to Alan Breck and John Splendid'.*

Buchan's implicit comparison with Stevenson was made explicit by the anonymous reviewer in the leading London literary periodical The Bookman *who stated confidently that: 'Mr Munro has won to the position that many tried to gain, and now stands forth bravely as the legitimate successor to the author of* Kidnapped.'

Remarking that it 'was quite the best piece of work that Mr Neil Munro has yet done' the reviewer concluded that: 'He is now one of the chief writers of the modern romantic school – perhaps indeed the chief.'

Munro's publisher, George W. Blackwood, wrote to him a week after publication: 'The reviews have been absolutely first rate, and should send the public flocking to buy copies of a work which can merit such praise.'

Indeed, the initial sales were encouraging – the pre-publication subscription for the title had been high and re-ordering had started. However the overall sales of The New Road *were undoubtedly depressed by the outbreak of the First World War in August 1914, and Munro's attention went from writing novels to reporting the War from the Western Front and the problems of running a newspaper. He spent a month in France in the first autumn of the War with the British Expeditionary Force and then returned to full-time work as acting editor of the* News.

In April 1915, when acknowledging a royalty cheque from Blackwood's which had been accompanied by an enquiry about the possibility of a new story, Munro wrote: 'I fear I can show you no successor to Ninian Campbell for some considerable time yet. I have a story simmering though – of the same period and character, and gathering material for it, and hope before very long to plunge delightedly into its execution.'

The eleven chapters of The Search, *which are here presented in published form for the first time, are the start of this promised sequel to* The New Road, *uncompleted at the time of Munro's death more than fifteen years later.*

In 1918 he told George Blackwood, 'I have actually begun a Romance for you' and at the end of 1919 Blackwood asked 'Are you making any progress with the new novel?' – an enquiry repeated by the ever-patient Blackwood in 1921, 1922, and 1923. In 1923 Munro was able to report that 'I have a new novel blocked out and partly written which should suit you to a T . . .' In May 1924 Munro advised Blackwood that in a couple of months he hoped to be free of his newspaper editorial role and be able to 'plunge into a new adventure of Ninian Campbell's'. Unfortunately he was not able to free himself from his newspaper work but in September 1924 advised that he was once more: 'on the trail with Ninian Campbell. I have every confidence that I can finish with him in four or five months.'

Blackwood reserved a slot for the first instalment of The Search *for the January 1925 issue of* Maga *but it never appeared, and in March 1926 Munro wrote to apologise for his failure to deliver. A year later* The Search *was again on Munro's mind and pending file but in October 1928 George Blackwood would still wistfully write: 'A real Munro novel for 1929 would be the very thing for* Maga' *and in September 1930, just three months before Munro's death, he wrote to Munro: 'I am always, as you know, hoping to hear from you about the new novel . . .'*

Why, in view of the literary and commercial success of The New Road, *was Munro not able to follow this up with a second novel centred on Ninian Macgregor Campbell? The period and theme were central to Munro's interests; the response to* The New Road *highly encouraging. Munro was a very productive writer: the years 1898–1903 had seen him publish four major novels:* Gilian the Dreamer, Doom Castle, The Shoes of Fortune *and* Children of Tempest *as well as turn in two columns a week for the* News, *and a vast range of other freelance literary work, ranging from reviewing to a weekly literary column for a new magazine,* St Andrew, *and starting a fortnightly column for* The Oban Times. *Although George Blake in* The Brave Days *suggests that Munro was a slow writer of creative fiction – often only achieving 750 words a day – as opposed to his much swifter rate of progress in journalistic writings, this still does not explain why the 30,000 words of* The Search *took 15 years instead of 6 weeks to write. Nor does it explain his apparent confidence that the novel could be finished with a few months' work, freed from the demands of the newspaper.*

Some of the reasons are probably just those that Munro gave to George Blackwood – the disruption of war and his wartime and post-war involvement as editor of the News. *However, it may perhaps be questioned if this is the full story. Munro, despite his oft-stated distaste for journalism, never really managed to break away from it. When at last he gave up the editorship of his paper, he immediately accepted a contract to serve as a Director of the company that owned it and to act as Literary Editor. When, in 1927, he finally gave up his connection with the* News, *he promptly started writing a series of reminiscences and opinion pieces, under the pen-name 'Mr Incognito' for the* Daily Record.

Part of the motivation for this was probably financial. Munro had been extremely successful commercially as well as artistically in the pre-war years. His diary records annual earnings ranging from £606 to £1343 in the years 1901–10. It is hard to express this in current values, but some indication of the more than comfortable level of his earnings is given by the fact that the large house – 3 public rooms, 5 bedrooms – he bought in Gourock in 1902 cost £875 – or around an average year's earnings for Munro at this time. Another indication of his very secure economic status is the fact that he could afford to send his oldest daughter, Effie, to a finishing school in Switzerland in 1907/08. The War brought a considerable change: paper rationing resulted in many titles going out of print and, for example, the mass-market cheap edition of The New Road *had to wait until the end of the war before it appeared. Munro enjoyed a fairly expensive lifestyle – in 1918 he moved from his Gourock home to an even grander Regency villa in Helensburgh. Starving romantically in a garret was not part of his life-plan and the regular income from journalism was a comfort that he had never been prepared to renounce. Even when, in 1897, he gave up his staff post on the* News *he kept on his two weekly columns and sought other freelance work.*

Nor was his interest in journalism purely a mercenary one. In 1904, at the height of his literary success, he accepted the office of Chairman of the Glasgow & West of Scotland District of the Institute of Journalists. It is probably fair to conclude that Munro had printer's ink in his veins and, despite protestations about 'the jawbox', as he called daily journalism – being shackled to journalism like a housewife to her sink – he delighted in the excitement and camaraderie of the newspaper.

The more solitary life of the novelist, the financial risk that would have been involved in a single-minded dedication to fiction, the emotional impact of the loss of his son Hugh, who was killed in action on the Western Front in September 1915, all these doubtless had something to contribute to the apparent writer's block which saw the much-promised The Search *stick at eleven chapters despite fifteen years of intermittent effort. Without descending too far into psychological speculation it is also possible to wonder if, coming back to fiction at the end of the War, he suffered a loss of nerve and hesitated before completing a sequel to his masterpiece,* The New Road.

After The New Road *Munro's creativity undoubtedly deserted him, at least in the field of literary fiction. His collection of short stories,* Jaunty Jock, *appeared in 1918, but this was a collection of stories which had been written much earlier – some as early as 1902.* Jimmy Swan *appeared in 1917 and a third collection of Para Handy stories in 1923, but these had been done as part of his newspaper work. The post-war years saw only one book appear – the* History of the Royal Bank of Scotland 1727–1927. *This work, which he said he had been pressured to undertake by a friend who was a Director of the Royal Bank, occupied much of his time and energies from 1925–27 and involved 'a lot of research and reading little to my inclination'.*

There are, in the collection of Munro's papers in the National Library of Scotland, two pages of manuscript (MS 26915 f.107/8). These are the first two pages of Chapter 1: 'The Newcomer', of a novel called The Windfall. *The story has a post-World War I setting and the manuscript is dated 19 January 1920. It might possibly have been intended to be no more than a short story, but the division into chapters does suggest that a novel was planned. Unfortunately there is no evidence that this project was taken any further.*

Quite how the decision to spend his time on hackwork such as the Royal Bank history can be reconciled with his frequent protestations of anxiety to devote himself to fiction and to finish The Search *is unclear. In one letter to George Blackwood he recollects how he used to be happy to agree to*

the serialisation of a novel with only enough written to supply three of the dozen or so instalments, '. . . but so many trivial engagements turn up unexpectedly that now I dare not venture it.' This recollection of earlier more productive days rather contradicts George Blake's assessment of Munro's very measured pace of writing. Failing physical powers and perhaps the lack of confidence which this engendered may have had something to do with this reluctance. While the immediate cause of Munro's death on 22 December 1930 was a cerebral haemorrhage in early November, the death certificate also noted a ten-year-old history of *arteriosclerosis, and he reported to George Blackwood that he had had, in the summer of 1921, the first serious illness of his life.*

The Search *itself is set in the late summer of 1746 with Charles Edward Stuart (or 'Morag' as he is referred to in code by all the characters, Jacobite and Hanoverian alike) on the run in the Highlands with a price on his head. John Derry, an agent of the London government, travels to Inveraray to make contact with Sheriff Campbell of Stonefield, and arranges to travel north with Ninian Campbell. He finds Inveraray in a state of disorder; the old castle and township are being swept away in the elaborate scheme of the third Duke, to be replaced by a new castle and a new planned town. The changes in Inveraray, which were planned from 1744, although the main reconstruction of the town was somewhat later than the period of the story, are a useful symbol for the changes in the post-Jacobite Highlands. Derry and Ninian leave on their journey north, but first retrace Derry's footsteps to Dumbarton on the River Clyde to see a Jacobite prisoner held in the Castle there and then prepare to travel on by way of Stirling and Doune.*

The surviving typescript of the text ends at Chapter 10. Some notes and part of Chapter 11 exist in Munro's manuscript. All the material is presented with minimal editing. In a number of places Munro has set down alternatives, left blanks or question marks, or provided himself with notes on developments.

We are very grateful to Margaret Renton for transcribing the typescript and manuscript and thus facilitating access to this unknown sequel to Munro's greatest novel.

Every reader of The Search *will wonder how the story was intended to develop and wonder if the apparent complexity of the plot may have been a factor in Munro's inability to bring it to a satisfactory conclusion. What is the role of the enigmatic Hannibal Lamont? What exactly is the mission of John Derry, and how is he likely to capture 'Morag' when all the military and naval forces of the Crown cannot pin him down? Could Derry's mission be to avoid the embarrassment of having the Young Pretender caught and tried for treason? Has he been sent to get him quietly out of the country? What will happen to Colina Drummond and why does she dress as a man? How did Craigbarnet escape so readily from Dumbarton Castle? Alas, we will never know.*

How good is The Search? *Again, every reader will be able to form his or her own opinion on this. The opening chapter is somewhat awkwardly written and makes a poor first impression, but the descriptions of eighteenth-century Inveraray, Dumbarton and Stirling, and as always with Munro, the Scottish landscape, are vivid. The evolving relationship between Ninian and*

Derry promises much, and the potential for romantic interest exists with Colina Drummond. It is impossible, and possibly unfair, to judge the work on the basis of what can only amount to about a third or a quarter of the whole. However no lover of Munro's work can surely regret renewing acquaintance with Ninian Macgregor Campbell or regret reading this final tantalising fragment from the pen of one of Scotland's leading novelists.

THE SEARCH
CHAPTER 1

Delivered at last from that hilly desolation, and the glen where night, quick-fallen, had seemed more like a stagnant pool of elemental darkness than the effect of sunset; down to the level of the sea again, and on a good hard road but lately made by soldiery, John Derry dismissed his guide. They had crossed a stream that frayed out in a delta. There was a smell of fresh-cut timber, and more faintly of burning turf. A dog barked distantly. Somewhere in those young woods were dwellers.

'It will beat you to make any error now,' said the guide in unpracticed English.

'Nine miles at the most and you're into the town. There is only one slated house 'twixt here and the place you're seeking, but I'll wager you'll never see it!'

Here at last was the longest speech the fellow had made since he had hired him in the morning: kept apart from real communion by mere difference of tongues, their conversation all the way had been little more than gestures and ejaculations. The man, who had insisted on his money forehand, turned his horse round as he spoke, and trotted back to the mountain pass wherefrom they had just emerged.

Derry, abandoned, halted till the clattering hoofs were silent. He had been deceived! The guide, after all, had a better knowledge of the English language than he first pretended. Clearly he had played the dumb man to escape interrogations, and Derry, thus bereft of a link between this wilderness and the world he knew, felt in a new way lonely. Never before had he had this uneasy sense of his dependency on fellow-creatures.

There is a loneliness of towns, even sparsely populated countryside, that is but a vague discomfort, a weight on the spirit that will lift at the light of a shop or a snatch of fiddling; this was an almost aching sense of solitude inimical. Something more than night, conspiring winds and watery mutterings was gathered round in this extraordinary country at the moment lapsed into ancient tumults and intrigues.

On his right, as he pursued his way, hills steeply lifted, close-thicketed to their base with trees that overhung the road, only to be conjectured dimly; on his left but a few yards seemed to lie between him and the tide that swished through shingle, disengaging seaweed odours. Sometimes tatters in the drifting clouds revealed but momentarily that stars were spying. Strangely, too, the clouds themselves, in a patch still far ahead of him, at times glowed with a luminance that wavered and quenched as though caused by wildfire or the Merry Dancers.

Those nine miles covered at a trot by a horse left mainly to its own volition, were but two-thirds compassed when a sudden detour to the west showed Derry, by the glow from low-hanging clouds and only for an instant, that his path lay round a broad expanse of bay in the long sea-inlet, the nature of which he for the first time comprehended.

The clouds had darkened again as suddenly as they had tinctured, but in that glimpse, as fantastic as anything in a play-house, he saw a little frigate moored, a salient cone-shaped hill, and a headland jutting beyond the bay, with lit houses. This last wonderfully comforting! Even the horse gave a whinny, surmising the stall and oats.

Ten minutes later and the cloud-banks glowed again; he had but time to turn his head and see on the peak of the conical hill, about a thousand feet above him, a tower with a beacon-fire in a deep recess of its southern wall. It flared, and died to an ember; brought a flush from the heavens; revealed again the frigate at her anchor with a feeble riding-light, and all about the bay with its tide-bared sandy floor vociferous with sea-birds of the night, thick-wooded mountain billows. Then darkness more profound than ever. Only the windows lit – not many for a metropolis – on the foreland.

There was a ramshackle bridge of a temporary wooden kind to cross; John Derry went over it; quitted the road and traversed the sands the quicker to reach the lighted dwelling, which seemed the only one awake. He had an intuition that it was the inn.

At the moment when John Derry took to the sands for a short cut, and while yet his approach was a secret of the dark, three men were standing outside the door of the house he made for – a rough-cast, lime-washed three-storey edifice with dormer windows, a sign-board with 'The New Inn' painted on it over the second storey, and a bracket above the door suspending a gilded bunch of grapes on a much bigger scale than those brought from the valley of Eschol to the camp of Kadesh-Barnea.

Behind the inn, which stood by itself on the edge of the short peninsula, were old high trees which spread some upper limbs above the roof, and sang to the wind, drowning all other noises save a curlew's screaming and the melancholy plaint of a river spilling over weirs that had held it back a little in some fish-pools before its final plunge to the sea.

The men at the door were silent – loungers merely; the innkeeper himself in a silken skull-cap, another with a hat and greatcoat which seemed to indicate the casual passer-by; the third a strapper in his shirt-sleeves. Through the open door a warm light from internal candles gushed on the roadway and the narrow sea-bank opposite, which sloped gradually to the beach. The radiance revealed them as through a slit in night's old privacy, a secret violated. They had, in this situation, in their immobility and silence that completed spiritual aloofness which in brooding souls gives to a transient group at a snow-bound ferry or to a solitary ploughman, paused against sunset at the furrow's end, a baffling sad significance as if it were some gesture of dead history petrified: a moment later, and the tale should move again, the planets swing!

Meanwhile their attention vaguely wavered between the mast-light of the frigate and the dying fire on the hill-top. The bay seemed filled with sandpipers of whom but one of the listeners took notice, cocking an ear, distinguishing some new note in the birds' commotion. A sudden scrabbling sound beyond the seabank in a moment after put an end to immobility; down on his forehead the man with the greatcoat tugged his hat and took two steps aside in the shadow.

As it were from the tide, a phantom of the deeps, a rider rose on the beach; hung for a little suspended on the verge of the human world with a hand above his eyes like its first discoverer. They saw the face of him, long and pallid, no body under it, as if it drifted in the wind; a stirrup glinted.

'Lord! Here he is at last! You would swear he had swum it,' muttered greatcoat. 'I'm off,' and instantly withdrew round the gable of the inn.

John Derry rode slowly over, dazzled a little by the New Inn lights, to find the innkeeper awaiting him on the threshold and the strapper at his bridle. At once the burden on his spirits lifted; it was like homecoming, for the host wore tightly-buttoned clothes of a slightly bygone London fashion and by his speech was obviously an Englishman.

'Good evening, sir,' he had said quietly, 'I shall have your horse put in and baited. You will find a bit of supper ready. But first, your room.'

There was an air about him warm and hospitable: when he snatched his skull-cap off, it was to show a head egg-shaped and bald and glossy, with a jowl that spoke good-cheer like a Smithfield brisket; the paunch of him was noble, and his legs were as sturdy as pilasters. John Derry had fancied this kind of host peculiar to France; he had come on none quite like it since returning thence.

The innkeeper's welcome, too, was grandly verified by the sense of smell; the most piquant odour, faint yet appetising, came from a chamber just within the entrance, with a door half-open that gave a glimpse of a furnished table, a pleasant fire of wood, and of candelabra on the sideboard throwing a cheerful radiance on decanters.

A cleanliness and freshness in the house immediately struck Derry, who in the last few days had most often quartered in unlicensed hovels. Even to its symbolic bunch of grapes which dipped into the gleaming entrance, it was manifestly new, with neither paint nor polish on its skirting-boards. The stair was plainly fresh from the mason's chisel, and on the landing, when Derry ascended hard on the heels of his host to be shown his bed-chamber, hung an odour of fresh mortar.

He had just begun to explain the absence of any baggage with him, when the bedroom door was opened by the landlord, and to his astonishment, in the light of the shaded candle picked up from a table on the landing by his host, Derry saw the lost portmanteau on a trestle beside the bed!

'Where in heaven's name did this come from?' he stammered. 'It's been in my mind like a sore finger for the last twelve hours.'

The landlord put his candle on the mantle, withdrew a silver snuff-box from his waistcoat pocket, tapped it delicately with a thumb-nail on the lid, opened it, and on his palm, as on a tray, proffered it to Derry.

'No doubt, sir' he said with deliberation. 'It was recovered three hours after you had set out today and brought here this afternoon by a messenger.'

'There must be shorter ways to this place then, than I took?'

'Not all of them convenient for a horse,' replied the inn-keeper. 'The bag was brought by a lad who came through the hills on foot, and took two ferries.'

'Did you pay him?' asked Derry.

'I gave him a plate of broth and some minced collops, sir, the best he's had, I'll swear, since his grandfather's funeral.'

'No more?'

'It was more than he expected, and as you may guess, it was his information that you were on the way made us ready for your reception.'

'How many miles, now, would this fellow cover to restore my property?' The landlord shut his eyes and calculated.

'Fifteen miles walking, – Scots – both ways, and say four both ways, for the ferries.'

'And he does it for nothing!' cried Derry. 'Damme, sir, the thing's incredible. The bag's intact, too, and a bag's a good deal easier to purloin than a cow.'

The landlord smiled; his chins expanded; to Derry he looked the soul of jollity though for the moment under a professional constraint.

'The lad,' he said, as he turned to leave his guest, 'came from what twenty years ago was regarded as the wickedest part of Scotland; and it's still not altogether wholesome. To look at him you would not trust him to carry an empty market-basket without stealing some of the wands.'

'Extraordinary honesty!' said Derry, and again the jowl of the innkeeper corrugated.

'Perhaps not altogether honesty,' he suggested. 'There is just a chance it was sheer stupidity. The fact that your bag was locked would seem to him a moral obstacle; it might never occur to him to slice it open with his knife. But that is the odd thing here, sir, – an incomprehensible people . . . In-comprehensible!'

He repeated the word with a kind of gusto – as though, chosen haphazard, it had agreeably surprised him by some unexpected quality of fitness or vocal charm. And he walked out backwards, bent a little from the hips shutting the door behind him.

'I have you now, my friend,' thought Derry, '– the emeritus butler', and left to himself, turned to his portmanteau.

The innkeeper, descending quietly, but with some precipitation, made through a back-door in the lobby to the stable-yard. By the light of a lantern, the strapper, hissing like a gander groomed the horse; beside him was standing the man with the greatcoat.

'Well, Mr Campbell,' said the innkeeper softly, 'Are you in the market for good riding cattle?'

'No, Mr Taylor,' said the other in a very different accent. 'I was just the least bit curious about this beast. Lennox-bred, I'll warrant you, and a good one! No brand on hoof nor fetlock nor nick on the ears, but a shilling under the skin.'

'Under the skin?' repeated the innkeeper. 'In-comprehensible!'

'Under the skin, Mr Taylor; where else would you look for a random shilling in Scotland these days? Feel that!' – and catching the innkeeper's wrist he drew the fingers over the horse's rump. 'That's a real Lennox brand and I doubt if it's even a shilling – a coin slipped under the hide and the cut healed up. And it hasna been long on the road this beast; its shoes are new and clinched in the lowland fashion by some silly fool too ready wi' the rasp. But the saddle's English pig-skin. It has done some travelling.'

Not a word more did he say, nor pause for any comment on a theme that seemed only at its start, but turned on his heel, and moved out of the yard into the night's oblivion.

Mr Taylor went out into the dark behind him, and stood for a little, musing. The rear of the inn, beyond the beech-trees, was a wilderness of gorse and bracken; no garden lent to it as yet amenity, and the tiniest pile of empty bottles ranged along a gable betrayed but a limited period of hospitality. Bracken and whin and bottles were invisible to Mr Taylor, but he felt their presence with a feeling of dreariness that comes as readily in solitude to fat jollity as to slim sober-sides; they were something not included in his life long dreams of inn-keeping. Clamant, the trees thrashed; from farther wooded cliffs fell the questioning cry of owlets; the rush of the river under its wooden bridge had a sound most dolorous.

'In-comprehensible!' he muttered to himself again; took a pinch of snuff, and went in through the cobbled yard to attend his guest.

John Derry was already at the table.

A trim, well-featured lass with good enough shoes on her waited on him, without a word of English in her cheek except for the names of viands, and she had the studiously imparted deferential air of one attendant on an English gentleman.

He was in the prime of life; very tall, lean-flanked, but a little bottle-shouldered, with cropped brown curly hair; clean-shaven, tanned in the complexion, with penetrating restless eyes, sloe-black, a disconcerting feature when they turned on her, as they did at times, with a smile too quizzical for mere good-nature. It was plain that he liked to see a lass.

John Derry had had but a cadger's dinner in the morning's tavern, scandalously rough and unready; he should have been the more in appetite for the tempting meal which Taylor's maid set forth, but he hurried through sizzling trout and the sappiest of brandered steaks without a glance at the entremets which flanked them, and not once stretched his hand to the decanters, an abstinence which fretted Taylor, who finally took a stance behind his guest and helped him. In a little he made to help him to some wine.

'You'll find it sound, sir,' he murmured, 'and not – not so new as the cellar. It's his Grace's favourite.'

Derry sipped a glass as good as the best he could have found in the land he came from, and finished it at a gulp, which made the innkeeper wince in spite of himself.

'The truth is that I'm in a hurry,' said the guest, who missed nothing. 'A delightful claret, and I wish I could do more justice to your excellent table.'

'May I ask, sir, if you mean to make a stay of any time?' inquired the innkeeper. Derry was already on his feet.

'Till tomorrow only, I hope. It's fairly late, I know' (and he looked at his watch) 'but tonight I must see the Sheriff. Is he far from here?'

'Ten minutes walking. Right in the middle of the town, beside the church; I could send a man with you.'

'No, no!' said Derry, assuming his hat from the peg he had hung it on in entering, with a muffler which he threw round his neck. 'No need for anyone to come with me. I'll find the place.' Already he was at the outer door.

Clouds still were scurrying, but to the south east, skimming a long low mass of hills, the moon was rising, invisible herself but wanly qualifying the earlier darkness of the night, and northwards stars were shining. The faintest ember of light was on the hill-top.

'What signifies the watch-fire?' Derry asked on the threshhold.

The landlord shrugged his shoulders. 'They are still a little timid here, sir, though I think, myself, there is no occasion for it now. But the soldiers only left on Wednesday; the ship out there is up for their guns and baggage.'

Derry moved out in front to the middle of the road and looked about him. For the first time, with bewilderment, he realised the absolute seclusion of the New Inn.

'Where the devil's the town?' he asked.

'You passed it coming in, sir' said Mr Taylor. 'Ah, no! – you came over the sand and wouldn't notice. It's round the bay there, in behind those trees; take the road to your left.'

Despite himself, and his professional dignity, he could not altogether suppress a chuckle.

CHAPTER 2

There was a strain of poetry in Derry, as there is in most of youth, till the clouds come down. Incapable of even one clinking couplet, or of finding words to express ideas other than the most prosaic, he was peculiarly inclined, when his stomach was full, to those moods wherewith the gifted make a kind of mordant for the dyed and patterned stuff of song. It was not only that a garish sunset, a lovely woman, or the most hackneyed flourish of conventional chivalry could affect his breathing, set him panting with vague and inexpressible emotions, or that he melted at the most banal melody heard in some soft appropriate hour: chords more unusual and subtle searched in him and found their own vibrations, there originating.

Too young to guess yet that we individually make our own world out of mingled trash and gems about us, which, themselves, are mere appearances, he saw in men and nature always, indications, symbols, clues, imposed on him, as he thought, but really sought for, and accepted because they confirmed his own desires and fears. There are nights when it seems as though the cares and apprehensions of mankind are shared by heaven; when the stars themselves, which should be tranquil, knowing not remorse nor expectations twitch with the pain of being. So Derry, riding in the dark from mountains which by day seemed horrible, by night piled the whole of the universe on the burden of his own private depression. As readily his spirits had lit up at the light of Taylor's candles and the smell of a decent supper.

But he had hardly walked two hundred yards from the security of the inn, pondering a little on the meaning of that final chuckle, when the mountains with their ambiguous menace seemed to close again about him. The road to the left that had been recommended to him forked from the highway he should earlier have followed round the bay, and had at its start a porter's lodge. It was starkly shuttered, with the faintest chink of light below its door; life was in it, plainly, with some confidence in merely tentative plans for human destiny, for it sounded with an air of suppliant psalmody. The language was unintelligible, but a droning quality in the melody to which adult and infant voices artlessly contributed – of resignation rather than of hope – left no doubt of it pious inspiration.

Nine o'clock was striking on a distant bell. Its slow deliberate strokes fell on the ear like something alien, intrusive on the wild and natural harmonies of the cascade and the wind. The final note, prolonged, and gradually vanishing, appeared to overtake and mingle with the silence.

Beyond was a dim expanse of fields, to their right the dark mass of the beacon hill, with its still red ember. The road, deep-rutted, led in that direction through a fringe of trees. It came to a ludicrous end against a wall, breast-high, of rudely-piled unmortared stones!

'The devil!' said Derry, and searched for an opening into the town whose immediate presence now was manifest in its odours.

The wall, he found on a closer examination, stretched probably to the bay on one side, and interminably inward on the other; no valid entrance of any dignity was possible. He realised the fuller significance of the innkeeper's hint at groundless fears – this was a hastily extemporised defence thrown up to close the triangle two-thirds formed by sea and river, in which the metropolis of his fancy squatted.

Clambering over the most convenient place that offered foothold, he found himself in garden-ground undelved, beside a ruined house. Mint was there; he smelled its perfume. But vaguely only – a passing whiff of an English autumn; and he had a flashing recent memory of a freckled girl. The prevalent odours were of fish, charred wood, lime dust, and something else more pungent which he found, a moment later, was the smouldering straw of paliasses. They had been tossed out in a lane and fired; an acrid reek still drifted from their sullen remnants.

The most fantastic – the most bewildering town! – were it really a town at all, and not a village; for twenty minutes he wandered round it, distracted from his immediate search for the Sheriff's house by wonder and speculation.

When Derry had got his orders at Whitehall, in the little secret room where three most important gentlemen had dropped their voices almost to a whisper as soon as it came to his more definite instructions, he had assumed that this first stage of his mission was to end in a scene more truly urban and august than this. In spite of some draughtsman's plans that were now again in his possession – too mediaeval for conviction – he had indulged his imagination with a stately chateau surrounded by parks of oaks and fallow-deer, on a terraced hillock preferably, with a thriving feudal town of shops, bakeries, charcuteries and cafés at its gates. France hitherto had been practically the only foreign country of his acquaintance.

No less, he had felt, could be expected from the country seat of the distinguished personage who in the little secret room had been the spokesman for the others; who had probed so cunningly, first, for Derry's own official conscience, and finding it sensibly pliant had proceeded cautiously to expound the incredible plot, yet had a name renowned, and specially clamant now through all the kingdom.

Even since he had crossed the Cheviots, Derry's expectations had been affirmed and heightened by all he gathered of his patron's consequence in the country; no more remotely than the house he had last night slept in, this place where he stood now, in darkness and the smell of squalor and destruction, was spoken of with a kind of awe as, at the moment, Scotland's veritable keystone. Here alone, of all places in the land, had Drummond unwittingly let out, could one count on single-mindedness and instinctive loyalty.

No scrap of his illusions now were left to him. He had come too late for chateaux and fallow-deer. There had manifestly been a siege here, and a vanquished town had been abandoned. It could never have had the urbanity or importance with which his fancy had endowed it, but in any case it was now an empty shell, over which curlews whistled and seagulls mewed with the very notes of desolation. Incorrigible, he gave another hue to his imagination, and visualised the elements of siege and sack.

The moon was up now; it was in her fitful revelations as the clouds scurried his impressions were assembled. First he moved through the outskirts – tanneries (by their odour) and coopers' sheds, fish-curers' yards, cow-byres, booths and butchers' stances and sinister cut-throat-looking vennels with single-storey habitations that had been thatched, but now were roofless, their ribs naked, with the straw in fringes hanging from the eaves. Doors and windows alike were gone; he went into some of those derelict dwellings, to find them uniformly empty.

So, too, with some wider lanes he crossed, with larger houses having patches of derelict garden-ground behind them; half the houses at least were stripped to the rafters; several with their gables fallen had been burned and blocked the lane with charred woodwork and limey debris. Those still intact were heavily shuttered outside on their lower windows, each shutter with a port-hole in it; and one long block that might have been a barrack had two rusted cannon at its door.

In the place, apparently, had been no deliberate design; it had grown haphazard, a congeries of domesticity and rural trade.

To get to its central parts – to its church or market square, was now his object; the noise of the river gave him his direction, and he went down a lane with deep cart-ruts in it which finally brought him to the riverside itself. Turning his back to the noisy stream, he looked between great tree-boles, and saw with some astonishment, two fortresses!

They stood less than two hundred yards apart – one high mediaeval keep of the simple kind he had seen on the Border with battered skyline, broken crow-stepped gables; the other smaller, habitable still, apparently, though with no hint of actual occupation. To the north of them behind him was a two-arched bridge of stone. He went to it; he crossed to its other end, which he found walled up with drystone building, within which had been piled a barricade of boats and carts. The further bank had its timber felled as far as he could see in the dim light; the trees, with all their branches cut from them, lay fallen and scattered in the fields, end-on to the bridge, to give less cover to an attack and a clear range for some little cannons whose trunnions swung on hurriedly masoned platforms midway between the parapets.

Once again was Derry seized with bodings, oppressed by a sense of human abandonment as complete as that which gave the scene about him an unutterable melancholy. Had he lost his way? Strayed into some forsaken *faubourg* only? Could the innkeeper have misled him? Where was the church which was to be his landmark? Even a sacked town would not have its church obliterated.

Only then did he recall the bell. Time at least was man's invention and must move by brassy mechanism. He plucked up spirit on reflecting that it must be somewhere near, presumably in a belfry. Re-traversing the bridge he hurriedly followed the road to which it ministered, passed some sleeping houses and a row of fishing-nets that swung on poles, and saw loom up a squat church tower with some lit windows in its neighbourhood – at last he had arrived!

But not yet was his dilemma ended; the obscuration of a cloud for a little plunged his steps in gloom, and he stumbled on the edge of a declivity. When the moon again emerged, he found himself on the brink of an enormous pit or quarry. At least it looked so at the first glance; more deliberate examination found it an area of at least two acres sunk in some natural cataclysm, blown out by mines, or scooped by human labour from rock and sand. Huge boulders strewed the bottom; in deeper depressions still lay pools that glinted. Round half the excavation, on its rim, were piled clay, loam and gravel, in which trees, mutilated, waded to their waists.

Scrambling over sandy mounds, he left behind him the enigma and sought the church whose tower appeared the only rational thing in a delirium. It stood intact at the head of a narrow street that ran south between lime-washed tenements ghostly in the moonlight; here at last was something tangible and living; there was the smell of household fires and frying herrings.

Next to the church, from which it was divided by a space with a market cross and a well, was a slated house of two storeys and attics, ivy on the façade of it and two lit uncurtained windows on the lower floor, with a main door, three steps up from the level of the street.

Derry took off the wrap he had put round his neck when leaving the inn and with it flicked from the polished boots recovered with his portmanteau the evidence of his stumbling walk through ashes, dust and sand. He felt in a pocket of his shirt for his credentials, pulled his waistcoat down, ran his fingers through his hair and smoothing hands down his coat skirts at the haunches, then briskly climbed the steps and tapped on an iron knocker.

A serving-woman of middle age, in her stocking soles with a shawl about her shoulders and a night-cap in her hand, opened the door. She stood in a lobby lit by a single candle.

'I wish to see the Sheriff,' said Derry with assurance; on a bust of Cicero in the lobby was a horse-hair wig of legal character, tilted over an ear, he had come at last on a sense of the jocular!

She summed him up at a glance. She let him in without a word. She opened a door on the left of the passage, and with a momentary pressure on his shoulder urged him, without ceremony, into a sitting-room. Behind him the door, green-baized, closed softly.

Every feature of the room appeared to him instantly definite and clear, with its own peculiar quality, though he stepped into a flood of firelight and candle. He blinked but once like a diver clearing brine from the vision on rising from sea depths to find the world the same bright joy he left it. Shining woodwork, jolly hangings, books and pictures; arm-chairs of the most inviting, the gleam of silver in a corner, and over the mantle-shelf a metzzotint, a portrait of the very man who had sent him here.

At the far end, by the fire whereon a cheerful kettle simmered, a burly, grey-haired, ruddy gentleman sat at a little table with a rummer of punch before him. He stood up on Derry's entrance; then he came forward a pace or two and scrutinized his visitor. Only standing was his figure seen in its full impressiveness; Derry was six feet tall, but he was over-topped by at least three inches.

'Sheriff Campbell?' Derry questioned, dipping this time, in a more secret pocket for his letter.

'At your service, sir' said the Sheriff, with an inclination, putting a clove in his mouth and pushing forward a chair.

'My name is Derry, sir, – John Derry. I have just arrived at the inn from London. A matter of secret service, which calls for some despatch and a little of your assistance, as you will find, sir, from this letter. I must make my excuse for so untimely an intrusion, but –'

'Not at all, Mr Derry! Not at all!' said his host with a smile. 'You find me at more leisure, and in better spirits than at most hours of the day', and a little gesture of the hands called humorous attention to the steaming punch-glass.

The missive Derry handed him was thickly smeared with wax, with a bold device of a boar's head on it; he scarcely looked at it before opening. Almost at a glance he mastered its contents of half-a-dozen lines, laid it open on the table, and turned on his visitor a gaze of even greater curiosity than on his entrance. Then, over his visage went a film of speculation; he stood abstracted, looking no longer through his eyes, which for a moment lost their lustre, inly occupied.

'So we have not got to the end of our troubles yet' he said at last without preamble, in a voice which, meant to be indifferent, or perhaps regretful, could not altogether hide an undertone which Derry felt suspiciously spoke a private feeling of relief. 'There was nothing, then, in that sack of sawdust?'

'Good lord!' cried Derry, 'did you know of that, sir?'

'I knew of it at least three days before you knew in London,' said the Sheriff quietly. 'I was a little dubious of that sack, Mr Derry . . . But also a little feared.'

He turned, as he spoke, and on flopping slippers shuffled across the room to a corner-cupboard, the lower part of which he opened. Stooping, he looked inside at the top shelf, searching. Derry leaned towards the table quickly, and read the open letter.

'Dear Sheriff,' it said, 'It is high time this endless search was coming to conclusions. We must find that young man Morag. The bearer, Mr Derry, one of our cleverest Trusties, is going North. He will need with him a good man of the country. There is none I can think of better than Ninian. Get him.' A single initial finished the letter with a flourish.

Derry was sitting back in his armchair contemplating the portrait over the fireplace when his host turned round with a secret rummer in his hand.

'You will join me in a glass of punch,' said the Sheriff softly. 'The elements are ready. It saves a lot of bother just to keep them all together in the kettle on the hob.'

The tone was cordial enough, but there had come a change of climate in the old man's air; a feeling – just the faintest – of withdrawal, as making room for the glass and kettle on the table he folded up the letter and put it in his pocket.

Derry bit his lip when he realised for the first time that the whole of the lighted room, himself included, was reflected in the latticed panes of the cupboard's upper half!

To smother his confusion he plunged a little wildly into the story of his journey. He had come from London in sixty hours, discarding horses, buying new ones on his way. Before that he had been called from France to look at the sack of sawdust, (having had for some years in France the closest opportunities to qualify him for declaring what the sawdust might contain.) A false alarm! Just sawdust – nothing really worth while in it! Dust in the eyes! In confidence he would admit he was relieved a little to find it so. France was a delightful country; he had hated to contemplate an end to his sojourn there through *trop de zèle* on the part of bungling amateurs. And now he was ordered North, where the amateurs seemed to have settled down to enjoy a summer's *fête champêtre*, and to have lost enthusiasm for the real business on hand. It was – officially – in secret little rooms in Whitehall – regarded as intolerable that any more time should be wasted in chasing rainbows.

It took him a little while before his narration steadied and he could forget the damning revelation of the cupboard; the bland demeanour of the Sheriff, however, finally made him hope he had been mistaken and that his professional indiscretion had been unobserved. That soothing thought, accepted gratefully by his will, he ended with a graphic and amusing sketch of his first impressions of Scotland.

'You haven't seen it yet,' said the Sheriff, dryly, pursing his lips. 'Had you supper at the inn?'

'I had,' said Derry, 'Excellent!'

'That's good! It's the best you're likely to have for some time. Take my advice, and if you start off tomorrow, make a hearty breakfast. You are now in the realm of short rations, even though Ninian Campbell forages for you.'

'I had planned to set out sometime tomorrow morning if he were conveniently ready,' said Derry.

'The odd thing about our Messenger-At-Arms,' said the Sheriff, 'is that he is always conveniently ready for anything. For twenty years I've been trying to take him by surprise, though by this time I ought to know better. Now, I'll give you a clew to native character in this land, Mr Derry; it may be useful to you. It is that even our commonest people are never surprised at anything. Take a peasant of ours and introduce him to a levee at St James's, or a corpse in a baker's oven; from his manner you would never suspect that the thing was new to him. I've tried, more than once, to fathom it, though I'm rather spoiled for judgment by a Parliament House career. It's partly that vanity some folk call pride, it's mostly something older, something we've forgot . . . The man's a Macgregor of the mist! Does that convey anything to you?'

'Not much,' said Derry, his thoughts were wandering through the window, into that nightmare town that lay around this snug inviolate dwelling; he itched to question.

'I thought not,' said the Sheriff. 'But the fact's pregnant. This is no countryside for the like of the Macgregors; they have aye kept well aloof from it. Ours is something of an oddity here, like a parrot brought by a sailor from the Indies. He bears the name of Campbell now, and officially he's Messenger-At-Arms, though for that part of it he never once lifted a fee that I remember. Most of the time we don't know where he is, but he covers a lot of Scotland in his wanderings . . . Are ye warm yet, Mr Derry?'

'I have an inkling,' answered Derry with awakened curiosity; he had calculated only on a simple guide among the mountains.

'We call him, between ourselves here, the *beachdar* – that means scout or tracker. I can guess that in France you had many a ticklish affair to deal with – it's your calling. You wouldn't be here with this letter if you were not of special distinction at the trade, but the – the person who sent you was wise when he decided you would be none the worse for having Ninian Campbell with you. In France the people you had to keep an eye on were never far away from a feather bed and a good kitchen. When folk hide here they keep away from reek and take like the polecat to the cairns.

There's not a parish 'twixt here and the Sound of Sleat where the man you seek for couldn't find a thousand skulking-places nobody could find except a native.'

He leaned forward across the table, to bring himself closer to his interlocutor, and lowered his voice to say 'There are other veils than mist, and other obstacles than morasses, Mr Derry. There's the mind of man – that's the only privy thing in nature after all. Ninian's branch of the profession may seem a little shabby to you, who have practised in the best society among people who wear perukes and ruffles, but believe me he's a far more influential man in these parts than myself, and I'm depute Baron Bailie as well as Sheriff of the shire – a most important personage, Mr Derry, if you saw me in something else than my slippers. The thing that puzzles me is, how you managed to my door without encountering him. It's most unusual.'

'Indeed' said Derry, jumping at the opening, 'to find your door was something of a puzzle, sir. Better advised I should have taken someone with me from the inn. What in heaven's name, has happened here? The place is devilishly battered. I had no idea you were in the zone of war.'

A flicker of amusement crossed the old man's face.

'So you were surprised already, Mr Derry?' he said. 'You haven't heard? No doubt you have come to your own conclusions. Ninian, in your circumstances, would have done so very quickly, found his own philosophy for our state, and never have given a stranger the gratification of seeing he was astonished. How did you come through the town?'

It was with some amusement, choking at his punch-glass, he heard Derry's recital of that mystified ramble in the moonlight, and realised how far a too-lively fancy had led the Englishman astray.

'I had quite forgot when you came in,' he said 'that our condition at present would puzzle you. The truth is that at this moment we're drinking punch – and not very much on your part, Mr Derry – in a town condemned.'

'Condemned?' repeated Derry, finding the word peculiarly equivocal.

'The fortresses as you call them above the river are the two old castles; the bigger one was an empty shell before the time of my great-great grandfather; the other has been vacant these two years, and the pit is for the founds of its successor. Had you come six months ago you would have discovered the builders working by flambeau light. Come back a few years hence and you'll find a palace.'

'I might have guessed that, I had a hint of it,' said Derry. 'But the ruined and empty buildings, the smell of fire?'

'That is simple too. A barrow-town, as we say, would be a scurvy environment for a palace, and a grand new town is to be planted on the foreland where you got your supper. You have seen the first of it – the New Inn, and I hope you found its host as clever a countryman of yours in an inn as he was in the castle, where he was the butler.'

'So I surmised,' said Derry. 'It was the wall that first misled me; I had to scale it.'

'That was Glendaruel's notion. Myself I saw no need for such precautions, but a week ago we had two thousand fencible men in arms here, quartered on us, and Campbell and Glendaruel were determined they should earn their rations. A bonny mess they made! They set a couple of tenements on fire, and the place is stinking yet with the bog-hay of their bedding. There are hardly a hundred women and children left with me in the burgh; they've flitted to the glens among their friends till the new town's ready. As for the watch fire, that might well be quenched now seeing the fermentation's all drifted north in papist country. In any case there's Ninian's vedettes on every pass within thirty miles of us. It perplexes me not a little, Mr Derry, that you seem to have escaped them.'

'I saw few living souls since I left this morning,' said Derry.

'Ay, but many a one saw you; you may take my word for it! A gentleman with a good hat, on a well-bred horse, cocks up pretty high over heather. I'll lay you five pounds, Scots, you occasion some curiosity this night to Ninian Campbell! Now when do you want to see him?'

At the very moment two gentle taps came to the Sheriff's window.

'Didn't I tell you!' he said triumphantly, starting to his feet and making for the door himself. 'Here's the very man! I'll let him in, myself, for my old servant Katrin's bedded.'

A moment later and the Messenger-At-Arms was with them.

'We were just wondering how we could send for you,' said the Sheriff.

'I guessed you would, my lord,' said Ninian Campbell; 'but it better suits with my bit offeecial dignity to come before I'm sent for, Sheriff.'

CHAPTER 3

John Derry, as they entered, got to his feet, with his back to the firelight and the candles which stood glass-shaded on the mantelpiece. Shaking hands with the incomer, he swept every aspect of him at a glance. And he was disappointed! He had had in his mind a younger man. This one might be his father. The feeling passed in a moment, however, for the figure, port and type of Ninian Campbell in the main conformed with the character he had built up for himself in his delightfully responsive imagination from the Sheriff's confidences.

A little under the middle height, with sturdy chest and shoulders; no fat about his person; his movements fluent and his manner self-possessed, the Messenger-At-Arms had the air of a forest creature all unconscious of being watched by man. His face was none the worse for a little roughening by smallpox; indeed the shallow pitting contributed to the strength of that distinctive moulding of the clean-shorn features, definite and bronzed. A sleet was at his temples; his hair, drawn back and knotted with a ribbon at the nape, was the hue of rusted brackens. Nothing in his dress arrested notice; he might be a prosperous burgess, but he had the hunter's eyes. Derry was not for a moment deceived by the fictitious unconcern that softened them when he looked up at the stranger; he had seen their glint and roll on entrance – a flash that comprehended everything and was quickly quenched; little could escape that lightning penetration!

'I am proud to meet you, sir,' said Campbell on introduction with a French excess of courtesy. The voice was quiet and mellow, with a quality and accent grown familiar to Derry in the last two days; now not wholly unpleasing; to begin with it had jarred on him like a *patois*.

'I have just been telling Mr Derry all about you, Ninian,' said the sheriff, breezily, fetching another rummer.

'Not all, I hope, sir' was the reply, with a grin of humour. 'Few of us could stand complete exposure, even over a friendly dram . . . I had been looking for you to arrive a little sooner, I suppose it was the dark delayed you, Mr Derry?'

He had now, as he sat, the Englishman's face in brightness; he turned on him a gaze a little disconcerting, vaguely quizzical (at the eyes).

The Sheriff chuckled. 'I told you, Mr Derry' he said, 'that you couldn't reasonably expect to reach my door without our friend's cognisance. I wish you had taken my wager.'

'I congratulate you on a good scout' Derry answered, not a whit abashed; he knew that the messenger who brought the bag had warned the innkeeper of his coming.

'Quite right, Mr Campbell. Quite right! For the last two hours of riding I was certainly not at a canter. It's a most amazing country. I gather you know Scotland well?'

'All that's worthwhile of it' answered Ninian blythly, 'and that's between the Water of Leven and Ben More in Assynt. They tell me there's a lot of shops to the south of it.' He said 'shops' with a snap that made the word contemptuous, and then revealed his teeth, drift-white, in an engaging smile. It appeared to be his way of taking the edge from irony.

'All the same, I doubt you're slackening, Ninian' said the Sheriff, mocking; 'it's always a boast of yours that nobody can cross the Garron bridge at night without your knowing his business. Well, let me ask you this, what is our friend here?'

For a little Campbell hesitated, but with no perplexity. He sought in Derry's face for something to excuse a response to the Sheriff's challenge. It was difficult to read that face, being one that like a pool in forest stirred with secret breathings, subterranean springs; and wavered with reflections from the things around, but the observer sought as for a hovering salmon in its deeps among steadfast boulders and yellow sands. Shrewdness and sentiment, coldness and amiability, restlessness and resolution, calculation; humour – all was there save the vulnerable part of youth he looked for – vanity. At once he took a liking to him.

'Whatever he is,' he said with great composure, 'he's a fine, strong, handsome young gentleman I could have a happy week with at the fishing.'

'Ah, you rascal; you evade the point!' said the Sheriff, shaking a finger at him.

'Not a bit of me!' answered Ninian coolly; 'With all respect to Mr Derry, I would say he had the cut of a kind of an architect.'

Derry was plainly staggered; the more since he saw in the speaker's watchful pucker something that he felt instinctively presaged more intimate revelations.

'Tut! tut! Man,' cried the Sheriff peevishly, chagrined at his prize-cock's poor beginning; he had looked for a brisker main than this false start gave promise of. Derry's mind went furiously back on every step of his northward journey. No indiscretion of his could have betrayed what he meant for a *secret de Polichinelle*, but had no occasion to parade. There were but two sources from which this man might have got an inkling – a precedent London letter was one of them. But no post-horses could have brought a letter to these outlandish parts from London so fast as he had ridden.

'I can only surmise you have got at my bag,' he said at last, without embarrassment.

'Shake hands on that!' cried Ninian, with a sparkling eye, putting out a hand impulsively. 'For a bit I was feared you might take me for a gentleman. You and me, I can see, will get on well together. There need be no polite palavering between us. I certainly got at your bag – a thing that foolish folk would think no gentleman would do. You and me know better, Mr Derry! I'm not a man to take my gentility out every now and then and polish it up like a trumpet, it's not an instrument, in any case, for dirty weather or for our trade. Myself, I have had a lot of droll experiences with namely gentlemen, and I found them just like common folk when it came to hunger, greed and fear. It was a man of mine who wandered your portmanteau; he brought it to my house this afternoon, and I had it open in a jiffy. The castle plans, with the name 'John Derry,

Architect' on them was enough for me, and I sent the messenger with the bag locked up again to Mr Taylor; I hope you found it all in order.'

To all this Derry listened with an air quite unperturbed; indeed it might seem – as the Sheriff thought, who watched him – with a secret amusement. He was back, here, in familiar country, not in dark mountain wilds which awakened curiosities they could not satisfy, held in their deep recesses mysteries of human nature to which he had no key; this was the bright land of *chicane*; he knew every foot of it.

'*Salut!* Mr Campbell,' he said, taking up his glass, with a flourish, and laughed with boyish gaiety. 'The Sheriff, I find, has in no way over-estimated your resource.'

A glance of the Sheriff drifted towards Ninian's face; what he saw there reassured him. It was benevolent, paternal! Something more was in reserve for the English cockerel!

'It's a great vexation to myself when I have to deal with locks,' continued Ninian, placidly, 'especially on portmantas, where they put me in mind of a woman's wedding-ring, that's only a plea for fair-play, no defence from gallantry. But you were near on the top of us Mr Derry, before I got the warning, and to find what you were I had to search your poke. It's none the worse for me, as you would find . . . I see you have your bonny boots on.' He threw an admiring glance at Derry's buckles.

The last remark alone touched Derry somewhere; he flinched a little.

'I was assured,' he said, without either malice or resentment, 'that I couldn't go far in these parts without exciting curiosity, but I scarcely thought myself worthy of all this attention.'

'What! In a time of war!' exclaimed the Messenger-At-Arms 'You took us cheap! Had you come last year in daylight, even with a drummer to play in front of you, nobody would have paid the least attention, for the Chiefs and Earls of Christendom come sooner or later to this quarter. But this is not a countryside for rambling in at present, and a stranger in a hurry on a horse is bound to set us wondering. Wondering about things like that and prying into them is what I'm paid for, like the bards of old, with a croft and three cows' pasture. Indeed I'm vexed about that bag of yours, but there was no time otherwise to find out what you were . . . And how are all the folk in France, Mr Derry?'

Derry stuck out his feet and surveyed his shoes with an interest exaggerated; they were certainly French on the face of them, though the last thing he would have dreamt was that their origin would be so obvious here, where shoes of any kind seemed so much a rarity. 'Quite right, Mr Campbell,' he admitted. 'My felicitations on your eyesight! I hope you admired my plans for the castle. They were meant for just such a casualty as befell my bag and for the eyes of the inquisitive. Bait, Mr Campbell – bait! I'm really not an architect.'

'Stop! Stop! Mr Derry!' cried the Sheriff, putting up a hand, and shaking with merriment. 'Give our friend a chance; he'll have you yet!'

'I never said you were,' retorted the Messenger-At Arms, 'I only said you had the cut of one, as arranged by your employers. There was a good deal more in that bag of yours than you knew yourself. It was not a bad bait – for cod, but the sea-trout's wary! The plans might pass for the genuine article in London, but not in this part – did you ever see such nonsense? Moats, and loop-holes, draw-bridges and battlements! The gentleman you got them from laughed like to end himself when he saw them first five years ago – a real play-actor's notion of a Highland castle for this time o' day when we're all for peace and business. I thought they were thrown in the midden long ago. It's a very different kind of house that's going up in the hole behind us here, and Mr Adam its architect left here only yesterday! Architects are not going round the countryside in covies; they're as rare's the capercailzie.'

'Capital! Oh, capital' cried the Sheriff, thumping on his knees. 'It's better than a play! You're a bonny pair!' His eyes were streaming tears of smothered laughter.

But quickly a thought of passing time, the lateness of the night, and the urgency of Derry's business sobered him; he put aside the cock-pit mood by an effort of the will and assumed a shrieval dignity more becoming to the situation.

'There seems to be little need to explain anything to you, Mr Campbell,' he said drily. 'You'll have heard the latest?'

'No yet,' said the Messenger-At-Arms.

'Well, this is it – We're not out of the wood yet! Our young man Morag is still amissing! They haven't flushed him yet. You were right about the sack of sawdust – nothing in it!'

'That's what I was thinking to myself all along,' said the Messenger-At-Arms. 'It was too like the work of Providence to be possible. They'll never get him!'

Sitting back in his chair, with his knees crossed, and a dangling shabby slipper; his two hands brought together on his breast, and meeting at the finger-tips – an unconscious understudy of his professional hero, (Prestongrange) Lord Arniston – the Sheriff drew a long, thin upper lip while the lower jutted. Again his visage dulled with inner contemplation. When he spoke again, it was as to himself, like one who writes a letter. There were, he muttered, several ticklish aspects to the situation. This gim-crack *petit-maître* of a fellow, keeping honest folk awake who should be bedded, was no fit object for compassion. But one had to calculate on fools and hot-heads. Perhaps the best thing that could happen would be his escape. Better an empty house than a bad tenant.

Derry maintained an air inscrutable through a long monologue wholly on this line, though its nature startled him. It was almost a paraphrase of what he had heard last night from Drummond. Could all these old, slow-pondering men be waverers? Or were they slyly testing him? Had he not apprised himself in a clumsy fashion of the letter he had brought himself from London, he might have suspected another possibility.

The uncurtained windows of the chamber looked out on a darkness which his mind could still invest with every startling and mysterious feature he had seen there half-an-hour ago. Again the clock was striking. He counted the strokes. Ten. Only ten! They seemed miraculously uplifted on the squat church tower over the town condemned, a brazen voice aloof from human plottings; it seemed incredible that in sixty minutes he should have traversed so many extraordinary sensations. The final note was no sooner thinned away to a wisp of sound and swallowed by the silence, than all outside – the ruins, and the litter, and the rearward menace of the hills – came through the fire-reflecting panes and stood round Derry like a dream's creation. He had a sense of ambush – singular thing in a well-lit room with such a portrait on its walls.

'I get your point, sir,' he said. 'No doubt there is something in it, but luckily my orders are explicit. I've got to find this young man somehow, and my business ends there. After that – *vogue la galère!* – I'm done with him!'

'And so is that phase of your occupation,' said the Sheriff, quietly. 'No more France for you in that case, Monsieur Derry. A dripping roast ruined! But I should be the last man to try to shake your resolution by any reflections of mine in the key of mere expediency and personal sentiment. I am just hinting at a state of mind that is not uncommon on this side of the Cheviots. Get your man, by all means! But I warn you it will be a ticklish business – a very different thing from strolling round St Germain's or Avignon. No one knows that better than the man who picked you for the task.'

He turned to Ninian Campbell. '*Beachdar!*' he said; 'You are to go North with Mr Derry tomorrow. It's time you were off to pack your knapsack.'

'It's packed already, my lord, and I have hired two horse,' replied Campbell, with composure.

Derry's brows came down; his visage darkened. This omniscience went too far for his peace of mind. 'So you know you are going with me; how?' he asked abruptly.

'You brought the news yourself,' said the Messenger-At-Arms.

There was manifestly some of the play-actor in him; it was with a keen eye to the effect of deliberation and suspense he put a hand behind his hip and produced an antique map which he unfolded on the table, without a spoken word at first to detract from the surprise it was to quicken in the Englishman.

'Old Blaeu! Old Blaeu of Amsterdam!' he said at last in a sardonic key. 'Old blethers! You might as well go wood-and-moorland-wandering with an almanac! I found it under your saddle-rug, Mr Derry. Myself, I always see my horse unsaddled, and I never leave its baiting to a change-house strapper so long as fodder is cheaper than oats.'

'I could have sworn that map was in my pocket!' stammered Derry.

'So it was – at ten o'clock this morning. But a fellow of mine just picked it from your pocket an hour or two after your bag was on its way to me. A clever lad! He saw that a horse for you was something less than a companion, and chanced my being at hand when its bellyband was loosened . . . Just you listen a jiffy, Mr Derry, I'm not going to start making pretence to you that I'm a fool; I'll ease your mind on that point. I'll admit that the plans in your bag were at first a disappointment to me; knowing the quarter they must have come from I could see you were travelling on the best authority, though what you were after I couldna fathom. That your boots were bought in France, and not so very long ago, was easy guessing; every countryman of mine who comes here to the markets for French recruiting wears the identical; it's enough to jyle them! But it wasna till your horse came in, and I got your bit map, I saw your whole contrivance in a flash. You packed your bag with great sagacity, Mr Derry, but your plans and your map were a peetiful mistake, with all respect to the gentleman who gave them to you. Every bit of your route to the North is marked on Blaeu with the pricking of a compass, and my name is on the side of it for your remembrance, in a hand of write there's nobody knows better than myself or his lordship here, the Sheriff. That was enough for me; you were come for Ninian Campbell! The innkeeper tells me you are setting out tomorrow, so I trysted two fresh horse and went home to pack my bag.'

To all this, Derry, recovered quickly from his first vexation, listened with a mask of smiling imperturbability; only a little surprised that craftiness should be the same here as in France or England, that a cunning no way different from what he used himself in his profession should be found in this mountain person whose practice could only be among barbarians. The baiting of the bag with the castle plans was no device of his own invention; their owner in Whitehall had proposed it to give colour to the rôle of architect in a neighbourhood where an English rider could hardly escape the most prying curiosity.

'You're a bonny pair!' exclaimed the Sheriff, chuckling. 'Do you know what you're going for with Mr Derry, Ninian?'

'Fine!' said the Messenger, getting to his feet. 'There is only one concern would bring a man from France here in such a devilish hurry that one horse couldn't carry him, to take me away from my ordinary occupations. And if I'm to be on the road tomorrow it is high time I was bedded.'

Derry rose, too; if anything of chagrin at so easy a discovery of his purpose was in his mind it was not revealed in the twinkling glance he threw at the Messenger-At-Arms.

'I must go, too,' he said, 'Perhaps you will do me the service to show me a better way back to the inn than the one I took coming. I shall sleep all the better tonight for knowing I'm to have so shrewd a *confrère* with me.'

'You said *two* horses, Ninian,' remarked the Sheriff, showing them to the door. 'Is Mr Derry's foundered?'

'Not a bit of it! A sturdy beast; there's fifty miles in him for tomorrow, if need be. The other two horse are for me and my body-servant.'

'Your body-servant!' exclaimed the Sheriff, 'Who on earth are you taking with you?' He had opened the outside door; Derry already was on the steps, sniffing that odour of fired bedding, uplifting eyes to the mountain fort whose flames were now apparently sunk to ashes – the faintest star in a sky now star-bespattered.

'I am taking Hannibal Lamont,' answered the Messenger, softly for the Sheriff's ear alone.

'Hannibal Lamont!' echoed the Sheriff in a tone incredulous. 'What, in the name of fortune, are you going to do with Hannibal?'

'Oh! Just to finish his education,' answered the *beachdar*, coolly.

'I'll see about this tomorrow morning,' said the Sheriff drily and, wishing good night to his visitors, re-entered and closed the door.

'Han-n-i-bal Lamont!' he muttered as he shot the bolts. 'God pity Mr Derry with Hannibal at his heels! Ninian's fair daft!'

CHAPTER 4

Town bells were ringing eight o'clock next night when the three men crossed a bridge and clattered noisily up a cobbled street to an inn at least a hundred years older than Mr Taylor's, to judge from its appearance, and Derry saw again the Rock with its white-washed prison in a cleft between its pinnacles, the wide grey estuary with its wherries. Across the water lights were already twinkling.

'Well, we're here at last, and what are we going to make of it?' said Ninian, with an eye askance on those further shires to which he always felt himself a stranger.

Derry made no reply. His new companion's disapproval of this Low-country road, as he called it, had been manifest since they set out in the afternoon. Their first day's traverse had been the subject of debate between them and the Sheriff in the morning, and the Sheriff, like Ninian, was all for their going through the land of Lorne and striking the New Road at the springs of Orchy. To seek anywhere south of that, he declared, was wasting time. Their man was in the North – far further north than Orchy; a week ago he had been on the hills of Badenoch.

In vain the *beachdar*, on Blaeu's discredited map, showed Derry all the more obvious parts of the country to be rummaged first, and the quickest ways through the glens to them. The legends on the map he treated with disdain; with a thumb that pounced on a feature here and there of the Dutchman's symbols for mountain ranges, valleys, streams and lakes, he ejaculated the names of tribes – Macdonalds, Camerons, Macleans and Frasers. 'That's where the fleas are,' he said, 'They're not named on the map, these clans, but *they're* the country. High land is all the same and mixty-maxie in any part of Albyn; it is only the folk who differ. It's hopeless for a man to hide in hills unless the glen is friendly; round about there we must look for Morag. What in the name of God do ye want to go back on your tracks for unless ye have a lass there, Mr Derry?'

Derry had laughed at this, and hinted at a possible clue, at first too lightly considered, which now appeared to call for further inquiry into. But it took him all his time to beat down opposition. Ninian and the Sheriff were surprised to find this seeming pliant Englishman like granite on a point a countryman of theirs would surrender amiably at the slightest opposition – with the hope of getting round it successfully some other way, or gaining, later, some more vital point in exchange for its concession. This last manoeuvre, so common in Highland tactics, was, indeed, so probable that Ninian finally acquiesced in the Lowland road with a great show of heartiness, so preserving, as he thought, a strong place for the next move in Derry's game of dambrod.

But nevertheless, once launched on the journey back in the tracks of Derry's ride of yesterday, the *beachdar* felt a whole day at the very least was being lost ridiculously. A score of times, between the marches of

Argyll and the Firth that bounded what he thought was truly Scotland – that had, beyond it, worlds to him unknown – he had made that purely ornamental 'body-servant' Hannibal, a sharer in his discontent. They spoke in Gaelic – what speech there was, for Hannibal was taciturn – Derry on horse ahead of them nearly always, more hurried than they, and even more amazed by the aspect of the country in broad daylight than he had been by its appearance under the veils of gloaming.

To Derry, from the first, this Hannibal was an enigma. He had joined them in the forenoon in the New Inn yard, with a silly sword at his haunch, and a Dettingen hat of a martial cut, well-cocked, which went grotesquely with a russet suit of homespun clothing; a baking-girdle and a little poke of meal swung on his back in lieu of a knapsack. He was, apart from his equipment, a fellow to take the eye – a little over twenty, under middle height, all gristle, with a fierce moustache, a chin uplifted truculently, a dark, wild, roving glance that intermittently dulled to the abstraction of a trance; with a soldier's brisk alacrity of movement that made him spring to anything he did like an automaton, when ordered, but left him, when unoccupied, scratching his buttocks, initiative dead, an awkward lout.

Not altogether a fool by any means, had Derry later on decided. He spoke a more conventional and easy English than the Messenger-At-Arms, who had two varieties of Derry's language – one very Scots and homely for the tavern folk, the other gentled down to an Englishman's comprehension, yet with curious foreign turns of phrase that were manifestly literal translations of the tongue in which he did his thinking. In Hannibal's constipated speech was a bookish quality; on the top of the poke of meal was disclosed, when he emptied it into the stable bin by Ninian's orders, a tattered copy of Caesar's Gallic War! It was all dog-eared, stained with grease, and lacked half its binding, but the lad seemed very proud of it.

At the sight of the sword, and the martial hat, and the meal-poke on him, Ninian was confounded.

'The devil take you, Hannibal!' he exclaimed. 'Do you think you're for the field of Flodden?' There's neither sword nor girdle needed where we're going; myself I have not even a knife on me. Put off that spit of yours this instant, and throw that meal into the corn-bin.' But this command had a tender note, as if he spoke to an erring son.

Surely as strange a couple as Scotland could produce, John Derry thought, as he rode ahead of them towards the glen whose utter abomination he could only guess at last night in the dark. When, climbing the track that rose for miles from the sea through moors of a hideous purple, the clack of horse-shoes silenced in the slow ascent through turf and gravel, he could hear the guttural muttering of the Messenger-At-Arms and that farcical body-servant, and he wondered what they talked about. But sometimes what he thought their speech was, as he later realised, the chattering of streams in hollows near at hand, the gluck and suck of falling water in some peaty hole behind a boulder. What a country for conspiracy, where men and waters doubtless understood each other, and could keep a stranger out of their confidence!

At the top of the steep was a plateau with a lakelet where fish plashed, but having passed it, he was staggered to find himself on the edge of a precipice wherefrom he giddily saw below him, wholly unexpected, the glen in whose deeps last night was a deeper dark than night, primeval, fluid dimness clotted. No vision he had conjured up in the dark of his surroundings was half so repellent as the truth revealed now at his feet.

It was with a frantic jerk of the reins he pulled his horse back on the edge of the declivity; his breath had thickened and choked a little in his breast at the first glimpse of the deeps where another step would have thrown him. Below him, the saddle of the hills fell steeply to the floor of the upper valley at whose head was a huddle of wretched cabins, crouching to the earth as if they apprehended his immediate fall upon them. For a moment the reeking houses held his vision, with his fears transferred to them; it seemed to him as if the mountain saddle itself was quaking under his horse's weight, and would fall in avalanche. Then his eyes swept down the glen to find the hamlet was the only living thing it held, thrown up, as it were, and stranded on the silt at the foot of the mountain barrier by some catastrophic tide that had burst into this wide cleft in a world not yet completely fashioned, smoothed and firmed, and then receded.

Indeed the waters were not yet wholly gone; still were the mountains wet, exuding brooks that fell down their precipitous flanks and, foaming, leapt the terraces with an amazing noise, to join a meandering stream that tarried on the swampish level, gathering in the seepage of the flood.

Mountains were not wholly unfamiliar to Derry; he had, onetime, to cross the Alps into Italy in a diligence, and came back by sea, so much he disliked the experience. But never, hitherto, had he seen such horrid hills as these, without a tree or vineyard terrace on them, stripped to the rock on their pinnacles, their buttresses a dismal gloomy brown as of clotted blood, or an acrid green whose very contemplation gave him a taste of poison. On the wake of the flood had tumbled from those peaks that rose, blunted or jagged to the sky on either side the glen, cataracts of shingle, and enormous boulders, with the size and shape, sometimes, of houses, and these had assumed in time a look of plan and occupancy from the thatch-like heath that grew on their upper planes. But beyond the cluster of hovels which smoked below him, no other human dwelling was in view.

It was a desolation over which his eyes roamed in vain for a single feature whereon to fasten human association – a shady path or grove for love, a field for the reapers' song, a wall for winter shelter, a bush for the song of birds. So prone is the man of the cities to think all nature tamed and made subservient to his will that Derry had a sense of exasperation, to see this useless savage valley, only half revealed by the cloudy afternoon, for at its distant end a filmy mist, like smoke, was drifting in the hollow, concealing aspects, it might be, even more repellent.

Though now he perceived the track he should have followed, which bent sharply to the left and in zig-zag fashion reached the plain, he remained where he was till joined by his companions, curious to see how they should regard a scene so disturbing to himself.

'It is well you were not coming this way alone in the dark, Mr Derry,' Ninian said lightly. 'Blaeu wouldn't be much use to ye at this point. Now, isn't that a gallant prospect?'

And he was quite in earnest, no irony was in a comment that contradicted every feeling in Derry's mind! At the very abomination of desolation spread before him, the *beachdar* gazed with an air of pleasure, and Hannibal, in a mood exalted, his head uplifted, scratched his bottom ecstatically and sniffed like a stag.

'I think it most depressing, Mr Campbell,' said Derry. 'Good Lord! Was there ever a dance or marriage in this appalling gully?'

'Aye, and many another ploy!' said Ninian, his eyebrows up, 'and generations born and perished, and strife and peace, and hopes and heart-breaking. God bless my soul! Mr Derry, it is a glen of great renown; where would we be in this part of the realm without it? – shut up between hills and tides like silly mice. It is here a man must come, were he King himself, for the doors of Gaeldom and the ferries to the Isles. There is not a handier road in the world for a messenger like yourself in time of trouble, though I wish to heaven you werena so keen on coming back on it.'

'But it's frightfully lonely,' Derry urged.

'No place is lonely between here and Assynt,' Ninian retorted. 'There was plenty of jovial company in the Hie'lands up till lately. Even in a glen like this where are not many tenant bodies, you needn't be lonely if you can put up with ghosts. Consider, you, all the folk that have been here at sometime, making love and war or wandering. I know some story or other about every rock ahead of us; many a cheery night I spent below there in the clachan.'

'Well, I have never seen anything like it,' stammered Derry. 'Is there much more of it further north?'

Even Hannibal grinned at this; Ninian laughed outright, 'This glen, Mr Derry,' he said, 'is like a bit of a lady's garden compared with the rugged bounds I'll take you through in Arisaig or Morar; that is the way I am keen to see them. Stop you, Mr Derry, and you'll see some splendid wicked places!'

In the mention of Arisaig, Derry found something to keep him in meditation for another mile. That name was graven on his mind by Whitehall confidences he had thought were secrets of State. Yet this surprising Messenger-At-Arms spoke of it casually with an implication that could scarce have been more direct if he knew every detail of Derry's mission, though Derry had not yet even hinted at his plans nor given any clue to his probable destination.

Throughout the afternoon, on the long bleak miles of that doleful glen, and round the sea-arms, and by the shores where women gathered shellfish; and the whole land seemed in the care of aged persons or of ragged barefoot children – not a young man left in it – such a phlegm possessed him he fell back but rarely to their company, and Campbell, quick to sense a stranger's mood, unfounded on discourtesy, respected his aloofness.

'A sober, quiet gentleman, with a lot to think about, Hannibal; not like you and me,' said the *beachdar* to his servant. 'It's his first time on the brindled hills, and he must be wondering. We'll get on together, splendid, by-and bye.'

'What is he, anyway?' Hannibal asked; the first sign he had given of any interest in the stranger, who for him was manifestly of subordinate importance to Ninian Campbell. 'Do we need to take him?'

'We'll *need* to take him, little hero,' Ninian replied. 'Isn't he our Englishman who carries the money, though it's little use he'll find for it where we're going to.'

The nearer they got to the end of their journey for the day, the more was Derry harrassed by a certain problem.

How far could he trust this man? How much was it prudent to conceal from him?

Derry had always, in his calling, worked single-handed, hiring tools where needful, but the tools, hitherto, had been of his own selection, and chosen always for a certain degree of dullness lest they should cut his own hands. He had been assured in Whitehall of a guide who could be trusted absolutely; nothing had been said of an accomplice; yet it was already plain that this was a tool of a razor-edge; and one, moreover, who at any moment might assume command of the most delicate situation on the strength of seniority, his own important office and his knowledge of the country. His heart was doubtless in the hunt – not like the Sheriff's; the Sheriff was a waverer. But that very fact made the *beachdar* dangerous. More than once Derry put his hand inside his waistcoat to feel the pocket in his shirt and assure himself there were still there one or two documents which, meaningless to most people, might be transparent clues for one who rifled bags and had eyes for the faintest prickings of a compass.

It was that he might find out, discreetly, more particulars regarding Campbell, that Derry had delayed on various pretexts setting out in the morning to retrace his steps of the previous day, though the thought of return to that town beneath the rocky citadel was peculiarly agreeable, and every moment of delay vexatious. Yet nothing had come of it. Any allusion of his to Ninian Campbell evoked from Taylor or the Sheriff but vague expressions of unreasoned trust in his ability to do anything demanding craft and courage. Had the letter to the Sheriff been a little more explicit, one question answered by his lordship would have settled Derry's mind, but it was a question which could not be put in the circumstances.

Oddly enough, for both the Sheriff and the innkeeper Hannibal Lamont's part in the expedition appeared the most striking feature of it. They had been incredulous when his going was mooted first; and when it appeared imperative, they could not quite conceal that they felt some element of drollery in the very idea. This atmosphere confirmed a feeling of Derry's that a servant might be a serious incumbrance – a suggestion Ninian Campbell firmly put aside with arguments which Derry, as a stranger to the country, could not meet. He had learned that Lamont was a student of divinity, the son of an honest weaver. The prospect of a gloomy and pedantic sprig of the church at his heels was by no means agreeable to Derry, but, at the first sight of the Dettingen hat and the sword, he recognised a kindred spirit, and was reconciled to having for company a lad of the kind with a taste for dramatics. Ferocity and arms were what he had looked for in this country; till now he had come but on old men, soft spoken, flaccid eyed, uncommunicative, their only weapon an ell-wand or a shepherd's crook – a shock to his expectations. Indeed it chagrined him a little that the Messenger-At-Arms should interdict the sword; Derry himself had a pistol down his back for the first time in his life. Never before had he come so close on warfare; he had rarely seen a lethal weapon used in his whole career; which had been wholly confined to a war of the wits.

CHAPTER 5

Not till they had got on to rough town *pavé*, smelled sea-coal fires, and eaten a meal, did Derry come at last to some decision on the attitude he should observe to those two curious participants in the machinations of Whitehall.

Now that the sadness of the hills was gone, he was almost gay, again possessor of himself and confident. It was plain that Hannibal must be regarded, not as a menial, rather in the light of a poor relation; his own obliviousness to social differences or discreet rebuffs made any attempt to put him in his place ridiculous, and his master, Ninian, in any case, from the first had put the lad on a filial footing only deliberate rudeness could seek to qualify. So Hannibal supped with them at a common table in a smokey room, quite at his ease if no great conversationalist. The Messenger-At-Arms it was who must be handled with all the subtlety of a politician. Frankness, up to a point, must be the key for Campbell.

At the first opportunity of getting him by himself when a hurried supper ended, Derry threw off reserve.

'Now that we are here,' he said, 'I may tell you why I stood out so firmly for doubling back on yesterday's tracks through that loathsome valley – with due respect to your fancy for it, Mr Campbell. I want to see a man called Stirling of Craigbarnet, who is a prisoner in the Castle.'

'Craigbarnet!' said Ninian. 'I know all about him! I doubt you'll no' make much of old Craigbarnet. How did ye get in to see him? You would get a permit from Captain Turnbull?'

Derry looked mysterious. 'There are permits and permits, Mr Campbell. I happen to have one that franks me for most places, above all, the forts and garrisons. But Governor Turnbull is from home, and his official deputy at the moment is a sick man, Drummond, bailie – as they call him – of the town. Drummond got out of his bed to gratify my curiosity about his latest batch of prisoners, and I had a talk of twenty minutes with Stirling, among a host of gentry of his own complexion, mixed with the scum and dregs of marching regiments, mutineers, thieves and common drinkers. He was captured only a week ago, still very high and mighty.'

'You would tickle him like a trout, I hope, Mr Derry,' said the Messenger-At-Arms. 'That's the way to play even the biggest fish in autumn.'

'Exactly! I thought I had got everything I desired from Stirling when I found what force had captured him. But night brings council. I was half-way over the hills when it came to me that Drummond, who stuck by me throughout the interview, had been more ill at ease than his prisoner, and could scarcely get us parted quick enough. I had gone to the prison with no particular object beyond seeing what human stuff was in it, to get, perhaps, a first glimpse of your disaffected persons; and spoke to Stirling on an impulse, mainly because he looked sick of the lousy crowd that were with him in his captivity. That's a mood as you know, Mr Campbell, in which a man will sometimes blab unthinkingly for sheer exasperation.'

'Capital!' said Ninian. 'You know your trade! But if you knew the Lennox country better, it is not in its bounds you would be looking for blabbing from Craigbarnet. The man's at home here; half the lairds about us are his kith and kin and would excuse his blabbing less than his poleetical defection. There are things a man can do abroad he darena' do at home, even to save his neck.'

'Well, anyhow, I thought I had got all I wanted from him, with no particular strain on his fidelity. But the more I thought of it afterwards, and the more I think of it now, I'm eager to see him again without the presence of Mr Drummond.'

'We have lost a day over an ill man hauled out of bed and anxious to get back to it, I'm afraid,' said Ninian bluntly. 'We might, by this time, have been through Breadalbane. But the tune's your own, sir, since it's you that pays the piper. Where are we going now?'

'First to Mr Drummond's house, and then for a talk with Stirling. He's likely to be more communicative with you as a countryman of his own.'

Ninian firmed his jaw. 'Drummond if you like,' he said, 'but not for me the prison! Far too many of my kin have suffered in it; I would not, for a ransom, put my foot there, Mr Derry. The long and short of it is I hate this place! It has always a dungeon smell for me though I never was in trouble in it. Give me the wilds! It is in the wilds we'll find young Morag; not on filthy causeways. The sooner you get your business by, the better; we'll make a real start in the morning.'

Leaving Lamont to his Caesar, they went into the street. The town was on a flat peninsula made by the windings of a tributary river and contiguous flooded meadows – a compact little place with one main thoroughfare running east to a secondary stream that made it practically an island. Fantastic pyramids of brick behind the inn had puzzled Derry when he saw them first; they were now explained to him by Ninian as the vents of glass-works. Not many folk were moving out of doors; the main street, wholly unlit by lanterns, or even by shop or household windows, these being closely shuttered, had a Sabbath loneliness; its salient features a jail midway, and a kirk with a slated steeple at the landward end of it. The houses were reared on principles of architecture which showed no desire for the slightest uniformity – some flush with the roadway, topped by an overhanging storey; some recessed, with sombre bushes and scabby grass in a plot in front of them; the unbroken gable of a tenement, at times, incongruously next the façade of a house of some pretentiousness, having chamfered lowered courses and carved scutcheons. Thatch was the prevalent covering.

Only when the kirk was passed was the Rock to be discerned – gigantic, black, and sinister, a basalt hill, with its summit cleft, uprising from the ooze of a lagoon on the one hand and on the other from the brackish estuary. It captured the eye, like an Ararat gone adrift in the universal deluge, and stranded in the shallows of a continent submerged. Though night was come, veiled moonlight qualified the dark; revealed the citadel in a definite shape against the wide and swampish plain to which it was so alien. Chaffer fires were burning somewhere, between its stoney paps; the ramparts, embrasures of batteries, and the prison blocks sprung momentarily into vision now and then when the flames got mastery; it seemed like an attic flat in cloudland. A bugle blew.

They had stopped a moment at the head of a transverse lane to look at this mount, the Messenger-At-Arms repugnantly, Derry finding a consolatory thought in its assurance that here at least ran English law, and sounded a familiar tattoo.

It was he, with a brisk, expectant manner, a cheerful Derry stroking his hair, and twitching his coat-cuffs, and humming the bugle-call, who led the way to Drummond's house, to which Ninian was apparently a stranger. It lay at the back of the town, beyond a mill on the verge of the flooded meadows.

There was a scurry within, when they knocked, and a minute or two elapsed before the door was opened. A little servant lass, with an agitated manner, showed them into a room where a girl was sewing. Such a flush was on her face as she rose and saw the visitors, such was the warmth of Derry's greeting for her, that the *beachdar* on the instant doubted the excuse that was made for coming here. It had, he thought, a suspicious air of pre-arrangement; it had all the features of a tryst except the kissing.

'Oh Mr Derry!' she exclaimed, with a hand on her breast. 'I had no idea you were here yet! I had thought you were leaving yesterday.'

She spoke with brightened eyes and the parted lips of gratification, all her first attention for the Englishman, then turned to Ninian Campbell with an air quite different, somewhat cooled, the smile continuing yet not concealing wholly an inward apprehension. For a moment she held the *beachdar*'s hand and dipped in his eye courageously without a quiver of recognition or curiosity though Derry presented him as 'Mr Campbell'. Ninian had never seen her before, and had every excuse for gazing back as steadily as herself. He recognised at once that the lass was apprehensive of him; he had already got her in a lie – the pretence that she had been ignorant of Derry's two days' absence, from a town where the entire community generally knew each day what a stranger might have for dinner, was too transparent! He might, possibly, have regarded so disingenuous an opening as dictated by the wish of an unpractised young philanderer to give to a tryst the look of a casual meeting for an elderly observer like himself, but silly though her words were, they had some more significance than that.

She was acting a part for the Englishman alone; she had really been taken unawares; her palpitating welcome for him, just a little overdone, was meant to conceal a dismay created by her recognition of the man he had brought back with him.

He was certain she knew him, and needed no presentation by Derry of his 'Mr Campbell'; her reception of him as a total stranger, which might have hurt his vanity in other circumstances, was a spur to his curiosity. Instantly he decided that she knew what he and Derry were after. Had she betrayed the slightest interest in what brought them there he would have been disappointed; his suspicions were confirmed when, for several minutes, she kept up a bright exchange of badinage with the Englishman as if he were a pedlar.

Ninian was the better pleased to be left out of Miss Drummond's attention since it gave him the opportunity to use his eyes.

The room they had been shown into was a small one, simply furnished with a round up-tilted table, a set of birch-wood chairs, a 'scritoire with its flap down as if lately used for writing, a little settee and a spinet. Above the fireplace were hung a gun, a powder-horn, and a sling for shot; two bright new samplers by 'Colina Drummond', framed, were on a wall within reading distance of Ninian where he sat on the left of the fire, and between them a shadow portrait of a lad with the beak of a kestrel, much too long to be other than a droll exaggeration of the artist. On a stool was a tobacco-pipe, and within the hearthstone kerb was a sliver of pinewood charred. A boot-jack under the settee caught his eye, and a pair of muddy boots thrown in along with it gave a sloven note in an interior otherwise trim and tidy.

From the most casual glance at all these features the Messenger-At-Arms again turned his regard upon the girl. In years she could hardly be more than nineteen or twenty though care or illness had put a few years more beneath her eyes and temporarily spoiled the curve of the cheeks, which, for a freckled girl, were now unnaturally pale.

The profile was the profile of the shadow portrait between the samplers – the same small firm chin, the curled, short upper lip, the heavy eyebrows, the cowslick kink of the hair above the forehead. The nose, to most observers, would appear a normal feature, yet Ninian found in it a little curve that in the rougher profile of a man might comically suggest the kestrel.

A bonny lass he would have thought her, on her face alone, even if her hair, nut-brown, and thick, with a cockle curl in it, had not been cut behind to the shortness of a boy's in a way that showed the shaping of the neck and head delightfully and gave her a spice of deviltry. Had he been younger, with no daughter of his own, his interest might have dwelt on her appearance; as it was he was the last man in the world to be drifted into the deluding stream where Derry now seemed fairly launched, the whole ostensible purpose of his coming to this house forgotten.

Not on the flesh of the shapely lass herself did the *beachdar* waste admiration; he had come to the age when men judge women-kind by ear and not by eye. He was listening to a gay palaver, meant, as he knew, to keep himself no less than the young man at arms-length from the actual woman. All things in the room about him at a glance had given him, coldly speculative, an idea of the household; he saw its usual occupants in a series of pictures, guessed at their daily life; that settled, he was now in search of something in the air more faint yet more significant than the odour of burning pine – a secret something – a moral exhalation – a presence hidden from all bodily senses – the family skeleton.

As for Derry, he had surrendered at once to an illusion flattering to his manhood. Here again was the one thing comprehensible and attractive in a country that up till now in its people was as ambiguous as its nights and mists, and almost as repugnant as its lumpish landscape. For Derry there was no particular, exclusive, ideal woman; he was yet at the age when most of a woman's charms are contributed by the masculine observer, like the dreams and thrills that are conjured up by music and make it holier than monotonous thrush-song in the thicket. Any comely girl for Derry found a responsive girl within him far removed from the world of cunning and intrigue that was his home.

He saw in her none of the dusks and lines of fear or tiredness so apparent to the *beachdar*; as if she knew they were there she kept him to her eyes and lips. The most amazing eyes, he thought – under their thick brows, their flickering long lashes that alternate screened and lifted like a challenge to enjoy, the orbs had fire and ice, wonder and childish innocence, banter and invitation. Not these were the forces to storm a citadel like Derry, the walls of him were breached by something new to him in eyes – a hint of landscapes wild and strange, still pools of privacy in evening forests, communion with the fairies!

Her speech even Ninian found curious and pleasing; to Derry it was a transport – so un-Scottish, so evocative of feelings stirred in him before by women's voices he had sometimes heard in France in sympathetic quiet hours in bowers and alcoves. No superficial echoes from the nose impaired her utterance; it came a little masculine in timbre clean out from the vibrations in her bosom, level and soft and musical, not smoothly polished like a sword – just a little roughened with a bloom on it like the dust on grapes; a voice that was at once an almost whispered confidence and a caress. No hint could be discovered of Caledonia in it beyond the landscape and the fairies he himself supplied; she spoke a neutral English more devoid of provincial tones and accents than his own.

From the first glance of her, the first words from her lips, he knew that not any real interest in Craigbarnet had brought him back, that he had returned for refuge from the threatening hills to a room where, two nights previously, he had, for the only time in four hundred miles of travelling, felt *sans souci*, a sense delectable of *rapport*; he had, now facing her, one of those momentary revelations of himself as a humbug that mercifully come at times to gay young men.

'Well,' she said, when he told her of his absence and where he had been, 'you have seen our horrid mountains. Didn't I wager they would drive you back?'

'I never lost a wager with less regret' he said, meaningly, with an uneasy thought that this opening was as good as a confession to the *beachdar*. 'What a pity we did not put the customary stake on it! You promised to tell me what saving grace they had, your mountains?'

She gave a little laugh, so deep in her breast it was a chuckle.

'It is too soon yet, Mr Derry; you are going back to England without really seeing more than the fringes of them. Now, if you were going North –'

'I'm on my way there now,' said Derry, and at these words Ninian Campbell stiffened in his chair.

'In that case you'll have time to observe for yourself the saving grace of the hills. They charm while they repel; they'll put enchantment on you, Mr Derry.'

'Is that a quality shared by the mountains too?' asked Derry, smiling with the unequivocal effrontery of the gallant.

'Oh la! La! Monsieur Derry!' she said with a shrug of her shoulders, a tone of gentle mockery, and Derry was abashed. He felt of a sudden, like a boy in Devon discovered in an orchard.

'*Ce que Mademoiselle parle français?*' he stammered.

'*Tant bien que mal*' she answered curtly, with a flicker of her eyes towards Ninian, and turned to English instantly. 'You want, no doubt, to see my father? I am so sorry; he has gone to sleep some hours ago; he has been ill again.'

Derry expressed his sympathy, concealed admirably his relief from the only thought that had troubled him before entering – how he should get to Stirling's presence again without the company of Mr Drummond.

'I had hoped he might be able to come with me to the prison again' he said quietly. 'It is urgent that I have a talk again with one of the prisoners.'

'Which?' she asked deliberately.

'Stirling of Craigbarnet.'

'You can't, Mr Derry. He's gone!'

Instantly the gallant and the boy abashed made way in Derry for the secret agent; he looked so staggered that the *beachdar*'s interest in the pair before him was transferred to Stirling of Craigbarnet. It was only a wavering attention he gave to the rest of the conversation; there had jumped to his vision an elderly awkward-moving man coming down on a rope and swinging like a pendulum, and it set up speculations not to be satisfied by anything that might be said by a girl now plainly determined to keep the Englishman out of the range of things that most concerned her. When it became apparent that Derry had now abandoned any idea of going to the prison, and was again the frank philanderer, just a bit too oblivious of his companion's presence for politeness, the latter got to his feet with an excuse for leaving them.

'Now that I'm in this part of the country,' said he, 'I am going to take a chance of seeing an old friend there may be little time to look for in the morning. I bid you good night, Miss Colina, and I hope your father will soon be on his soles again.'

Derry seemed, on the whole, relieved by this withdrawal, he could not see; the girl, as he expected, was not so satisfied.

Outside the gate of Drummond's ground, he stood and looked back at the house more minutely than on his coming, and at its outside offices – a byre or stable with a granary loft; then at a lively step walked south and out of the town completely, following a road that led to the Rock, and that, midway, passed the twisting-posts of a rope-walk. He quitted the road, went up the rope-walk two or three hundred yards through whin and ragweed, and came to the shed that was the roperie itself. It was shut for the night, but contiguous to it was a cottage and someone playing a fiddle in it.

A minute later and the *beachdar* was with the fiddler in a bachelor kitchen, lit by an evil smelling fish-oil cruse, and half furnished from the driftwood of the tides.

'I thought I would give you a cry in the passing, Fletcher,' he said, with no preamble to the fiddler in his shirt sleeves – a young man with an eye of quick intelligence and another slightly at variance with its neighbour. 'What's this I'm hearing about Craigbarnet? Has he taken his feet for it?'

'It's you that is not long of learning things, Mr Campbell,' said the householder. 'What way in the world did you get here?'

'What way but on a horse?' said the *beachdar* – 'a beast I always hate to be hampered wi'. It's dangerous at both ends and anything but feathers in the middle. Never you mind about that, but tell me this, for I'm in a hurry – who let Craigbarnet free?'

'If I knew that I would be as wise as yourself,' said the other, pricking up the cruse-wick with a nail.

'And what in God's name do I keep you here for? I get you the place at some great trouble to myself that you might keep your eyes about ye when ye werna twisting yarn. Craigbarnet must have passed your very door when he made evasion, unless he swam the rivers.'

'But it was at night,' explained the fiddler, eagerly. 'He was gone at the roll-call in the morning, and fifty fathom of hawser swinging from the Regent battery. I canna stay up all night to watch things, Mr Campbell.'

'Ye could if ye would play the fiddle less, Fletcher,' retorted the *beachdar*, 'Music's the very devil to distract a man from his occupations; it's worse than drink. Could he have crossed the ferry?'

'There's no a boat amissing, and every boat was on the hard this morning, exactly where it was left last night. I can tell you, Mr Campbell, there has been great commotion here this day, and if the man's not got it's no' for the want o' searching. The bylie's out o' his wits for fear they'll blame it on him. He put every likely hiding-place in the parish through a riddle.'

'I thought Drummond was ill?' said the *beachdar*.

'He might be ill, but there's no appearance of it; from the scriech of day till half-an-hour ago he was the nimblest man on the track. There was no use searching far afield, for Craigbarnet couldn't take the highroad, being cripple.'

'Was he a cripple?' questioned the *beachdar*, with new interest.

'Cripple's no' the word for't; the man couldn't walk on his own legs twenty yards without the lend of an elbow. He was wounded when they took him prisoner in Arisaig.'

'When was he brought here?' asked the *beachdar*.

'Just three days ago, with twenty others, some of them very namely gentlemen.'

'He hasna taken long to make arrangements for a rope. Had ye the sense to look at it?'

'Yes' said the fiddler, 'and I knew it like my hand, for I was at its twisting.'

'Who does it belong to?'

'It was made for Bylie Drummond's sloop a year ago, was borrowed without question last July by a gang of free-fishing folk from the other side of the water. They were caught with it and the nets and the fish in them, and clapped in cells, where their gear has been lying ever since. The rope was taken last night from the jail – I knew its history.'

'Did ye mention it to Drummond?'

'Not a word' said Fletcher, slyly. 'I was waiting for him to mention it first. And he never let on he saw it before.'

'Capital!' said the *beachdar*. 'Ye're no altogether without your wits about ye. Half the rogues in the world escape through honest men being in a hurry to show how clever they are. Keep your eye on Mr Drummond!'

'But it couldna be Drummond' said the fiddler. 'Craigbarnet and him's at daggers drawn for years back over a law-plea. You should see the way that Drummond scoured the town for him!'

A little taken aback by this disclosure, the Messenger-At-Arms stood for a moment pondering, but made no comment. He went to the door, looked out on the night, and the cliff below the landward battery lit by the chaffer fire. The rope-work stood alone, a dreary place like a lazarette, pitched midway between the town and the estuary, chosen for his spy for the deliberate purpose of keeping an eye on the garrison. No human sounds came near it; brisk fiddling, the *beachdar* felt, was needed to make the nights agreeable to a lonely man in such a situation; he could not be surprised at his emissary's manner of passing time.

'She's a brave bright lass that Colina one of Drummond's' he remarked, turning in again and shutting the door. 'Where did she get her schooling?'

'By all accounts she got the best of it in France.' Said Fletcher. 'Her mother had a brother there, under a cloud.'

'Who is he?'

'He's dead; he was a Macdonnell from Morar.'

'Just that!' said the *beachdar*, tapping his teeth with his finger-nails. 'A gallant people, but daft for politics the whole of them! Is there not a son to Drummond? – a fellow with a beak.' – and with a thumb and forefinger to his face, he signified the kestrel.

'I never saw him,' said Fletcher. 'He's in the law in Edinburgh; Patrick they call him.'

'There's one thing of it – he has a clever sister, anyway!' And you wouldn't believe it – she never heard of me, and she doesn't know me!' said the *beachdar*, and put on his hat. 'I must be going, for I'm leaving in the morning early. Keep your eye well-cocked and your ears without caulking in them, and let our man in Luss know anything that's stirring. I can assure you *he's* not a fellow that wastes time at fiddling when the hare is in the corn. Good night to ye, Peter.'

He was off in a flash, and back ten minutes later at the house where he had left the Englishman. Opening the gate noiselessly he stepped in on the grass and walked all round the domicile. Five windows looked to the front – one of them that of the room he had been in, with curtains on it through which lights feebly showed it had still an occupant. But no sound of speech came from it; he concluded Derry was gone.

At the back of the house, two windows were lit on the ground floor, both with outside shutters having screened portholes cut at the top to let in the morning light, both having iron stanchions. On the sill of one of them were pot-brooms and dishclouts dried; it must be the kitchen. From the path that went round the house he picked up a handful of gravel, withdrew to a clump of laurel and lightly threw a pebble or two at the other window which he took to be that of a bedroom. It had no result; for the moment at least, though lit, it appeared to be unoccupied. For a house in which three people must still be awake Drummond's house seemed oddly silent.

He had almost got back to the gate, reluctantly quitting a place where every curiosity of his seemed doomed to be unsatisfied, when he noticed, for the first time, a chink of light under the granary door in the upper part of the outhouse. Headstalls jerked and rattled underneath; there was a smell of horse. For a minute or two he listened with his ear against the lower door; somewhere aloft was the sound of a low conversation.

He tried the door; it was on a hasp which his thumb pressed on as lightly as on a trigger; pushing it open with precaution, his breath suspended in a fear of the creak of hinges, he looked in on a two-stall stable with two horses showing dimly in the feeble light that fell through a trap-door in the ceiling, to which a perpendicular ladder built close against the wall, with grip-holes reached. For a moment or two again he stood like a heron, listening; the talk aloft went on monotonously but in a tone too quiet to be intelligible.

Out he went into the darkness, softly closing the door behind him; threw gravel at the granary door and slipped to the gable of the outhouse where were growing hollies.

On the granary ladder feet clumped hollowly; the stable door was opened, and a man came out, leaving the door open behind him. The rattle of the sand on the granary door would seem a kind of signal with which he was familiar, for he made no pause to look about him for its origin, but walked deliberately over to the house and entered.

No sooner was he gone from view than the *beachdar* plucked two sprigs of holly and darted for the stable. He stuck a twig under each horse's tail, and they began to kick with fury, tossing their heads, till the headstalls went like thunder. In the commotion he went up the ladder softly, lifted his eyes only above the level of the granary floor and looked at what he could see by the light of a lantern hanging from the rafter.

One look he gave – no more – and descending as quietly as he had mounted, ran from the yard, burst through the gate to Drummond's property and trotted down a bye-way which led, as he knew, circuitously to the inn.

CHAPTER 6

Colina Drummond, a woman entirely altered from the sparkling girl who had so artfully engaged the interest of John Derry, was writing furiously at the bureau, her knuckles wet with her tears, when her father entered.

She turned to him, strained, and almost sobbing. 'Why in God's name did you leave your boots there under the settle?' she demanded harshly, as if every filial sense in her were frozen. 'It was only five minutes ago I noticed them, just when I was happy thinking I had smoothed things out!'

Drummond stared at her, astonished. Only twenty minutes had elapsed since he had gone across to the granary, leaving a daughter agitated to a natural degree from her interview with her unexpected visitors, yet still with her virginal manner of affection. He was tired to exhaustion, as she knew, and the prey of alarms that had made three nights sleepless for him, never man more needed sympathy; yet here she was in a fury at him!

'What does it matter, Col, about the boots?' he asked with a bewildered look at them. 'I had no time to think what was to be done with them when the knock came to the door.'

He had such a mortified, uncomprehending air as he stood before her, haggard with fears and vigils, that she softened to him.

'It can't be helped now, father,' she said in a more natural tone. 'It is foolish of me to blame you, since I saw you throwing them there and thought no harm in it. But when my eyes fell on them again they drove me demented.'

'What ails you at the boots, my dear?' he asked. 'I am not usually so untidy; they can be shifted.'

'Sit there!' she said impulsively and urged him into the chair that Ninian Campbell had occupied. 'Now look about you! Is there anything more conspicuous in this room than those boots that should never be in it except on your feet? Have a look at them, father! The man who sat in that chair a little ago couldn't imagine they were mine nor think we are in the habit of throwing muddy boots in a slovenly way like that about in a parlour. Boots have tongues to them, father; yours were fairly bawling out for notice from the one man on earth who could understand their language.'

'What does it matter?' said her father. 'We have something far more terrible to trouble us than that an Englishman should see your room in some disorder.'

She threw up her hands. '*Mon Dieu!*' she cried, 'Can you so misunderstand me, father, as to think at a time like this a silly thought like that would vex me? It surely matters something that a man like that should see your boots with the wet mud on them in a place like that after I had told him you were ill in bed. Haven't I said I am in terror of him?'

'You said nothing of the kind, Col,' said her father peevishly. 'You gave me to believe he was easy to beguile.'

'That was Derry, father. I may have managed to beguile him for a little in a fashion I'm half ashamed of, though I'm not so sure, for there's something curious in reserve in Mr Derry. I'm speaking now of Ninian Campbell; it was he who sat in that chair and looked about him. It beats even me to keep two men's eyes on me at once; there's something to be done in that way with young men, but not with a sly old rogue like Ninian Campbell, and his very presence turned my blood cold. I daren't come close beside him for fear he should hear my heart, nor look at him lest I should lose the command of my eyes. All the time he sat there, the boots of you were crying 'liar!' to my story; it couldn't be worse if your feet were in them. When he rose and left Derry and me after hearing of Craigbarnet being missing I knew at once he had got all he wanted here and was off to push inquiries elsewhere.'

'Tach! The man is not so devilish clever as all that, Col,' said Drummond. 'It's Derry that I'm feared for. It took me all my time to get him away from Stirling in the Castle the day before yesterday.'

She frowned, dubiously; puckered up her mouth a moment, as one weighing a new misfortune.

'I think you were wrong there, father,' she said, 'Craigbarnet would never have repeated what he told you; for all that has come and gone between you, he wouldn't have done that.'

'I know that now, but I was anxious. As ill luck had it, he wasn't two hours on the Rock when Derry was on him. I hadn't even time to warn him, and seeing Derry with me, he might have let something slip in all innocence.'

'It wasn't Derry you had to fear at all, but the man he was seeking to help him. Derry never once mentioned to me who he was going to look for yesterday morning, and I thought he was just a messenger from London, but when he came in here with Ninian Campbell I knew in an instant what he was and who had sent him into Scotland. *They'll find him, father!* I'm terrified! The Englishman is a boy in some things, but he is not so simple as he looks. I'm always in two minds about Englishmen; they beguile themselves, but when they know what they want that is a great advantage to them, and they're not so easily beguiled by other people. If he were just the depth he looks, he would never have been sent here to pick up Ninian Campbell. That two such men should be on the scent is a calamity! You know what the *beachdar* is! – all the Macgregor cunning under one bonnet; I felt like a child when I stood before him, trying to throw dust in his damned grey eyes!'

'That is no language for a lady, Col!' cried her father, shocked. 'Remember you're not a fishwife!'

'I wish I were!' she said, 'and this very night I would take a creel and cry herring all the way to Arisaig! If those two men get up to Arisaig within the next week we are done for, and our darling's doomed!'

No bloom of the grape was on her voice now; it was jangling like sheets of brass. She sunk into a chair, with every sinew of her unrelaxed, a picture of despair.

'It is not so black as all that, my dear,' said her father, with his hand on her shoulder.

'If there is any creature on earth who can find him in the land where Craigbarnet saw him last, it is Ninian Campbell!' she stormed. 'Everybody here knows where Craigbarnet came from; it was no use trying to hide that from Derry if he was curious in that direction, but the trouble we took to hide it is just the thing to make Campbell guess there was something else to hide of more importance. And these men are going North tomorrow morning!'

'Going North,' repeated Drummond shaken.

'Of course! What did you think they were here for? From the first I suspected the Englishman was a spy, and I manoeuvred to get him to come back this way that I might find out a little more about him. But I little thought he would come back with keener eyes and far more wits than he went away with. I'm writing to Jean in Colasa telling her to warn the country. You'll have to get a man to set out on horse with my letter tomorrow morning. Someway or other your boots have terrified me.'

'All this about a pair of muddy boots is quite beyond me, Col,' said her father, 'I thought you would be in your bed by this time, but now that you summoned me what do ye want?'

'Summon ye?' she repeated, wondering. 'How did I summon you?'

'Did you not throw gravel at the granary door?' he asked quickly.

'Good heavens, no! I haven't been out of this room since you left me.'

'Then somebody is spying on us!' said Drummond, and laying her head on her arms, she sunk across the table weeping.

Not much of an ill man, he rushed out to the yard and was back immediately, breathless, panic-stricken.

'The cattle have been disturbed,' he said hoarsely; 'there has been someone in the stable.' She jumped to her feet, her features twisted.

'Is your man still there?'

'Sound sleeping! He can have seen and heard nothing.'

'Then it is for you to think what's next to be done in that direction; for me there's only one thing – I must go North myself! The need to warn them there is far too urgent for a man to be the messenger; I have no trust in men. Every hour is precious when that devilish *beachdar* is on the track; I'll take four hours' sleep and be off by daybreak.'

'Do you think he is in such danger, Col?' inquired her father, tremulous.

'Danger! He was never in worse! Poor lad! Poor lad! He's in the very heart of danger!'

She began to tidy up the room hastily like one who had made a habit of leaving all things orderly behind her.

CHAPTER 7

Derry was far away from Scotland and its hostile hills before Ninian Campbell got to the inn again: it is Captain Sleep who is the best of all skippers to sail a young man out of tribulation. Once out of the disturbing presence of Colina Drummond, the Englishman found himself dog-weary, and went straight to bed; a bolted door met the Messenger-At-Arms when, returning from his scrutiny of the Drummond domicile, he sought to consult his travelling companion on their plans for the following morning.

It was for Derry's chamber he made first; when that proved consecrate to a privacy even a *beachdar* must respect, he sought further along a pitch-dark lobby for the room he was to share with Hannibal Lamont. With his thumb on the snatch of the latch he paused for a little, his ears cocked for a curious padding sound that went on within, as if its occupant were in some dire strait, or at the dancing.

Hannibal would seem to have someone with him in the room; it shook like a booth at a fair and panted like a bellows; short, snarling, half-choked cries of 'Harlaw!' and 'Ardlamont!' reached the listener who took off one boot preparatory to entering.

The body-servant, with his heels hammering on the floor, his breath gasping, was so far away in time and clime from anything that might reach his bodily senses that he did not hear the click of the latch nor see the eye of Ninian stare in on him through an inch of opened door. He had cast his footwear, coat, and waistcoat, and was only in shirt and breeches. Two candles guttering on the chimney showed he had piled on the bed the chamber's plenishing of chairs and table to get a clear space on the floor for his fantastic exercise with a poker. Half-crouched on his stocking-soles, with his left arm in the air, he advanced and retired in confrontation of some phantom fencer, in a series of feints and false attacks, ripostes and counter-ripostes, with the ludicrous weapon thus extraordinarily aggrandised from its ordinary office of stirring coal or peat. He thrust and slashed with venom, hissing, his teeth revealed below a moustache that bristled, his eyes ferocious.

They lost that crazy flame when the door pushed fully open and the *beachdar* entered limping, himself a little foolish-looking with a boot swung in his hand for use if trouble threatened.

'Splendid! Splendid altogether!' cried Ninian in Gaelic. 'I thought I was in time to help you with the heel of a boot, but I'm too late now for anything but your funeral. You were dead from the start with a guard like that if anything but air was facing you. It is not a guard at all, my little hero, but a hearty invitation! If ever you are in a habble, Hannibal, try to bring yourself out of it with song or story; your sword-play is beyond redemption! Who were you thinking you were fighting?'

'I was letting on I was at Harlaw,' answered Hannibal, not very much put about.

'And what side were you on, my warrior? Donald of the Isles, or Mars'?'

'I'm not very sure in my mind yet, but I was on the right side anyway,' said Hannibal, still panting from the heat of his attack on a foe phantasmal.

'I never saw a lad of any spirit on the wrong side yet when it came to the hour of battle; it is just the same with wild-cats. It is time you were getting your claws clipped, lad. And you with a college education! You can't fence worth a snuff; you're not a credit to your clan or the land of Cowal.'

It was there he reached Hannibal's shame; the lad, confused, grew red as a raspberry and clashed his weapon down on the hearth.

'What could you expect of me,' he cried, 'and me with only a poker? If you had only let me keep my sword! It was my grandfather's.'

The Messenger-At-Arms picked up the poker, and looking at it, found the cause of Hannibal's infatuation; it had been, in its youth, a claymore's blade; years and rust and fireside drudgery had worn it to a spit.

'It is something of an omen, Hannibal, lad-o'-my-heart,' said the *beachdar* quietly, putting it down on the hearth again. 'I doubt it means that for you and me the wars are over.'

'Devil the bit!' exclaimed the lad. 'I never had my chance yet! Is it not a war we're going to? And me without a weapon to take the bare look off me! I might as well be a lowland pedlar.'

'Better without a weapon, *laochain*!' said Ninian, lifting a chair from the bed and sitting down on it to take off his other boot. 'I carried, myself, for many a day, a sword with the name Grey Colin to him, and he always got me into trouble. I'm done with him! The dirk is more discreet, or a wee Doune pistol, but even that I'm better wanting; my rages never rise in me when my hands are empty. I am all for peace now, and a pair of fireside slippers like the Sheriff's. You're all ajee in your notions about wars, my scholar; stop you, and I'll show, where we're going, that there's not a more unhandsome thing 'twixt the four brown boundaries of the world than a young man's corpse and he a sacrifice to old men's notions he had no concern in. Go we to bed, like good bairns, for we're starting early in the morning.'

'Where is the Captain?' asked Hannibal, clearing the bed of its burden.

'What Captain?' asked the *beachdar* with surprise.

'The Englishman.'

Ninian regarded him with admiration. 'Good for you, Hannibal!' he exclaimed. 'There's something in good schooling after all! You have got the very title for him! Was I not bothering what I was to call him in the North to make it reasonable that I should be in his company and under his command, and there you are with the very rank for him! "Captain" a gallant name to travel with – I couldna better it! "Captain Derry" – *air m'anam fein*, it's like a line of song! There's a touch of the warlock in you, Hannibal; tell me this – what do you think of the Englishman?'

'Oh, good enough, for the tribe!' replied Hannibal. 'Flippant enough on his feet, and his mother taught him manners! But he hasn't the cut of a sodger, and he never read the Commentarii.'

'Neither did I,' said Ninian bluntly. 'Far better a book of ballads or the Word of God! And it's not a sodger that's wanted on the trip we're going; it's a man of some contrivance. I canna make up my mind about the Captain. He wouldn't be here if he was not something special, and I have a feeling in my bones he's going to quirk me.'

'Men and love! Mr Campbell, it would beat him to do that!' said Hannibal with an air so innocent that the *beachdar* laughed.

'Indeed I'm not new off my mother's lap,' he said, 'and I'm not the man to be tricked like a linnet by a riddle and a piece of string, but I never before came athwart a Sassanach, and I'll have to travel a bit with this fellow yet before I find out if he is so ready as he looks to listen to the music of the wind and put his own words to it . . . Do ye follow me, Hannibal?'

'Fine!' said Hannibal, and his face as blank as the underside of a halibut, back to his scratching, nothing now upon him but his shirt.

'It is not here we should be at all this night, but over Orchy.'

'That's just what I was thinking to myself in the Latin language, Mr Campbell,' said the youth. 'Where are we here but *in partibus infidelium*?'

'We're here in a place where a man with the time to spare could get much amusement studying something deeper than the Latin – the tricks of men, and women too, the darlings! I saw a lass a little ago that looked like having our Captain on a hook, and faith I thought she had him, but he snapped. I'm wondering if he got his head above the water and saw the gaff. I don't believe he did. He's young enough to think it was for his bonny eyes she angled him, though I, being up in years, knew different. It was not even for the sake of practice she was casting; she had her eye on *him*, but all the time her mind was on the wee red otter sitting watching . . . and that was me! Tell me this, Hannibal, are you curious where we're going and what we're going for? You never asked me.'

'Time enough to find out that when we get there,' Hannibal answered cheerfully. 'It's some place where the storm-cock whistles, or you wouldn't be going there. Whatever we're out for, we're for King and country.'

Ninian sunk his chin and with his eyebrows twitching with amusement, looked askance at him.

'That's but a battle-cry, Hannibal,' he said. 'You never saw your King but on a sign-board and your country's in the clouds. Let me tell you you're for nobody but Ninian Campbell and he is out for another man they call MacCailen. We needna go beyond that. But if you'll take my advice you'll keep your mouth shut about "King and country" where we're going; you are just an honest *sgalag* going with your master, and that's me, for cattle. Just you give a squint on that.'

He produced from a pocket of his coat a wallet of home-made leather fastened with a thong, and drew from it a document he passed to his companion, who read:

Permit the Bearer, James MacNab, Drover in Craig of Orchy, who goes with two servants to purchase and bring back black cattle from Kintail and the Isle of Skye, to pass to and from these countrys with their arms.

A. Campbell of Stonefield, Advocate.
Sheriff Depute of the Sheriffdom of Argyll.

To All Officers Civil and Military.

'*A chiall!*' cried Hannibal, 'Does the Captain ken he's to be a drover?'

'He'll never ken unless the need arises, and he has plenty of permits of his own complexion. I always like to have a letter of my own, for nowadays a good tale's better than a pistol, anywhere above Druim-Albyn. Get you to bed, oh hero! I'll pinch out the light.'

Hannibal got 'twixt blankets, lay on his back and stretched himself out like a figure of stone on an island tomb. The whitewashed ceiling, pocked and scarred by fallen plaster, had a patterned look and moved to the fire's twinkling; he saw on it the vague stuff of his dreams, a world of battles.

CHAPTER 8

The Messenger-At-Arms was not quite wakened; was yet in the shallows of sleep, when Derry appeared at his door, yet fifteen minutes later he and Hannibal with the Englishman were at a drover's breakfast of white puddings, oaten bannocks, cold mutton-ham and ale, which Derry contemplated ruefully more often than he tried them on his appetite. For a body-servant, or a servant of any kind, Hannibal was more than ever plainly never meant by his Creator; he would have sat at those mealy puddings while even a skim of them was left, had not the *beachdar* hinted in the most off-hand fashion that it might be well to see that the horses were being saddled. At that he went out at a jump, with a chaplet of pudding half consumed thrust into his coat pocket.

'He's getting on, the young one!' chuckled Ninian. 'The great thing in the Hie'lands is always to make sure of your next bite . . . What's the plan this morning, Captain Derry?'

Derry was one of those whose breakfasts have the dregs of sleep in them and who take some time to adjust themselves to a new day and all its irritating contacts. Up till now he had hardly exchanged three sentences with his companion; this brevet-rank, so unexpectedly conferred on him, shook him into all his faculties.

'Captain!' he repeated with some astonishment. 'How could you think of that, Mr Campbell? It happens to be the very cloak I have been searching for to put over my civilian clothes.'

'That was my idea, too,' said Ninian, blandly. 'I couldna go far through the Rough Bounds without having some excuse for you that would satisfy my curious friends. There would be no use clapping a kilt on you or a crofter's drugget trews; you haven't the shape for it. It's a great misfortune you couldna pass for anything but a gentleman; it must be a drawback in your calling. Hannibal it was who got the style for you; he called you Captain Derry just on your appearance.'

A discernment so flattering evidently gratified the Englishman; it was the first evidence he had that the roving eyes of that ridiculous body-servant ever came down to earth.

'Captain is a good travelling name,' pursued the *beachdar*, 'especially in a country full of them. Plenty of Captains who were wearing cockades six months ago are now back at the farming and the droving, hoping they'll be overlooked, and an odd one here and there with the leisure to stravaig the country is only to be expected. You can be a Major for the forts and garrisons if it suits you, but we're not going much about them, I hope, and for haunts of another complexion, you had better stick by the Captain, if it's only just to spare me the need for making up stories. There, nothing folk in Scotland are more concerned about than to know how a stranger makes his living. And "Captain" has this advantage; it's not like a cockade, it does for any side at a time of trouble.'

Not a word was said of the fiasco that had wasted a day for them; that, it seemed, was to be a chapter closed for both of them. They were in the best of humour in spite of a pauper breakfast; Derry secretly assured that at least he would have a decent dinner, the *beachdar* happy to think that now they were done with causeways, and that noon would find them in the woods. Disillusion came to him like a blow on the stomach. 'How many miles is it to the Forth?' Derry asked him.

'Two-and-thirty,' stammered Ninian, 'But God be about us! You're not in the notion to go to the Forth, surely? It's off the road for us altogether, and ye canna have a lass there too, Captain Derry.'

(*Ninian had concluded that Derry would want to go up Glen Falloch, the sooner to reach the Arisaig district. Colina went up Glen Falloch.*)

All the arguments of yesterday were thrashed through again; Derry was as dour set on his own arrangements; he must be at the Forth that night if he had to walk it. Letters of marque cachet were waiting for him there, and he daren't go North till he had got them. What letters-of-marque were Ninian decided to find out at the earliest opportunity from Hannibal, not this time out of craft did he concede the Englishman's way of it, but in despair of a character so foolish as to make so much of a running jump at a wall that had to be painfully climbed in any case.

It was still the dawn when the trot-trot-a-trot of their going woke the street. Not so much as a cat was stirring on the cobbles; only a bakehouse would appear to have life in it from the smell of fresh-burned wood mixed with the stale strange odour of oak ashes and hot oven-sole. Two miles out, from a rise, they saw the plain they had quitted filled with misty vapour, wherefrom the black Rock jutted like a skerry of the sea, the gulls about it. On the shoals of the broad still stream whose bank they followed, herons stood knee-deep contemplative; goats tethered behind poor little cabins browsed on low ragged beechen hedges; dew dripped from every growing green thing, giving the fields, with gossamer carpeted, a fluid aspect, stirred by the breeze into ripples as if they had been silvery ponds. It was broad day before the travellers had got clear of the little sleeping hamlets; the sun smote on a great expanse of water to the west, with woody islands, prisoned in by hills whose pinnacles appeared like astral emanations, almost a transparent blue against the deeper blue of sky.

All Derry's detestation of the mountains woke again; it was gladly he saw them sink from view at a dip of the ill-made road that led down to a ford across a fretful little river where, of a sudden, the *beachdar* halted and jumped from his horse.

'Endrick Water!' he said with some emotion; 'my folk have fished it!' and without another word of explanation, hurried along the bank some fifty yards; took off his coat, rolled up a shirt sleeve, lay on his belly, and dipped to the armpit in a pool, with questing fingers. '*Sin thu!*' cried he, and up with an astonished sea-trout, flapping!

In less than fifteen minutes he had got six; strung them on a twig of willow, tied them to his pommel and mounted. 'Now,' said he, 'we're safe at least for a dinner.'

They got, in a while, into a land of trees. From a thicket that bordered the road, to which it fell from rocky terraces, a shot rang out with an appalling echo, and a moment later a man with ragged garments, a gun, and a canvas sack slung on his shoulder was ahead of them on the roadside. He gave but a glance at them and darted back to shelter.

Again was the *beachdar* off his horse. 'Fie on the free-hunter!' he said, laughing. 'I'll bring my fish to market and make a bargain wi' him.' So saying he dashed into the thicket whence in a little he brought the man and got in exchange for two of his trout two brace of birds.

For many miles before they reached the Forth they saw its castled crag uprise above the great wide plain ahead of them; it had, for Derry, a look of Lombardy. It was noon before they came to a hamlet on its outskirts and the Englishman was so hungry he fell in without demur to a proposal of the *beachdar's* that they should there and then have a meal, though where it was to come from was not obvious in a community that could not even boast of an ale-house.

But the Messenger-At-Arms made little of this difficulty; at a tidy-looking cottage, through the open top-half of a door, he saw a woman busy making scones. 'We're into the Land of Plenty, Hannibal,' said he; dropped from the saddle again, took a fish and a moor-hen and went boldly to the entrance.

'Beloved of all women of the world,' said he with a merry eye, 'What are we but wanderers, and hunger on us? Wouldst give us some scones and butter swop in swop for the finest trout in Endrick Water and a hen of the heath?'

'Oh man! Isn't he the gallant!' said Hannibal transported.

It was but the opening of Ninian's siege to her domestic privacy; five minutes later and he and Hannibal were gutting fish and plucking fowl; he had somewhere in a pocket salt and spices; very soon, with sticks from the garden, he was roasting fowl and fish, and then, at a table dragged out to the rear of the house, the three men sat to a meal which Derry found had most of the appetising qualities of an *al fresco* meal in France, save that the wine was wanting. They sat in a tiny patch of garden, under rowans, the scent of tansy, musk, and briar about them, and a crimson little flower flamed up the wall behind them to the eaves of thatch. 'What are we to drink?' asked Derry.

'Devil the thing but water!' answered Ninian and produced a jugful. 'There's nothing better for the health.'

Derry gave a grimace. 'No doubt, friend,' he said, 'but I'm spoiled for it as a beverage. It tastes all alike to me.'

Whereupon the *beachdar*, with a ludicrous fervour, garrulously upheld the virtues of mountain wells. No two waters, he declared, tasted alike till a man had ruined his palate. Of water's mildness, coolness, lightness, clearness, sparkle, he discoursed in a lyric note. To its potable qualities, went, he swore, far subtler preparations than the vine press and the rack, in itself, as it fell from the clouds an insipid juice, it was savourless, otherwise men might swill it from rain-casks, but from heath and thyme and the myrtle of the bogs it drew an essence of garden wilds far subtler than the vineyards. Nor even then was it fit for man; it must settle for a while on sands, to be sifted of its dusty particles, seep through the old fir tree roots of the peaty moor to get the tang of ancientry, toss over rock to get its sparkle, run underground to get its cool.

'There are noble, splendid, glittering wells in the lands where we're going, Captain Derry,' he said, 'with names to them for a thousand years. Many a time and oft I walked miles off my road just for a taste of them. Neither pumps nor the breathings of men have dirtied them; when I was young I could get drunk on them!'

As he spoke, two singular figures passed on the highway – a file of soldiers with shakos over their ears and trailing sabres, blue uniforms, long, fair, waxed moustaches curled up to their eyes, pig-tails hanging behind, and pleated love-locks on their temples.

'God's splendour! What have we here?' broke out the bard of water, astounded. 'The like of that I never saw but in a picture.'

'Germans,' said Derry, a little elated to see them. 'The Prince of Hesse-Cassel's horse; I guessed we should find them somewhere here.'

Hannibal looked after those strange figures with admiration and envy; they would seem to him, to judge from his transport, creatures of his books and dreams, great shapes of chivalry; he cocked his Dettingen hat unconsciously, to the Messenger-At-Arms' amusement.

'Just penny sodgers, Hannibal!' he remarked. 'Ye can buy them in the shops in London. If I were you I wouldna cock my bonnet for them. By all accounts they use them here for stopping holes; they havena wet their weapons yet.'

Their meal concluded, Derry proposed that he should go into the town alone on foot, and leave the others to rest the horses for an hour or two, joining them later, when he had done his business in the Castle.

CHAPTER 9

The afternoon was warm and sunny; downy clouds with silvery edges drifted, lazy, from the west; in a haze the distant hills to the north seemed almost vapour too. Derry, walking towards the citadel through purlieus with filthy gutters running down their cobbles, where ragged men sat on the kerbstones eating bread and onions, had again a feeling that it might be Italy. In the higher parts of the town it had the right Italian blend of faded grandeur and modern squalor that makes up so much of the picturesque for which folk travel abroad. There came to his remembrance suddenly a hill-town in which he had one time slept – Bergamo. A cousin, sure, to Bergamo this, when in an ascending thoroughfare he looked down alleyways or lanes that sank precipitous from the ridge, and saw at their further ends long vistas of the campagna that stretched to the horizon, the river links, great verdant parks, patches of coppice, what might be villa gardens, and an abbey's towers.

There was an appropriate air of lassitude and unkemptness in the women sitting on stools at the entries of the tenements, knitting, small-bone combing children's heads, and gossiping; an odour of garlic, an attack by beggars, or arcades and *antichita* would have made the illusion perfect; instinctively he glanced over broken tiles for a darting lizard.

No less Italian seemed the view to the south from the castle-ramparts; he was in the Citta Alta of Bergamo, and that shoreless plain was Lombardy – a little Lombardy. Such a generous flat expanse, such verdure, such fertility, could not conceivably be Scotland.

He had come up a wynd that was thronged with the Hessian soldiers lounging in the sunshine, outnumbering the *jupe court* fellows with knotted knees who gabbled Campbell's language. There were a few troopers of Cobham's horse, some of De Jean's grenadiers, and a squad of the rank and file of Barrell's regiment kicking a ball in a yard and swearing in honest English; all of their distinguishing accoutrements he had learned by heart on the counsel of his employers in Whitehall.

Unlike that other Rock he had left behind in the morning, this one, brother to it, had a tail that stretched far and gradual to the river: at the top of the slope the shabby tenements with their washing out like banners ended and there was a wide parade with a company of foot at drill on it. On the edge of the precipice crouched stark squat buildings that were seemingly casernes, with a mediocre palace carved in the Latin fashion with heavily-stanchioned windows, shattered statuary, bastions, embrasures, and mediaeval guns. Bergamo for a ducat! Within must be a Maroni Madonna of priceless value or an altarpiece of Paul Veronese. Derry felt that if passion were fluid and soaked into the scenes of history, one could not scratch his name here on a wall without extracting blood, nor pluck a wild flower from the cranny that had not its roots in the red heart of things forgotten. He had, for a moment, one of his poetic moods and felt that could the Arab of the story touch his ears whereby his sluggish senses might be quickened, he would hear the ultimate waves, that still exist in space, of sounds that went back to the roar of chaos crystalling into shape, and hear this only half-English outpost terrible with drums and trampings; its walls would be intolerable for the cries of struggling people, stranded for a moment on that crag, to be swept away again and whelmed in death and time.

At a postern gate he asked for the quarters of the Governor, and was taken into a bare little chilly cell where a fat red-faced officer, crumbs of pie on his waistcoat, his uniform coat unbuttoned, leant paunchily over a table with a map spread on it, playing some solitary game with pins and the crimson berries of the mountain ash.

Derry, in key with the captaincy conferred on him by Hannibal Lamont, gave a salute and produced a letter.

'No message here for you, Mr Derry,' said the Governor, having read it and buttoning up his coat fastidiously. 'We have not seen a courier since Wednesday. I hope it's nothing urgent.'

'Not urgent, really,' said Derry gaily. 'I only came this way as a precaution to assure myself the situation was unchanged; that our sweet young friend was still at large.'

'So much at large that he covers most of this map where you find me marking the disposition of affairs at noon yesterday. Spring-heeled jack!

Takes a whole shire at a bound! If I had legs like that I would take a shire or two in my stride and be south of the Tweed by supper-time. You don't know how I hate being here like a rook in the mist, not knowing really what is happening round about me, nor why it's happening, nor when the whole tragic farce is to be ended.'

'I am pushing on to Fort William,' said Derry.

'Lucky man, to be pushing on anywhere! I can only wish you joy in your perambulation, and I hope you know your way, for I haven't a single man to spare to go with you, and look at this –'

He took Derry to the window that gazed loftily on the plain, closed to the north by those mountains that a little ago had looked so airy and iridescent. Over them was thunder. They had taken on now an inky hue; come closer; showed their teeth.

'There you are!' said the Governor with a bitterness in his tone. 'That's the edge of it. Into that and you might as well be in the moon! A welter! And it will soon be winter. Even now one might as well search a hundred-acre field for a corncrake. Did you ever see a corncrake, Mr Derry?'

'Never.'

'Neither did I, though there are several in a meadow down below there that spoil my sleep at night with their rasping. Nobody ever sees a corncrake on the wing, though it comes from foreign lands. What's to prevent it flying back again without notice? I'm sometimes half-convinced our particular corncrake's gone where came from and that we are a pack of fools.'

'Oh no!' said Derry cheerfully. 'He is certainly not gone yet, or I should not be here.'

'One cannot be sure of anything in this amazing country,' said the Governor. 'I get a dozen reports of him every day, all contradicting one another. Spring-heeled Jack! No later than Tuesday he was said to have gone through the Blair of Athole with a gang; lifted seven horses and twenty bullocks, put torch to granaries, staved in a cellar, and chased the women to the hill. Next morning there was news of him being captured on the Tay, disguised as a pedlar in a lodging. He killed two men who came on him, and was, as the story went, badly wounded himself, but got on a horse and made his escape.'

'Do you believe one word of it, sir?' asked Derry.

'I'm too long in this part of the world to believe a damned thing I hear except the shot of a musket. It's best for you to believe that he's still alive and at liberty, and a desperate fellow who will certainly get wind of you as soon as you stick your head above the heather.'

Derry smiled, slyly. 'You are, sir, if I may say so, jumping at conclusions. Take it as not unlikely that I may be on a purely diplomatic mission.'

The other grunted; picked some rowan-berries off the map and chewed them with a grimace. 'Mum's the word, Mr Derry!' he said. 'I'm all discretion – We have in the Army our own short word for that kind of diplomatics. Have you been in there before?' – he made a gesture indicating the portals of an unknown world that might stretch to Polar regions.

'I have never been north of Durham till now,' answered Derry. 'But a good guide is with me. I have left him outside the town to rest the horses. My notion now is to push on till night fall.'

'A Highlander?'

Derry nodded.

'Then watch him! That's all I say – watch him! It seems to be a point of honour with all these gentry to mislead anyone in breeches. This land will never be safe for the like of us till breeches are compulsory. Your man is just as likely as not to give the corncrake cry in the fields where there's not a living bird.'

'I have the best credentials with him from the best of quarters,' said Derry. 'He is a man with the King's Commission.'

In the words 'the King's Commission' was a hesitancy due to Derry's doubt if a Messenger-At-Arms had really regal script; the Governor noticed it and gave a side-long glance at the young man, who seemed effeminately vain of his finger-ring as he fiddled with the top button of his sage-green coat. That it was a broken button, and half gone, no doubt accounted for so trim a fellow's consciousness of its untidy look, particularly in the presence of a soldier point device.

'How do you purpose going?' said the Governor, attending him to the door and half way to the postern. 'There are two roads only. If you want to be on the line of sutlers' carts and what there may be of intelligence, go by Crieff and Killiekrankie. Those cursed refugees have eaten up the country; what comes to us in the garrison comes to us on the hoof, and I'll not deny it's wholesale pillage. The other road is by Callander and Rannoch – shorter, maybe, but it's not cleaned up yet and the hills are full of bandits who would dirk you for the sake of your boots.'

'The latter is nearer the sea, is it not?' said Derry reflectively.

'It's nearest the devil! By all accounts it's a route where you see nothing but smouldering thatch, where life would seem snuffed out entirely but for the human tricks that make it a perfect hell for decent soldiery. Perhaps the road by Callander might be the best road for you, though, as you show no arms; I have long had a feeling that we are working too far to the east on wheel-tracks, that nothing but sawdust sacks will come to us from that direction.'

'At all events, sir, *I'll* not send you any sacks of sawdust,' Derry responded cheerfully, and, saluting, passed the sentinel and descended to the town.

(In Stirling Derry had learned from the Commandant where Craigbarnet had been arrested – a fact Ninian had found out before him in Dumbarton.)

CHAPTER 10

He got back to his companions just in time to rescue the body-servant Hannibal out of the hands of a picket of Barrell's foot who had put snitchers on his wrists and were starting off with him to the town. The Messenger-At-Arms was nowhere visible; the horses were gone. It did not take long to gather an idea why Hannibal was in bonds; his master and he having groomed the horses as carefully as if they were for a market, Ninian had taken the three of them without a word of explanation down a road that led to the riverside, with orders to the lad that he should wait beside the saddles and their bags for the return of Captain Derry. Hannibal had got tired waiting; the road to the town grew livelier with promenading Hessians; a low black slattern house behind a nail-work seemed to have some attraction for them; fascinated by the glitter of the warriors, Hannibal had followed a squad of them and found himself in an unsuspected boozing-den. Not a word did he know of the soldiers' language, nor they of his, though he tried them in dog Latin, but apparently they had drunk together some bad ale, and there was brawling. Hannibal plucked at a giant fellow's love-locks and they came away in his hand; the Hessian Horse, it seemed, eked out its martial aspect with borrowed hair. The picket had burst in on a squabble that made an appalling din, but had no more of serious bloodshed in it than a wake; it promptly grabbed him as the only friendless man in a crowd coherent in spirit if not language, and found he had a pistol in a belt below his waistcoat.

'I never put a hand on it, Captain Derry!' cried the culprit. 'I carry it just to take the bare look off me, and I haven't a grain of powder.'

'You are an idiot to have such a thing about you when you know it is forbidden,' Derry told him, pricked a little in his conscience by remembrance that he had in the tail of his own coat a more effective weapon of the kind than Hannibal's, which was a rusty tool with no flint in the jaws of it.

They stood on the road, in front of the cottage where they had cooked their dinner. The housewife, terrified to be discovered harbouring strangers likely to get into trouble, had taken the saddlery and the bags from the garden bench behind where the Messenger had left them, and thrown them into the gutter at the front, gone in and barred the door to escape interrogation. Every child in the hamlet stood with a bubbling nose round the picket, Derry, and the prisoner; the Prince of Cassel's mercenaries had completely disappeared; in sight was not one shako.

Derry was in a quandary. The disappearance of the horses concerned him most. It was impossible to believe that Campbell meant to bolt with them, yet the Governor's warning to beware of Highland guides was still in his ear, and it beat him to think of any innocent reason for a step which had already, indirectly, got the body-servant into an awkward scrape. The picket corporal was a man of Somerset by his tongue, and civil enough to a countryman who had, to judge from the prisoner's address to him, an army rank though in civilian garments. But no blandishments of Derry's would make him release the peccant Hannibal, till Ninian Campbell all of a sudden appeared on the scene from a side road, astride on a bare-backed-horse with another two in tow.

'*Mo creach*!' he exclaimed dismounting hurriedly. 'What's this of it? Are we into battle, Captain Derry?'

The circumstances were explained to him; he took out the sealskin wallet containing the *laissez-passer* and produced it for the corporal's examination. 'There you are, my gallant fellow,' he said. 'It's all in order.'

The Corporal scratched his head as he read the document; assured that Derry was the drover in spite of his captaincy and English tongue, and the other two the servants, and handing it back to him, he brusquely commanded the release of Hannibal, to whom he retransferred his pistol.

'Where are the horses?' Derry asked, when this exciting incident was ended, and the picket moved off townward. The string of three which Ninian now so unaccountably had in hand was made up of lively enough beasts, but shockingly ungroomed, with last winter's hair on them and thickly feathered on the fetlocks.

'There is a coper here by the name Gillespie, everyone in Scotland knows for his stock in riding cattle,' said Ninian coolly. 'I made a swap wi' him. Our two horses had another thirty mile in them at the least, but yours was sorely saddle-galled and as good as foundered. Still, it would never do for Hannibal and me to be mounted on stable horse and you on one from the hill, so I swapped them all for this leash of sturdy fellows, and three saxon pounds – there's your New Bank note for you, Captain Derry, and you can have first pick.'

'But you should have told me,' broke in the Englishman.

'There's something in that,' agreed Ninian, 'but if you're comin' to the hills wi' me, you must put up wi' my decision on the best way to get through them. It's no' a country to parade on shiny bestial, there hasna been the leisure time to groom a horse there for the last twelve months, except it was a dragoon's charger. I was sorry enough to part wi' three good horse that wanted only a hot mash and a night of rest to put them in condition, but at the same time they were foolish for our purpose. If the folk we met didna take us for dragoons in civil clothing, they would credit us at least wi' plunderin' a barracks. What's more, I have made a bargain wi' Gillespie to keep the horses till we come back – if we come back by this way.'

'It's just as well, perhaps,' said Derry at last; 'for we're going on at once by way of Callander.'

'Capital!' said Ninian, 'That's something like the thing!' and he hurried to the saddles. Ten minutes sufficed to put them on the road again, skirting the town by a bye-way, twice bordering two loops of the river that finally had to be crossed at a village where they halted half-an-hour to let past them the most astounding herd of cattle Derry had ever witnessed. It filled all the width of the road between the ditches; seemed unending in its length; the afternoon was loud with bellowing. Rough black and yellow beasts they were, with enormous horns and a general aspect of ferocity little in accord with their docility before the cudgels of the soldiers driving them, as it were in, and with gentle speculation in their hair-fringed eyes. There were at least a thousand, many of them lamed by walking, many bleeding, from their cudgelling or the prick of swords, all of them gaunt with hunger.

They were, it seemed, the latest sweepings from Lochaber; many such droves had passed through in the past few weeks, gathered in from the disaffected country, to be sent to the south for marketing to the King's credit. There was a stoppage of the drove for a while at the village confines, where a canteen stood by the side of the road for the herdsmen's entertainment. Rain was falling. The afternoon had a sombre, saddened hue. Everything seemed wretched to John Derry, above all the *gémissement*, the plaint of these creatures, reft from their familiar fields and strangers to each other. That they were starved with hunger was manifest from the eagerness with which they took advantage of their halt to plunge across the ditches when they could and browze greedily in wayside fields that had not been cropped that autumn.

The village itself seemed almost desolate; few folk came out to look at the invasive tide of cattle; the only evidence of activity was in a smithy where armourers were busy at the anvils and the grindstone.

'This was a great place,' said Ninian, as they looked in on the smithy, 'for its Hielan' pistols. For three generations was a family here that made the finest dags in Europe. No gentleman of courage was complete without a pair of them. The worst of them was worth three bullocks. You never in all your life saw pistols that were so pretty; a man of taste would sooner be shot by a Doune pistol than break his leg at the dancing.'

Hannibal looked, goggle-eyed, at the Vulcans who were English soldiery, and not the usual tenants of the smithy. To Ninian he expressed a wonder if here he could make up for the lack of flint in the private weapon that had got him into the scrape two hours ago.

'Tach, I wouldna be bothered wi' a flint,' said Ninian; 'It'll just get ye into mischief. We're well enough girt for battle, the three good fellows of us, with nothing but our wits.'

They spoke in English, as they always did in Derry's presence, though otherwise they more naturally fell into Gaelic. But light though Ninian's spirit might seem in English, an inner old man in him was stricken by the sight of English armourers at Maclauren's anvils, by that lamentable, unending drive of pillaged cattle. When the last poor heifer had passed on the way to Stirling and the Trysts, and he and his companions again were mounted, and into a countryside of woods, he expressed a cynic bitterness.

'That is war for you, Hannibal! The songs and battle-cries are always about King and Country, but when you find folk fighting out of their own country, you'll find there's nothing bonny about war; it is nothing more nor less than an excuse for pillage, with all respects to our good friend Captain Derry.'

Derry laughed. He had begun to find in those two curious fellows – one still an enigma – a quality of grotesqueness that was at least amusing.

'By all accounts,' he said with gaiety, 'pillage is an ancient industry in this part of the realm; you can hardly blame us for taking a hand in it. But I see you're a man of peace, Mr Campbell?'

'I am!' said Ninian, firmly, 'I'm all for the kindly word, no ill-will to anybody, and a pair of slippers like the Sheriff's.'

'Supposing now I kicked you on the buttocks?' suggested Derry, with a twinkle.

Only for a moment was the *beachdar* staggered by a remark that he knew was meant in fun but yet had something of an argument in it. Then he looked at Derry with admiration.

'You have me there! I can see that you and me will get on well, together,' he said at last. 'Indeed it's not myself; it's a lot of wild Macgregors dead in the kirkyard at Balquidder that would make up my mind for me, if I was kicked. I doubt in that case if the kindly word would be on the tongue of me.'

Only when the gloaming came did Derry propose a halt till morning.

They had come to a lake, but seemingly it must be rounded; at the top of it, half a mile off, was a village on fire. The flames lit up the sky, and sparks were flying over the water.

The typescript ends here. What follows is copied from Munro's own manuscript.

Munro's Notes

Colina: after Chapter 10, is heard of only as a lad. She has gone north in masculine clothing and stirred up the country to retard the spies, so that she may secure the safety of? Pat before they come on the scene.

Her first obstacles to them are laid down at Tyndrum. She has called early in the morning on a lady friend there [*Lady of The Manse conspirator*]; revealed herself and her purpose, and finds in this lady an ingenious confederate. Between them, they devise plans for letting it be supposed in the district that this handsome young fellow (Colina) who moves about so mysteriously – is Morag, with the enemy on his heels. – This rumour goes around the country in a few hours. Everybody conspires for his protection. Men come in from the hills, and in groups watch all the roads and passes on the outlook for 3 men who are chasing 'Morag'. These 3 men (Derry, Ninian, Hannibal) are – by Morag's desire – not to be harmed, but everything must be done to stop them by arrest or otherwise.

It has been surmised by Colina that the 3 men, on leaving Stirling, will make for Arisaig. Their inevitable route, therefore, she decides, must be by Doune, Callander, Balquidder and Glen Dochart through Tyndrum. [*lead mines at Tyndrum*]

The Hill men (the watchers), therefore, have particularly watched this road, and from their retardive schemes come various obstacles and adventures into which the 3 spies are projected between Balquidder and Fort William. First cheque [check] in Balquidder.

CHAPTER 10
[Stirling to Balquidder]

The Doune pistols.
The lifted cattle.
Ninian's lecture to Hannibal on war and cattle. The songs and battle cries are always about King and Country – not a word about the cattle. But always, where you'll find folk fighting out of their own country, there are

cows to lift. In Derry's presence Ninian and Hannibal speak English, so Derry hears this conversation and takes part in it.

N – What made ye take this road?

D – I saw the disposition of things on a map. (Not Blaeu)

N – You were wise: it's the road we should have been on this morning.

D – explains why he went to Stirling – to find out about Craigbarnet; where he was arrested.

N – I could have told you that last night if you werena so soon bedded. There was no need to come round by Forth to find that out. Why your curiosity?

D – (frankly) – On his coat, when I saw him first in prison, there was a broken button – just like mine. [Hannibal is not listening now] (He explains the purpose of the button) Odd as it may seem to you, Mr Campbell, I was relieved to learn he had escaped from the Rock, though annoyed at myself for not asking where he had got the button and come from.

N – Drummond was relieved too. Leave it to the Bylie; he has yonder in his booth, left the poor old *bodach* and his button. [Tells where Craigbarnet is, and that when they went into the house last night a half button was on the desk where Colina had been sewing, and a coat, along with the boots, under the settee.]

D – Curious! (speculates) Justice – Justice is a daylight job.

Fire in Balquidder.

The stolen horses.

Chapter 11. 15 miles to Tyndrum.

CHAPTER 11

There was, on the part of Derry, a disquieting sense of being spied on by unseen observers. For an hour at least, with one exception, they had seen no moving man or beast in any place they passed. The fields had neither arable crop nor cattle on them, were deplorably run to weed and bracken. At the best the countryside could never have been very populous: there was hardly a dyke or hedge to it anywhere. Cottar-houses were dispersed at wide intervals, and all of them abandoned: at least from none of them came the reek of household fires. A company of soldiers, with carts of what looked like bedding and pots and pans, had passed down on the other side of the river in what Campbell called a strath a little less than an hour ago. A recognition of them as his own countrymen made Derry feel it was happier with him were he with them going south, than going with those odd companions of his into a land which he now surmised must be picked to the bone as retribution for its sins.

It was just before they came in sight of the water and the flaming roofs beyond it he suspected a furtive dodging of some figures in the wayside thickets. But he had said nothing of it, fearing to betray what after all might be a foolish apprehension. Now, his interest in a flaming hamlet, that seemed to him like tinder in spite of falling rain, was hardly more intense than the curiosity with which he saw for an instant at least half-a-dozen stalkers in a beechwood close at hand.

'It is my opinion,' he said impetuously, 'that we're being followed.'

'That's just what I was thinking to myself,' said the Messenger. 'They have come a couple of miles with us, at no great convenience to themselves, and I'm wondering what they are. They're not sodgers, for sodgers in this country keep close together in all their strength, particularly after burnings. Besides that, this fire is the King's job, and the people engaged in it need fear nothing from the like of you and me.'

He gave, of a sudden, the hoot of an owl with a little twist to the end of it, and, pulling up his horse, stood listening. There was no response.

'I thought it might be some of my Macgregor friends, but no,' he explained. 'And still it is somebody watching us without King's protection.'

'Have you friends here?' asked Derry.

'God knows! By the lowing of these houses there's not much chance of anything being left at all but ashes. It is here, Mr Derry, my people came from, and abode, though my father and I have been wandered ones of the hill, and I have always feared that there might be little friendship left for us in Balquidder. It is the first time in my life I have dared come near it. On my soul! It's a warm welcome that I'm getting, but that's the Butcher for you! I wish we had come on a colder night . . . I'll tell you what we'll do. We'll not go into that town at all until morning; we'll go back to that empty byre we passed at the cross-road, tether the horse in the planting and take a sleep to ourselves.'

They retraced their way a few hundred yards, unsaddled, tied the horses to trees and went in with their baggage to a dry-stone edifice where old brackens were left that gave them at least a chance of lying down. Hannibal snored as soon as he was stretched.

'What made you come this road?' asked Ninian, having lit a spark of fire. 'There is not a change-house within fifteen miles of us.'

Derry felt –

'Does the road not please you?' he asked.

'It's a road that doesn't abound in victuals, you can see, but otherwise ye couldna get a better. I'm wondering how a man with nothing but Mr Blaeu behind him hit on the only road that's any use to us if we're to be on the track of Morag.'

Then Derry explained. He had chosen the road from a study of another map than Blaeu's – from the big chart of the country used by the castle governor to mark out day by day where the troops were. There was no use going further east than the forts; their man was inside a cordon that stretched from Linnhe to LochHourn.

'Of course!' said Ninian. 'Isn't that what I always told you. But for the fancy that you have for garrisons, Captain Derry, we might have been there tonight, and on the heels of our young friend Morag in the morning. Our way to start it should have been up Glen Falloch. Are ye no' trusting me?'

'No one in our profession quite trusts a new acquaintance wholly till he's tried –'

'That's right,' said Ninian heartily.

'Now I'll tell you exactly why I came back to Drummond's, and how what I learned there sent me on to Stirling . . . Craigbarnet, when I saw him in the prison, had on a coat with only half a button at the neck –'

'The same as yourself.'

'Exactly. It's – a signal – a protection. A man with such a button was the last man I should expect to find so far away just now from – let us say Fort William – and particularly in a prison. I came back because I wanted to see him by himself about where [?] he had got it, where he had been arrested, and, if possible, to secure his release.'

Ninian listened with grave attention.

'If ye didna go to bed so early I could have told you about it last night,' he said quietly. 'Craigbarnet was captured in Arisaig. It was his coat Miss Colina was sewing another button on when we went in on her last night; I saw the broken button on her desk and the coat itself below the settee, though I never paid much attention to either. And as for poor Craigbarnet, it was Drummond let him out of prison; Craigbarnet needna worry ye; he spent last night in Drummond's loft, and by this time he'll be clear of Clydeside.'

'You see, Mr Campbell, I was right in not quite fully trusting you; if you had told me that this morning, there would have been no occasion for us to come to Stirling' [except for disposal of troops].

'I wasna going to risk being kept another day in a locality, Captain Derry, where Colina Drummond was at hand to waste your time with. I have been, one time, young myself, and that's a clever lass and bonny.

You're better out of her road. I was most annoyed when you told her we were coming North. It's the last thing I would let her know, myself; she's far too clever, yon one.'

'Tell me about her, Mr Campbell,' said Derry eagerly.

'Ye know as much about her as I do. Let us hope the chapter's ended. If you'll just take your boots off and rest ye for a little, I'll go out and see if there's anything of meat for us on the griddle that was once Balquidder.'

Then he went out in the rain, went cautiously through the smouldering hamlet, into a tacksman's house. A careful search discovered for him food – a cooked hare in a pot overlooked in the pillage, a basket of oatcakes disdained by English soldiery, and in a hole in the wall a spirit bottle. He was gone well nigh half an hour, and when he returned to the byre, both of his companions were sound asleep, unconscious that the horses they had tethered at the back were gone!

'I wonder . . . I wonder . . .' he puckered his face and almost closed his eyes in a moment's speculation. 'Damn it, I canna be sure about that Englishman! There is something sleek about him. I'll wager he's the champion fox of England. He has at times a kind of half laugh to himself the way a man would have that has a trump card I am forgetting. Old Lovat would be a baby to him! . . . Did he see the gaff? That's what bothers me. My hope is that he's young enough yet to think it was for his bonny eyes she angled him.'

cf. *Sitting watching*. Anyway, we must get him out of here as soon as we can; it's a terrible place for clash and there are things to learn that would keep him another week. He dragged us here for a talk on a man that's missing and I thought at first it was for a lass, and perhaps the lass was part of the attraction, but I can tell you, Hannibal, he's not a man, even with a lass, to forget his own wee bits of business. For all the lassie's eyes he was honestly put about when he heard his man had bolted. And what for was he put about? – I'm thinking to myself about that. – I could bring him to his man in fifteen minutes, sleeping snug an' ??, but I know all the man could tell him. A decent man though a kind of idiot, but I'm eager to be on to where there's better game for shooting. Tomorrow we'll be on the Moor of Rannoch – Tell me this, Hannibal –